The Politics of Criminology

Deviance and Social Control

edited by

Stratos Georgoulas

(University of the Aegean, Greece)

Volume 1

LIT

Stratos Georgoulas

The Politics of Criminology

Critical studies on deviance and social control

LIT

Bibliographic information published by the Deutsche Nationalbibliothek
The Deutsche Nationalbibliothek lists this publication in the Deutsche
Nationalbibliografie; detailed bibliographic data are available in the Internet at
http://dnb.d-nb.de.

ISBN 978-3-643-90186-6

A catalogue record for this book is available from the British Library

©LIT VERLAG GmbH & Co. KG Wien,
Zweigniederlassung Zürich 2012
Klosbachstr. 107
CH-8032 Zürich
Tel. +41 (0) 44-251 75 05
Fax +41 (0) 44-251 75 06
e-Mail: zuerich@lit-verlag.ch
http://www.lit-verlag.ch

LIT VERLAG Dr. W. Hopf
Berlin 2012
Fresnostr. 2
D-48159 Münster
Tel. +49 (0) 2 51-620 320
Fax +49 (0) 2 51-23 19 72
e-Mail: lit@lit-verlag.de
http://www.lit-verlag.de

Distribution:
In Germany: LIT Verlag Fresnostr. 2, D-48159 Münster
Tel. +49 (0) 2 51-620 32 22, Fax +49 (0) 2 51-922 60 99, e-mail: vertrieb@lit-verlag.de

In Austria: Medienlogistik Pichler-ÖBZ, e-mail: mlo@medien-logistik.at

In Switzerland: B + M Buch- und Medienvertrieb, e-mail: order@buch-medien.ch

In the UK: Global Book Marketing, e-mail: mo@centralbooks.com

CONTENTS

CONTRIBUTORS

Emma Bell is senior lecturer at the University of Savoie in Chambéry where she teaches British history and contemporary British politics. Her research aims to situate British penal policy in its wider social, political and historical context. She has just published a book which attempts to understand the so-called 'punitive turn' in British criminal justice policy under the New Labour administration and examine its links to neoliberal political economy (*Criminal Justice and Neoliberalism*, Palgrave Macmillan, 2011).

Toulina Demeli holds a PhD on Social Anthropology and History, University of the Aegean. She is a lawyer, working as an UNHCR Legal Consultant.

Konstantinos (Costa) Delimitsos, sociologist/criminologist, prepares a PhD thesis on the questions of delinquency, social reaction and public expertise while teaching at the department of sociology of the University of Nancy and at the Social Work Regional Institute of Lorraine.

Christina Ericson is M.Phil. in Criminology and is working for The National Board of Health and Welfare in Sweden. Her main areas of interest are violence in intimate relationships and criminal policy.

Stratos Georgoulas is Assistant Professor of Criminology and Director of the Laboratory EKNEXA in the University of the Aegean in Greece His working experience concerns amongst others several legislative committees and special advising at the Greek Ombudsman, the Ministry of Justice and the Scientific Committee on Preventing Juvenile Delinquency and Victimization. He has been Visiting Professor in FSU, USA (Fulbright Scholarship), University of Toronto (International Council for Canadian Studies scholarship), University of Damascus- Syria (Greek State Scholarships Foundation), Slovak Academy of Science (Slovak Republic National Scholarship Programme) and University of Amman (Jordan). He has published several books, chapters in edited volumes and journal articles in Greek and English; he is a member of editorial boards in several scientific journals in English and editor of the journal "Youth, Crime and Society".

Jane Harris lectures in Criminology, School of Education and Social Science at the University of Central Lancashire. Her teaching and research interests include state responses to children in trouble with the law, critical pedagogy and research methods.

Mark Hayes is Senior Lecturer in Criminology/Politics at Solent University, Southampton UK. He has published material on a wide variety of topics, including the New Right, Fascism, Political Violence, and Football. However, much of his research interest has focused on Northern Ireland, particularly British government policy, and the nature of Irish Republicanism. Mark has also conducted work for the Ex-Prisoners Assistance Committee in Ireland, and has made journalistic contributions to a variety of publications.

Anastasia Karamalidou is Lecturer in Criminology at Middlesex University, London. She has an BA (Hons.) in Criminology from Middlesex University (2000), a MSc in Crime, Deviance & Control from London School of Economics (2001), and a Ph. D. in Criminology from Middlesex University (2010). Her current interests revolve around penology and human rights.

Angeliki Kitsiou is sociologist, Msc of "Applied Social Research", and PhD candidate at the Department of Sociology of the University of the Aegean. She has worked as teaching staff of the Hellenic Army School of Cadet Petty Officers, as a research staff of the Therapy Centre for Depended Individuals (ΚΕ.Θ.Ε.Α.), and also as a research staff in several European Projects.

Christos Kouroutzas is Ph.D Candidate in the Department of Sociology, School of Social Science, in the University of the Aegean. He has studied Sociology, and he had finished his Msc, in the same department in the program of postgraduate studies in 'Development of Innovative Local and Regional Policies and Social Cohesion'. He is member of the Laboratory, of Sociology of Youth, Leisure and Sports. His research interests is about Forensic Genetic Science and Criminology, 'Global crime', 'new social control' and 'new biological rights'.

Margaret S. Malloch is a Senior Researcher at the Scottish Centre for Crime and Justice Research at the University of Stirling.

Bill Munro is a Lecturer in Criminology and associate of the Scottish Centre for Crime and Justice Research at the University of Stirling.

George P. Nikolopoulos is Associate Professor of Criminology at the Panteion University of Social and Political Sciences (Athens) and President of the Adminstrative Board of "Epanodos – Centre for the resettlement of ex-prisoners", a juristic person of private law under the auspices of the Greek Ministry of Justice. He is graduate from the Law School of the National and Capodistrian University of Athens (1982) and Ph.D. in Criminology (1993) from the Catholic University of Louvain (Belgium).

Recent publications: "*State, penal power and european integration. A criminological approach*", Kritiki Publications, Athens, 2002 and "*The European Union as a criminal policy actor. The 'Hague programme' and its implementation*", Nomiki Bibliothiki Publications, Athens, 2008 (both in greek), «*La construction européenne d' un espace de liberté de sécurité et de justice: les enjeux sociaux et politiques des contraintes représsives supraétatiques*» (pp. 279–300) and «*Crise de la gouvernementalité européenne: quelles implications pour l'agenda du contrôle social supraétatique?*» (pp. 301- 325), both in Th.Papathéodorou & Ph.Mary (Éds.), *Mutations des politiques criminelles en Europe*, Groupe européen de recherches sur la justice pénale & Université de Peloponnèse, Éditions Papazissis, Athènes 2006.

Paul Norris is a Senior Lecturer in Criminology and Politics at Southampton Solent University. He has written on Northern Ireland, and antiterrorism measures in Britain.

Dave Orr is currently a Senior Lecturer in Criminology at the University of Central Lancashire, where he has been one of the team responsible for writing and delivering the criminology degree at the university. Prior to this, Dave Lectured at the Centre for Studies in Crime and Social Justice, Edge Hill. Following the completion of his Masters there in 1999, Dave set up the online Hillsborough Disaster archive for the Centre for Studies in Crime and Social Justice, and worked on the ESRC funded national *Violence Project* with the historian Dr John Archer. Dave's own research has largely been historical and class based analysis of the prison system and criminal justice in the nineteenth-century England and Wales. More recently, Dave has also written papers concerned with children, sexuality, 'mental illness', criminal justice in early Nineteenth-century London, Financial Crime and Sex Trafficking. Dave is about to publish '*The Foul Conspiracy to Screen Salisbury and Sacrifice Morton': A Micro-history of Extortion, Resistance and Same Sex Intimacy in Early Nineteenth-century London* in The Journal of the History of Sexuality.

Caterina Peroni graduated in Political Sciences-International Policies in 2006 at the University of Padua (Italy). In 2008 she obtained the Master title in Critical Criminology, Prevention and Social Security supervised by Prof. Mosconi. Currently, she is attending a PhD. course in Law Sociology at the University of Milano (Italy) and she is lecturer of the following subjects: Political Parties and Lobbies in the EU and Equal Opportunities Policies in Italy and Europe. She is a collaborator of

CIRSPG (Interdipartimental Research Centre for the study of gender policies) of the University of Padua where she is responsible for the organization of seminar cycles on gender issues.

Nikos Rinis is a sociologist, Msc of "Applied Social Research", of University of the Aegean and a PhD candidate in the Department of Sociology- University of the Aegean. He is a member of the Laboratory of Sociology of Youth, Leisure and Sports of the University of the Aegean (EKNEXA).

Vincenzo Ruggiero is Professor of Sociology at Middlesex University in London (UK), where he is Director of the 'Crime and Conflict Research Centre'. He has conducted research on behalf of the many national and international agencies, including the Economic and Social Research Council (ESRC), the European Commission and the United Nations. Among his latest books: *Crime in Literature* (2003), *Understanding Political Violence* (2006), *Social Movements: A Reader* (2008), and *Penal Abolitionism* (2010).

Dimos Sarantidis is a PhD student at the University of the Aegean, Department of Sociology and a member of the Laboratory of Lab for Sociology of Youth, Leisure and Sports. His PhD thesis is on the notion of police culture in Greece. He has cooperated with several NGOs by providing legal assistance and counseling to migrants.

Demetra Fr. Sorvatzioti, holds a LLB, MA in Criminology and a PhD in Criminology. She is a Lecturer in the Law Department of the European University Cyprus and a specialized lawyer in Criminal Law.

Panagiotis Sotiris teaches social and political philosophy at the Department of Sociology, University of the Aegean. His publications include *Communism and Philosophy. The theoretical adventure of Louis Althusser* (In Greek, Athens: Ellinika Grammata, 2004). His research interests include social theory, Marxist philosophy, social movements and the theory of imperialism.

Aimilia Voulvouli is Adjunct Lecturer at the Department of Cultural Technology & Communication – University of the Aegean where she teaches cultural theory. Her research focuses amongst others on social movements, urban conflicts and environmentalism in the eastern Mediterranean (Turkey, Greece, Cyprus). She is the author of the book *From Environmentalism to Transenvironmentalism: The Ethnography of an Urban Protest in Modern Istanbul.*

INTRODUCTION

Stratos Georgoulas

A short history of the politics of criminology

From Howard Becker's 1967 exhortation, 'Whose side are *we* on? [1]' the issue of the politics of criminology has continued to be a significant theme in academic debate, policy implementation and legal reform. Variously identified as 'technicians of the State' or 'apologists for criminal justice', administrative criminologists have been criticized as functioning primarily to 'manage' the consequences and conflict of structural inequalities in advanced democratic states. They are repre-sented as necessary and willing functionaries in what Nils Christie termed the 'social control industry[2]'.

These conventional criminologists are inspired by one desire: the modification of human behaviour to fit into a social context (since the individual, and not the society, owes to change), having (almost always) honourable intentions, but being trapped in the cage of partiality of the object of their pursuit, without being able to discern the holistic nature of the phenomenon they try to artificially explain.

The risk to disengage the research object from its (social) origins, may lead to the legalization of status quo. For example, when scientific questions about the nature of crime are specialised during the attempt of discovering this nature, as if they study "another" reality, then these sought answers drive them to the recording of a technical knowledge, by experts that work within in vitro conditions. Although they approach with positivism the scientific results as recorded through the use of sci-entific methods and techniques, however, their action framework is ide-alistic. The main ideology supported in this way is the ideology of con-servation and perpetuation of particular social conditions which neither are subjected to scientific research nor are examined in relation to their effect to the way of posing the fundamental scientific question. If the posed scientific question has a positivist tone (which is the cause? which is the result of this action?) and issues of cultural, historical, financial

---

[1] Becker,H. (1967), "Whose Side Are We On?" *Social Problems*, 14/3: 234–47
[2] Christie, N. (1993), *Crime control as industry*, Routledge. The above paragraph was part of the call for papers from the 38th Annual Conference of the European Group for the study of deviance and social control, held in Mytilene- Lesbos in September 2010, and was written by Phil Scraton

aspects are excluded, then, the answer in advance is teleological and absolutely conservative, and results to an academic justification of the existent policies of discrimination in the institutions of the formal social control.

If we do not wish to follow this track we should be ready to bring policy back to what it was a conversation on technical issues of application, we should deal with society as a whole. As the authors of "New Criminology" [3] wrote, this is nothing but an old criminology which renegotiates the same problems encountered also by classic social scientists. In fact, it is about a sociological study of the entire social framework of the inequalities of power, wealth and authority which is the result of class relations of industrial society with a simultaneous critical rejection of analytic individualism, either in the idealistic form of neo-classicism, or in the form of individual positivism. A study based on the tradition of dialectical materialism where freedom of will and absolute determinism are vitiated; a study where anti-positivist radicalism will be promoted beyond the world of personal interpretations in the critique of history and structure of society; a study where the criminological interest is orientated to the great questions of social structure and interactions of humans with the structures of power and rule within the framework of which criminal phenomenon as a process takes place. There is no need for the different to be approached as pathological, since crime cannot be considered as a marginal phenomenon, but as an endemic phenomenon dispersed in the society. On the other hand, the opposition to this - criminalisation – as integral part of the totality of the phenomenon is approached through the aspect of conflict.

What critical analysis has established is that in official definition, popular discourse and state intervention 'crime' and 'conflict' are political; in the processes of recording and reporting, measurement and targeting, policing and punishment.

This Criminology was and still is an adventurous undertaking in the field of Social Sciences (and not only). Its constant scientific practice raises issues and poses questions concerning the role that science of criminology and criminologists should play; questions that have been posed throughout its historical course and it's for the best to recall them.

Let's start our journey with the first human societies where the term crime was something unknown. At that time, when something "evil" happened in the small social group - and by the term "evil" we

---

[3] Taylor, I., Walton, P., Young, J. (1973), *New Criminology,* Routledge and Kegan Paul

mean something that threatened the life and the cohesion of this group - this evil, after being attributed to the effect of a bad spirit-demon, was punished either with physical extermination (death) or exile. What was evil for the human group was determined by terms such as totem (the symbol of the family co-existence), and taboo (the action which was evil for the group). The forbidden - evil actions were sexual intercourse among persons of the same totem (a form of incest) and the threat against persons in authority (chief, sorcerer) or persons who were casually weak (pregnant women, infants).

Every other action identified today as crime was not subjected to the group's collective reaction. Even homicide was punished only with private vengeance, either through death or usually repayment. This continued until the organisation of men into clans and the establishment of kingship as form of authority. Homer presents Aias blaming Achilles for perpetuating his enmity after the murder of Patroklos, despite the custom of receiving compensation even for a murdered brother or son, as was the case with Hector who stopped the vengeance. The first written law in Greece, the Law Code of Gortys (Dodekadeltos) in Crete (6th century BC) made reference to private repayment for every kind of offence, and, of course, not to a collective reaction (penalty).

The weakening of clans and their progressive disintegration was parallel to the strengthening of the state authority and the right of state intervention to the penal suppression. Solon's but mainly Kleisthenis' laws attempt to limit the private vengeance, but not the money compensation as a penalty for most of the crimes. Taboo, as offence of a person, became offence of an institution (regime or religion) and the new evils were sacrilege, treason and introduction of new deities. The punishment for these was death, property confiscation and exile (ostracism). For the rest, thefts, homicides etc. there were certain compensation rates not depending on the action, but depending on the social position of the perpetrator and the victim. As a rule, if the perpetrator was a slave and the victim was a free man then the penalty was heavier.

History until almost 18th century shows that every dominant group could define an act as evil, crime, and punish it as it could and only if it could. The decisive intervention of Pope in political events of Roman Empire shows for the first time a new aspect of the meaning of deviant behaviour, the sin. Free sexual relations regardless of gender are strictly punished, while the dispute of Pope's authority is punished with public torture and execution by fire as sorcery.

In 13th century, the plague exterminated 1/3 of the population in England. Landowners lost manpower/serfs. Then the crime of beggary was discovered, where those who had fled away from the landowners and wandered in the trade centres of that time begging, were punished with death if they did not return to their master. The penalty for such crimes was public tortures and execution by fire only when a central authority existed to award it. When in some periods in the middle Ages, feudal lords disintegrated the states, then, the usual penalty was again private vengeance.

Despite the fact that through this historical retrospect it was obvious that each authority defined which action was a crime, if, and how it would be punished, nevertheless, the study on criminal behaviour withheld this fact. With the bright exception of the ancient sceptic philosophers, it was common place that there was a natural law given by a deity that determined evil and good and no one could question it. Anyone that did otherwise was a criminal.

The demonistic and theocratic beliefs about crime were prevalent, inhibiting any scientific knowledge on the issue of deviation, which, after all, was not necessary for the level of development of social organization. Apart from Aristotle, some pre-Socratics, such as Alkmaion from Kroton, Epicureans and Stoic philosophers, who searched for biological, psychological and social causes of the malevolence of criminals, no other rational reference has been recorded.

However, as social and economical evolution proceeds, scientific knowledge evolves in parallel. The emergence of new social strata, such as the urban one, and their claim for a share in power, leads the society to social as well as political revolutions, most important of which is the English Glorious Revolution in 1648 and the French Revolution in 1789. The first demand is the disengagement of the social evolution from the strict boundaries of political arbitrariness of monarchs and religious monocracy regarding the way of perceiving reality.

Thomas More in his famous work "Utopia" in 1516 states that criminal behaviour is not the result of a demonised soul but a product of poverty, while Beccaria, following the dictates of European Enlightenment thinkers, in 1764 published his work "On Crimes and Punishments". In this work arbitrariness and cruelty of sovereigns regarding definition and punishment of crimes are condemned and he demands the precise determination of punishable acts and the direct, formally defined response to the offence, after a public trial.

It is the time when the need for greater accumulation of capital by the urban strata leads to the need for labour intensification. The exclusion of several members of the society from the production procedure as it happens with criminals, who are punished usually with death and torture, is not an option. All the lower social strata should work. For this to happen, the ultimate target of penalty should be the reformation of criminals and not their absolute extermination.

Social sciences were born then, with main purpose the safeguard of such a labour continuity and hence the structure of a social policy used as safety net. So, criminology is created, with the objective to understand the reason that one becomes criminal and in what way this could be originally prevented and confronted in the future, remedying the conditions that generate crime.

Then, the sentence of imprisonment was broadly implemented; the use of death penalty was limited, while in 1777 John Howard declared the significance of labour within an institution as a means for the correction of criminals. All these developments lead to the publication of the work by C. Lombroso "The Criminal Man" in 1876 and in the foundation of the Italian School of Positivist Criminology with his disciples Garofalo and Ferri. It was then that Darwin's theory of Evolution had just caused sensation in the scientific world, and Lombroso considered useful to also apply it in the study of deviation, through scientific methods.

According to this theory, a criminal is a man who has not been normally evolved and is found a little behind in relation to other normal people of our society and for this reason is driven to deviant behaviour. Due to his non-normal evolution this man has some physical characteristics – hereditary stigmata on his face and body, which if we manage to associate with particular types of crimes, then it is easier to confront the crime. Through the examination of convicted criminals' craniums, he made this association and suggested the marginalization in advance of such "primitive" humans in order to avoid affecting the rest and so the criminal element in the society to be limited.

The reactions to Lombroso's theory were directly expressed by all of the social sciences which had started being fully developed, promoting the study of deviant behaviour to new levels of knowledge, by implementing social researches and testing the credibility of their conclusions. Crime was connected to individual factors such as heredity, birth defects, organic dysfunctions, psychic diseases, mental retardation, and immaturity. When, however, researchers realized the limits of an individualistic approach and study of crime, they turned towards the effort to articulate social terms of the generation of deviation aiming at recording suggestions of social anti-criminal policy.

In this effort, they rediscovered researches, such as this of the French Querry and Belgian Quetelet, which connect criminality to climatologic conditions, as well as terms such as anomie of the sociologist Durkheim. In the early 20th century the well-known Chicago School of sociology carries out a very important research in order to discover the social causes of criminality that hits the slums and suggest measures for its treatment. In parallel to the Chicago School, researches are conducted trying to connect crime with problematic families, problematic education, mass media influence.

The famous sociologist Merton gives another impetus to the term *anomie* of Durkheim. When a person, adopting the broader objectives and values of contemporary society without having the means to achieve them, then, he/she is driven to an anomic behaviour which often may become criminal. Another sociologist, E. Sutherland, would explain some years later that criminal behaviour may be learnt through the constant contact of the individual with groups which adopt delinquent values in their behaviour and at the same time the lack of his/her ability to communicate with groups which express normal values for a society.

Common element of all these theories is a principle: common feature of all crimes is that they consist of acts that are condemned by the totality of the society (consensus model). All of the healthy conscience in a social system is called (as defined by Durkheim) collective conscience, while every deviation from it is determined as anomic behaviour. Crime is such an anomic behaviour, that as act offends the collective conscience and brings social condemn which can reach even the formal punishment. Deviation with its after-effects (e.g. condemn, punishment of the criminals, etc) contributes to the confirmation/definition of the values of the society.

In other words, common feature of all these theories is the prerequisite that the totality of a society's members has mutually decided which action is beneficial and which is censurable. This decision is a product of total consensus, having as a result when someone acts illegally, all the rest to react, judging negatively his/her behaviour and supporting the suppression of this behaviour, legitimising the action of the formal agents of social control, e.g. police intervention or court decision.

However, something is missing from this approach on the study of deviant behaviour. Something that Karl Marx, a few years before Lombroso wrote "Criminal Man", implied in his theories on surplus value[4].

A philosopher produces ideas, a poet poems, a clergyman sermons, a professor compendia and so on. A criminal produces crimes. If we look a little closer at the connection between this latter branch of production and society as a whole, we shall rid ourselves of many prejudices. The criminal produces not only crimes but also criminal law, and with this also the professor who gives lectures on criminal law and in addition to this the inevitable compendium in which this same professor throws his lectures onto the general market as "commodities. This brings with it augmentation of national wealth, quite apart from the personal enjoyment which—as a competent Witness, Herr Professor Roscher, [tells] us—the manuscript of the compendium brings to its originator himself. The criminal moreover produces the whole of the police and of criminal justice, constables, judges, hangmen, juries, etc.; and all these different lines of business, which form equally many categories of the social division of labour, develop different capacities of the human spirit, create new needs and new ways of satisfying them. Torture alone has given rise to the most ingenious mechanical inventions, and employed many honourable craftsmen in the production of its instruments. The criminal produces an impression, partly moral and partly tragic, as the case may be, and in this way renders a "service" by arousing the moral and aesthetic feelings of the public. He produces not only compendia on Criminal Law, not only penal codes and along with them legislators in this field, but also art, belles-lettres, novels, and even tragedies, as not only Müllner's Schuld and Schiller's Räuber show, but also [Sophocles'] Oedipus and [Shakespeare's] Richard the Third. The criminal breaks the monotony and everyday security of bourgeois life. In this way he keeps it from stagnation, and gives rise to that uneasy tension and agility without which even the spur of competition would get blunted. Thus he gives a stimulus to the productive forces. While crime takes a part of the superfluous population off the labour market and thus reduces competition among the labourers—up to a certain point preventing wages from falling below the

[4] http://www.marxists.org/archive/marx/works/1863/theories-surplus-value/add1.htm

minimum—the struggle against crime absorbs another part of this population. Thus the criminal comes in as one of those natural "counterweights" which bring about a correct balance and open up a whole perspective of "useful" occupations. The effects of the criminal on the development of productive power can be shown in detail. Would locks ever have reached their present degree of excellence had there been no thieves? Would the making of banknotes have reached its present perfection had there been no forgers? Would the microscope have found its way into the sphere of ordinary commerce (see Babbage) but for trading frauds? Doesn't practical chemistry owe just as much to adulteration of commodities and the efforts to show it up as to the honest zeal for production? Crime, through its constantly new methods of attack on property, constantly calls into being new methods of defence, and so is as productive as strikes for the invention of machines. And if one leaves the sphere of private crime: would the world-market ever have come into being but for national crime? Indeed, would even the nations have arisen? And hasn't the Tree of Sin been at the same time the Tree of Knowledge ever since the time of Adam?

So, crime should be seen as a social product of our society without seeking to reveal abnormal conditions in order to be explained; there should be a different approach to deviant behaviour. This is the aspect of conflict. This aspect considers that criminal behaviour has different origin and presupposes the existence of conflict of interests.

The required consensus of all of the members of a society, regarding which act is criminal and which is not, is questioned. Instead of this, what is present in every society is the conflict of opposite social groups with opposite interests. When a social group prevails in this conflict, then its estimation on what is evil and what is good for society prevails, too. These estimations are turned into formal rules governing the action of the rest of the people. In this way laws are created which actually protect the goods of the dominant group, but remain also binding for the rest of the society.

Conflict theories define crime as an act which questions a value of the dominant social group, it questions the predominant morals. A criminal, that is, the man who violates such a formal code, is "produced" accordingly. When there is a law infringement, the offender confronts the mechanism of formal social control.

However, in the operation of police as well as in judicial system there are successive infiltrations. A man becomes suspect for police when he/she has the suitable profile of a guilty (e.g. person of a lower social status). Within legitimacy, he/she receives different sentence depending on whether his/her socioeconomic features constitute the stigma of a criminal – ergo of a dangerous individual for the society.

On the other hand, if someone does not bear these features, does not "look like" criminal, he/she is not a usual suspect and may be punished or not– if he/she ever goes to trial - with the lightest sentence. According to these theories (of conflict) it is reasonable for such a criminal to come from a dominated group.

Instead of searching for fake and idealistic causes of crime, we should prove how crime is politically and economically fabricated through the social control institutions within the framework of political economy of the capitalist society. This involves that our priority should be also the study of those institutions and the suggestions for their change. At the same time however, the wider spectrum of thinking should focus on the suggestions of social and economical change of the current reality within which the criminal phenomenon is developed and preserved. Besides, a criminology which is not orientated to the abolition of the wealth and power inequalities is a criminology that would end to serve the interests of the financially and politically strong, by scientifically legitimising their actions. It is not enough to question the criminological stereotypes, constructing "alternative phenomenological realities". It is not enough to discover alternative penalties for imprisonment, or in general alternatives of social control. The main objective should be the structure of a new, rightful society, where the elements of human differentiality cannot be subjected to the power of criminalization

These principles, in fact, invite us to search beyond simple answers, to seek the difference and some times, to make it ourselves, when we have to explain social phenomena, when we should understand the world we live in.

Finally, this is the generative power for this publication, which was based on the 38th conference of the EG where papers were presented on every aspect of the theme, including theoretical debates and controversies in critical analysis, primary research, global trends and international comparisons.

Outline of the book

We have given Part 1 of the book the title "Critical Criminology: from the past to the future". The chapters comprising this part provide some crucial theoretical debates on critical criminological theory through the history. Stratos Georgoulas, for example, asks genealogical questions about the constitution of the discipline of criminology stating that history becomes essential to an understanding of the modern criminological enterprise -discipline's relation to institutional practices and concerns, - key terms and concepts that structure the discourse. He uses the example of Hesiod' poems (the first Greek poet who reinvent Gods and rituals, and the first who revealed the new social needs of his era- 8th century BC), providing evidence that these poems written in an era of drastic social changes from a poet with explicit class conscience represent the spirit of this era and as for the genealogy of terms of criminological thought, as there are included elements of critical thought on crime, sentences and justice. Margaret Malloch and Bill Munro examine the application of the concept of Utopia as a political perspective within social science discourse and the practical political value of utopian thinking for criminology, questioning whether criminology can be political, which is to say critical and even subversive, or whether it is necessarily re-appropriated and co-opted by the social system of which it is part. Emma Bell brings us back to the present studying penal policies in Britain and France. The neoliberal transformation of the state from provider of social security to facilitator of market solutions has meant that regulating the crimes of the powerless has become an increasingly important means for governments to attempt to secure legitimacy and the 'rebalancing' (of the criminal justice system in the interests of victims and 'consumers' of justice 'services') that has taken place has rather been away from individual citizens and towards the state and the private sector with whom it has increasingly come to share a vital 'correspondence of interests'. Vincenzo Ruggiero provides us with an important theoretical argument crucial for the present and the future of critical criminology. He answers to the institutional efforts (as well as criminological analyses lending their theoretical support to them) to address organised crime and political violence jointly and treat them as a single issue, by examining the differences between organised crime and political violence and presenting the crucial distinction between 'organised behaviour' and 'organised identity'.

With Part II (Contemporary Critical Criminology- case studies) we address several topics, such as policing and prisons, migration, gender and sexuality. In the first case, Dave Orr, using the case of Lehman Brothers, and the report published in March 2010 regarding their bankruptcy and the dubious and fraudulent activities of Lehman and Ernst and Young, argues for enforced compliance and tougher regulation of all corporations, with a specific focus upon policing and regulatory bodies as a means of preventing large scale financial fraud and increasing corporate accountability, while assessing Obama's current proposals for increased financial regulation. Paul Norris drawing on recent experiences of policing public protests in the UK and the use of tactics at the G20 protest in London in 2009 examines critically public order policing in the UK, stating that there is a move towards a more 'paramilitary' policing style, at both protests and football matches. He also reopens the debate about public order policing and policing styles (such as neighbourhood policing). Mark Hayes examine the nature and purpose of internment in Northern Ireland in August 1971, providing an explicit answer to the emerging consensus amongst some academics and commentators that internment was either relatively unimportant and/or moderately successful, given its military/security aims and objectives. They state that this issue is absolutely central to understanding the subsequent configuration of the 'troubles', and raises critical criminological issues about the contemporary role of state power, authority and legitimacy, incarceration, neo-colonialism and the politics of resistance. Konstantinos Delimitsos presents the rhetoric, the means of reasoning and the representations that the new security experts in France convey. He also emphasizes on the new security experts' proposals for an appropriate course of actions in order to face violence and delinquency, advanced like technical solutions and therefore supposedly external to political and/or social antagonisms. Anastasia Karamalidou focus on the educative and emancipatory potentialities of human rights that were born out of prisoners' conflicting statements, drawing on data gathered from 64 English and Dutch prisoners. Finally Demetra Sorvatzioti in her research, conducted during the years 2006-2009, in Greece, proved that equality (as one of the basic principles of prison life) does not exist. Huge differentiation is driven due to the economic status of the prisoner. Basic human rights are violated. Poor prisoners are forced by the powerful ones to serve them and often to commit more crimes. Leaves and conditional releases are not provided for poor prisoners by the Council of Prison and the length of their sentences becomes longer.

Concerning migration, George Nikolopoulos proposes to shift the focus of the debate about the social control of immigrants away from the measurement of their criminality, to the criminalization of the immigration policy itself, i.e. to the study of the institutional and social conditions which drive the immigrants into the realm of the penal system, examining all the relevant discourses and practices, the formal and informal norms, the attitudes and representations, in short, the complete social apparatus which sets into motion the social reactions, "spontaneous" or organized, towards immigrants. He concludes that the over-representation of immigrants among the "clients" of the penal system is nothing else but a self-fulfilling prophecy about their criminality.

The last topic that we address in this part is gender and sexuality. Within this topic Christina Ericson presents results from an evaluation project, where the aim is to find out if a selection of batterer intervention programmes in Sweden are effective. Caterina Peroni analyses the public debate on gender violence and criminal law in Italy, focusing on the analysis of the campaign "Transgender" (May 2010), whose goal is to criticise the symbolic use of gender violence as a pretext to criminalise immigrant men, and of the social construction of gender violence itself, through a post-feminist critical approach. Jane Harris argues on the decline in the presumption of innocence of children by discussing a case study in the UK, to highlight the criminalisation of children's expressive sexuality which is perceived to be unsafe or dangerous by 'knowing' adults.

The last part of this book aims at introducing the critical criminological thought in the University of the Aegean in Greece, by presenting the work of my colleagues and students in the laboratory EKNEXA (Lab for the Sociology of Youth, Leisure and Sports). Panagiotis Sotiris examines the December 2008 Rebellion of the Greek Youth by providing an overview and analysis of the discoursive displacements that lead to this notion of "movement as deviance" and how these displacements are conditioned by the prevailing neoliberal orthodoxy and the general trend towards dealing with social inequality and discontent mainly in terms of "technologies of power". Aimilia Voulvouli aims at initiating a discussion concerning the suppression of gay-identity in countries of the Eastern Mediterranean as a result of the uneven contact with the West. In doing that, she proposes that the usage of the Foucaultian concept of biopolics can be extremely fruitful as it opens the door to the examination of gay identity as an identity carrying with it a lot more than the pure sexual liberation demand. This discussion could lead in the shaping of a theoretical framework on which scholars dealing with gender suppression in these countries could base their research. Toulina Demeli follows imprisoned women in Closed Central Women Prison of Korydallos while entering prison, and observes the interpersonal relations and solidarity networks created. Angeliki Kitsiou analyzes focus group research method in order to examine social construction of crime via free software movement's activities and Dimos Sarantidis tries to identify some basic characteristics of the phenomenon of police culture in Greece through participant observation at a detention centre for asylum seekers and immigrants at Lesvos Island. Finally, Nikolaos Rinis uses a qualitative analysis of the movie Hoodwinked in order to research if the cinema version of the classic fairytale is a reproduction of stereotypes and values about crime and criminal and Christos Kouroutzas examines critically the association between the forensic investigation of crime and criminology in Greece.

PART 1

CRITICAL CRIMINOLOGY: FROM THE PAST TO THE FUTURE

1.

RADIX OF RADICAL CRIMINOLOGY- HESIOD

Stratos Georgoulas

1. a. Many authors have tried to outline the origins of contemporary criminological theory through the consensus-conflict debate of human societies since the period of classical Athens and through Plato's and Aristotle's' theories (Bernard, 1983). In this article an effort is made to illuminate a period of the past, and one of the first two poets of Ancient Greece, without, however, disregarding the questions constantly raised (Garland 2002) about epistemology of criminology. This historical review cannot be part of the criminological thinking, which has been formed in contemporary historical and social circumstances in a strict methodological framework of research and discourse. On the other hand, this historical background may be proved important for the understanding of contemporary science of criminology within the framework of genealogy of terms and concepts that form the theory of criminal behaviour (Garland, 2002:9).

b. The criminal phenomenon constitutes a social relation; hence it should be examined within the framework of social organization and hierarchy and in the specific historical environment in which it is developed. Embracing the position that such a phenomenon appeared at the beginning of the class division in ancient societies, the criminological approach of a period of social upheavals, structural revolutions, a century of Greek "renaissance"- as 8th century B.C has been characterized-, presents great interest. In addition, one of the first written ideological products of European literature, representing the Bible of Greek mythology on the one hand (Hesiod –Theogony), and the first historical writing dealing with current issues of that time (Hesiod – Works and Days) on the other, are worth examining. However, the above-mentioned "innovations" themselves do not present an interest for critical criminology. The works of Hesiod and the genealogy of criminological terms should be approached as ideological products with socially relative character, taking into consideration the fundamental importance of financial factors and mainly of the production relations, the class formation, the conflict of interests and finally their connection with the structures of authority as they are shaped in an environment of social change and finally legitimised through the specific produced discourse.

2. Around 12th century B.C. at the geographic area of today's central and south Greece, a large movement of population took place which lasted until the 10th century B.C., having as a result the enfeeblement of the previous socio-political patterns of the Mycenaean period. The so-called "descent of the Dorians" would be accompanied by the introduction of iron tools and weapons, more resistible than the previous ones made of copper, having as social consequence the democratization of warfare and the political "localism" (McNeil, 1963:241). The Big-Man, hereditary head of kingship of the past era, is replaced by a general aristocratic council of men with great land property. The land and the livestock supported by it (horses, cows) acquire great significance for the economy and warfare (being a major part of the productive mechanism) and as a result, their possessor realises his great political power[1]. This new leading group that takes part in the new government, starts pursuing its establishment close to the seat of administration, which gradually loses the feature of a castle-palace and acquires the character of a city around the castle or within it.

The city life was not originally urban (commercial or artisanal), but aristocratic. The new socio-political model, the "city-state", replaces the "nation-state", and the king becomes simply one of the many aristocrats. Permanent residence, and agriculture and livestock farming as a main mode of production are accompanied by the dominant production relations between aristocrats/land owners of the city and the rural farmers who possessing small and poor land -if possessing any- leased land from the nobles, by paying the taxes to the aristocrats themselves (as state tax collectors). As McNeil states, "By the 7th century B.C. in many parts of Greece population pressure had become a serious problem. Farms were subdivided, so that in bad years a poor farmer might be obliged to borrow seed or food from his richer neighbours. In return he pledged his land or his liberty, which became forfeit if the loan were not paid" (McNeil, 1963:245). In this case, he would become either hired labourer (*thetes*) by the year, but when there was no production he

---

[1] As Mann states, although origin was important, it was never developed into a caste or class consciousness. Wealth easily overset the discriminations based on descent and the predominant ideal was the participation in public issues and not the hard work or hand labour. (Mann, 1986:277)

would be dismissed from the land (De Ste Croix, 1981:244), or slave. In every case, he ended to the bottom of the class pyramid of a society which has been characterised as slave economy, but as De Ste Croix refers, it had also features of serfdom, due to the large number of free men and women living not much above the subsistence level who were exploited by the ruling class, to some extent individually and directly (the leasehold tenant by his landlord and the freeholder by his mortgagee), but partly through indirect and collective forms of exploitation such as taxation, military conscription, etc. (De Ste Croix, 1981:293).

As a consequence of all the above, there was an outburst of strong class conflicts suppressed by the military supremacy of knights (*hippeis*). However, as the population growth, combined with the growth of agricultural production due to the use of more resistible iron tools, led to the ability of forming a great army of *hoplites*-infantry (the phalanx as a formation of heavy-armed infantry operating in unison which could prevail even against cavalry) the aristocrat military power faded away.[2] Free peasants who were objects of exploitation gradually acquired political power. Access to political power, which was a privilege of hereditary aristocracy, starts being questioned and the exploited peasants constitute a new distinctive social class, the "demos", which asserts and in some occasions accomplishes its legal protection against the rich (e.g. legislation of Lycurgus in Sparta and Solon in Athens). Merchants, artisans, ship-owners joined forces with them; social groups with growing financial power due to the development of Greek trade in 8th century B.C., preserving at the same time, however, their low symbolic value. In the 8th century in several regions of the Greek territory, a social revolution took place through the evolution of the aristocratic city-state to a city-state of free citizens with equal rights, which often was expressed as political rebellion with the overthrow of aristocracy and the establishment of tyranny, which, as Aristotle mentions, originated from the demos (people) and the masses, in order to oppose to the upper classes so that the demos should not suffer injustice at their hands. (De Ste Croix, 1981:358-9).

Boeotia, where Hesiod lived and wrote, passed through similar phases of social evolution; an exclusively rural region where the class issue prevailed, with small farmers who turned into *konipodes* (barefoot), working occasionally (*thetes*) or begging, while also the "crea-

---

[2] The use of iron is extended to the arms of simple peasants, replacing wood and goat skin which until then were broadly used by them (Marangoudakis 1999)

tors", artisans with limited political power, were in almost the same position. The time that Hesiod wrote his works was a transition period, as it was described, where the established aristocracy did no longer enjoyed majority's legitimisation. Besides, the new era is combined with a renaissance in cultural and ideological terms; first, a revival of ideas, images and skills from the Mycenaean Age that they had been forgotten, as it seemed by the works of Homer. Furthermore, as soon as the power of kingship faded, religion ceased to be a privilege of the royal house; its rituals exceeded the boundaries of palace and became a public activity with the full participation of aristocrats. However, at that time, and since the literates grew in number,[3] the issue of religion as part of the ideology of the new era changed in character. Together with the predominant cult of Mysteries which were conducted only by initiates, were unknown to public and kept secret and confidential through the mediation of a priesthood, Mycenaean gods were rediscovered. They had a new form, influenced by ideas and rituals of the East, and heroes were presented as semi gods, who cover the new social need of shaping a common identity of a particular place, of the new city-state. So, heroes are "localized" in a way that the *demos*, and the aristocrats attributed their origin and their right of land ownership to the ancestry of the "heroic" era[4]. In any case, however, the presence of these newly emerged deities was indispensable for the survival of the city-state as an entity of equal political rights, either as guardians of a city-state, as its first inhabitants, or using it as place of burial (Nilsson, 1940:248). Hesiod is the first who reinvents and assists in the establishment of gods and rituals (in his work "Theogony") which are not primordial (Mann 1986:287), but a product of transcription from previous "sacred books" of Eastern cults (Hesiod's origin is from Kymi at the coasts of Asia Minor)[5] and new social needs which he does not hesitate to thoroughly reveal in his work "Works and Days".

3. The two poems attributed to the historical figure of Hesiod, were written in 8th century. The particular connection of Hesiodic poetry to an ac-

---

[3] The simplicity of alphabet, the trade needs, the homogeneity of dialects of the Greek speaking tribes and the political need for written laws, led to this outcome (Murray 1993:140)
[4] The ones claiming a new social position in the transition period, and the others to secure their place in authority under the new ideological terms.
[5] Kymi, the greatest Aeolian city together with Mytilini (according to Stravon) had very early developed close relations with Phrygians, while, having a rich inland with large fields and fertile earth, agriculture was its main resource. Hesiod's father left from there, because of the bad financial conditions

tual person has received various critiques. It has been mentioned that actually responsible for both poems is an oral poetic tradition (Tsaggalis, 2006), greater than one person, as well as that each of the poems has been written by different people, while an array of other poems or abstracts have been attributed to Hesiod. In any case however, there is no disagreement that it is in vain to argue on the issue of identification and it is more important to examine the position of these poems in the world of archaic society, by observing the very same images they present (Ragos, 2006), without questioning what is common place for scholars, that is, that Hesiod lived in 8th century and was already known since Herodotus time (Histories, 2:53), while "Theogony" and "Works and Days" were definitely his works (Allen and Rambaut 1915, West 1970, Lamberton 1988, Peabody 1975, Evelyn-White 1964). These poems have been survived in Alexandrian papyri since as early as the 1st century BC, in copied manuscripts after 11th century, while the first printed edition was issued in 1493 by Demetrius Chalkondylis in Milan[6].

---

[6] Papyri-Manuscripts of "Work and Days":
- S Oxyrhynchus Papyri 1090
- A Vienna, Rainer Papyri L.P. 21-9 (4th cent.).
- B Geneva, Naville Papyri Pap. 94 (6th cent.).
- C Paris, Bibl. Nat. 2771 (11th cent.).
- D Florence, Laur. xxxi 39 (12th cent.).
- E Messina, Univ. Lib. Preexistens 11 (12th-13th cent.).
- F Rome, Vatican 38 (14th cent.).
- G Venice, Marc. ix 6 (14th cent.).
- H Florence, Laur. xxxi 37 (14th cent.).
- I Florence, Laur. xxxii 16 (13th cent.).
- K Florence, Laur. xxxii 2 (14th cent.).
- L Milan, Ambros. G 32 sup. (14th cent.).
- M Florence, Bibl. Riccardiana 71 (15th cent.).
- N Milan, Ambros. J 15 sup. (15th cent.).
- O Paris, Bibl. Nat. 2773 (14th cent.).
- P Cambridge, Trinity College (Gale MS.), O.9.27 (13th-14th cent.).
- Q Rome, Vatican 1332 (14th cent.).

Papyri-Manuscripts of "Theogony":
- N Manchester, Rylands GK. Papyri No. 54 (1st cent. B.C. - 1st cent. A.D.).
- O Oxyrhynchus Papyri 873 (3rd cent.).
- A Paris, Bibl. Nat. Suppl. Graec. (papyrus) 1099 (4th-5th cent.).
- B London, British Museam clix (4th cent.).
- R Vienna, Rainer Papyri L.P. 21-9 (4th cent.).
- C Paris, Bibl. Nat. Suppl. Graec. 663 (12th cent.).
- D Florence, Laur. xxxii 16 (13th cent.).
- E Florence, Laur., Conv. suppr. 158 (14th cent.).
- F Paris, Bibl. Nat. 2833 (15th cent.).
- G Rome, Vatican 915 (14th cent.).

In the poem "Theogony" there is a thorough reference to cosmology and birth and evolution of Greek deities. These elements that present influences from respective sacred poems of the East (Mpezantakos 2006) are the main reference framework of the features forming ancient Greek mythology. The second poem "Works and Days" written on the occasion of an heir dispute between Hesiod and his brother Perses, is a detailed record of agrarian life in archaic Boeotia. In both poems (mainly in the second one) there is biographical information about the author. This lead to the conclusion that Hesiod was a peasant, with no great land property, and Aeolian origin from his father's side who had left his home place due to the adverse economic conditions. As a consequence, it appears that the writer belonged to a specific social class of his time, as it was described above, underlined the importance of labour (which was opposed to the predominant values of the aristocrats of his time), while he tried to transcribe religious hymns and traditions making them broadly known, contrarily to the past, where religion as an ideology was monopolized by the few initiators[7].

However, Hesiod's work is the only source of information (together with Homer's works) about judicial procedures and the meaning of crime in ancient Greece before the 7th century BC (Mac Dowell 1978), while the principle of the dipole "positive-negative" is the main common principle governing the ideas of all of his work (Manakidou 2006).

In "Works and Days"[8], Hesiod's brother took the greatest part of their heir, winning the trial by bribing the lords/judges, characterized as imbeciles. Besides, according to Hesiod, the time he lives is a period where "might makes right". In a Hesiod's parable, lords are like hawks

---

- H Paris, Bibl. Nat. 2772 (14th cent.).
- I Florence, Laur. xxxi 32 (15th cent.).
- K Venice, Marc. ix 6 (15th cent.).
- L Paris, Bibl. Nat. 2708 (15th cent.).

[7] In G.K. Kordatos "Prolegomena to the Homeric problem, Part 5", a detailed reference is made on the fact that to this effort of Hesiod as spiritual leader of the farmers, there was strong reaction by the aristocrat authority. Religious hymns and traditions with religious, philosophical and historical content were taboos and monopole of the old priesthood in the palace. The punishment of those who broke this taboo might be to become blinded (as it is believed that happened to Homer), while censorship was certain. Plato believed that a special law should be enacted that on the one hand it would force the poets engaged in religious hymnology to ask permission from priests, and on the other hand everyone violating the orders of the priesthood censorship to be punished (www.mikroapoplous.gr/homer/kordatos5.htm#e34).

[8] We are going to use the translation by Hugh Evelyn- White which is easily accessible via internet in www.sacred-texts.com/cla/hesiod.htm.

that torture nightingales, without accounting to anybody; while the judicial system passes through crooked procedures of people that accept the unrighteousness of the lords.

Perses, lay up these things in your heart, and do not let that Strife who delights in mischief hold your heart back from work, while you peep and peer and listen to the wrangles of the court-house. Little concern has he with quarrels and courts who has not a year's victuals laid up betimes, even that which the earth bears, Demeter's grain. When you have got plenty of that, you can raise disputes and strive to get another's goods. But you shall have no second chance to deal so again: nay, let us settle our dispute here with true judgement which is of Zeus and is perfect. For we had already divided our inheritance, but you seized the greater share and carried it off, greatly swelling the glory of our bribe-swallowing lords who love to judge such a cause as this. Fools! They know not how much more the half is than the whole, nor what great advantage there is in mallow and asphodel.

As we are in an era where...

The father will not agree with his children, nor the children with their father, nor guest with his host, nor comrade with comrade; nor will brother be dear to brother as aforetime. Men will dishonour their parents as they grow quickly old, and will carp at them, chiding them with bitter words, hard-hearted they, not knowing the fear of the gods. They will not repay their aged parents the cost their nurture, for might shall be their right: and one man will sack another's city. There will be no favour for the man who keeps his oath or for the just or for the good; but rather men will praise the evil-doer and his violent dealing. Strength will be right and reverence will cease to be; and the wicked will hurt the worthy man, speaking false words against him, and will swear an oath upon them. Envy, foul-mouthed, delighting in evil, with scowling face, will go along with wretched men one and all.

Kings and princes – according to Hesiod- are hawks who torture the nightingales without the fear of justice.

And now I will tell a fable for princes who themselves understand. Thus said the hawk to the nightingale with speckled neck, while he carried her *high up among the clouds, gripped fast in his talons, and she, pierced by his crooked talons, cried pitifully. To her he spoke disdainfully: `Miserable thing, why do you cry out? One far stronger than you now hold you fast and you must go wherever I take you, songstress as you are. And if I please I will make my meal of you, or let you go. He is a fool who tries to withstand the stronger, for he does not get the mastery and suffers pain besides his shame.' So said the swiftly flying hawk, the long-winged bird.*

While concerning justice....

There is a noise when Justice is being dragged in the way where those who devour bribes and give sentence with crooked judgements, take her.

In "Works and Days", Hesiod records the production procedure of justice and injustice, crime and lawfulness, as a process which in human society is developed through the conflict of the mighty and the weak, a process which is distorted by the bribery of the judges/lords who make the decisions. In the world of deities (in "Theogony") another procedure of power conflict is described, where the winner has the absolute authority by setting his/her terms. The first god, Uranus, gives birth to Themis (guardian of justice).

After them was born Cronos the <u>wily, youngest and most terrible</u> of her children, and he hated his lusty sire.

The relations of the first master and the subsequent king (Kronos) are not at all developed through social consensus.

For of all the children that were born of Earth and Heaven, these were the most terrible, and they were hated by their own father from the first. And he used to hide them all away in a secret place of Earth so soon as each was born, and would not suffer them to come up into the light: and Heaven rejoiced in his evil doing. But vast Earth groaned within, being straitened, and she made the element of grey flint and shaped a great sickle, and told her plan to her dear sons. And she spoke, cheering them, while she was vexed in her dear heart: `My children, gotten of a sinful father, if you will obey me, we should punish the vile outrage of your father; for he first thought of doing shameful things.' So she said; but fear *seized them all, and none of them uttered a word. But great Cronos the wily took courage and answered his dear mother: `Mother, I will undertake to do this deed, for I reverence not our father of evil name, for he first thought of doing shameful things.*

Besides, king's offspring were Titans, who made nefarious acts, Nemesis -disaster for mortals-, Apati (=Deceit), Erida (=Strife), while his grandchildren bore similar characteristics.

But these sons whom are begot himself great Heaven used to call Titans (Strainers) in reproach, for he said that they strained and did presumptuously a fearful deed, and that vengeance for it would come afterwards. ...Also deadly Night bare Nemesis (Indignation) to afflict mortal men, and after her, Deceit and Friendship and hateful Age and hard-hearted Strife. But abhorred Strife bare painful Toil and Forgetfulness and Famine and tearful Sorrows, Fightings also, Battles, Murders, Manslaughters, Quarrels, Lying Words, Disputes, Lawlessness and Ruin, all of one nature, and Oath who most troubles men upon earth when anyone wilfully swears a false oath.

The only person who never lies but tells always the truth is Nereas who is not the king's son.

And Sea begat Nereus, the eldest of his children, who is true and lies not: and men call him the Old Man because he is trusty and gentle and does not forget the laws of righteousness, but thinks just and kindly thoughts.

It is of great interest the way Hesiod presents the genealogy of the term "Power (Kratos) and Force (Via)". They are always assistants and companions of the new king[9].

And Styx the daughter of Ocean was joined to Pallas and bare Zelus (Emulation) and trim-ankled Nike (Victory) in the house. Also she brought forth Kratos (Strength) and Via (Force), wonderful children. These have no house apart from Zeus, nor any dwelling nor path except

---

[9] Later on Aeschylus too, in his tragedy "Prometheus Bound", mentions: "Kratos and Via, your charge from Zeus already has its end, and nothing further in the way. For the mind of Zeus is hard to be hanged; and he is wholly rugged who may newly rule"

that wherein God leads them, but they dwell always with Zeus the loud-thunderer...and Zeus honoured her, and gave her very great gifts, for her he appointed to be the great oath of the gods, and her children to live with him always. And as he promised, so he performed fully unto them all. But he himself mightily reigns and rules.

While another of his protégées, Hecate, plays a relevant role in judicial procedures and the socialization of youngsters.

Hecate. ...she will she greatly aids and advances: she sits by worshipful kings in judgement, and in the assembly whom she will is distinguished among the people.... she is honoured amongst all the deathless gods. And the son of Cronos made her a nurse of the young who after that day saw with their eyes the light of all-seeing Dawn. So from the beginning she is a nurse of the young, and these are her honours.
During Zeus' dominion as absolute master, penalties are set for those who might think to rebel.

But when strife and quarrel arise among the deathless gods, and when any of them who live in the house of Olympus lies, then Zeus sends Iris to bring in a golden jug the great oath of the gods from far away, the famous cold water which trickles down from a high and beetling rock. Far under the wide-pathed earth a branch of Oceanus flows through the dark night out of the holy stream, and a tenth part of his water is allotted to her. With nine silver-swirling streams he winds about the earth and the sea's wide back, and then falls into the main (24); but the tenth flows out from a rock, a sore trouble to the gods. For whoever of the deathless gods that hold the peaks of snowy Olympus pours a libation of her water is forsworn, lies breathless until a full year is completed, and never comes near to taste ambrosia and nectar, but lies spiritless and voiceless on a strewn bed: and a heavy trance overshadows him. But when he has spent a long year in his sickness, another penance and a harder follows after the first. For nine years he is cut off from the eternal gods and never joins their councils of their feasts, nine full years.

When the cycle of violence ended, new authority prevailed having the law on its side, or rather, part of his family.

But when the blessed gods had finished their toil, and settled by force their struggle for honours with the Titans, they pressed far-seeing Olympian Zeus to reign and to rule over them, by Earth's prompting. So he divided their dignities amongst them...Next he married bright Themis who bare the Horae (Hours), and Eunomia (Order), Dike (Justice).

At the same time, in the mortals' world, arrogant, unfair and impudent people were still in authority.

And the son of Aeson by the will of the gods led away from Aeetes the daughter of Aeetes the heaven-nurtured king, when he had finished the many grievous labours which the great king, over bearing Pelias, that outrageous and presumptuous doer of violence, put upon him.

4. In the novel by Marry Shelley, Victor Frankenstein was a scientist who, using flawless techniques and driven by his desire to give life, creates the Monster. This creation that takes place in an isolated village, does not take into account the negative social impact, having as a result the Monster to be driven to criminal acts.

Many conventional criminologists are inspired by a similar desire: the modification of human behaviour to fit into a social context (since the individual, and not the society, owes to change), having (almost always) honourable intentions, but being trapped in the cage of partiality of the object of their pursuit. As Frankenstein creates life out of an action without, however, taking into consideration the social reaction, in a similar way, criminologists cannot discern the holistic nature of the phenomenon they try to artificially explain. Crime and deviation have a necessary dual character of action and reaction, which cannot be separated into these two interacted features of it. Such a human act and behaviour has a distinctive dialectic relation with social reality and simultaneously a clear time and space definition, since it cannot be considered as a given and fixed element of a positivist approach which ends to become non-social as well as abstract, as a value and ideology.

The risk to disengage the research object from these origins, may lead to the legalization of status quo. Radical criminology does not follow this approach, but brings policy back to what it was a conversation on technical issues of application; it deals with the society as a whole. It is about a sociological study of the entire social framework of the inequalities of power, wealth and authority which is the result of class relations of industrial society with a simultaneous critical rejection of analytic individualism, either in the idealistic form of neoclassicism, or in the form of individual positivism. A study based on the tradition of dialectical materialism where freedom of will and absolute determinism are vitiated; a study where anti-positivist radicalism will be promoted beyond the world of personal interpretations in the critique of history and structure of society; a study where the criminological interest is orientated to the great questions of social structure and interactions of humans with the structures of power and rule within the framework of which criminal phenomenon as a process takes place. There is no need for the different to be approached as pathological, since crime cannot be considered as a marginal phenomenon, but as an endemic phenomenon dispersed in the society. On the other hand, the opposition to this - criminalisation – as integral part of the totality of the phenomenon is approached through the aspect of conflict.

The theoretical aspect of conflict as a conceptual instrument of sociological analysis of the reality constitutes a clearly defined framework of interpretation development, which is opposed to functionalism. The "indisputable evil" product of a social consensus, is replaced by the evil defined as the result of a procedure of criminalisation controlled by the socially strong-winners in the social conflict, against the socially weak-losers. Such a social conflict always ends to an attempt of conservation and perpetuation of the winner's authority. This takes place originally through the law which firstly protects the goods and values or behaviours of the strong and keeps on with the operation of mechanisms of formal social control that through their actions or omissions secure the result of the pre-existent conflict. The greater the social conflict is the more possible for the strong to criminalise the behaviour of those having questioned or questioning their authority and threatening their interests is. So, the analytical framework of record of crime followed by the radical criminology is set according to all the above, characterised by socially examined postulates-estimations, such as (Georgoulas 2008, Vold, et.al. 2002):

a. The values and interests of a person are formed by his/her living conditions. In modern societies, people live under different conditions, hence their values and interests are different.

b. People act according to their values and interests. When values are opposed to their interests then they adapt the values according to the interests.

c. Laws support the values and interests of people. When there are opposing interests and values, then the law supports the interests and values of the dominant social group or groups.

d. Usually the law implementation agents, since they operate within bureaucratic structures, are more efficient in simple cases than in more complex ones. Simple cases are these of infringements by individuals or groups that have a low political and financial power. On the contrary, complex cases refer to the infringements of powerful groups or individuals.

e. Exactly due to the previous discretionary operation of the law implementation agents, the officially recorded crime, which is a record of their action, will present features which are in accordance to the power distribution in a society. In other words, the majority of the criminals are expected to be people without financial and political power, violating values and interests of the powerful.

Instead of searching for fake and idealistic causes of crime, we should prove how crime is politically and economically fabricated through the social control institutions within the framework of political economy of the capitalist society, as well as historically in every social reality[10].

Hesiod's poems written in a period of social changes by an active man with clear class consciousness represent the spirit of that time regarding also the genealogy of terms, concepts and images of a criminological thought. Of course, they are not part of the clearly defined criminological "paradigm", however, they definitely contain elements of a critical thought about crime, penalties and justice. Society, just as gods that govern it, is characterized by conflicts and violence. The winners have the authority over the rest of the people and the agents being established to propagate this authority in the field of anti-criminal policy act with injustice, oppressively and for the interest of the ruling authority.

---

[10] This involves that our priority should be also the study of those institutions and the suggestions for their change. At the same time however, the wider spectrum of thinking should be focused on the suggestions of social and economical change of the current reality within which the criminal phenomenon is developed and preserved. The main objective should be the structure of a new, rightful society, where the elements of human differentiality cannot be subjected to the power of criminalization.

References

Allen, T. W. and Arthur A. Rambaut. (1915) 'The Date of Hesiod', *The Journal of Hellenic Studies*, 35, 85-99

Bernard, TJ. (1983) *The consensus – conflict debate: form and content in social theories,* NY: Columbia University Press.

De Ste Croix, G.E.M. (1981) *The class struggle in the ancient Greek world. From the archaic age to the Arab conques*t, London: Duckworth.

Evelyn-White, Hugh G. (1964) *Hesiod, The Homeric Hymns and Homerica.* Volume 57 of the Loeb Classical Library, pp. xivf., Cambridge: Harvard Press

Garland, D. (2002) "Of crimes and criminals: the development of criminology in Britain", in Maguire, M., Morgan, R., Reiner, R. *The Oxford handbook of criminology*, 3rd edition, Oxford University Press

Georgoulas, S. (2008) "Editorial", *Youth, Crime and Society*, Lab for Sociology of Youth, Leisure and Sports publications, University of the Aegean, 1, 5-12 (in Greek).

Lamberton, R. (1988) *Hesiod*, New Haven: Yale University Press.

Mac Dowell, D.H. (1978) *The law in classical Athens*, London: Thames and Hudson ltd.

Mann, M. (1986) *The sources of social power*, vol. 1, Cambridge: Cambridge University Press.

Manakidou, F. (2006) "Searching Work and Days. Dialectics of Kosmos of Hesiod and the structure of poem", in Mpezantakos, N.P. and Tsaggalis C.K. (eds), *Mousaon archometha. Hesiod and archaic epic poetry*. Athens: Patakis publ. (in Greek).

Marangudakis, M. (1999) N*ature and power, A Study of the Social Construction of Nature in Eurasia from the Stone Age to the Hellenistic*

Times, PhD Dissertation, Department of Sociology, McGill University, Montreal

McNeill, W.H. (1963) *The Rise of the West: A History of the Human Community,* Chicago, University of Chicago Press.

Mpezantakos, N. (2006) "Hesiod and the East", in Mpezantakos, N.P. and Tsaggalis C.K. (eds), *Mousaon archometha. Hesiod and archaic epic poetry.* Athens: Patakis publ. (in Greek).

Murray, O. (1993) *Early Greece,* London: Fontana Press.

Nilsson, M.P. (1940) *Greek Popular Religion,* New York: Columbia University Press

Peabody, B. (1975) *The Winged Word: A Study in the Technique of Ancient Greek Oral Composition as Seen Principally Through Hesiod's Works and Days,* NY: State University of New York Press.

Ragos, S. (2006) "Hesiod and philosophy: origin of truth of logos in Ancient Greece", in Mpezantakos, N.P. and Tsaggalis C.K. (eds), *Mousaon archometha. Hesiod and archaic epic poetry.* Athens: Patakis publ. (in Greek).

Tsaggalis,C. (2006) "Poetry and poetics in Theogony and Work and Days" in Mpezantakos, N.P. and Tsaggalis C.K. (eds), *Mousaon archometha. Hesiod and archaic epic poetry.* Athens: Patakis publ. (in Greek).

Vold, G.B., Bernard, TJ, Snipes, JB. (2002) *Theoretical criminology,* 5th edition, New York, Oxford: Oxford University Press.

West, M.L. (1970) "Hesiod," in *Oxford Classical Dictionary,* second edition, Oxford: University Press, p. 510.

2.

CRIME, CRITIQUE AND UTOPIA

Margaret S. Malloch and Bill Munro

'there is no alternative to Utopia'
Jameson (2005: xii)

Introduction

This chapter considers the relationship between Utopia and the political, and questions the practical political value of utopian thinking for criminology. In particular, it questions whether criminology can be political, which is to say critical and even subversive, or whether it is necessarily re-appropriated and co-opted by the social system of which it is part. Utopia in this case, following Jameson (1975, 2005), should not be seen as the representation of an ideal state of affairs, but as a heuristic device reflecting our inability to imagine Utopia in the first place. This inability to imagine a positive political vision of the future is not, according to Jameson (1982, 2005), the result of a failure of imagination, but due to the cultural and ideological constraints which bind us to the present.[1] The paper on which this chapter is based (Malloch and Munro, 2010) was a predominantly reflective piece that considered the need to combine theory and practice within a utopian metaphor for radical critique. The chapter continues this work in progress. It will outline the need for change, based on the view that without a vision, calls for change will be limited in their effectiveness at challenging broader social, political and economic systems. However, more importantly, it will question the nature of that vision. Can such a vision have content, as Levitas (1987) would argue, or does it exist merely as a negation or critique of what already exists? This chapter will outline the history and context of utopian

---

[1] This is also captured by Eagleton (2000: 31) when he writes that it is only in the language of the present that we are able to articulate what transcends the present; however in doing so, there is a danger of annulling our imaginings in the very process of expressing them. In other words it is impossible to transcend the present when attempting to imagine radical otherness; all 'utopia is thus at the same time dystopia, since it cannot help reminding us of how we are bound fast by history in the very act of trying to set us free from that bondage'.

thought; consider the relevance of utopian thought for a critical criminology; and finally, outline some potential areas for supporting social
change.

I

The concept of Utopia as a political perspective has been given a renewed vitality within recent social science discourses (Cohen and
Rogers, 1995; Roemer, 1996; Bourdieu, 1997/1998; Bowles and Gintis,
1999; Fung and Wright, 2003; Ackerman et al, 2006; Wright, 2006 and
2010; Gornick and Meyers, 2009). The term utopia covers a variety of
meanings and interpretations: mythological, geographical, historical,
psychological, sociological, which differ in content, form, political
alignment and intention (Goodwin and Taylor, 1982; Goodwin, 2001).
However, one of the key characteristics of utopian politics lies in the
imagining of political systems radically different from existing contemporary ones (Jameson, 2005). The key question here is the relation between Utopia's fictional expression and the historical conditions in
which it is produced. Marin (1984) argues that Utopia is not 'other' to
the 'real' world, but a fictional reconstruction of it, that has displaced
this 'reality' through its imaginary representation. In this way, Utopian
representations can foreground the social and economic contradictions
of a society in ways not available to 'realist' models. For Marin (1984:
161), Utopia exposes such contradictions in the forms of ruptures that in
turn question the 'naturalness' of existing conditions. Although this critique can never be total, as Utopia itself is unavoidably entangled in history, it can be read as an ideological critique of the dominant ideology.

Kumar (1991) argues that it is this very relationship between history and Utopia that is problematic. He notes that it has often been
viewed as unnecessary and misleading to speak of a history of Utopia.
Utopia in this sense was traditionally viewed as a timeless and unchang-
ing construct, a habit of the mind that manifests itself in all times and
places; an *ur*-type of the human social imagination. Others, such as
Wallerstein (2001) argue, that different meanings and usages of the concept of utopia reflect different moments of the history of the modern
world as reflected in its intellectual currents.

A Brief History of Utopia

Western cultural formations of Utopia suggest a hybrid concept born of Judeo-Christian beliefs and Hellenic myth, 'the crossing of a paradisaical, other-worldly belief' with the 'myth of an ideal city on earth' (Manuel and Manuel, 1979: 15). This naming took place in an enclave of sixteenth century scholars excited about the prospect of an Hellenic Christianity. However, it is important to note that religious and political utopias are not exclusive to Judeo-Christian and Hellenic traditions. Blessed isles and paradises are part of the imaginary world of all cultures. The wanderings of the Guaraní tribe in search of a 'Land-without Evil'[2] have been tracked over the length and breadth of Brazil (Métraux, 1948; Levi-Strauss, 1973; Manuel and Manuel, 1979; Gott, 1993). Al-Azmeh (2009) writes of the utopian elements of Islamic political thought and their complex and distinct relations to both historical and fundamentalist Islam. The 'ideal Islamic city', in this case lies in the historical past in the form of the Medinan Caliphate; however, as Al-Azmeh points out, contrary to orientalist assumptions, this is not an ideal divorced from reality but is historically grounded and embodied in legal statute.

By the end of the sixteenth century the adjectival form 'utopian' was born[3] and by the seventeenth century, Utopia made its way into other European languages (see Bacon, Cervantes and Shakespeare). Utopia was not only a poetical or imaginary place but had come to denote general programs and manifestos for ideal societies promoted by the authors directly (Milton, Leibniz) and realised via political action. Following on from the original *Utopia* of Thomas Moore in 1516 and throughout the 1880's with the writings of a plethora of individuals, a range of literary utopias emerged (Francis Bacon, 1627; Henry Neville, 1627 – see Bruce, 1999 for both; William Morris, 1890/1995), some presenting a vision of a new society; others presenting a blue-print for

---

[2] 'Ever since the European conquest of their lands in the sixteenth century, the Guaraní Indians to the east of Paraguay river have been stirred up from time to time by messianic revivals. Sometimes a prophet announces the end of Spanish rule and the beginning of a new golden age. Sometimes the nation abandons its territory and goes on a great pilgramage to the west, in search of the Land Without Evil' (Métraux, 1948, cited from Gott, 1993).
[3] I thinke if men, which in these places live
Durst looke for themselves, and themselves retrieve,
They would like strangers greet themselves, seeing then
Utopian youth, growne old Italian. (John Donne cited in Manuel and Manuel (1979:2).

possibilities that could be applied in practice (i.e. Robert Owen writing between 1813-49, see Owen, 1991); Karl Marx and Fredreich Engels, 1872, see Marx and Engels, 1964, 1970, 1975; Charles Fourier writing between 1808 and 1836, see Fourier, 1971; Peter Kropotkin, 1902 and 1906, see Kropotkin, 2006, 2007) .

Marx and Engels (1970) in the *Communist Manifesto*, argued against utopianism. Engels (1970) outlined his critique of Utopian thought in *Socialism: Utopian and Scientific* originally published in 1892 where he referred specifically to the work of Saint Simon, Fourier and Owen – although not unsympathetically. He noted that while the ideas that their utopias were based upon were important and progressive[4], they were limited by the embryonic stage that the proletariat was at, at the time of their development; thus leading the proponents of these progressive ideals to appeal to the bourgeoisie for their acceptance. Similarly, Gramsci writing between 1929 and 1935 noted: "The utopians, in as much as they expressed a critique of the society that existed in their day, very well understood that the class-State could not be the regulated society. So much is this true that in the types of society which the various utopias represented, economic equality was introduced as a necessary basis for the projected reform. Clearly in this the utopians were not utopians, but concrete political scientists and consistent critics. The utopian character of some of them was due to the fact that they believed that economic equality could be introduced by arbitrary laws, by an act of will, etc." (*Selection from Prison Notebooks, p257-258* in Hoare and Nowell Smith, 1971*).*

Marx and Engels opposed Utopian thought not because they rejected the idea of a radically transfigured society - a position that more conservative critics have taken against Utopian thought (see Popper, 1945) - but because they rejected the notion that a new society could emerge into the present from a-historical imaginary blueprints for a perfect future. Indeed, Marx and Engels' belief that the revolutionary potential of the proletariat had developed sufficiently for the overthrow of capitalism and its exploitative system, (i.e. Marx and Engels, 1970) led to criticisms that they themselves were utopian. However, for Marx, the opposite of Utopia was not realism however it may be defined - as Eagleton (2000) notes, there is nothing more idly utopian than a prag-

---

[4] Engels refers to Owen's advance from social reform to Communism and the consequences he faced for challenging private property, religion and contemporary marriage (Engels, 1970: 24-5).

matic realism that assumes the future to be very much the same as the present - the opposite of an idealist Utopia for Marx was immanent critique. As Harvey (2010) notes, it was Marx's negative critique of Utopian socialism in *Capital* that gave the work itself its Utopian impulse.

Utopia and Crime.

The issue of 'crime' has been of central importance for utopian thinkers and has been directly related to the structural organisation of society. In particular, the driving impetus of poverty as the motivating factor for envisioning new social structures is evident; as is the subsequent social exclusion that distinguishes between citizens and non-citizens. For example, More's critique on crime and its punishment was embedded in a broader critique of property and early capitalist society in the name of egalitarian ideals. It is one of the earliest accounts of 'accumulation by dispossession' (Harvey, 2005: 48) as he related the source of much sixteenth century crime to the plight of the peasants dispossessed through the enclosure of common land. Theft and vagrancy were neither a matter of choice nor of individual morality, but the necessary recourse of those whose livelihoods have been taken away. This predicament chimes with contemporary accounts of neo-liberal economic restructuring where the 'redistribution through criminal violence' has become 'one of the few serious options for the poor', and where 'whole communities of impoverished and marginalised populations' have been criminalised[5]. For More (1999) the only way of overcoming these problems was to eradicate what the book claimed to be their fundamental cause: private property. Thus More (1999) identified the gap between the concrete historical situation, outlined in part one of the book, and its solution, the description of Utopia itself, in the second. As Wallerstein (2001: 171) notes: More believed that the criticisms in book one could lead to social action, '[l]ike the good civil servant that he was, More believed that legislated reform could bring utopia into being'.[6]

---

[5] See also Linebaugh's (1991) book *The London Hanged* for an account of redistribution through custom and its criminalisation in the 18C. Here Linebaugh reveals the relationship between the organised death of living labour (capital punishment) and the oppression of the living by dead labour (the punishment of capital) in the 18th century spectacle of hanging. Here hanging was not simply a form of punishment but a way of forcing the poor to accept the criminalisation of customary rights and new forms of private property.

[6] Wallerstein (2001: 171) notes that More's Utopia does contain one inequality. It would appear even in Utopia that there is 'dirty and heavy work' to be done that requires the labour of

Owen too (1991: 22) considered 'crime' to be directly related to the social structures in place, and also believed (initially), that reform through legislation and social awareness (in addition to his very practical social reform schemes and co-operative villages) was the way forward, asking: *"How much longer shall we continue to allow generation after generation to be taught crime from their infancy, and, when so taught, hunt them like beasts of the forest, until they are entangled beyond escape in the toils and nets of the law? when, if the circumstances of those poor unpitied sufferers had been reversed with those who are even surrounded with the pomp and dignity of justice, these latter would have been at the bar of the culprit, and the former would have been in the judgment seat".*

The shared recognition that poverty (and correspondingly) general 'crime' is related to economic and social structures rather than the 'fecklessness' of the poor underpinned these calls for a new social order. They also contained the germinating recognition that some crimes were punishable i.e. those of the poor; while elsewhere in society, significant acts of injustice (such as enclosure of the land) were largely unchallenged, except by the dispossessed themselves whose resistance was itself criminalised. Acknowledging these concepts, utopian thinkers went on to develop, and often to introduce, radical reforms aimed at creating a new social world. Utopian thinking provides a potential critique for existing social, political and economic conditions, while at the same time, setting out a vision for change for a new society (although the basis for this and means of achieving it differ).

Relevance to Criminological thinking

The importance of developing a social critique has resulted in the spectre of dystopia as a frequent presence in criminological thinking. Indeed, it could be argued that there are more images of dystopias both in current critiques of penal development (Parenti, 2008;Wacquant, 2009) and future visions of society (Nellis, 2006) than there are of actual utopias. Zedner (2002) warns of the 'dangers of dystopias in penal theory, noting that the insecurities of late capitalism can cause greater fear than the fear

slaves recruited among convicts, prisoners of war and 'criminals worthy of death' brought from foreign countries and the hiring of mercenaries for the defence of Utopia. This echoes Adorno's (1998: 32) observation that it 'is peculiar to the bourgeois Utopia that it is not yet able to conceive an image of perfect joy without that of the person excluded from it'.

of crime. Wacquant (2009) also makes the point that concerns about 'security' need to go beyond the limited spheres of crime and justice. The dystopic visions of the future set out by critical criminologists to precipitate change has led Zedner (2002) to argue that the 'political project' this originally entailed (attempts to precipitate structural change necessary to transform the social order), has largely been abandoned.

The political potential of 'the academy' to promote social change in relation to 'crime' and social control developed in the early 1970's with the emergence of a *New Criminology* from which *Radical/Critical Criminology* emerged. In summary, this heralded an alternative to the administrative criminology which had had taken precedence and provided a critique which challenged the very definition of crime and institutions of 'social control'. While some of the key proponents of this approach challenged the very notion of 'criminology' as a discipline (i.e. Stan Cohen) the ideas proposed were crucial in the development of criminological thinking. Importantly, by questioning the basis of 'crime' as a concept and employing an analysis which took into account political economy, the New Criminology provided for an examination of both the criminalisation of the poor, and the crimes of the powerful.

By the 1980's the founders of the *New Criminology* had been (problematically) categorised as following one of two strains: realist and idealist. While those of a 'realist' persuasion turned their attention to the reality of crime and sought ways of addressing this asking, for example, *What is to be Done about Law and Order* (Lea and Young, 1984; Young, 1988) others retained their critique of the existing structural relations of society and maintained an abolitionist perspective (i.e. Mathieson 1974, Hulsman 1986, Davis, 2003; Sim, 2009, Ruggerio, 2010).

Elbert (2004) asks what happened during the 1980s to the 'utopian energies' that characterised critical criminology. Elbert notes: *The answer is quite visible today: it ended an ideological and theoretical common ground on which many critical criminologists of diverse nationalities and academic fields somehow managed to gather in the years previously. A more or less common 'object of critique' also seems to have been lost: the capitalist state and its modes of 'social control'.* (Elbert, 2004: 385). He notes the emergence of administrative criminology's elaborate plans 'to protect the middle classes' (388). *"This then is administrative criminology's utopian horizon: communitarian participation and the negotiated solution of conflicts".*

Looking back to the early days of the New Criminology, Paul Walton notes that *"To recognise the utopianism of the The New Criminology is to recognise its critical semiotic strategy. It seeks to produce a community of readers who are wedded to social change. It is this radical textual strategy that entitles The New Criminology to be taken as an intellectually serious rather than merely a respectable, professional contribution to human knowledge"* (Walton, 1998: 4). However, as Stan Cohen (1998) points out, the pursuit of immediately achievable goals in the short-term can obscure the longer-term revolutionary alternatives; a tension that has been prevalent between utopian vision and reformist practicalities. For example, Loader (1998) calls for 'utopian realism' which retains an affinity to left realism and which he argues should be 'systematic', 'normative' and 'prudent'.

Peter Young (1992), more optimistically, suggests that the existence of utopia within critical criminology has been evident in the arguments for 'rehabilitation', and abolitionism, presenting a challenge to the 'penal dialect' (i.e. Hulsman, 1986, 1991; Christie, 1993) and creating a 'competing contradiction' (Mathieson, 1974); he notes that by contrast, appeals to realism can often end up as a defence of the status quo (see also Walton and Young, 1998; Ruggerio, 1992; Lippens, 1995).

Abolitionists, meanwhile, have continued to call for an end to the prison, and subsequently for changes in the entire mechanism of the distribution of punishment (Davis, 2003). They have acknowledged the need for these changes to be embedded within social and structural change (the prison industrial complex). However, the challenges that abolitionists face in being heard above the clamour of the current rhetoric on crime and punishment, and the difficulty in positing an alternative to the prison (for starters) means that they can often remain grounded in the critique (the need for critical analysis as resistance has been emphasised consistently by critical criminologists i.e. Cohen, 1998; Scraton, 2002). To obtain some level of credibility in the broader criminological/sociological and policy-based environments often pre-empts the space for going further by envisaging what a broader alternative would look like. As Angela Davis (2003: 105) asks: 'Why should it be so difficult to imagine alternatives to our current system of incarceration'? Here lies the distinction from utopian thinking, which requires some consideration of future alternatives, and the space to dream a little. What would society after the prison (and its carceral companions) look like? As Davis (2003: 108) notes: "Alternatives that fail to address racism, male dominance, homophobia, class bias, and other structures of domination will not, in the final analysis, lead to decarceration and will not advance the goal of abolition".

But to continue to develop the questions raised by an abolitionist perspective requires that the focus of attention does not stop at critique. Following the 'utopian impulse' requires further consideration of the vision required to go beyond critique, and the action required to make changes.

II

Applying Utopian Thought to Critical Criminology

While there is much to be said about the potential for development here, and this chapter reports on work in progress, some general points for consideration are outlined. They take the form of critique (through theoretical engagement) and change (through action). This requires some consideration of directions for moving forward. The current interest in 'utopian thinking' provides an opportunity to raise a number of issues that need to be addressed in order to consider new possibilities in terms of social, political, economic and philosophical thought. In the current climate of neoliberal entrenchment (Jacoby, 1999; Dean, 2009; Wacquant, 2009; Zizek, 2009) utopian visions are all the more relevant, although perhaps increasingly distant.

By continuing to consolidate and develop a critical criminology, it may be possible to contribute to the ongoing debates about the current crisis in criminal justice systems and their development, and in the wider social, political and economic sphere. This may require consideration of the emergence and continuation of 'oppositional sites' while at the same time, considering the role of critical criminology in supporting alternative forms of collective action (as proposed by Elbert, 2004; and more broadly Bourdieu, 1997). Indeed Elbert (2004) accuses New Realism of supporting the 'human face of late capitalism' in the UK and Latin America. Instead, he argues, critical criminologists should be describing and interpreting the dynamics of late capitalism and its consequences, and searching for alternatives to oppressive systems of social regulation.

Outwith criminology, a number of developments in this direction can be noted: the emergence of new social movements with the aim of social transformation (i.e. global resistance and anti-capitalist movements) which set out the inequities of neo-liberalism as a basis for critique; and actively seek to transform the existing social, political and economic landscape by direct action.

Perhaps the real challenge for utopian thinking is how to bridge the gap between the academic critique of existing societies which forms an accepted basis of theoretical enquiry, and the development of visions for social change (Cohen, 1998). This can come about through academic engagement with activist struggles (see Sudbury, 2005; Wacquant, 2009) but ultimately, how far can critical criminology go in making these changes and what can be put in place as a 'compass' for moving forward (Wright, 2006)?

A potential area for consideration lies in the action of small 'grass root' organisations which are able to create 'oppositional spaces' and in doing so, provide us with alternative examples of responses to crime and/or challenges to current institutional responses to crime[7]. These 'pockets of resistance' allow for the retention of a vision for alternatives, and can inform possibilities for the future. As Peter Young (1992: 429) points out, "utopias are intimately connected with hope. Utopias are inherently optimistic and continually argue for a brighter future".

Bearing in mind the historical utopias described above, it is also possible to draw upon examples of communitarian societies, which have attempted to provide models of utopian vision. If crime and deviance are viewed as environmental, and therefore cannot be controlled in conventional society, then utopian communities may be the logical alternative (Albanese, 1982). They can be considered as 'utopian' in their vision of a new place and creation of a visible site that is not the wider society. However, while intentional communities do exist, the historical visions discussed previously, became obsolete a long time ago. There are few examples in operation today, and few have been operationalised in previous years.

By considering their legacy however, it is possible to consider what alternative 'communities' have to offer by inspiring and sustaining a space for potential social change. They provide examples of different forms and meanings of 'justice', encapsulated in different forms of living (Hostetler, 1974; Abrams and McCulloch, 1976; McLaughlin and Davidson, 1985; Sawatsky, 2009). There has been increasing emphasis in Scotland on 'communities of recovery' emerging out of the 'recovery

---

[7] See for example the activist work outlined by the contributors in Sudbury (2005) in response to the increasing incarceration of women internationally.

movement' from drug and alcohol and drawing upon the development of therapeutic communities (White and Kurtz, 2005 and 2006). However, as Christie (1989) notes, these communities are aimed at preparing the individual for integration into wider society rather than the transformation of that wider society.

It is also important to be cognisant of the way in which current 'community'-speak often masks the role of the state in criminalising and distributing punishment (justice). The current social, political and economic climate has resulted in decimated communities and real contention over the very meaning of community (see Young, 1999; Brent, 2009).

Some Concluding Thoughts

Starting from the premise that crime is socially constructed and created, how then can social structures be changed and what, if any, role can critical criminology play in achieving change? And in 2011, what would change look like? While continuing to develop critiques, it is also necessary to highlight the need for new visions, visions which can become potential oppositional forces in their own right; however, as this paper has highlighted such visions may end up supporting those structures which need to be challenged. Midgley (1996: 24) notes: "If this distant view is never seen – if a society simply never takes the trouble to notice how far it is from fulfilling its supposed ideals – then there is nothing to stop it becoming complacent about its present state". As Goodwin and Taylor (1982) argue Utopian politics can only emerge from the historically specific political dilemmas which the concept embraces. It is the practical and historical characteristics of the Utopian impulse that place it beyond the false oppositions of idealism and realism. As Jameson (2005, xii) writes in relation to Utopia, today 'there is no alternative'.

References

Al-Azmeh, A. (2009) Islams and Modernities London: Verso

Abrams, P. and McCulloch, A. (1976) *Communes, Sociology and Society,* Cambridge: Cambridge University Press.

Ackerman, B. Alstott, A. and van Parijs, P. (2006) *Redesigning Distribution: Basic Income and Stakeholder Grants as Cornerstones of a more Egalitarian Capitalism*, Volume V of the Real Utopias Project Series, London: Verso.

Adorno, T. W. (1998) *Beethoven: The Philosophy of Music,* Cambridge: Polity Press.

Albanese, J.S. (1982) 'Deviance in Utopia: The Criminology of Ideal Society', *World Future Society Bulletin,* Jan/Feb, p25-29.

Bourdieu, P. (1997) *A Reasoned Utopia and Economic Fatalism,* speech of acceptance of the Ernest-Bloch Preis der Stadt Ludwigshafen, 22 November 1997.

Bourdieu, P. (1998) 'A Reasoned Utopia and Economic Fatalism' *New Left Review* I/227, January-February.

Bowles, S. and Gintis, H. (1999) *Recasting Egalitarianism: New Rules for Accountability and Equity in Markets, States and Communities*, Volune III, Real Utopias Project Series, London: Verso.

Brent, J. (2009) *Searching for Community,* Bristol: Policy Press.

Bruce, S. (1999) (Ed) *Three Early Modern Utopias: Thomas More: Utopia / Francis Bacon: New Atlantis / Henry Neville: The Isle of Pines,* Oxford: Oxford World's Classics.

Carrington, K. and Hogg, R. (eds) (2002) *Critical Criminology,* Cullompton: Willan Publishing.

Christie, N. (1989) *Beyond Loneliness and Institutions: Communes for Extraordinary People,* Norway: Norwegian University Press.

Christie, N. (1993) *Crime Control as Industry,* (second edition), London: Routledge.

Cohen, S. (1998) 'Intellectual Scepticism and Political Commitment: The Case of Radical Criminology', in P. Walton and J. Young (Eds) *The New Criminology Revisited,* Hampshire: Palgrave.

Cohen, S. (2001) *States of Denial,* Cambridge: Polity Press.

Cohen, J and Rogers, J (1995) *Associations and Democracy*, Volume I, Real Utopias Project Series, London: Verso.

Davis, A. (2003) *Are Prisons Obsolete?* New York: Seven Stories Press.

Dean, J. (2009) *Democracy and Other Neoliberal Fantasies: Communicative Capitalism and Left Politics,* Durham: Duke University Press.

Eagleton, T. (2000) 'Defending Utopia' *New Left Review*, 4 Jul-Aug, 173-176.

Elbert, C. A. (2004) 'Rebuilding Utopia? Critical Criminology and the difficult road of reconstruction in Latin America', *Crime, Law and Social Change,* 41, 385-395.

Engels, F. (1970) *Socialism: Utopian and Scientific,* Moscow: Progress Publishers.

Fourier, C. (1971) *Design for Utopia: Selected Writings of Charles Fourier,* New York: Schocken Books.

Fung, A and Olin Wright, E. (2003) *Deepening Democracy: Innovations in Empowered Participatory Governance,* Volume IV of the Real Utopias Project Series, London: Verso.

Gott, R. (1993) *Land Without Evil: Utopian Journey's Across the South American Watershed,* London: Verso

Goodwin, B. (Ed) (2001) *The Philosophy of Utopia,* London: Routledge.

Goodwin. B and Taylor, K. (1982) *The Politics of Utopia: A Study in Theory and Practice*, London: Hutchison.

Gornick, J. and Meyers, M. (2009) *Gender Equality: Transforming Family Divisions of Labor* London and New York: Verso.

Harvey, D. (2005) *A Brief History of Neoliberalism,* Oxford: Oxford University Press.

Harvey, D. (2010) *A Companion to Marx's Capital,* London: Verso.

Hoare, Q. and Nowell Smith, G. (1971) *Antonio Gramsci: Selection from Prison Notebooks,* London: Lawrence and Wishart.

Hostetler, J. (1974) *Communitarian Societies,* New York: Holt, Rinehart and Winston, Inc.

Hulsman, L. (1986) 'Critical Criminology and the Concept of Crime', *Contemporary Crises,* 10, 63-80.

Hulsman, L. (1991) 'The Abolitionist Case: Alternative Crime Policies', *Israel Law Review,* 25, 3-4, 681-709.

Jameson, F (1975) 'World Reduction in Le Guin: The Emergence of Utopian Narrative', *Science-Fiction Studies*, no. 7, p. 230.

Jameson, F (1982) 'Progress versus Utopia, or, Can We Imagine the Future?', *Science-Fiction Studies*, no. 27, p. 153.

Jameson, F (2005) *Archaeologies of the Future: The Desire Called Utopia and Other Science Fictions,* London: Verso

Jacoby, R. (1999) *The End of Utopia,* New York: Basic Books.

Kropotkin, P. (1902; 2006) *Mutual Aid,* Mineola: Dover Publications Inc.

Kropotkin, P. (1906; 2007) *The Conquest of Bread,* Edinburgh: AK Press.

Kumar, K. (1991) *Utopianism,* Buckingham: Open University Press.

Lévi-Strauss, C. (1973) *Mythologiques: Introduction to a Science of Mythology Vol 2, From Honey to Ashes* London: Cape

Lea, J. and Young, J. (1984) *What is to be done about law and order?,* London: Pluto Press.

Levitas, R. (1997) 'Educated Hope: Ernst Bloch on Abstract and Concrete Utopia' in J. Owen Daniel and T. Moylan (Eds), *Not Yet: Reconsidering Ernst Bloch* London: Verso

Linebaugh, P. (1991) *The London Hanged: Crime and Civil Society in the Eighteenth Century,* London: Allen Lane

Lippens, R. (1995) 'Critical Criminologies and the Reconstruction of Utopia', *Social Justice,* Vol. 22, No. 1, p 32-50.

Loader, I. (1998) 'Criminology and the Public Sphere: Arguments for Utopian Realism', in P. Walton and J. Young (Eds) *The New Criminology Revisited,* Hampshire: Palgrave.

Malloch, M. and Munro, W. (2010) 'Crime, Critique and Utopia', paper presented at the European Group for the Study of Deviance and Social Control, *Politics of Criminology Conference,* University of the Aegean, Mytilene, Lesbos, Greece, September 2010.

Manuel, F. and Manuel, S. (1979) *Utopian Thought in the Western World,* Oxford: Basil Blackwell.

Marin, L. (1984) *Utopics,* New York: Humanity Books.

Marx, K. and Engels, F. (1964) *The German Ideology,* Moscow: Progress Publishers

Marx, K. and Engels, F. (1975) *The Holy Family, or Critique of Critical Criticism,* Moscow: Progress Publishers.

Marx, K. and Engels, F. (1970) *The Communist Manifesto,* New York: Pathfinder.

Mathieson, T. (1974) *The Politics of Abolition,* Oxford: Martin Robertson.

McLaughlin, C. and Davidson, G. (1985) *Builders of the Dawn,* Tennessee: Stillpoint Publishing.

Métraux, M. (1948) "The Guaraní" in J. Steward (Ed) *Handbook of South American Indians, Vol 3: The Tropical Forest Tribes* New York: Smithsonian Institution.

Midgley, M. (1996) *Utopias, Dolphins and Computers,* London: Routledge.

More, T. (1999) 'Utopia' in S. Bruce, (Ed) *Three Early Modern Utopias: Thomas More: Utopia / Francis Bacon: New Atlantis / Henry Neville: The Isle of Pines,* Oxford: Oxford World's Classics

Morris, W. (1995) *News from Nowhere,* Cambridge: Cambridge University Press.

Nellis, M. (2006) 'Future Punishment in American Science Fiction Films' in P. Mason, *Captured by the Media,* Cullompton: Willan Publishing.

Owen, R. (1991) *A New View of Society and Other Writings,* London: Penguin Books. (edited and introduced by Gregory Claeys).

Parenti, C. (2008) *Lockdown America,* London: Verso Books, second edition.

Popper, K. R. (1945) *The Open Society and its Enemies Vol.2: The High Tide of Prophecy. Hegel, Marx, and the Aftermath,* London: Routledge & Kegan Paul.

Roemer, J. (1996) *Equal Shares: Making Market Socialism Work*, Volume II, Real Utopias Project Series, London: Verso.

Ruggiero, V. (1992) 'Realist Criminology: A Critique' in J. Young and R. Mathews (Eds) *Rethinking Criminology: the Realist Debate,* London: Sage.

Ruggiero, V. (2010) *Penal Abolitionism,* Oxford: Oxford University Press.

Sawatsky, J. (2009) *The Ethic of Traditional Communities: Studies from Hollow Water, the Iona Community and Plum Village,* London: Jessica Kingsley Publishers.

Scraton, P. (2002) 'Defining 'power' and challenging 'knowledge': critical analysis as resistance in the UK' in K. Carrington and R. Hogg, *Critical Criminology: Issues, Debates, Challenges,* Cullompton: Willan Publishing.

Sim, J. (2009) *Punishment and Prisons: Power and the Carceral State,* London: Sage Publications.

Sudbury, J. (ed) (2005) *Global Lockdown: Race, Gender and the Prison-Industrial Complex,* New York: Routledge.

Wacquant, L. (2009) *Punishing the Poor: The Neoliberal Government of Social Insecurity,* London: Duke University Press.

Wallerstein, E. (2001) *Unthinking Social Science: The Limits of Nineteenth-Century Paradigms,* Philadelphia: Temple Univercity Press

Walton, P. (1998) 'Big Science: Dystopia and Utopia' in P. Walton and J. Young, J. (eds) *The New Criminology Revisited,* Hampshire: Palgrave MacMillan.

Walton, P. and Young, J. (eds) (1998) *The New Criminology Revisited,* Hampshire: Palgrave MacMillan.

White, W. and Kurtz, E. (2005) *The Varieties of Recovery Experience,* Chicago: Great Lakes Addiction Technology Transfer Center.

White, W. and Kurtz, E. (2006) *Recovery: Linking Addiction Treatment and Communities of Recovery,* Northeast ATTC.

Wright, E.O. (2006) 'Compass Points' *New Left Review* 41, September-October.

Wright, E.O. (2010) *Envisioning Real Utopias,* London: Verso.

Young, J. (1988) 'Radical Criminology in Britain: The Emergence of a Competing Paradigm', *British Journal of Criminology,* Vol. 28, No. 2, p.159-183.

Young, J. (1999) *The Exclusive Society,* London: Sage Publications.

Young, P. (1992) 'The Importance of Utopias in Criminological Thinking', *British Journal of Criminology,* 32: 4, pp 423-437.

Zedner, L. (2002) 'Dangers of Dystopia in Penal Theory', *Oxford Journal of Legal Studies,* 22, 2, pp341-366.

Zizek, S. (2009) *First as Tragedy, Then as Farce,* London: Verso.

3.

NEOLIBERAL CRIME POLICY: WHO PROFITS?

Emma Bell

In order to answer the question posed in the title of this paper, it is first necessary to define exactly what we mean by neoliberal crime policy. The focus here is on the British context, although variants of neoliberal crime policies can of course be detected across most Western nations today. In many ways, neoliberal crime policy is not dissimilar to crime policies of the past: it targets the 'usual suspects', namely the poorest and most disadvantaged members of society, whilst largely turning a blind eye to the crimes of the powerful; it continues to rely on imprisonment to punish convicted offenders and to deter future offenders; and it aims to send out a moral message about the State's limits of tolerance. However, in contrast with penal policies of the past, particularly those associated with social democracy, neoliberal crime policy is supported by a greatly-extended penal apparatus in the form of new surveillance technologies, extensive new regulatory powers and the rise of out-of-court penalties. This intensification of the punitive capacity of the State is justified by the need to prevent crime before it occurs. Whilst the optimism of the previous era centred on the State's capacity to rehabilitate and reintegrate offenders, contemporary penal optimism centres on the State's capacity to control risky behaviour.

Consequently, following Wilson and Kelling's 'broken windows theory' (Wilson and Kelling, 1982), governments of all political hues since the mid-1990s onwards have focused their attentions on combating low-level disorder. To this end, New Labour invented the ASBO[1], the Penalty Notice for Disorder[2] and the Dispersal Order[3], alongside a range

---

[1] ASBOs were created by the *Crime and Disorder Act 1998*. They may be handed down to anyone aged ten or over who is thought to have acted in an anti-social manner, that is to say, "in a manner that caused or was likely to cause harassment, alarm or distress to one or more persons not of the same household as himself". Breach of an order demanding that a person refrain from engaging in antisocial behaviour may result in a sentence of imprisonment.

[2] The Penalty Notice for Disorder (PND), created by the *Criminal Justice and Police Act 2001*, gives police, community support officers and other 'accredited persons' the power to give on-the-spot fines to those responsible for behaviour which is considered to provoke 'harassment, alarm or distress', as well as to those guilty of more specific offences such as criminal damage or the purchase of alcohol for a young person aged under 18.

of social intervention measures such as Youth Inclusion Programmes[4] and Family Intervention Programmes[5]. At the high end of the punishment spectrum, indeterminate prison sentences have proliferated in the name of protecting the public from recidivist behaviour[6]. Although preventative penalties existed in the past in Britain, notably the indeterminate sentence created under the Prevention of Crime Act 1908, they were in practice little-used on account of their failure to respect sentencing proportionality (Radzinowicz and Hood, 1990: 283; Bailey, 1997: 302). Today, by contrast, disproportionality in the penal system has become commonplace. In addition, there is a renewed focus on the individual responsibility of offenders who are once again to be considered as fully rational actors, responsive to incentives and disincentives to engage in criminal activity. Neoliberal theory (along with classical liberal theory, for that matter) certainly favours such a view of criminal behaviour: just as individual citizens are considered to act in ways which will best maximise their own interests, potential offenders are thought to commit crime only when the benefits of crime are greater than the costs incurred. Consequently, should society wish to reduce crime levels, it must increase the relative costs of criminality by rendering punishment more certain and severe (Becker, 1968; Zedner, 2009). However, such logic clashes with disproportional sentencing. As Joseph Stigler, a key neoliberal economist explained, where such sentences are used 'the marginal deterrence of heavy punishments could be very small or even negative' (Stigler, 1970: 527). This would suggest that disproportionately severe

---

[3] The *Antisocial Behaviour Act 2003* created the Dispersal Order which gives senior police officers the power to disperse groups of two people or more from a public place when he or she has reasonable grounds for believing that *their presence or* behaviour has resulted in, *or is likely to result in*, one or more people being intimidated, harassed, alarmed or distressed.

[4] Youth Inclusion Programmes (YIPs), created in 2000, bring together all those who participate in local Crime Reduction Partnerships, from police to social services and voluntary associations, to share information about eight to 17-year-olds at risk of engaging in criminal or antisocial behaviour. The young people are then invited to participate in a YIP, which may function as a kind of local youth group, providing social and educational services as well as extra-curricular activities

[5] Family Intervention Projects, first introduced in 2006, aim to work with deprived families to tackle the causes of their antisocial behaviour. Sanctions for families who fail to cooperate can be severe: for example, they may be evicted from their social housing, have their children taken into care or have their social benefits withheld.

[6] For example, the Indeterminate Sentence for Public Protection (IPP), introduced in April 2005, allow judges to impose a minimum period of imprisonment (tariff) on offenders, after the end of which they must remain in prison until the Parole Board considers that they no longer pose a threat to the public, at which point they may be released on licence.

punishment such as we are witnessing today is not intrinsic to neoliberalism itself, as experts such as Loïc Wacquant have suggested (Wacquant, 2009). It is instead argued here that penal severity results from the peculiar political conjecture that neoliberalism produced in the UK.

That peculiar conjecture was one where the two major political parties in the UK were suffering severe crises of legitimacy. In 1993, the year to which the so-called 'punitive turn' is usually dated, the Conservatives were struggling to deal with the socially destructive legacy of Thatcherism, whilst the Labour Party was attempting to come to terms with neoliberal hegemony and to shed what it had come to consider as its left-wing baggage. The Conservatives' crusade on crime was part of a wider campaign to rebuild the moral foundations of society, creating what Harvey has described as 'social glue' (Harvey, 2007) capable of uniting the nation around a common project – that of neoliberalism. For New Labour, adopting a tough stance on crime was a way for it to divest itself of its unjustly-earned image as being 'soft on crime' whilst providing it with an issue that could appeal to voters across class lines, thus also enabling the party to shed its lifelong association with the working classes and move into the political mainstream. Indeed, once the party had reconciled itself to the new neoliberal order, it found itself relatively powerless to assume the key function of the social-democratic State as it had been understood since the beginning of the 20th Century – guaranteeing the social security of its citizens. Although, in government, it did attempt to manage the socially deleterious effects of neoliberalism, thus inaugurating a new, less destructive 'roll out' neoliberalism in opposition to the 'roll back' neoliberalism of the Thatcher era (Jamie Peck and Adam Tickell 2002), its commitment to neoliberal orthodoxy, which focused on individual rather than state responsibility for social problems, rendered any attempt to tackle social injustice entirely futile. Crime policy can thus be understood a way of managing the neoliberal transformation of the State from provider of social security to facilitator of market solutions (Leys, 2003). Wacquant is correct to describe punitive penal trends as part of an ongoing *political* project, designed to consolidate the authority and legitimacy of the neoliberal state.

Indeed, as David Garland has argued, toughness in the face of the crime problem is a means for the State to demonstrate its capacity to protect citizens from the risk posed by crime whilst it remains relatively powerless to protect them from the various risks posed by what he describes as 'late modernity' (Garland, 2001). Rather than speaking of late modernity, I think it is more appropriate to speak of neoliberalism, which is surely the overarching political orthodoxy of contemporary times. It is specifically neoliberalism which has both exacerbated social problems and rendered the State impotent in face of them. It has done this by forcing a profound restructuring of the labour market and also by fostering a culture of hedonism in the economic sphere whilst simultaneously encouraging a culture of authoritarianism in the social sphere. Ironically, as irresponsibility has come to characterise the world of finance, increasing focus has been placed on the need to encourage individual responsibility for social problems. Consequently, all of New Labour's attempts to tackle the social problems which it identified as key causes of crime were focused primarily on the need to encourage, or even force, individuals and families to take responsibility for turning their lives around. In the penal sphere, welfarist measures were underpinned by coercion, leading to the extension of punishment through welfare.

Here, we see in operation what Garland has described as 'sovereign state' and 'adaptive' strategies for dealing with the crime problem. The first involves the State reasserting its power to punish whilst the second involves it effectively admitting its weakness in face of the crime problem as it attempts to offload its responsibility in that regard onto communities themselves. Both strategies were adopted by successive New Labour governments in Britain. On the one hand, the State's 'power to punish' was reasserted as a huge number of new offences were created and increasing numbers of people found themselves criminalised. On the other, communities were encouraged to join in the fight against crime by becoming members of Crime and Disorder Partnerships or by volunteering their services as Police Community Support Officers, for example. These two strategies are complementary rather than contradictory since they both facilitate the dispersal of state power throughout society. They also help to absolve the Neoliberal State of responsibility for the crime problem: the first strategy responsibilises the offender whilst the second responsibilises citizens and communities. It is in this sense that the State 'profits' from neoliberal crime policies. The profits are not pecuniary – indeed, spending on law and order has been increasing wildly in recent years – but should rather be understood in terms of the legitimacy they can confer on those States which apply them. It is true that in practice New Labour failed to either to foster a culture of responsibility or to successfully legitimise its own power. It has instead fostered a culture of irresponsibility towards others by fostering a form of exclusive, egotistical individualism. Moreover, no matter how tough New Labour governments got on crime, it was still perceived to be 'soft' in this respect. Nonetheless, in the context of the neoliberal transformation of the State, crime, like immigration, represented one of the few 'popular' issues which it could regularly invoke in an attempt to appeal to the public at large. It may thus be understood as an attempt at legitimation at a time when governments can no longer seek legitimacy by presenting themselves as providers of social and economic security.

Yet, the State is not the only one to profit from neoliberal crime policies. The private actors who form part of the 'security-industrial complex' also benefit considerably. They have influenced the punitive direction of these policies and then reaped the benefits, using crime control to protect their own commercial imperatives. Increasingly, as government has come to see its key role as facilitator of market solutions, it has, according to Joe Sim (2010) come to share what Hall and Scraton (1981) once described as a 'correspondence of interests' with the private sector. Governments in post-war Britain tended to share commonality of interests with civil service and academic élites, both of whom tended to see themselves as the 'platonic guardians' of the public interest, entrusted to govern the country as they saw fit (Loader, 2006). These élites shared a common view that the science of government demanded the application of highly-specialised professional (meaning academic) expertise to specific social and economic problems: politics was above all to remain neutral, impervious to the high emotions of public opinion or to personal whims (Loader, 2006: 568-570; Clarke and Newman, 2006: 4-8). They shared a common interest in preserving their (relatively privileged) professional status. Today, neoliberal governments have come instead to share an interest with the private sector in applying market solutions wherever possible. For example, the commodification of public services provided a significant financial opportunity for private business whilst enabling government to preach the discourse of modernisation and to claim to be reducing the cost to the public purse (even if this did not actually occur[7]). In terms of criminal justice, both parties benefited in this way when criminal justice services were opened up to contestability. The private sector has been able to compete for contracts to run criminal justice services from prisons to probation and, in some cases, it

---

[7] In actual fact, expenditure on prisons and probation increased substantially in the UK between 1999 and 2009 (*cf.* Mills, Silvestri and Grimshaw, 2010).

has been given a significant advantage over the public sector: in one particular case, a contract for prison management was awarded to the private sector despite the fact that the public sector bid was actually less costly (Barnett, 1999). The private sector has been able to make phenomenal profits as providers of a wide variety of security services, from prison escort services to new surveillance technologies. It is estimated that the private security company Serco makes over £50 million a year from managing four adult prisons alone (PPRI, 2005).

In addition, tackling the highly visible forms of crime and antisocial behaviour which are perceived to threaten business both helped to protect business interests and enabled government to be seen to be responding to the kind of behaviour which most worries the public. It should not be forgotten that a key plank of the Labour Party's transformation from 'old' to 'new' Labour entailed the forging of close links with the business community in an attempt to gain a wider support base and to prove its competence in economic matters. For business, a focus on street crime has enabled it to divert attention from the crimes and social harms that it might cause. Indeed, business is more usually seen as a victim than a perpetrator of crime. Alongside the increased regulation of the powerless, there has been a corresponding deregulation of the crimes of the powerful. There has been a serious failure to persecute crimes perpetrated *by* businesses, such as the failure to respect their duty of care towards their employees, particularly those employed in the construction industry (Coleman *et al.*, 2005). According to Tombs and Whyte, there is a serious 'crisis of enforcement' as state agencies routinely fail to effectively regulate breaches of health and safety regulations in the workplace (Tombs and Whyte, 2008; 2010). Sim refers to this as the 'non-governance' of social harms (Sim, 2009: 88). This occurs despite the fact that the Health and Safety Executive estimates that two thirds of accidents at work are caused by companies breaching their duty of care with regard to health and safety regulations (Tombs and Whyte, 2008: 5). The law is more usually employed to protect businesses. For example, nine people were arrested under the *Antisocial Behaviour Act 2003* for holding a demonstration outside Caterpillar's offices in Solihull, Birmingham, in protest against the sale of machinery to the Israeli army (Statewatch, 2010), whilst section 132 of the *Serious Organised Crime and Police Act 2005* modified the *Protection from Harassment Act 1997* to enable it to apply to the harassment of two people or more, thus permitting it to be used against protesters lobbying against the government or a business, for example.

Business has been welcomed into government circles as a key partner in fighting crime, as was symbolically demonstrated by the 1998 *Crime and Disorder Act* which places a duty on members of Crime and Disorder Reduction Partnerships (CDRPs) to develop crime-fighting strategies in consultation with local businesses. In some cases, key aspects of crime control have even been handed over to private companies. For example, Business Improvement Districts (BIDs), created under *The Local Government Act 2003*, are partnerships between local authorities and businesses which aim to create conditions favourable to commerce. Businesses present in certain designated areas are given free rein to make any changes they think necessary to meet this aim. For example, they may decide to recruit private security guards to patrol the area and/or to forbid certain kinds of behaviour. Consequently, the notion of 'public' space is being redefined to fit with the concerns of local businesses. Certain areas in Britain's cities are no longer freely accessible to any member of the public but rather to those who might contribute to the economic prosperity of the area: consumers, investors and tourists. The main priority of urban crime control policy has thus been to eliminate all those who may dissuade potential consumers from visiting city centres. This is not about tackling crime *per se* but rather about ensuring that people feel safe. The notion of crime is thus extremely widely-defined to encompass all such behaviour which consumers may find off-putting. Under the influence of corporate interests, the British government has been applying a form of what van Swaaningen has described as a form of 'revanchist urbanism' whereby the poor, rather than being incorporated within public spaces, are held responsible for crime and the decay of the inner cities and are thus deemed to have forfeited their right to inhabit 'public' space (Van Swaaningen, 2005). Meanwhile, control of these spaces is handed over to private business. Business is thus granted further opportunities for profit maximisation whilst government can vaunt the benefits of urban regeneration projects.

Despite the managerialist rhetoric about the need to satisfy the 'consumers' of criminal justice services, it is this group of people who profit the least from neoliberal crime policies. It is useful here to ask who exactly government is referring to when it speaks of the 'consumers' of these services. For New Labour, the consumers were clearly considered to be the victims of crime and the public at large in whose interests the criminal justice system needed to be 'rebalanced'. The interests of the other 'consumers' of criminal justice services – namely offenders themselves – were, however, routinely ignored. Laws intended to protect the interests of the former tended to undermine the interests of the latter, such as the abolition of the 'double jeopardy' rule[8]. Yet, in practice, none of these groups have benefitted to any significant extent from neoliberal crime policies. Although the voice of victims of crime is now more likely to be heard by the courts via, for example, Victim Personal Statements which allow courts to hear about the impact of certain crimes on their victims, legal conflicts very much remain the property of the State (contrary to Nils Christie's advice delivered almost 35 years ago – 1977). This fact is demonstrated by the hijacking of restorative justice programmes by the State[9]. The general public also fails to 'profit' from neoliberal crime policies in any significant way. As taxpayers, the public suffers considerable pecuniary loss through increased expenditure on the criminal justice system. It is not even possible to argue that this is good value for money since it is notoriously hard to prove any link between such expenditure and falls in crime rates. Furthermore, government failure to tackle social injustice and the structural causes of reoffending has meant that the poorest and most vulnerable members of society – those who suffer most from crime and antisocial behaviour – are even more likely than ever to become victims of crime. Despite New Labour's professed commitment to 'left realism', the poorest tenth of the population are considerably more likely to be murdered than the rest of the population (Dorling, 2006), whilst those living in the poorest areas of England and Wales are more likely to feel that they are affected by anti-social behaviour (Thorpe and Hall, 2009: 101). It might also be argued that they are also more likely to suffer from unofficially-defined forms of antisocial behaviour perpetrated by companies which employ them in dangerous, low-paid jobs without respecting health and safety regulations. Society as a whole has also suffered from the general erosion of civil liberties which, it has been claimed, is the price to pay for greater public

---

[8] This legal rule, according to which an offender cannot be tried twice for the same crime, was effectively abolished by the *Criminal Justice Act 2003* which permits the Court of Appeal to annul an acquittal and order a new trial when there is 'new and compelling evidence against the acquitted person in relation to the qualifying offence' provided that a new trial would be 'in the interests of justice'.

[9] A case in point is Northern Ireland where restorative justice emerged as an alternative to formal justice procedures but has now largely been subsumed under the latter (*cf.* Convery *et al.*, 2008).

protection. Finally, whilst some offenders have experienced a slight improvement in the material conditions of their detention (such as the end of slopping out), many more others have found themselves subject to worsening conditions in overcrowded jails or to an erosion of the centuries-old protections designed to protect them from miscarriages of justice – we mentioned the abolition of the double jeopardy rule above, but we can also list the admission of hearsay evidence into criminal trials, the limitation of the right to choose trial by jury, the decline in the quality of legal protection offered to defendants on account of the severe limitation of legal aid; not to mention the blurring of the boundaries between the civil and the criminal law via the creation of hybrid measures such as the ASBO. We might also note the disgraceful treatment of those suspected of having committed, prepared to commit, or merely promoted acts of terrorism.

It might be asked whether a change in direction in penal policy is at all likely under the current coalition government in the UK. I would suggest, rather pessimistically, that the chances of this occurring are slim. Despite the coalition's declared commitment to civil liberties and the new Justice Minister's much-publicised indirect criticism of the 'prison works' philosophy which has dominated sentencing policy since at least 1993 (Ministry of Justice, 2010), it would appear that neoliberal crime policies will remain in place. The coalition's commitment to neoliberalism is firmly anchored. It would be a mistake to regard plans to increase state regulation of the financial sector as a retreat from neoliberalism. As Dardot and Laval point out, neoliberalism cannot be reduced to the notion of laissez-faire (2009). Furthermore, just like the state interventions in the economy in 2008 and 2009, which involved the part-nationalisation of the banks, future interventionist measures are likely to be regarded as emergency measures only, designed to ensure the survival of the neoliberal order rather than to herald the beginning of a fundamental transformation of capitalism (Callinicos, 2010: 128-9). Yet, as I suggested earlier, punitiveness in penal policy is not intrinsic to neoliberalism. Nonetheless, given the renewed crisis of legitimacy of the neoliberal order, it is likely that the coalition, as the New Labour governments before it, will turn to issues such as crime and immigration in a desperate attempt to appeal to the electorate across class lines and consequently try to secure its legitimacy, particularly in the context of massive public spending cuts which will inevitably exacerbate social and economic insecurities and undermine its already fragile popularity. Indeed, in the recent general election, these issues continued to be a hot topic for debate amongst all three major contenders for office, situated in second and third places behind the economy in the public's list of 'Most Important Issues' facing the country. A closer analysis of the detail of crime policy reveals that a more libertarian approach in this respect is skin-deep only. It is only the civil liberties of the law-abiding that appear to be of concern to the current government. Rather than repealing legislation which has led to the blurring of the boundaries between the civil and the criminal law and the rise of out-of-court justice, the coalition government plans to extend the arsenal already available to the police, reducing 'timewasting bureaucracy' and amending the health and safety laws that 'stand in the way of common sense policing' (HM Government, 2010). This would suggest that the civil liberties of offenders are somewhat less sacrosanct. Indeed, the Conservatives promised to repeal the *Human Rights Act 1998* which they claim has rendered the fight against crime more difficult by protecting the human rights of criminals. Furthermore, plans to halt the current wild expansion of the prison population are likely to be difficult to pursue in practice: both parties to the coalition support the toughening up community sentences which is likely to mean that such penalties will continue to act as additions rather than alternatives to imprisonment. A commitment to 'honesty in sentencing' may mean that prison sentences will continue to lengthen. It is finally important to note that business will remain an important partner in the formulation of crime policy and the delivery of criminal justice services. Indeed, its role with regard to the latter is to be extended in the context of current budget cuts. Government is thus likely to continue to share a considerable 'correspondence of interest' with the private sector in prosecuting the crimes of the powerless whilst ignoring those of the powerful. Both parties will continue to profit from neoliberal penality.

References

Bailey, V. (1997) 'English Prisons, Penal Culture, and the Abatement of Imprisonment, 1895-1922', *Journal of British Studies*, 36(3), 285-324.

Becker, G. (1968) 'Crime and Punishment: An Economic Approach' *Journal of Political Economy*, 76(2), 169-217.

Callinicos, A. (2010) *Bonfire of Illusions: The Twin Crises of the Liberal World* Cambridge and Malden: Polity Press

Christie, N. (1977) 'Conflicts as Property', *British Journal of Criminology*, 17(1), 1-15.

Clarke, J. and Newman, J. (2006) *The Managerial State*, 2nd edn London and Thousand Oaks: Sage.

Coleman, R., Tombs, S. and Whyte, D. (2005) 'Capital, Crime Control and Statecraft in the Entrepreneurial City', *Urban Studies*, 42(13), 2511-2530.

Convery, U., Haydon, D., Moore, L. and Scraton, P. (2008) 'Children, Rights and Justice in Northern Ireland: Community and Custody', *Youth Justice*, 8(3), 245-263.

Dardot, P. and Laval, C. (2009) *La nouvelle raison du monde: Essai sur la société néolibérale,* Paris: Éditions de la Découverte.

Dorling, D. (2006) 'Prime Suspect: Murder in Britain', *Prison Service Journal*, 166, 3-10.

Garland, D. (2001) *The Culture of Control: Crime and Social Order in Contemporary Society,* Oxford and New York: Oxford University Press.

Hall, S. and Scraton, P. (1981) 'Law, Class and Control' in Fitzgerald, M., McLennan G. and Pawson, J. (eds.) *Crime and Society,* London and New York: Routledge.

Harvey, D. (2007) *A Brief History of Neoliberalism*, 2nd edn, Oxford and New York: Oxford University Press.
HM Government (2010) http://programmeforgovernment.hmg.gov.uk/, date accessed 26 May 2010.

Loader, I. (2006) 'Fall of the 'Platonic Guardians': Liberalism, Criminology and Political Responses to Crime in England and Wales', *British Journal of Criminology*, 46(4), 561-586.

Leys, C. (2003) *Market-Driven Politics: Neoliberal Democracy and the Public Interest*, 2nd edn, London and New York: Verso.

Mills, Helen, Silvestri, Arianna and Grimshaw, Roger (2010) *Prison and Probation Expenditure 1999-2009*, London, Centre for Crime and Justice Studies.

Ministry of Justice (2010), *Breaking the Cycle: Effective Punishment, Rehabilitation and Sentencing of Offenders*, Cm7972, London: HMSO.

Peck, J. and Tickell, A. (2002) 'Neoliberalizing Space', *Antipode*, 34(3), 380-404.

PPRI (2004) 'United Kingdom: Private sector: lower pay, longer hours, higher turnover', *Prison Privatisation Report International*, 65, http://www.psiru.org/justice/ppri65.htm, date accessed 26 May 2010.

Radzinowicz, L. and Hood, R. (1990) *The Emergence of Penal Policy in Victorian and Edwardian England,* Oxford: Clarendon Press.

Sim, J. (2010) 'Review Symposium: *Punishing the Poor – The Neoliberal Government of Insecurity* by Loïc Wacquant', *British Journal of Criminology*, 50 (1), 589-608.

Sim, J. (2009) *Punishment and Prisons: Power and the Carceral State,*(London and Thousand Oaks: Sage.

Statewatch (2010) http://www.statewatch.org/asbo/asbowatch-mentalhealth.htm, date accessed 21 December 2010.

Stigler, G. (1970) 'The Optimum Enforcement of Laws', *Journal of Political Economy*, 78(3), 526-536.

Thorpe, K. And Hall, P. (2009) 'Public Perceptions' in Walker, A. *et al.* (eds.) *Crime in England and Wales 2008/09 Volume 1: Findings from the British Crime Survey and police recorded crime,* London: Home Office.

Tombs, S. and Whyte, D. (2010) 'A deadly consensus: worker safety and regulatory degradation under New Labour', *British Journal of Criminology*, 50(1), 46-55.

Tombs, S. and Whyte, D. (2008) *A Crisis of Enforcement: The decriminalisation of death and injury at work*, London: Centre for Crime and Justice Studies.

van Swaaningen, R. (2005) 'Public Safety and the Management of Fear', *Theoretical Criminology*, 9(3), 289-305

Wacquant, L. (2009) *Punishing the Poor: The Neoliberal Government of Social Insecurity, Durham* and London: Duke University Press.

Wilson, J. Q. and Kelling, G. L. (1982) 'The Police and Neighbourhood Safety: Broken Windows', *Atlantic Monthly*, 249(3), 29-36.

Zedner, L. (2009) 'Opportunity Makes the Thief-Taker: The Influence of Economic Analysis on Crime Control' in Newburn, T. and Rock, P. (eds) *The Politics of Crime Control: Essays in Honour of David Downes*, 2nd edn, Oxford and New York: Oxford University Press.

4.

CRIMINAL ENTERPRISE, IDENTITY AND
REPERTOIRES OF ACTION

Vincenzo Ruggiero

Although it is commonly recognised that there are fundamental differences between organised crime and terrorism, it is also often stressed that the two have much in common. Obviously, differences and commonalities will emerge, or fail to do so, depending on the respective definitions we provide of the two. Thus, those adopting a definition of organised crime as 'criminal activity by groups of three or more individuals who engage in criminal activities collaboratively, with a degree of structure and coordination' may end up finding similarities among a wide variety of diverse acts (Grabosky and Stohl, 2010: 5). Three or more individuals may possess a degree of structure and coordination to beat up a fellow secondary school student because he does not look 'cool', or because of the colour of his skin. Three or more children may be coordinated in regularly stealing sweets from a corner shop; or three politicians may be well structured in illegally financing their party, as three police officers may use structure and coordination in deploying prohibited techniques of crowd control. Finally, three Prime Ministers, say Bush, Blair and Berlusconi, may get structured and coordinated for the illegal invasion of a country.

There is, simultaneously, an official effort to address organised crime and terrorism jointly and treat them as a single law enforcement issue (Schmid, 1996; Hutchinson and O'Malley, 2007). It would be intriguing to investigate how members of organised criminal groups and violent political groups respectively react to such official effort. In my own memory, when the 'mafiosi' happened to share a prison institution with members of the Red Brigades, they would steer away from those idealist Communists who got nothing out of killing. The former, when overcoming the disgust they felt in the presence of those who in their eyes adopted an incomprehensible political stance, and perhaps even a despicable sexual lifestyle, would simply suggest: "don't make revolution, make money, you cretin!". The latter, in their turn, would deal with the former as one deals with yet a different version of the economic and political power against which they fought. Echoes of this are found in an example coming from Greece itself, where the Courts have attempted to term 'common' rather than 'political' the offences attributed to the Revolutionary Organisation November 17.

The fact that organised crime is guided by material motivations and terrorism by political ones may be seen as irrelevant by official agencies pursuing the objective of degrading the 'enemy' whoever that might be. Therefore, the ceremonies of degradation, including the choice of an ad hoc vocabulary, may well serve the task, as the mad, the drug user and the terrorist constitute an undistinguishable mob in the face of which quibbling differences may just obstruct the criminal justice process.

The purpose of this paper is to try and clarify a number of issues that we encounter when dealing with organised crime and political violence respectively.

Professional crime and political violence

Let us start with the hypothesis that organised political groups, in order to finance their activity, are often forced to resort to forms of serious criminality. While such criminality may at times include drug trafficking, it is likely to be a general rule that political groups purporting to represent disadvantaged communities would avoid involvement in activities that might damage those very communities. Moralistic and Robin Hoodesque in their own self-perception, ideally, political groups will opt for 'robbing the robbers', namely the wealthy who are favoured by the exploitative system against which political action is addressed. Lucrative hold ups, for example, or kidnappings of tycoons, according to this logic, would be the preferred sources of financing for violent political organisations.

Organised criminal groups and terrorist groups, however, may engage in similar activities, such as money laundering (ibid: 2). But even when carrying out such financially rewarding exploits, are we sure that political organisations mimic their criminal organised counterparts? In order to answer this question it is necessary to identify some peculiarities of organised crime and political violence respectively.

Conspiracies and enterprises

There is confusion and eclecticism as to what exactly constitutes organised crime. There is also a tendency to avoid the problem of its definition, as if the obvious need not be defined. In a statement issued by the US President's Commission on Organized Crime, it is stressed that, while there is acceptance and recognition of certain acts as criminal, there is no standard awareness as to when a criminal group is to be regarded as organized. 'The fact that organized criminal activity is not necessarily organized crime complicates that definition process'. We have seen one definition at the beginning of this paper. Other descriptions range from 'two or more persons conspiring together to commit crimes for profit on a continuing basis' to more detailed accounts of what these crimes are. Organised crime can be simply equated with serious offending, although serious crime may be extremely disorganised. On the other hand, organised crime can be identified as one single, self-perpetuating, criminal conspiracy (US agencies in the 1960s). It may also be seen as constituted by 'crime families', hence the use of the notion of bureaucracy, suggesting hierarchically structured groups, characterized by formal rules and consisting of individuals with specialized and segmented functions within the hierarchy. A few individuals and families, in the past, were therefore deemed to centralize and coordinate all organized criminal activities.

Critics suggest that a credulous sociology was led to believe in the big conspiracy: The Organization. This sociology, 'innocent of such notions as informal organizations and patron-client networks, fixed the sociological frame of organized crime around conspiracy' (Block, 1991: 10).

While bearing these controversies in mind, I suggest that the best-known definitions of organized crime can be classified very roughly as follows. Some hinge on strictly quantitative aspects: the number of individuals involved in a criminal group is said to determine the organizational degree of that group (Johnson, 1962; Ferracuti, 1988). Organized crime is said to differ from conventional crime for the larger scale of its illegal activity (Moore, 1987). Some others focus mainly on a temporal variable that is on the time-span during which illegal activities are conducted. The death or incarceration of a member of organized crime, for example, do not stop the activities in which they are involved.

Criminologists who focus attention on its structural characteristics observe that organized crime operates by means of flexible and diversified groups. Such a structure is faced with peculiar necessities due to its condition of illegality. Firstly, the necessity, while remaining a 'secret' organization, to exert publicly its coercive and dissuasive strength. An equilibrium is therefore required between publicity and secrecy that only a complex structure is able to acquire. Secondly, the necessity to neutralize law enforcement through *omertà* (conspiracy of silence), corruption and retaliation. Finally, the need to reconcile its internal order, through specific forms of conflict control, with its external legitimacy, through the provision of occupational and social opportunities (Cohen, 1977).

Frequently, definitions of organized crime revolve around the concept of 'professionalism': its members, it is suggested, acquire skills and career advancement by virtue of their full-time involvement in illegality. Mannheim (1975) only devotes a dozen pages of his voluminous treatise to organized crime. The reason for this may perhaps be found in his preliminary general statement, where it is assumed that all economically oriented offences require a degree of organization, or at least necessitate forms of association among persons. In this light, the term 'organized crime' should be applied to the majority of illegal activities.

Other authors prefer to concentrate on the collective clientele of organized crime. This is therefore identified with a structure involved in the public provision of goods and services which are officially defined illegal. Organized criminal groups, in other words, simply fill the inadequacy of institutional agencies, which are unable to provide those goods and services, or perhaps officially deny that demand exists for them. The contribution of McIntosh (1975) is to be located in this perspective. She notes that organized crime is informed by a particular relationship between offenders and victims. For example, even the victims of extortion rackets often fail to report the offenders, less because they are terrified than 'because they see the extortionist as having more power in their parish than the agents of the state' (ibid.: 50). It may be added that the victims may also recognize their 'protector' as an authority which is more able than its official counterpart to distribute resources and opportunities.

The descriptions and definitions mentioned so far share a central element: they are, to varying degrees, related to the notion of 'professionalism'. This seems to allow for an original approach to the subject-matter, because such a notion alludes to a plausible parallel to be drawn between organized crime and the organization of any other industrial activity. However, one crucial aspect which characterizes the crime industry is neglected. This is that the crime industry itself cannot limit its recruitment to the individuals who constitute its tertiary sector or middle management. In order for the parallel with the licit industry to be validated, it has to be stressed that organized crime also needs a large number of unskilled criminal employees. Professionalism and unskilled labour seem to cohabit in organized criminal groups, and their simultaneous presence should be regarded as a significant hallmark of organized crime.

In my opinion, therefore, what connotes large criminal organisations is their internal division of labour, which transcends the technical skills of their members, displaying a *social* differentiation between those enjoying decision-making power and those devoid of it.

Let me now give a provisional answer to the question posed above: even when carrying out financially rewarding exploits, are we sure that political organisations mimic their criminal organised counterparts? I would suggest that, even when committing serious crimes, political organisations cannot be assimilated to organised crime, but rather to varieties of professional criminality. In this type of criminality the distribution of roles, typically, is based on specific individual skills, while a relative collegiality presides over decision-making, so that the planning and execution of operations are enacted by individuals close or known to one another. On the contrary, contract killers or drug couriers working for large criminal organisations, for example, hardly know the identity of the final beneficiary of their acts. They may engage in a long-term career while ignoring the strategy, motivations, let alone the face, of their employers.

Considering that some organised criminal groups do not limit their activities to conventional offending, some supplementary observations are needed. Successful organised crime manages to establish partnerships with the official world, particularly with business people and political representatives. When unable to do so, it remains a form of pariah organised crime, operating in the underworld, and destined to exhaust its resources and energies within the restricted realm of illicit markets. Organisations leaping onto the overworld, by contrast, are required to adopt a business style, a conduct, a strategy and a 'vocabulary of meaning' helping them to blend in the environment receiving them. In an environment saturated with corruption, within the political as well as the economic sphere, organised criminals will learn the techniques and the justifications of white collar criminals, now their partners. They may still 'commute' between licit and illicit markets, but their new status will force them to identify allies, sponsors, mentors and protectors. In brief, they will be required to develop the negotiation skills characterising an economic consortium or a political party. Even when groups, while operating in the official economy, find it opportune from time to time to use violence, this violence will still be inscribed in the 'vocabulary of meaning' belonging to political parties and competing economic actors. Killing, therefore, may become in this case part and parcel of the negotiation process.

Political violence and criminology

Looking at the work we have inherited from the founding fathers, it comes as no surprise that political violence was central to the analytical efforts of early criminology. Cesare Beccaria and Jeremy Bentham, for example, dealt with 'sedition' and 'crimes against the state' respectively, and their analyses, which also addressed institutional violence, were triggered by the revolutionary movements of the eighteenth century. The Positive School, in its turn, was engaged in understanding the turmoil of 1848, the violent events occurring during the Commune of Paris, as well as the attacks carried out by anarchists, revolutionary socialists and individual nihilists. Last but not least, Durkheim was compelled to differentiate between socialism as a 'reasonable proposal for change' and communism as an 'abnormal programme of destruction' (Ruggiero, 2006).

Moving to the current times, it seems that only after the events of 9/11 has criminology resumed any specific interest in political violence, at least in its variant commonly termed terrorism. Thus: 'Criminology can play a major role in helping us understand the aetiology of terrorist behaviour. Again, contributions in this area have thus far been limited, but we are already seeing traditional criminological theories being applied to explain terrorism' (LaFree and Hendrickson, 2007: 782).

There are scholars advocating the application of criminological theories of 'common' violence to the analysis of political violence, who argue that both types of violence are directed to the achievement of goals. Thus, one of the definitions of terrorism proposed is: 'An act or threat of violence to create fear and/or compliant behaviour in a victim or wider audience for the purpose of achieving political ends' (Grabosky and Stohl, 2010: 5). This definition, however, neglects the fact that, commonly, organised crime seeks to create fear by targeting precise official individuals who hamper their criminal enterprise, while terrorism, at least in the fashion it presents itself in recent international attacks, tends to create fear by hitting at random people who do little to hamper them. More definitional precision is therefore necessary in this respect.

For example, both organised crime and political violence aim at extracting something from someone; moreover, at least by perpetrators, both are presented as the outcome of provocation by the victims. When institutional-anomie theory (value clash) is applied to the study of terrorism, this is described as a clash between supporters of primordial institutions against 'a rootless world order of abstract markets, mass politics, and a debased, sacrilegious tolerance' (LaFree and Hendrickson, 2007: 786).

From a different perspective, the suggestion has been made that the principles of situational crime prevention should also be applied to terrorism. According to this view, after identifying and removing the opportunities that violent groups exploit to mount their attacks, situational measures implemented through partnerships among a wide range of public and private agencies will assist with this task (Clarke and Newman, 2006). In other contributions the point is put forward that conventional crime is characterised by tensions and dynamics that underpins many forms of terrorism. Issues of shame, esteem, loss, and repressed anger, alongside the pursuit of pride and self or collective respect, which provide important tools to criminological analysis, may also help establish a taxonomy of terrorism. That criminological theories can migrate into the area of political violence is empirically probed by authors who apply a rational choice theoretical framework to a specific examples of political violence and terrorism.

This notwithstanding, it is still appropriate to claim that most of the literature on political violence is produced by experts in political sciences, international studies and law. It is worth specifying, in fact, that most criminological studies available do not focus on political violence or terrorism, but rather on the official perceptions, the institutional responses to these phenomena, and the effects that such responses produce in the social and political sphere.

It is not uncommon for criminologists to address the consequences of state intervention against terrorism, particularly in terms of human rights violation, its impact on civil liberties and policing, but also in respect of corporate and state crime. Themed sections of academic journals and professional magazines have also focused on 'trading civil liberties for greater security', 'anti-terrorism and police powers', 'terrorism and criminal justice values' (Zedner, 2008).

It may be contended that the state of criminology with respect to political violence is similar to the state once observed by Becker (1963: 166) with respect to gangs and juvenile deviance. 'I think it is a truism to say that a theory that is not closely tied to a wealth of facts about the subject it proposes to explain is not likely to be very useful'. In other words, one may look at violent political actors with the same dissatisfaction with which Becker looked at young delinquents, and lament the paucity of information available around what they think about themselves and their activities. Some criminologists, perhaps stimulated by such paucity, have followed an alternative analytical route.

Elements of criminological theories are used by Hamm (2007), who refers to Sutherland's notion that criminal behaviour is learned through interaction and interpersonal communication. While Sutherland argued that the learning process involves specific techniques to commit crime as well as rationalisations for the crimes committed, Hamm supplements these with 'a third element in a person who is willing to use it as a tactic: fanatical dedication to a cause' (Hamm, 2007: 115). Rationalisations are intended by Hamm as ideology, therefore 'the confluence of skill, ideology, and fanatical dedication has been the engine driving most terrorist groups throughout history'. Drawing on classical sociological thought, the author also introduces the variable charisma, that he applies to specific characters in the contemporary history of terrorism such as Carlos the Jackal and Osama bin Laden. Charisma, or the power of the gifted, is regarded as the fourth dimension of terrorism, a quality that elicits loyalty and unquestioned action. For charisma to express its strength, however, a crisis has to erupt in specific spheres of collective life. Charismatic leaders, therefore, are capable of responding to crises through their unique gifts, which may fall in the spiritual domain, in the economic arena or in the political sphere. 'If the crisis involves political conflict, the gifts will be in the realm of oratory. And if that conflict leads to violence, the leader is likely to be gifted in military tactics' (Hamm, 2007: 115). The author, however, mainly looks at 'terrorism as crime' from a particular angle, as he is less interested in political violence per se than in the crimes committed for the provision of logistical support to that violence. His analysis, therefore, focuses on crimes aimed at providing terrorists with money, training, communication systems, safe havens, and travel opportunities. These crimes are seen as the 'life-blood of terrorist groups', and include counterfeiting, bank robbery, theft, fraud, kidnapping, espionage, drug smuggling, gun running, tax evasion, money laundering, cell phone and credit card theft, immigration violations, passport forgery, extortion, and prostitution. Hamm's goal, therefore, 'is to examine terrorists' involvement in these crimes and describe law enforcement's opportunities to detect and prevent them' (Hamm, 2007: 3). In this way, one may opine, criminological theories are mainly applied to the analysis of 'auxiliary' common offences rather than precise political ones.

Arena and Arrigo (2006: 3) claim that the extant literature 'examines the causes of terrorism from within a psychological framework'. There is, in effect, an abundance of studies addressing violent political conduct as a function of the individual's psyche, or even attempting to identify specific personality traits 'that would compel a person to act violently'. This search for the terrorist personality, in reality, is a long-standing effort and echoes the analysis of Lombroso and Laschi (1890), according to whom individualistic political offenders (as opposed to revolutionaries) are characterised by 'congenital criminality and impulsive instincts, which converge in a form of epilepsy associated with vanity, religiosity, megalomania and intermittent geniality' (Ruggiero, 2006: 43). Arena and Arrigo suggest that the identity construct is too often deemed a contributing factor in the emergence and maintenance of extremist militant conduct, and while noting that knowledge around identity and terrorism is limited, they propose an alternative social psychological framework grounded in symbolic interactionism. The concepts utilised include symbols, definition of the situation, roles, socialisation and role-taking.

Fuzzy actors

As I said earlier, organised crime may use violence as a supplementary tool of negotiating their presence on markets, or with the system. Violent political groups, on the contrary, use violence as a signal of their unwillingness to negotiate with a system they would rather demolish. Their action transcends the immediate result they achieve, and prefigures, realistically or not, a different set of arrangements which will be valued in a future, rather than in the current society. Of course, some political groups may use violence as a supplementary form of pressure to accelerate a specific negotiation and pursue a concrete, material objective. But in this case, the word 'terrorism' becomes inappropriate, and such groups might be described as engaging in 'armed trade unionism'. Are official governments prepared to do so? The ad hoc vocabulary of degradation, alluded to above, would prohibit it.

Finally, the development of networked organisational forms by both terrorist and conventional criminal groups is deemed yet another aspect of their similarity. On the contrary, it is indeed the evolution of organised crime into structures commonly described as networks that may makes comparisons between the two forms of violence increasingly far-fetched. When we focus on organised crime, networks imply the alliance between highly heterogeneous groups and individuals, each with a distinctive cultural and ethnic background, who may establish common goals on an occasional or long-term basis. Actors operating in organised crime networks are socially 'fuzzy', in the sense that their exploits and careers overlap with those of others who are apparently radically different from them. Networks are a reflection of grey areas hosting diverse cultures, identities, values and motivations, areas in which the diversity of activities results from the development of points of contact, common interests and strategies between licit, semi-licit and overtly illicit economies. I am thinking of 'dirty economies' consisting in encounters which add to the respective cultural, social and symbolic capital possessed by criminals, politicians and entrepreneurs, who interlock their practices. Networks, mobility and fluidity are metaphors that aptly describe the flows of people and groups engaged in some of the most successful forms of organised crime.

Such forms of organised crime, in sum, see the participation of diverse collective or individual entities each pursuing their own goals in a style and against a set of values that are consistent with their own specific cultural, ethnic and professional background. As collective actors, participants display a form of *organised behaviour* without showing signs of an *organised identity*. None of this applies to networks set up by terrorist groups, which require a high degree of homogeneity among participants, in terms of political, religious and philosophical creed, along with a common understanding of the outcomes pursued by their acts. Terrorist networks may be fluid and diverse, but participants display an *organised identity*, in the sense that they do not pursue their individual differentiated goals, their main goal being the affirmation of a common idea or state of things. But let us now shift to a more specific set of considerations pertaining to political violence.

Violent political groups do not pursue material gain, and when they do, this is related to the acquisition of symbolic status, namely a capacity to step up their propaganda and hence their visibility. Although criminology does provide analytical tools to deal with symbolic or expressive violence, there are other characteristics in political violence which make this specific conduct hard to locate within a criminological framework. A short overview of theories will help clarify this point.

Anomie theorists may interpret the behaviour of armed groups as the effect of a lack of social integration and regulation, namely of cohesion, collective beliefs and mutually-binding constraints allowing smooth interactions. However, violent political groups claim to represent highly integrated and regulated groups, such as classes, political formations or religious communities. In other words, their lack of solidarity with the dominant social groups is counter-balanced by a high degree of solidarity proffered to what are deemed dominated groups, thus describing a situation of anomie with respect to the former and one of strong normativeness with respect to the latter. In their case, therefore, it is not anomie, but its opposite, namely solidarity and integration that provide crucial preconditions for action.

Adopting the concept of social disorganisation, it might be suggested that political violence is a possible solution to the dilemmas of exclusion and impotence. However, it should be noted that similar solution is embedded in a process of empowerment in which 'boundary creation' is paramount. All social relations occur within boundaries between those involved, and while at the individual level, these boundaries fall somewhere between *you and me*, at the collective level they fall between *us and them*. Boundary creation between *us and them* is crucial for the formation of identities, and in the case of social movements and groups it also involves the recognition of existing inequalities as unjust. The concept of disorganisation may explain 'oppositional behaviour', not 'oppositional identity'. The latter involves identifying with an unjustly subordinated group, recognising the injustice suffered by that group, opposing it, and forging a collective identity of interest in ending that injustice (Ruggiero and Montagna, 2008). This implies a high degree of organisation and purposefulness, rather than aimless social disorganisation. While it is useful to explain dysfunctional processes and behaviours, it is also important to describe how some processes are functional to the promotion of shared consciousness, to the identification of collective interests and the building of organisational capacity to act on those interests. Political violence is one of the outcomes of such functional processes.

In the perspective of learning theories, violent behaviour is transmitted in enclaves of peers and through mimetic processes triggered by role models. Learning opportunities, however, are accompanied by 'claim making' about social justice and the perception of viable ways of pursuing it. Such claims become political when groups and organisations holding means of coercion are addressed. On the other hand, strain theorists would posit that political violence is one of the possible deviant adaptations to an unsatisfactory situation. The impossibility of achieving goals through legitimate means, in this type of adaptation termed 'rebellion', is turned into the imagining of alternative goals and the promotion of alternative, including violent, means to achieve them. Rebellion, however, which implies a 'genuine transvaluation', namely a full denunciation of officially prized values, also includes a sense of frustration, a degree of resentment, and ultimately the perception of one's impotence due to lack of resources. Although questioning the official monopoly of imagination, rebellion as described in strain theory remains anchored to a deprived social condition hampering the constitution of alternative reservoirs of imagination. Such a reservoir, on the contrary, can be regarded as an important resource without which movements as well as violent political groups could not produce action. Resource mobilisation theorists, for example, suggest that availability of resources, rather than absence of them, makes groups capable of undertaking concrete action. Resources include material and non-material items, such as finances, infrastructures, authority, moral commitment, political memory, organisations, networks, trust, skills, and so on (Ruggiero and Montagna, 2008). In brief, while strain theorists tend to see social action as the result of a deficit, organised social action, whether violent or not, can also be interpreted as the outcome of a surplus.

Political violence may be prevalent in contexts where control efforts eschew negotiation or accommodation, and are themselves characterised by violence. In this sense, the activity of some violent political groups could be understood as violence against the establishment, on the one hand, and as one of the effects of violence perpetrated by the establishment, on the other (Ruggiero, 2006). If this relational dynamic seems to be successful in explaining political violence, conflict theory, which also contains relational elements, proves too general for the task. It is true that institutions do not represent the values and interests of society at large, and that norms of conduct may only reflect the norms of the dominant culture. But to state that political violence is a manifestation of two sets of norms violently clashing does not account for the fact that in most contexts, where also the norms of conduct only reflect the norms of the dominant culture, there is a negligible degree of contentious politics and political violence. The analysis of the specific context in which political violence occurs is crucial if the generalisations of conflict theory are to be avoided. The existence of repertoires of action, accumulated through long periods of conflict, is in this respect paramount. Repertoires consist of a legacy, made of cultural and political resources, available to political groups. They contain sets of action and identity deriving from shared understandings and meanings; they are cultural creations that take shape in social and political conflict.

Some of the techniques of neutralisation identified in criminology may well describe the ideological process whereby violent political groups come to terms with the effects of their acts. The denial of the victim is operated through the perception of the victim as wrongdoer, the condemnation of the condemners through their association with immorality, and finally the appeal to higher loyalties through the appropriation of the ideals and practices of one's political or religious creed. Techniques of neutralisation, however, seem to belong to an ex-post repertoire of motivations mobilised by offenders in order to fill the moral void they presumably experience. They are, in sum, a defensive device which may temper moral disorientation. Political violence, instead, combines defensive and offensive strategies, a combination without which action could hardly be triggered. Such strategies may include ways of overcoming a presumed moral disorientation, but must provide, at the same time, strong, unequivocal orientation for individuals and groups to act. This combination of strategies coalesce in the form of collective identity, which transcends pure role or group identity, in that it refers to shared self-definitions and common efforts towards the production of social change. Collective identity offers orientation in a moral space and gives rise to a sense of self-esteem and self-efficacy; it also prompts what is worth doing and what is not in *organisational terms*, leading individuals to appreciate their capacity to change the surrounding environment.

Conclusion

Political violence, therefore, is one of the outcomes of *organised identity* and entails high degrees of subjectivity, so that some features of social life are no longer seen as part of misfortune, but of injustice. Along with techniques of neutralisation, political violence needs to elaborate an interpretive 'frame alignment' with the activists it intends to mobilise.

Against the backdrop of control theories, political violence could be examined as the result of a lack of attachment, commitment, involvement and belief. On the contrary, most armed organisations possess all of these in exceeding measure. In turn, adopting 'propensity event theory' may prove problematic, as the violence of the organisation does not reveal a deficit in self-control and an inclination to impulsivity, but an extremely developed ability to postpone gratification (the perfect social system to come) and an equally patient capacity to plan actions.

In brief, in political violence what is 'organised' is not crime or behaviour, but identity. And yet one may opine that organised crime and political violence could still be analysed jointly, because both require scientific investigations and interpretations of their structure, their internal make up, their external interactions, their targets and their changing physiognomy. The sociology of organisations, in this respect, could well be mobilised for such a joint examination. But this specific branch of sociology is certainly also useful for the analysis of other organisations, for example, universities, companies, bureaucracies, and so on. Why then limit our joint analysis to organised crime and terrorism? One could propose that, say, the next edition of the Oxford Handbook of Criminology contains a chapter on 'Organised Crime and Universities', or 'Fundamentalist Violence and the Post Service'.

References

Arena, M.P. and Arrigo, B.A. (2006), *The Terrorist Identity: Explaining the Terrorist Threat*, New York: New York University Press.

Barnett, A. (1999), "Prison Service banned from jail contract", *The Observer*, 31 October.

Becker, H. (1963), *Outsiders: Studies in the Sociology of Deviance*, New York: New Press.

Block, A. (1991), *Perspectives on Organizing Crime. Essays in Opposition*, Dordrecht: Kluwer.

Clarke, R.V. and Newman, G.R. (2006), *Outsmarting the Terrorists*, Westport: Praeger.

Cohen, A. (1977), 'The Concept of Criminal Organization', *British Journal of Criminology,* 17 (2): 97-111.

Ferracuti, F. (ed.) (1988), *Forme di organizzazioni criminali e terrorismo*, Milan: Giuffré.

Hamm, M. S. (2007), *Terrorism as Crime*, New York: New York University Press.

Johnson, E. (1962), 'Organized Crime: Challenge to the American Legal System', *Criminal Law, Criminology and Police Science*, 53 (4): 1-29.

Grabosky, P. and Stohl, M. (2010), *Crime and Terrorism*, London: Sage.

Hutchinson, S. and O'Malley, P. (2007), 'A Crime Terror Nexus? Thinking on Some of the Links between Terrorism and Criminality', *Studies in Conflict and Terrorism*, 30: 1095-1107.

LaFree, G. and Hendrickson, J. (2007), 'Build a Criminal Justice Policy for Terrorism' *Criminology & Public Policy*, 6 (4): 781-89.

Lombroso, C. and Laschi, R. (1890), *Il delitto politico e le rivoluzioni*, Turin: Bocca.

Mannheim, H. (1975), *Trattato di criminologia comparata*, Turin: Einaudi.

McIntosh, M. (1975), *The Organisation of Crime*, London: Macmillan.

Moore, M. (1987), 'Organized Crime as Business Enterprise', in Edelhertz, H. (ed.), *Major Issues in Organized Crime Control*, Washington, DC: Government Printing Office.

Ruggiero, V. (2006), *Understanding Political Violence*, London/New York: Open University Press.

Ruggiero, V. and Montagna, N. (ed) (2008), *Social Movements: A Reader*, London: Routledge.

Schmid, A. (1996), 'Links between Transnational Organised Crime and Terrorist Crimes', *Transnational Organized Crime*, 2: 40-82

Zedner, L. (2008), 'Terrorism, the Ticking Bomb and Criminal Justice values', *Criminal Justice Matters*, 73: 18-19.

PART 2

CONTEMPORARY CRITICAL CRIMINOLOGY- CASE STUDIES

5.

LEHMAN BROTHERS, OBAMA AND THE CASE FOR CORPORATE REGULATION

Dave Orr

For over two decades, neo-liberal economists, socio-legal academics and politicians argued that deregulation and a *laissez faire* approach to financial capital and corporations are crucial to economic growth. When the banking crisis began almost three years ago, the international cost of deregulation became clear. Using the case of the Lehman Brothers' bankruptcy and the dubious and misleading activities of Lehman and accountants Ernst and Young, this paper will argue for a tougher enforcement approach by regulatory bodies as a means of preventing large scale financial fraud and to increase corporate accountability. In view of this, proposals outlined in *'Financial Regulatory Reform (2010)'*, produced by The Department of the Treasury, will also be considered. First, however, let us revisit the specifics of the Lehman Brothers' case.

1. The Lehman Brothers Case

In January 2008, two months after the collapse of Northern Rock Building Society in Britain and ten months before the banking crisis reached its peak, Lehman Brothers declared record profits of $4 billion for the previous financial year. This statement added 30 million to Lehman's' share value, and seemed to indicate that the holdings company was stronger than it had ever been. Eight months later (September 15th 2008) Lehman Brothers filed for bankruptcy after 95% of its share value had been wiped out (Report of Examiner Valukas 2010:2). According to Anton Valukas, Examiner for the US Bankruptcy Court, the roots of the collapse date back to 2006 when, 'Lehman made the deliberate decision to embark on an aggressive growth strategy, to take on significantly greater risk, and to substantially increase leverage upon its capital' (Valukas 2010:4). This involved substantial investment in the so-called sub-prime residential mortgages at a time when the sub-prime market was already experiencing difficulties. However, confidence in the strength of the US economy was high. In August 2007, Henry Paulson, US Secretary of the Treasury, declared that the US economy was strong enough to absorb any 'fallout' from the subprime mortgage market. Despite these assurances, the sub-prime market collapsed at the end of the year, and Lehman Brothers lost billions of dollars (*'Paulson Sees Sub-prime Woes Contained'*, Boston Globe, August 2007). In an attempt to recoup these loses, Lehman began to take greater risks, and 'repeatedly exceeded its own internal risk limits' (Valukas 2010:4).

In March 2008, Bear Sterns Investment Bank, who had also invested heavily in sub-prime mortgages narrowly avoided collapse. The Federal Reserve Bank of New York effectively loaned JP Morgan Chase $30 million dollars to facilitate a merger with Bear Sterns, and offset its debt. Consequently, investors began to look at other companies involved in sub-prime mortgages, and most notably Lehman Brothers. At this point, 'to buy more time, to maintain that critical confidence, Lehman painted a misleading picture of its financial condition' (Valukas 2010:5). At the end of the second quarter 2008 Lehman was forced to announce a quarterly loss of $2.8 billion, and told by the US treasury to find a buyer (ff40, Valukas 2010:10). However, Lehman had failed to disclose that they 'had been using and accounting device (known within Lehman as Repo 105 (Valukas 2010:6). Although operating within permitted accounting regulations, Repo 105 allowed Lehman to hide loss on assets or loss making assets sold and re-purchased within days of the sale for the purpose of raising finance, and thus gave a false impression of Lehman's liquid assets (Valukas 2010:7). In contravention of the Sarbanes-Oxley Act (2002/US), which I will discuss in the next section, neither financial regulators nor board of directors were informed of this arrangement. Investors were also kept in the dark, but 'Lehman's auditors Ernst & Young were aware of but did not question Lehman's use and nondisclosure of Repo 105 accounting transactions' (Valukas 2010:8). In short, Lehman was in bigger trouble than it had admitted, but needed to present a false picture of liquid assets in order to borrow more, so the company could continue trading, and perhaps trade its way out of trouble. In fact, 'a substantial portion' of the alleged liquid assets were nothing of the sort, and 'significant components of Lehman's assets generally had lost any monetary value. So, although Lehman declared liquid assets of $41 billion on September 10th 2008, the real amount available (disclosed after Lehman's collapse) was less than $2 billion. On the same day, Lehman announced projected losses of $3.9 billion for the third quarter of 2008 (Valukas 2010:10). Lehman had no rescue plan nor had it secured or sought a prospective buyer. By September 12th, Lehman share price was $3.95, a fall of 94% on the January 2008 price. At the same time, US treasury investigators realise that Lehman did not have the assets it claimed, and nor did it have sufficient funds to prevent a collapse. Thus, when the Barclays deal to save Lehman was blocked by the FSA in Britain on September 14th 2008, Lehman filed for bankruptcy, and set off a chain of events that forced the US Government to put together the Troubled Asset Relief Programme (TARP), a $700 billion package designed to prevent further collapse of financial corporations and the US economy generally.

Controversially, the US treasury examiner rejected the claim that the collapse of Lehman had triggered the global meltdown of financial institutions, and that the Lehman situation was more a product of bad judgement than fraudulent business activities (Valukas 2010:2-3). However, the collapse of Lehman, and the far reaching and global consequences of the run on the US banking system should provide a salutary lesson for those who supported the deregulation of financial institution over the past three to four decades. Thus, the mismanagement and misleading activities of Lehman now lead us to discuss corporate regulation in the US at the time of the collapse.

2. Regulating Corporations

It is untrue to say that financial institutions are not regulated by the US state. This is the case now and was prior to the beginning of the banking crisis in November 2007. As Tombs and Whyte (2007:145) note, 'states do a great deal of regulating' of business. States set the parameters of entry into (financial) markets and of business activity therein. In the US, the major piece of regulatory legislation governing the conduct of financial institutions prior to the collapse of 2007 was the Sarbanes-Oxley Act (2002/US). The act required all *issuers* or corporations to submit accounts for scrutiny by the appropriate state regulatory organisation. As a first step, the act required issuers to establish,

> *by and among the board of directors an audit committee to oversee the accounting and financial reporting processes of the issuer and audits of the financial statements of the issuer' (HR 3763-3, par 3a).*

In the absence of such a committee, *'the entire board of directors of the issuer' (HR 3763-3, par 3b),* was to act in this capacity. Second, the act required, *'an examination of the financial statements of any issuer by an independent public accounting firm' (HR 3763-3, par 2).* This is where Ernst & Young enter the Lehman's case as the first stage in the external regulation of Lehman, and why Treasury Examiner Valukas was so critical of Ernst & Young's part in the collapse of Lehman Brothers. Only when financial statements of issuers had been checked, *'by an independent public accounting firm'*, were they submitted to the appropriate regulatory agency. In other words, financial organisations were largely trusted to regulate themselves, with external auditing and scrutiny acting as a check upon regulatory compliance and ensuring that accounts offered a true reflection of a corporation's business activities.

Whilst in hindsight this type of self-policing or compliance may now appear naive, it must be remembered that many corporations did and still do operate in this way. Secondly, this approach to corporate regulation was rooted in both a prevailing neo-liberal commitment to the free market and regulatory theory predicated upon the notion of corporate self-regulation. Lending regulations in the US had gradually been relaxed in the three decades prior to the collapse of Lehman with the intention of encouraging growth in the US financial sector. In 1980, the Carter administration relaxed regulations on mortgage lending with the Depository Institutions Deregulation and Monetary Control Act (US/1980). Two years later, the Garn St-Germain Depository Institutions Act (US/1982) was passed by the Regan administration. Not only did this facilitate take-overs of failing financial institutions, but it also permitted savings and loans organisations to offer some banking services and increase lending facilities by up to 30%. Acts in 1999 (The Gramm-Leach-Biley Act) 2000 (Commodity Futures Modernisation Act) and 2004 further relaxed lending restrictions, and opened the way for the rapid development of the so-called sub-prime market.   In 2007, Henry Paulson, the then US Secretary of the Treasury, re-affirmed US commitment to the free market just before the banking crisis when he stated that "An open, competitive, and liberalized financial market can effectively allocate scarce resources in a manner that promotes stability and prosperity far better than governmental intervention' (Bloomberg.com. September 24, 2008). The commitment to neo-liberalism and compliance based strategies was reflected in some academic writing on corporate regulation (e.g. see Hawkins 1990; Hutter 1997). This literature argued that over-regulation, regulation inflation or red tape inhibited the functioning and development of private business, and that corporations had, from a market point of view, a vested interest in complying with regulatory bodies. Furthermore, compliance theorists argued that over-enforcement of corporations was counter-productive, and that negotiation and self regulation was more likely to produce ethical corporate behaviour. Clearly these arguments are derived from and sympathetic to neo-liberal economics.

Counter arguments took a variety of forms. Parker (2002) concluded that compliance strategies had spawned a bureaucratic rather than regulatory system, which had thus far been used by corporations to manage appearance. This was clearly the case with Lehman who, with the help of Ernst & Young, appeared to comply with US financial regulations whilst hoodwinking investors and the Federal Financial Authority. Pearce and Tombs (1990), much to the chagrin of Keith Hawkins, argued that compliance based regulation did not provide sufficient protection for workers exposed to the harmful, and too often fatal, consequences of corporate safety breaches. Nor did it provide sufficient deterrence to stop profit-hungry corporations breaching safety regulations. In fact, they argued, it was a misnomer to assume that the corporation was a moral entity, capable of making ethical decisions regardless of profitability. In the case of Lehman, the roots of the problem lay in attempts to increase profit at the expense of some of the poorest people in America by capitalising upon the sub-prime market. As problems mounted, survival drove senior employers to make decisions and engage in duplicitous and ultimately destructive activities. This is amoral rather than moral or ethical behaviour, but one can hardly expect anything else from a corporate system driven by competition and profit. Ayres and Braithwaite (1992) proposed a regulatory model based upon compliance and enforcement (in the case of non-compliance), whilst Slapper and Tombs (1999) and Tombs and Whyte (2007) argued that stronger regulations and regulatory enforcement by more powerful regulators to police corporations. Despite these critiques, regulatory policy on the 1990s and the first decade of the new millennium tended to lean most heavily towards compliance based models of regulation because these models were most sympathetic to state sponsored neo-liberal and global economic strategies. However, given the weaknesses of compliance based strategies exposed by recent events, the Obama administration began a re-examination of corporate regulation in the financial sector. The following section examines current political thinking on corporate regulation with a review of *'Financial Regulatory Reform: A New Foundation'*, published earlier this year by the Treasury Department.

3. The Proposed Reforms

The growth of financial capital in the last three decades has largely been predicated upon debt. In part, this is because incomes in the US and Western Europe (particularly Britain) have failed to keep pace with inflation. So, in order to access material good, maintain lifestyles and pay for an increasing raft of privatised services, including housing, many resorted to loans (Harvey 2010). As I have noted, this development took place alongside regulatory reform that increased access to debt, and led to unprecedented growth in western financial capital. The so called subprime mortgage arose out of this development and the drive to open up new debt markets. Thus, both corporate and individual debt underpins the contemporary US economy. It is hardly surprising then, that the final draft of *Financial Regulatory Reform: A New Foundation (2010)* begins by stating that the 'challenge' faced by the US government is, to revive our financial system so that people can access loans to buy a car or home, pay for a child's education or finance a business' (Financial Regulatory Reform, 2010, 2). Not surprising, but not encouraging either for those looking for concrete and long-term reform, albeit reform delineated and limited by capitalist economics.

The FRR then highlights reasons for the financial collapse and collapse of certain large financial institutions like Lehman Brothers. In statements resonant of the Lehman case, FRR identifies 'complacency', 'lack of transparency', 'failures in consumer protection' and 'gaps and weaknesses in the supervision and regulation of financial firms' at the level of the state as the major causes of the collapse (*Financial Regulatory Reform, 2010:2*). These statements indicate criticism of compliance models.

At no point is a reason given for this nor is it suggested that this comes out of purposeful deregulation intended to facilitate the growth of financial institutions in the frenzy of neo-liberalism that castigated regulation as red tape. In other words, not only did the US (and other) states fail to regulate; they actively created the conditions which led to the 'complacency' and 'lack of transparency' of financial corporations.

4. Conclusion

As ever, western capitalist states are caught between a rock and hard place. In order to maintain legitimacy, liberal democracies must be seen to respond to harmful and socially damaging activities. When dealing with relatively powerless individuals or social groups, those responses have, since the 1970s, become increasingly punitive. As I have noted, this has not been the case when the perpetrators of harm are also viewed by the state as essential to economic and social stability, and their harmful activities have yet undermine that stability. That is not to suggest that western financial corporations are unregulated or beyond state regulation, but it does explain, in part, why FRR, and other post-banking crisis responses have focused on the recovery of financial institutions rather than their increased regulation or regulatory powers. Indeed, at a time of neo-liberal economic dominance, the introduction of greater regulation and more powerful, better resourced regulators would involve a radical paradigm shift, but would also increase corporate accountability and protection for the less powerful from corporate harm. Whilst the impact of these suggestions may be modest in the face of global capital, and certainly do not address inequities inherent in capitalism, it does at least offer a recognisable way to reduce corporate harm.

References

Ayres, I. and Braithwaite, J. (1992) 'Responsive Regulation: Transcending the Deregulation Debate', Oxford: Oxford University Press, cited in Slapper, G. and Tombs, S. (1999) *Corporate Crime,* Harlow: Longman/Pearson Education Ltd

Harvey, D. (8th May 2010) *Hardtalk Interview,* BBC

Hawkins, K. (1990) 'Compliance Strategy, Prosecution Policy and Aunt Sally: A Comment on Pearce and Tombs', *British Journal of Criminology, 30(4) 444-446*

Hutter, B. (1997) *Compliance, Regulation and Environment,* Oxford: Clarendon Press

Lawder, D. (August 1st 2007) *Paulson Sees Subprime Woes Contained,* Boston Globe

Parker, C. (2002) *The Open Corporation: Effective Self Regulation and Democracy,* Cambridge: Cambridge University Press

Pearce, F. and Tombs, S. (1990) 'Ideology, Hegemony and Empiricism: Compliance Theories of Regulation', *British Journal of Criminology, 30 (4)423-443*

Slapper, G. and Tombs, S. (1999) *Corporate Crime,* Harlow: Longman/Pearson Education Ltd

Tombs, S. and Whyte, D. (2007) *Safety Crime,* Cullompton: Willan Publishing

US Congress (107/2 2002) *Sarbanes-Oxley Act,* HR 3763

US Department of the Treasury (2010) *Financial Regulatory Reform: A New Foundation: Rebuilding Financial Supervision and Regulation*

Valukas AR (March 11th 2010) *Lehman Brothers Holdings Inc. Chapter 11 Proceedings, Examiners Report,* United States Bankruptcy Court, Southern District of New York

6.

PUBLIC ORDER POLICING IN THE UK: FROM PARAMILITARY POLICING TO NEIGHBOURHOOD POLICING?

Paul Norris

This paper will outline how the police in the United Kingdom came to develop a paramilitary style of policing when it came to policing political protests, strikes and demonstrations (and also football matches). Some examples of paramilitary style policing will be given, with the problems that this caused. The recent publication of the HMIC report, *Adapting to Protest: Nurturing the British Model of Policing* (2009), poses the question will the police move towards a neighbourhood style of policing in public order situations?

The expression of democratic rights is an essential part of a liberal democracy, and being able to protest is part and parcel of participation in political life. Thus it could be argued that there is a moral dilemma in the policing of public order. On the one hand there is the democratic right to peaceful protest, and on the other the police keeping order. The core issue is that the police are dealing (for the most part) with law-abiding citizens who are expressing their democratic right of protesting. Peaceful protest is not criminal, thus there is a contest of moral equals.

As Fielding (2005) has pointed out *'the police work at the heart of social conflict'* (xi). One of the main reasons for the establishment of the police in 1829 was to maintain order. Prior to those troops were used, for example at the St. Peterloo massacre in Manchester in 1819. Even after the formation of the police troops were used in industrial disputes such as the miners strike in 1893 at Featherstone in Yorkshire (2 miners killed), 1919 in Liverpool, 1920 Glasgow, and the 1926 General Strike. But by the mid twentieth century protest and the policing of it was polite and on the picket lines it was mainly pushing and shoving. This was the *'golden era'* of British policing. However, cracks were starting to appear in the late 1960s, as a new generation of youth were less subservient to the established order, and some trade unions elected left wing leaders.

The first signs were the demonstrations against the Vietnam War. On the 28th March 1968, and Grosvenor Square became a battle ground between the police and the demonstrators. The demonstrators came close to storming the American embassy and it was clear that the police did not have a strategy, tactics or equipment to deal effectively with this situation. On the 30th August 1976, the Notting Hill Carnival ended in a riot. Relations between the police and the local black community had completely broken down, due largely to the application of the 'sus' (suspected person) procedure contained in the Vagrancy Act of 1824. Once again the police had no strategy, tactics or equipment to deal with the situation. They used dustbin lids as shields to defend themselves. One hundred police officers and sixty carnival goers were taken to hospital, and sixty people were arrested.

The move towards Paramilitary Policing

By the 1980s a Conservative government had been elected, with Margaret Thatcher as Prime Minister, who took a potent 'law and order' approach. The 1980s were dominated by the politics of the recession (industrial decline, high unemployment, monetarism), and there was cultural, industrial and political dissent. The Conservative government supported the police, by giving them extra central funding, with better pay and increased numbers, but at the same time cutting other public services (Fielding 2005). The spring and summer of 1981 saw the inner cities erupt with riots in London (Brixton), Liverpool (Toxteth), Birmingham (Handsworth) and Leeds (Chapletown). As Leech notes *'These were not 'race riots' in the sense of conflicts between races...At the heart of the disturbance, was not racial conflict but rather conflict with the police as symbols of white authority and white racism. They were certainly racial disturbances in the sense that racism, State racism, racism in the policing and criminalization of black communities were perceived to be the underlying issues'.* (Leech 1988: 71). During the riots the traditional methods used, passive restraint through cordons, were seen to be a failure. The equipment and tactics used were no longer suitable for the increased levels of violence, which would culminate in the death of PC Keith Blakelock at the Broadwater Farm Estate (Tottenham) in October 1985.

There was also renewed industrial conflict by steelworkers, print workers and miners. The major industrial conflict was the year long miners strike from March 1984 to March 1985.

There was an uncompromising application of the law. The dominant strategy used by the police was *escalated force*. There was a lack of communication and negotiation between the police and the strikers, and a readiness to apply force by the police. During this period there was the ideological vilification of dissenters, as Margaret Thatcher coined the phrase *'the enemy within'*. There were allegations by some of police repression and partisanship, as the miners called the police *'Maggie Thatcher's boot boys'*.

It was during the miners strike that one saw the changed appearance of the police and the adoption of 'the riot squad'. The police wore a helmet with a visor, a flame retardant suit with body armour and shields, and often with no collar numbers. They looked formidable, invulnerable and also continental. It was very different to the traditional image of the British 'bobby'. By the end of the 1980s and beginning of the 1990s there was a debate amongst British criminologists about paramilitary policing. The main two protagonists were Tony Jefferson (1990) and P.A.J. Waddington (1993), although other academics joined the debate throughout the 1990s. By the 1990s there was an element of the 'strong arm of the law', with the police 'tooled up' for action. Some commentators wondered if the police were bringing the tactics used in Northern Ireland to Britain. The 1990s also saw a shift from 'class'/'ethnic' politics to 'issue' politics, such as ecology/environment, animal welfare, third world poverty and sexuality. The protestors involved were more middle class, and there was not a clear political consensus among the protestors, which was a challenge to police legitimacy. What also emerged in the 1990s as a result of the Broadwater Farm riot (1985), the Hillsborough Disaster and The Poll Tax Riot (1990) were better police training and a clear command structure for public order situations. So by the twenty first century all police forces in the UK were trained to a national standard and had standard equipment. The basis used for public order training is based up on 'classic crowd psychology'. This holds that crowds are *'irrational, dangerous and open to easy exploitation by agitators and therefore implies that physical crowds are single psychological entities posing inherent dangers to public order'* (Stott 2009: 3). Stott goes on to argue that the theory is prejudiced as it fails to explain crowd behaviour and the surfacing of collective conflict (Stott 2009: 3).

The G20 Protest

So as the police prepared for the G20 demonstration in April 2009 it was based on the classic theory. But there had been plenty of evidence of policing based on the classic theory at previous demonstrations and also of policing football supporters. Paul Lewis of the Guardian also made the point that, '*In the four years leading up to the G20 protests, the TSG, the specialist unit of 730 officers at the centre of controversy after the G20, received more than 5,00 complaints, mostly for "oppressive behaviour". Of those, only nine-0.18%-were substantiated after an investigation by the Met's complaints unit*' (Guardian 1ˢᵗ April 2010).

There had been problems in London at May Day protests in 2000 (95 arrests), 2001 (1,000 people 'kettled' into the centre of Oxford Circus for 7 hours), 2002 (50 arrests), 2003 (32 arrests). 'Kettling' is one of the most controversial public order tactics that the police because of its impact on civil liberties. The police prefer the term 'containment', but it has been nicknamed 'kettling' because it raises temperatures to boiling point (on both sides). Numerous humanitarian groups and civil rights organisations have called for the police to abandon this tactic, but police have legitimised its use by saying there is "no alternative" (Skrimshire 2005). Other tactics that the police use are interception and obstruction of protestors and the use of no protest zones. Also, as in the miners strike, many officers did not wear identification numbers.

Although policing at demonstrations was based on classic crowd psychology theory, some academics have claimed that there has been a move by the police towards the use of negotiated management when dealing with protestors (see Della Porta and Reiter 1998; Waddington and King 2005; Vitale 2005). This approach is where agreements are reached between the police and protestors that limit the scale and scope of demonstrations, but does not actually prevent them from happening. This of course requires the cooperation of the protestors to succeed. New laws requiring cooperation with the police, such as seven days notice of a demonstration and a route stated by the police, may appear to have put restrictions on protestors, but most appeared to have accepted this. However globalisation protests attract many disparate groups and the police may not attempt to negotiate with certain groups (as certain groups will not want to cooperate with the police). Thus, negotiated management may not be applied in every context (Rosie and Gorringe 2009). The police therefore have a number of '*preventative measures, of varying de-*

grees of overtness and legality' (Waddington 2007:16) to deal with protests.

There had been two very large demonstrations prior to G20 in April 2009. There had been a demonstration in Scotland in 2005 at the G8 conference (see Gorringe and Rosie 2008), and also in London in January 2009 in protest against the Israeli invasion of Gaza. In both demonstrations the police created conditions, which would provoke collective conflict. Besides kettling other tactics included intimidation (full riot gear, dog squads, horses), undifferentiated use of force, discrimination and arbitrary handling of the laws, which only served to delegitimise perceptions of the police in the eyes of the protestors. It should have come as no surprise that the police did the same thing at the G20 demonstration in April 2009. It wasn't helped that prior to the G20 protest (and also the G8 protest) that the newspaper reports prior to the protests were predicting 'chaos' and 'violence' (Rosie and Gorringe 2009; Greer and McLaughlin 2010) As Gorringe and Rosie have noted *'Cops read papers too'* (2008:699).

The big difference between the G20 protests and the previous ones was the death of Ian Tomlinson, a 46-year-old newspaper vendor who was not involved in the protests, but was walking home. It was amateur footage which showed Tomlinson walking away from police officers with his hands in his pockets when a police officer hit the back of his legs with a baton. The same officer then dived on Tomlinson sending him sprawling to the ground where he hit his head on the pavement (Guardian Editorial 2009). Rosie and Gorringe (2009) note that there was a noticeable shift in the tone of some media coverage. It was not the first time a protestor had been killed because of police actions. In April 1979 anti-fascist Blair Peach was killed, but in1979 there was no CCTV or mobile phones to record this. Over the next few weeks there emerged a number of complaints about police violence, which the media highlighted.

The HMIC Report

In response to the media outcry about the issue of kettling and the policing of G20 the HMIC set up a review team to look at the policing of public protest. The final report was published in November 2009, *Adapting to Protest: Nurturing the British Model of Policing.* Dr Clifford

Stott submitted evidence to the HMIC, *Crowd Psychology and Public Order Policing: An Overview of Scientific Theory and Evidence* (2009).

He argued that the 'classic' crowd psychology *'position is outdated, unsustainable scientifically and it is critical that training is updated to reflect contemporary theory and evidence'* (2009: 3). Stott goes on to assert that such a theory is prejudiced, and thus fails to explain crowd behaviour and how collective conflict occurs (2009: 3). Stott's evidence was based on the Elaborated Social Identity Model (ESIM); in light of its successful employment by the Portuguese Public Security Police at the UEFA Football European Championships (see Stott et al 2007). The HMIC report took on board the evidence presented by Stott.

The final HMIC report was 200 pages, which advocated an *'approachable, impartial, accountable style of policing based on minimal force'* (2009: 5).

The report pointed out that public order events have exposed inconsistencies in the training, standards and leadership of public order policing, in particular:

- An absence of clear standards on the use of force.
- Inappropriate use of public order powers such as stop and search and overt photography: Police use of overt photography and the retention of the images raise human rights issues.
- Variation between forces in understanding of the law.
- Inconsistent equipment and tactics: There is no common standard for public order personal protection uniform and different approaches to training - 19 forces train with intermediate and round shields, 2 with long and round shields and one with all three types.
- Out dated training and guidance: The current tactics-training manual was written in 2004 and has not been revised since. (2009: 5-7)

Some of the key areas addressed in the report were a recommendation that public order training should be overhauled, with an emphasis put on communication strategies and the understanding and management of crowd dynamics. This is not new, as some commentators had previously argued this. (see Adang 2002; Reicher et al 2004; Fielding 2005)

The report makes a number of other recommendations, including:

- The adoption of a set of fundamental principles on the use of force, which run as a golden thread through all aspects of police business.
- Codification of public order policing to ensure consistency in public order training and use of equipment, tactics and police powers.

- Clarification of the legal framework for the use of overt photography by the police during public order operations and the collation and retention of photographic images by police forces and other policing bodies.
- Review of the status of the Association of Chief Police Officers to ensure transparent governance and accountability structures, especially in relation to their quasi- operational role of the commissioning of intelligence and the collation and retention of data.

The policing of the Climate Camp in London, August 2009, suggested that the police had taken on board the lessons of G20, as they adopted a more tolerant approach. It may have been significant that both senior officers who were in control of tactics were both women, Superintendent Julia Pendry and Inspector Jane Connors. Was the policing of the Climate Camp a first step towards 'neighbourhood policing' of protests and public order?

One Constabulary where some senior officers are advocates of Stott's principles is Hampshire. They had a chance to put these into practice at the FA Cup game between Southampton and Portsmouth on the 14th February 2010. This is one of the fiercest rivalries in football. But Hampshire police viewed it as a public safety event rather than a public order event. The policing style was 'safer neighbourhood plus', with officers in normal uniform and riot officers held in reserve. The operation was deemed a success as '95% went as planned' (interview 2010). Hampshire police adopted the same policing style and tactics a month later when Southampton played Leeds United. Again this was a success. A senior officer commented, 'we have cultural issues in the police we have to get the mind set right. If you deploy NATO kit and long batons you are creating a mindset of trouble. So we want to look like ordinary community Bobbies, with sticks and helmets in the van' (interview 2010).

Although there are some officers in Hampshire Constabulary who are fully behind the HMIC report and are big supporters of the principles by Clifford Stott, a note of caution needs to be applied. Policing football crowds is very different from policing political demonstrations. The key word here being *political,* which football matches are not. Also, it may not be down to individual senior officers in regional constabularies when it comes to policing protest. At present, surveillance of demonstrations and the collection, retention and dissemination of information is managed by three units, with an estimated spend of £9 million, set up and managed within ACPO.

The largest of these is the National Public Order Intelligence Unit (NPOIU), which runs a central database containing details of thousands of so-called domestic extremists. In addition, ACPO runs the National Extremism Tactical Coordination Unit (NETCU), which advises companies on how to manage political campaigns, and the National Domestic Extremism Team (NDET), which pools intelligence gathered by investigations into protesters across the country (Evans, Lewis and Taylor 2009). So there could well be tensions between ACPO and the HMIC when it comes to managing political protests.

Not everyone thought the policing of the G20 was a failure A report published by the Home Affairs Select Committee in June 2009 summarises that *'The policing of the G20 Protests was a remarkably successful operation; more than 35,000 protesters demonstrated in the centre of London with a police presence of several thousand, yet there was a minimum of disruption to the City. Aside from a few high-profile incidents, the policing of the G20 Protests passed without drama... The policing of the G20 Protests was a remarkably successful operation; there was a minimum of disruption to the City'*

If the police's primary role is to facilitate peaceful protest and act as public protector, then there is no doubt that their operation was anything but 'remarkably successful'. However success for the Home Affairs Select Committee is considered to be seen as minimising 'disruption to the City', therefore preventing interruption to trade and disallowing protesters to effectively demonstrate their anger towards capitalism and government outside of an isolated area.

The Impact of the HMIC Report

In nine months since the publication of the HMIC Report in November 2009 have there been major changes in the way police political protests? Well it is probably too early for an in depth assessment. As pointed out earlier, Hampshire Constabulary has used the new guidelines at football matches, but not all police forces in England and Wales have followed suit. There have been several marches by the far right English Defence League and counter demonstrations by United Against Fascism, all of which have ended in violence and arrests. This perhaps is not surprising as you have two diametrically opposed forces facing off against each other with the police attempting to keep them separate and keep the peace. Violence has frequently marred protests in which the English Defence League has been involved in. At one such event in Bolton, 20th March 2010, 'Kettling' was used, and 'snatch squads were used to dive into crowds to pull out so-called troublemakers. There were 74 arrests after the day's confrontations, with at least 55 anti-racist campaigners arrested. (Tracy McVeigh: 2010). This was perhaps due to the fact that the police appeared to arrest the most vocal UAF activists, regardless of whether they had broken the law. These arrests seemed to anger the crowd rather than pacify them, as did the policy of threatening to arrest those who were trying to give legal advice. Of those arrested only three were prosecuted.

It comes as no surprise, therefore, that how the police deal with some left –wing protestors has come under scrutiny. This is particularly true of anti-globalisation and anti-war protestors. They used the tactic of the pre-emptive arrests of protestors in Nottingham as 114 environmental protestors were arrested on the charge of conspiracy to commit aggravated trespass in on the 13th April 2009 (Matthew Weaver: 2009). The police also make regular use of Forward Intelligence Teams to photograph protestors, and still use the controversial tactic of 'kettling'. At an anti-fascist protest in Brighton on the 30th August 2010 police seized a film cassette of a local man under Section 19 of the Police and Criminal evidence Act 1984, and police tactics used against the protestors who demonstrated at the arms dealer EDO MBM/ITT in Brighton in 2010 did not appear to be those of neighbourhood policing when 53 out of approximately 150 protestors were arrested. (Marc Vallee 2010). As well as public order legislation Sussex Police made use of a little-known by-law passed in 1998 by Brighton and Hove City Council under section 235 of the Local Government Act 1972. It was introduced for "good rule and government" for the "prevention and suppression of nuisances," namely in the form of shouting, singing, playing musical instruments or using electrical equipment in streets or public places. It was not intended to prevent political protest.

A key point in the evidence to the G20 inquiry was that all crowds are not all the same and that they are not homogeneous. The police need to make a distinction between peaceful protestors and those who are intent on violence, as Hampshire Police have tried to distinguish between football supporters and football hooligans. A year after the death of Ian Tomlinson, the Crown Prosecution Service took the decision not to prosecute the police officer who struck Ian Tomlinson which raised the question of whether the police are beyond the law[1].

Conclusion

The 1980s saw the militarisation of the police in response to industrial unrest and political protests and in an attempt to preserve the state's monopoly of legitimate force. Over the last 30 years we have witnessed paramilitary style policing of demonstrations and football matches. This has raised the question of what kind of policing do we want in a liberal democracy?

The police decision making in public order situations is of course complex, but the principles of keeping public order have not really changed since the Peterloo massacre in 1819, when the police following their formation in 1829 took over the task of quelling civil unrest from the military. Quite simply their job is, and always has been, to keep the peace, using minimum force. The difficulty is getting the balance right. It may make a difference to how you police an event depending on how you view it, for example – public order or public safety. There is a need to take into account of how decisions on strategy and tactics influence the crowd, and the work of Stott and others is important here. The police need to utilise intelligence, communication, differentiation and facilitation strategies which avoid the situation of them treating a crowd as a homogeneous mass.

However, the reviews and proposals published so far have do not go far enough because they treat the problem as a tactical issue. It is not just about police tactics, the problem is deeply rooted in the politics and culture of the police. How will the police react to how people protest against the economic cuts? Is it possible to adopt 'neighbourhood policing' against demonstrators who it maybe perceived are threatening the state? Will they police with the velvet glove or the iron fist? History has shown that when the state is perceived to be under threat, then the velvet glove is removed[2].

---

[1] On the 29th November the family of Ian Tomlinson lodged a further complaint with the Independent Police Complaints Commission. The IPCC have been asked to investigate the claim that a senior Metropolitan Police officer misled those investigating the cause of the death of Ian Tomlinson by alleging that Ian fell onto the ground before the assault incident with the police officer (which was captured on video).
[2] This paper was presented on the 2nd September. Since then there have been two large demonstrations in London against the rise in student tuition fees and public expenditure cuts. The

References

Adang, O. (2002) 'Police Studies and public order maintenance', in A. Mellink and E.R. Muller (Eds) *Police Science and police Studies in the Netherlands,* Apeldoorn: Dutch Police Academy.

Della Porta, D. and Reiter, H. (eds.) (1998) *Policing Protest: The Control of Mass Demonstrations in Western Democracies,* Minneapolis: University of Minneapolis Press.

Evans, R., Lewis, P. and Taylor, R. (2009) 'How police rebranded lawful protest as 'domestic extremism', in *The Guardian,* 26th October 2009.

Fielding, N. (2005 2nd Ed) *The Police and Social Conflict,* London: Glasshouse Press.

Gorringe, H. and Rosie, M. (2008) 'It's a long way to Auchterarder! 'Negotiated management' and mismanagement in the policing of G8 protests', *British Journal of Criminology,* 59 (2): 187-205.

Greer, C. and McLaughlin, E. (2010) 'We Predict a Riot: Public Order Policing, News Coverage and the Rise of the Citizen Journalist', in *British Journal of Criminology,* 50, 6: 1041-1059

Guardian Editorial (2009) 'G20 Protests: A Case to Answer', in *The Guardian,* 8th April 2009.

---

first demonstration was a national demonstration organized by the National Union of Students and the lecturers union, the UCU, on the 10th November 2010. The Metropolitan Police misjudged the number of students who would turn up, expecting the number to be about 15,000. Approximately 50,000 turned up and there were only 225 officers to police the event. There was only a handful stood at the entrance of the Conservative Party headquarters when some students broke away from the demonstration to enter the building. The press criticized the police for being caught off guard and for the way they handled the demonstration, which turned violent. One newspaper commented that *'yesterday we saw the fruits of the softly, softly approach proposed by Sir Dennis O'Connor, who conducted a report into policing of the G20 demos'.* (Daily Telegraph, 11th November 2010). So it was perhaps not surprising that the police took a tougher line at the student demonstrations on the 24th November. They reverted back to the tactics used at G20, police in full riot gear, 'kettling', and police on horseback charging students and schoolchildren. It appears that the police have not quite got the balance right yet when policing political demonstrations.

HMIC (2009) *Adapting To Protest: Nurturing the British Model of Policing,* London: Home Office.

Home Affairs Select Committee (2009) *Eighth Report: Policing of the G20 Protests,* 29th June 2009. Available at: www.publications.parliament.uk/pa/cm200809/cmselect/cmhaff/418/418 02.htm

Interview with Senior Police Officer of Hampshire Constabulary, February 2010.

Jefferson, T. (1990) *The Case Against Paramilitary Policing,* Buckingham: Open University Press.

Leech, K. (1988) Struggle *In Babylon: Racism in the Cities and Churches of Britain,* London: Sheldon Press.

Lewis. P. (2010) 'Untouchable Elite that seems ripe for reform', in *The Guardian,* 1st April 2010.

McVeigh, T. (2010) 'Dozens held in clashes at rightwing rally', in *The Observer,* 21st March 2010.

Reicher, S. (2001) 'Crowds and Social Movements', in M. Hogg and S.Tindale (eds.), *Blackwell Handbook of Social Psychology: Group Processes,* Oxford: Blackwell.

Reicher, S. Stott, C., Cronin, P. and Adang, O. (2004) 'An Integrated approach to crowd psychology and public order policing', in *Policing: An International Journal of Police Strategies and Management,* 27 (4): 558-572.

Rosie, M. and Gorringe, H. (2009) 'What a Difference a Death Makes: Protest, Policing and the Press at G20', *Sociological Research Online 14 (5) 4, www.socresonline.org.uk/14/5/4.html>doi:10.5153/sro.2047.* Accessed 26th July 2010.

Skrimshire, S. (2005) 'Anti-G8 Resistance and the State of Exception', in *Shut Them Down! The G8, Gleneagles and the Movement of Movements,* Autonomedia.

Stott, C. and Reicher, S. (1998a) 'How conflict escalates: the intergroup dynamics of collective football crowd "violence"', *Sociology,* 32 (2): 353-77.

Stott, C.J., Adang, O.M., Livingstone, A., & Schreiber, M. (2007) 'Variability in the collective behaviour of England fans at Euro 2004: public order policing, social identity, inter-group dynamics and social change'. *European Journal of Social Psychology,* 37: 75-100.

Stott, C., Livingstone, and Hoggett (2008) 'Policing football crowds in England and Wales: A model of good practice?' Policing *and Society,* 18: 1-24.

Stott, C. (2009) *Crowd Psychology and Public Order Policing: An Overview of Scientific Theory and Evidence,* [online] (Liverpool: University of Liverpool) http://www.liv.ac.uk/pyschology/staff/Cstoot/HMIC%20Report%20Crowd%Psychology%20Final%Submission%Draft%20%2814-9%29.pdf [accessed February 2010].

Vitale. Alex. (2005) "From Negotiated Management to Command and Control: How the New York Police Department Polices Protests", *Policing and Society* 15 (3): 283-304.

Waddington, D. and King, M. (2005) 'The Disorderly Crowd: From Classical Psychological Reductionism to Socio-Contextual Theory – The Impact on Public Order Policing Strategies', *The Howard Journal,* 44 (5): 490-503.

Waddington, D. (2007) *Public Order Policing: Theory and Practice,* Cullompton: Willan.

Waddington, P.A.J. (1991) *The Strong Arm of the Law,* Oxford: Clarendon.

Waddington, P.A.J. (1993) 'The case against Paramilitary policing considered', *British Journal of Criminology,* 33 (3): 353-373.

Waddington, P.A.J. (2003) 'Policing Public Order and Political Contention', in T. Newburn (ed.) *Handbook of Policing,* Cullompton: Willan; 394-421.

Weaver, M. (2009) 'Power station protest plot suspects released on bail', *The Guardian,* 14th April 2009.

http://www.marcvallee.co.uk/protest [accessed August 2010]

7.

THE IMPOSITION OF INTERNMENT WITHOUT TRIAL IN NORTHERN IRELAND, AUGUST 1971: CAUSES, CONSEQUENCES AND LESSONS

Mark Hayes

The state of "Northern Ireland" was created in June 1921. After the Government of Ireland Act became law Ireland was partitioned, and two separate parliaments governed in Dublin and in Belfast, with Northern Ireland remaining under British control. Partition was a pragmatic policy response to a Nationalist uprising, but also reflected the fact that the majority of people in the North-east corner of the island (mostly Protestants) retained their allegiance to Britain. The Stormont regime in Northern Ireland was therefore dominated by Protestant Unionists committed to Britain and their British identity, and hostile toward the political aspirations of Irish Nationalism and Republicanism. These Protestants, who were the descendants of the loyal settlers sent to Ireland to subdue the rebellious Catholics in the seventeenth century, were intent on preserving their cultural identity, which was enshrined in the Constitutional connection to Britain via the Monarchy. The Irish Catholic minority in Northern Ireland were, in effect, trapped within a state designed to secure a loyal British Protestant majority. It is now generally acknowledged that Catholics were subsequently discriminated against in terms of the distribution of housing, employment prospects, voting rights and opportunities for cultural expression (see White 1995 et al :334, Weitzer 1987).

Self evidently security became *the* critical issue in Northern Ireland and civil obedience was maintained, primarily, via the imposition of draconian laws. The most emblematic example of such legislation was the Civil Authorities (Special Powers) Act (Northern Ireland) 22 April 1922, which was the most potent symbol of the state's coercive capability. The SPA regulation 11 (1) and Section 12 permitted arrest and detention on the basis of suspicion that an individual had acted, was acting, or *might* act "in a manner prejudicial to the preservation of the peace or maintenance of order" (SPA cited in Boyle, Hadden and

Hillyard 1975: 58; see Walsh 2000: 51, Taylor 1998: 92, Donohue 1998:1089, and De Baroid 2000: 69). The Act, which had nine sections and thirty regulations, was also used to prohibit public expressions of specifically Irish Republican political dissent – the Home Affairs Minister could not only intern without trial, but arrest without charge or warrant, flog or even execute! The authorities were empowered to destroy buildings or requisition land, and banning orders at various times covered not only membership of certain groups but particular meetings, assemblies, processions, coroners' inquests, the flying of the Irish tricolour, the wearing of the Easter lily (as a cultural expression of support for the Nationalist uprising in 1916), the circulation of certain newspapers, the printing of particular documents, the construction of monuments and even the singing of certain songs! (see Donohue 1998 and White et al 1995).

This severely authoritarian legislation clearly reflected the fact that "Northern Ireland" was a fragile entity, where Unionist political leaders could not establish legitimacy via consent. For Irish Catholics Northern Ireland became essentially a police state. It is therefore evident that "from the creation of the state emergency legislation was entrenched and normalised as a daily part of state procedure...The centrality of emergency laws to the functioning of the Unionist regime is an early indicator of the abnormal political reality of the state" (Ní Aoláin 2000:21).

When the co-ordinated campaign by Northern Ireland Civil Rights Association (NICRA) to achieve equal civil rights for Catholics was met by systematic state repression in 1969, it precipitated serious social disorder. As Swann correctly points out, the political zeitgeist of "the consciousness of freedom" from Watts to Prague has to be factored in here (Swann 2008). Catholics in the 1960s were no longer willing to accept their subordinate status under the Stormont regime. Although the British Army was deployed in August 1969 to "restore the civil power", the initial optimism amongst some Catholics about the social reformist intentions of a Labour government in London proved unfounded. The spiral of mutual mistrust and hostility between an oppressed minority, and an intransigent Unionist government at Stormont, deepened dramatically. Moreover, the Army was ill-equipped to maintain social order and the Falls' curfew of July 1970, which led to the death of 11 innocent civilians, confirmed to many Nationalists the notion that the British military were there to simply sustain the Unionist regime at Stormont (Farrell 1992:273). It is certainly also worth noting that, in the summer of 1969, the IRA did not really exist as a significant force at all. The inter-communal violence and the evident need to defend Catholic areas, along with the evident aggression of the Army, made Republican armed resistance almost inevitable. Given the re-emergence of armed Republicanism as a factor, Unionist policy makers simply re-iterated their security agenda, and this led to the re-application of "special powers" and internment without trial in August 1971.

Internment was brought in with the agreement of the British government on 9 August 1971 – in effect British Prime Minister Edward Heath allowed Unionist leader Brian Faulkner, the architect of internment, to take an enormous gamble, and as Cunningham has pointed out, "while internment could not have been introduced without at least the acquiescence of Westminster, the policy indicated a shift towards greater influence for Stormont in what were previously jointly determined security decisions" (Cunningham 2001:9). In order to introduce internment without trial Britain had to derogate from Article 5 of the European Convention on Human Rights, but Faulkner stated unequivocally; "I have had to conclude that the ordinary law cannot deal comprehensively or quickly enough with such ruthless viciousness, I have therefore decided to exercise where necessary the powers of detention and internment vested in me as Minister for Home Affairs" (cited in Winchester 1974:166). The aim of internment was to destroy the operational capacity of the IRA, as O'Boyle says, "the underlying official policy beneath this introduction in 1971 was primarily to obtain more intelligence information about the IRA and to detain individuals on a preventive basis who could not be dealt with by the ordinary means of law" (O'Boyle 1977:675).

At around 4.30 on 9 August "Operation Demetrius" was implemented - 3,000 troops set out, ostensibly, to capture Republicans, and 342 men were arrested (O'Boyle 1977:675). No Unionists/Loyalists were arrested! (two were actually Protestants, but both were politically anti-Unionist). This is despite the fact that some pro-British paramilitary groups, such as the Ulster Volunteer Force, had been engaged in a relatively systematic campaign of violence against Catholics for several years! Moreover, the methods used by the British Army in expediting the internment warrants were often brutal. As McKittrick points out, "allegations that soldiers had in the process often used brutal methods were denied by the authorities but often substantiated by later inquiries and court proceedings" (McKittrick et al 2000:68).

Many volunteers in the Provisional IRA had heard days before that internment was to be introduced and so absconded south of the border, but a few activists were lifted in the initial sweep. Mickey Donnelly, a well-known Republican activist from Derry said "in 1971 our aim was to bring Stormont down, I didn't think civil rights would be successful because of the nature of the state. It couldn't be reformed" (interview 16.09.10). Donnelly, who would not have been surprised by his detention, relayed the precise circumstances of his arrest, "I was living in William's Street (Derry) at the time. I heard a noise downstairs and within seconds a whole gang of British soldiers were in the bedroom, as many as could fit in, maybe 10, or 12. I was made to put trousers on and a shirt and dragged out into the Land Rover. The Army troops were brutal in the back of the vehicle. I was taken to the barracks, but never actually told why I was arrested" (interview 16.09.10). However, in a significant number of cases civil rights activists were arrested. As Donnelly recounts, "I had quite a few family members and friends interned – some were not members of the Republican movement at all" (interview 16.09.10). The information supplied to the Army by Special Branch was woefully inadequate and many innocent individuals were caught up in the operation. Interestingly, the Army subsequently acknowledged the inadequacy of the intelligence used, as Colonel Michael Dewar later admitted, "the net was cast fairly wide and internees ranged from known terrorists to comparatively harmless pamphleteers" (Dewar 1996:53).

Paddy Joe McClean was one such civil rights activist: "I was not a Republican although I was interned before between 1956-60 – I had no trial at all. It wasn't even an issue. I was a member of the civil rights movement preaching non-violence. Every policeman I met knew that. I had a family background that was Presbyterian on one side. Everyone knew I wasn't a terrorist" (interview 17.09.10). He too recalls the circumstances of his arrest: "My wife's mother was in hospital, and I hadn't had much sleep. I heard them arrive at about 6am, RUC and Army. No indication was given then or subsequently about why I was arrested, but no excessive force was used. We were taken to the army barracks in Omagh, then onto Magilligan. I got the sense that the army were running the show. They contradicted orders given by the police about where I should go" (interview 17.09.10). McClean continues, "it was extraordinary that the British government knew the PIRA men, actually met them on occasion to negotiate with them, but they were not interned. I got the surprise of my life to see so many civil rights supporters interned. It was amazing to me. I was socialist orientated. We wanted fair play – borders didn't come into it" (interview 17.09.10).

Given the large number of completely innocent internees, and the circumstances surrounding their detention, there is no doubt that "internment caused irreparable damage to the relationship between the Catholic community and the RUC and the Army because so many individuals and families were targeted, often on the basis of spurious and inaccurate files...Although the use of internment might be viewed as a desperate attempt to bring order to a society increasingly undermined by conflict, it had the opposite effect" (Hayes et al 2005:15). Indeed, the reaction to internment was almost instantaneous in Nationalist areas in the North. As journalist Simon Winchester put it, "it was a dreadful, satanic night – and a time when many of us thought that the very fabric of civilised life was coming away at the edges, and some sort of Armageddon was upon us all...Violence of unimaginable proportions grew and grew that autumn, until by the end of 1971 so many had been killed and injured that all vestiges of normal life that Ireland had once known had disintegrated" (Winchester 1974:167-8 and 176). People queued up in Derry to join the Provisional IRA, "who were benefitting from increased hostility to the troops and attracted support principally on the basis that they alone were prepared to attack the army at every opportunity" (O'Dochartaigh 2005:235). As civil rights activist Eamonn McCann explained, "internment was a calculated humiliation which Unionist governments had, since the inception of the state, regularly visited upon our community. In the twenties, the thirties, the forties, and the fifties, the RUC had come storming into our areas at night, dragged our people from their beds and taken them off to camps and prison-ships, where they were often held for years; no charge, no trial, nothing. There was not a family in the area which had not had a relative or a neighbour interned. Now it was happening again", however "the days when the Bogside allowed itself to be kicked around like this were long gone...By dawn the area was hysterical with hatred...There were many dead...The twenty-four hours after internment were the bloodiest Northern Ireland had known for decades" (McCann 1981:91-92 and 93)[1].

---

[1] see White et al 1995:330, Hillyard 1988:204, De Baroid 2000:94, Coogan 1995:128, Fay, Morrisey and Smith 1999 – see statistics p.137 and 148. See also Spjut 1986:716 and Hadden 1975:315 who uses official statistics to illustrate the dramatic increase in the level of violence.

Internment "would be viewed by Catholics as the culminating act of a policy of uninhibited repression which had begun in early July 1971, and as a deliberate escalation of the conflict...the scale of this process of alienation locked much of the Catholic community, including moderates, into a basic rejection of the authority of the Northern Ireland state" (O'Dochartaigh 2005:230). As Boyle et al point out, "the level of violence in the main Roman Catholic enclaves in Belfast and Londonderry (sic) increased dramatically, and a number of 'no-go' areas were rapidly established from which the RUC and the British Army were effectively excluded and within which the IRA proceeded to build up its strength and direct its operations" (Boyle, Hadden and Hillyard 1975:56-57). Hadden and Hillyard therefore make the point that, "the Provisional IRA had clearly built itself into a strong and well organised military force with a fair measure of tacit support in the main Roman Catholic enclaves. The introduction of internment in August 1971 completed the process. The list of those arrested and detained was so out of date and haphazard, and the treatment meted out in the detention and interrogation centres...so harsh as to unite the Roman Catholic community in Northern Ireland behind the Provisionals as never before. Recruitment and financial support are reported to have risen dramatically on both sides of the border, and the phase of all-out guerrilla warfare began in earnest" (Hadden and Hillyard 1973; see O'Doherty 1998:84-5, Farrell 1992:283, Bowyer Bell 1994:217 and 224, Smith 1995:101, Coogan 1995:128). As Farrell says, "in August 1971 the British government sanctioned the introduction of internment: the anti-imperialist movement replied with all-out war" (Farrell 1992:330). As Mickey Donnelly confirms, "the effect of internment was massive. The Republican movement had a free hand for a while after. I think they actually realised it had failed, especially after 'Bloody Sunday' which was of course an anti-internment march – Stormont collapsed. Internment was the really big turning point" (interview 16.09.10).

Moreover, the antagonism of the area towards British authority was accentuated when word filtered out of the torture techniques being used on internees. According to De Baroid, internees were forced to run over cinders, barbed wire and broken glass in their bare feet, whilst soldiers beat them with clubs and boots (De Baroid 2000:74). The individual testimonies of internees, collected by fellow detainee John McGuffin (1973) are particularly disturbing, for instance that of Eamonn Kerr (:13), who had cigarette butts stubbed out on his neck, or Edward

Campbell who had his head shaven because he had the (fictitious) disease "venereal scabies" (p.18). The extent of the mistreatment was confirmed by James Magilton (aged 60) and John Murphy (aged 61) who were both badly beaten before being released within 24 hours (McGuffin 1973:119); by Patrick Fitzsimmons and William Joseph Johnston, who both given electric shock treatment (McGuffin 1973:124); and also by Tom Kearns who was given hallucinogenic drugs whilst being questioned (McGuffin 1973:125). These specific cases clearly indicated sadistic maltreatment, and accusations were made about the squeezing testicles, the use of cattle prods, beating with batons, insertion of items into anal passages, burning with matches, candles and electric fires, playing "Russian roulette", firing blanks into mouths, and urinating on prisoners (McGuffin 1973: 126 and De Baroid 2000:74-5, who both quote Fr Denis Faul and Fr. Raymond Murray; see Wilson 1997:68, Bardon 1992, Boyle and Hannum 1974).

Mickey Donnelly recalls his personal experience: "Four of us were separated and asked to give information – we were told if we were cooperative we could make it easier for ourselves. We finished in Magilligan army camp, in a corrugated tin hut guarded by army sergeants. It was strange and ominous. We got no sleep because of the noise they made, and the threats. Some of the lads were put in helicopters which they thought were miles over the Irish Sea, but were in fact stationary. They were told to talk or be pushed out of the door. It happened to me, and I remember the wind and the noise of the helicopter, and the shouting in my ear. I remember shouting something, I'm not sure what, then I was pushed from the door. The fall knocked the wind out of me. I thought I was going to die. Another time I felt I was drugged, I was so cold and couldn't control my limbs, and was hearing music. I remember thinking that this is all so mad they will never ever let me out to tell people about it" (interview 16.09.10). He continues, "…we were all lined up, hit with batons, even older people. One man had a plastic bullet fired into his stomach at point blank range. I tried to intervene to help the poor man because I knew his son but they hit me with rifle butts. They were actually looking for his son, but took his elderly father instead. He never really recovered. He had a series of operations afterwards, and died a few years later" (interview 16.09.10).

As well as such indiscriminate abuse, there was the more systematic application of the so-called "five techniques" of Sensory Deprivation (SD) used on particular internees. This so-called "experimental interrogation" (McKittrick et al 2000:68), took place between 11-17 August 1971, probably at Ballykelly airfield (Bowyer Bell 1994 :231, Newbury in Newbery et al 2009:631). The five techniques were: having a hood placed over the head; being forced to stand spread-eagled against a wall for long periods; denial of regular sleep patterns; irregular and limited supply of food and water; the playing of constant white noise (see O'Boyle 1977:675). In effect the human brain requires sensory stimulation, sugar and oxygen to function adequately – and the selected prisoners were deprived of all three (McGuffin 1974:40). Moreover, the artificial deprivation of such sensual stimuli can induce severe stress and trauma, leading to the impairment of cognitive judgement, diminution of rational behaviour and paranoia (McGuffin 1974:40). According to McGuffin, these techniques were used for six reasons (McGuffin 1974:156-57): to gain intelligence; secure "confessions"; mete out punishment; create a climate of fear in a given area; to create anxiety amongst younger volunteers of a guerrilla army; and to justify the position of the torturer by degrading and de-humanising the enemy (McGuffin 1974)[2]. Originally twelve men were subjected to "interrogation in depth", with two more subjected shortly afterwards – both Mickey Donnelly and Paddy Joe McClean were in the original cohort.

Both Mickey and Paddy Joe are clear about the process and its purpose: as Mickey says, "I was subjected to Sensory Deprivation on the basis of details supplied by an informer who gave my name as someone who supposedly had information. In the morning the RUC came in and the hoods were put on. I was punched and abused by an RUC man who clearly enjoyed what he was doing. I was handcuffed extremely tightly so it hurt, beaten and taken away in a helicopter. We landed and I was led inside somewhere. I was put in a boiler suit. I heard the noise, very strange and hard to describe, it penetrated your head, a mixture of high and low pitches – I have never heard anything like it since. It must have been designed to drive people out of their mind. I was made to stand

---

[2] see McGuffin (1974) p.105; see O'Boyle (1977) p.676-79; see also McGuffin (1974) chap 7 pp.104-115. See the Memorandum submitted by Amnesty International to the Parker Committee on Interrogation Procedures, Appendix I in McGuffin (1973) p.197. Amnesty invoked Article 17 of the Geneva Convention opposing physical and mental torture of prisoners, and claimed the techniques were "immoral, illegal and inexpedient" (cited p.210); see also the evidence submitted by the British Society for Social Responsibility in Science (McGuffin 1973:217) which recommended the prohibiting of such techniques, arguing that official utilisation would constitute a "misuse of science and technology, as well as a crudely behaviouristic view of the individual as an object to be manipulated mechanically by the State" (cited in McGuffin 1973 :220).

with my hands against the wall. I was quite fit but it catches up with you. I heard people scream as they fell and were beaten. There was just bread and water, which I refused because I thought I might be drugged. I heard later some of the others were given LSD, others electric shocks" (interview 16.09.10).

Paddy Joe: "I think the decisions were made at the headquarters of British intelligence, to conduct a psychological experiment. We were isolated from each other. My mind-set was that I was certain I was going to die – no-one would let me out to broadcast the details of what was done in the name of 'democracy'. They put me in an army uniform so I thought they would shoot me and say it was a case of mistaken identity. We don't know for certain where the special treatment was carried out, I assumed it was in Scotland. They made me stand at a wall, played constant noise and deprived me of sleep for days on end. I said to them 'I know what you are about – this is torture'. I decided not to follow their orders, and I got battered and abused" (interview 17.09.10).

Catholic and international reaction to the evidence emerging from the internees meant that the British government had little choice but to sanction an inquiry by Ombudsman Sir Edmund Compton (see McGuffin 1973:127 and 1974 chapter 5:78-91). Yet there were immediate procedural difficulties with the Committee of Inquiry: it was not held in public, did not have full judicial powers to summon witnesses or examine records, and there was to be no cross-examination of witness testimonies. Moreover, in its report the Committee found no evidence of torture or brutality, but did however acknowledge that there had been "ill-treatment". The Committee saw only one "complainant", and received a written submission of evidence from another, but heard, among others, 95 army witnesses, 26 police witnesses, 11 prison officers, and five military medical officers. Compton then infamously concluded that: "where...physical ill-treatment took place, we are not making a finding of brutality on the part of those who handled these complainants. We consider that brutality is an inhuman or savage form of cruelty, and that cruelty implies a disposition to inflict suffering, coupled with indifference to, or pleasure in, the victim's pain. We do not think that happened here" (Compton Report cited in McGuffin 1974:51). The crucial evidence, according to Compton, was in the minds of the interrogators, who were not indifferent to, nor did they take pleasure in, the victim's pain! (O'Boyle 1977:676; Taylor 1980:22). The report did not consider at all the psychological impact of the techniques. Nationalists, not unreasonably, regarded the findings with considerable scepticism, if not contempt – as Coogan argues "the name Compton became synonymous for 'whitewash' in the minds of many Irish people" (Coogan 1995:129).

The obvious inadequacies of the Compton Report lead, almost immediately, to the establishment of a second committee chaired by Lord Parker. However, a majority on the committee found the techniques, with some safeguards, justified in the circumstances because vital intelligence was gained (see McGuffin 1974:105-6), in effect justifying the techniques in terms of the intelligence dividend – it maintained that the outcome of the process had saved innocent lives. However, a minority report by Lord Gardiner reached a qualitatively different conclusion in that it expressed concern at the medical after-effects of the interrogations, and argued that they were not only contrary to domestic law, but morally unjustified even if certain intelligence "advantages" were secured (see McGuffin 1974:109 and Taylor 1980:15). The Report was published on 2 March 1972 and on the same day the Prime Minister Edward Heath announced that the government was minded to accept the findings of the Minority Gardiner Report - the techniques would be discontinued[3].

Internment ended in Northern Ireland on 5 December 1975, with the last detainee being released. This policy reversal was as a direct consequence of the Diplock Report (1972) which, by abolishing trial by jury and altering the threshold for the admissibility of evidence, provided another method of dealing with suspects. A range of laws – the Emergency Provisions Act 1973 and the Prevention of Terrorism Act (1974) which extended the powers of arrest, introduced exclusion orders, port controls, and proscribed certain organisations, effectively replaced the Special Powers Act.

---

[3] How far Heath's change of position reflected a substantive change in perspective is open to question, McGuffin for instance suggests quite plausibly that it was fear of embarrassment amongst new allies in Europe that provided the motivational dynamic, see McGuffin (1974) p.114. Years later on 2 September 1976, following individual applications filed with the European Commission on Human Rights, the episode was described as a breach of the Convention, and the "techniques" were referred to as, not just "inhumane and degrading treatment", but also "torture" (Coogan 1995:129; McKittrick et al 2000:68, De Baroid 2000:75, O'Boyle 1977:684). Article 3 of the ECHR stated explicitly, "no one shall be subjected to torture or to inhuman or degrading treatment or punishment" (cited in Taylor 1980:11) a right from which there could be no derogation. However, when the case went to the European Court of Human Rights two years later, on 18 January 1978, the finding of "torture" was rescinded, although Britain was still found guilty of "inhumane and degrading" treatment.

However, although the practice of internment was ended, the victims of such blatant state brutality received no justice for their suffering. As Mickey Donnelly says, "I suffered afterwards, but others had it much worse. I had bad nightmares, terrifying at times. I don't like enclosed spaces or darkness. I wasn't the same person – I adapted to things, but I wasn't the same. I don't waste time hating people, but I still feel the effects when I talk about it. Some of the men went around the bend – never came to terms with it. These techniques have a long history, my father told me about them being used. I knew people that were ex-British Army in Malaysia, and they told me the kind of things they got up to. Terrorising villagers, cutting off ears and heads – I had a first-hand account of this, so I knew what they were capable of. The torture confirmed that I was right – it was a corrupt rotten state and had to be brought down" (interview 16.09.10). In effect internment, as an extra-judicial coercive measure, merely represented a crude, coercive attempt to intimidate Nationalists into submission, and as Paddy Joe McClean succinctly put it: "internment was not successful at all because it created more gunmen – more young people who flocked to join the Provisional IRA" (interview 17.09.10). Moreover, as Walsh argues, "the concept of an arrest power which permits the detention of a person without charge and for an unlimited period merely on the subjective suspicion that he or she poses a threat to public order is a total negation of the law and the hallmark of a totalitarian state which pays scant regard to the basic principles of legality" (Walsh 2000:45).

The authorities in Northern Ireland engaged in systematic torture that was not only immoral and illegal in international law (e.g. under terms of the Geneva Convention 1949 and Article 5 of Universal Declaration of Human Rights), but which "produced intelligence of the most limited value" (Bowyer Bell 1994:218). This led directly to the perception that the security forces acted unfairly and that administration of justice was inherently corrupt. As McGuffin explains, "internment had succeeded in uniting the minority as nothing else had ever done...the violence of the army when patrolling, raiding and sacking the Catholic ghettoes cemented the alienation. The tortures and brutalities exacerbated it even further. The plain and simple truth is that the Unionist Government, the army, the police and the courts had all lost credibility" (McGuffin 1973:108 and 112). Injustice and oppression precipitated anger and resentment, and merely intensified and prolonged the conflict.

When the whole issue of internment is viewed in historical perspective it is quite clear that similarities with the contemporary "war on terror" are quite striking. Fundamental legal and constitutional principles such as habeas corpus have been effectively abandoned in the name of national security, with secret courts and extraordinary rendition to facilitate torture. Britain, as Gereth Peirce (2010) has eloquently explained, has been complicitous in criminal acts of the utmost gravity. This is why the personal testimony of the victims of state violence is so critical, in order to construct a truthful narrative to penetrate ubiquitous state secrecy and counteract official misinformation. Moreover, in a very tangible sense the experiences of Micky Donnelly and Paddy Joe McClean are analogous to those of Binyan Mohamed and Moazzam Begg. The parallels are certainly not lost on those who suffered internment in 1971 as Paddy Joe says unequivocally: "the same thing is happening today in Abu Graib, Kandahar, Guantanamo and elsewhere. The techniques are just being refined by the Americans. There are direct similarities (interview 17.09.10)". Indeed, Micky Donnelly noted, "I met Moazzam Begg, and we compared notes. It is exactly the same type of treatment – people being set up and sent away for no reason" (interview 16.09.10). Indeed both the civil rights activist and the Republican agree that the current emergency anti-terrorist legislation in Britain, which facilitates 28 days detention without trial, is a form of internment. As Paddy Joe McClean says "28 days detention *is* effectively internment", while Mickey Donnelly concludes "it is happening here again at the moment with the 28 days detention, people have been lifted off the street in Derry, beaten and abused for no reason at all". This can only fuel further discontent, the desire for retribution and, ultimately political resistance. As Peirce concludes, "we are very far along a destructive path, and if our government continues on that path, we will ultimately have destroyed much of the moral and legal fabric of the society that we claim to be protecting" (Peirce 2010:72). Those policy makers who fail to learn from the lessons that history has taught us, are condemned to repeat the very same mistakes!

References

Bardon, J. (1992) *A History of Ulster,* Belfast: Blackstaff

Bowyer Bell, J. (1994) *The Irish Troubles: A Generation of Violence 1967-1992,* Dublin: Gill and Macmillan

Bowyer Bell, J. (1998) *The Secret Army: The IRA,* Dublin: Poolbeg

Boyce, D. (1996) *The Irish Question and British Politics 1868-1996,* Basingstoke: Macmillan

Boyle, K., Hadden, T. and Hillyard, P. (1975) *Law and State: the Case of Northern Ireland,* Martin: Robertson

Boyle, K. and Hannum, H. (1974) "Individual Applications Under the European Convention on Human Rights and the Concept of Administrative Practice: the Donnelly Case", *The American Journal of International Law* vol 68, No.3 July, pp.440-453

Brecher, B. (2007) *Torture and the Ticking Time Bomb,* Oxford: Wiley-Blackwell

Brewer, J. (1998) *Anti-Catholicism in Northern Ireland 1600-1998: The Mote and Beam,* Basingstoke: Macmillan

Campaign for Social Justice in Northern Ireland (1971), *Northern Ireland – The Mailed Fist, A Record of Army and Police Brutality from August 9 – November 9 1971,* Dungannon: CSJNI in collaboration with the Association for Legal Justice

Civil Authorities (Special Powers) Act (Northern Ireland) (1922) http://cain.ulst.ac.uk/hmso

Compton Report (1971): *Report of the inquiry into allegations against security forces of physical brutality in Northern Ireland arising out of events on 9th August* Cmnd 4823 HMSO

Coogan, TP. (1995) *The Troubles: Ireland's Ordeal 1966-1995 and the Search for Peace,* London: Hutchinson

Cunningham, M. (2001) *British Government Policy in Northern Ireland 1969-2000,* Manchester : Manchester University Press

De Baroid, C. (2000) *Ballymurphy and the Irish War,* London: Pluto

Dewar, M. (1996) *The British Army in Northern Ireland,* London: Arms and Armour

Donohue, L. (1998) "Regulating Northern Ireland: The Special Powers Acts 1922-1972" *The Historical Journal* vol 41 No.4 December, pp.1089-1120

Farrell, M. (1992) *Northern Ireland: The Orange State,* London: Pluto Press

Faul, Fr. D. and Murray, Fr. R. (1972) *British Army and Special Branch RUC Brutalities, December 1971-February 1972,* Dungannon LHL

Fay, M-T., Morrisey, M. and Smyth, M. (1999) *Northern Ireland's Troubles: The Human Cost,* London: Pluto

Gardiner Report (1974): *Report of a Committee to consider, in the context of civil liberty and human rights, measures to deal with terrorism in Northern Ireland,* Cmnd 5847 HMSO

Hadden (1975) "The Debacle of Ulster Internment" *New Society* vol.2 p.315-17

Hadden, T., Boyle, K. and Campbell, C. (1988) "Emergency Law in Northern Ireland: The Context" chap 1 pp.1-26 in Jennings, A. (ed) *Justice Under Fire: The Abuse of Civil Liberties in Northern Ireland,* London: Pluto

Hadden, T. and Hillyard, P. (1973) *Justice in Northern Ireland – A Study in Social Confidence,* London: Cobden Trust

Hayes, P. and Campbell, J. (2005) *Bloody Sunday: Trauma, Pain and Politics,* London: Pluto Press

Hillyard, P. (1988) "Political and Social Dimensions of Emergency Law in Northern Ireland" chap 8 pp.191-212 in Jennings, A. (ed) *Justice Un-*

der Fire: The Abuse of Civil Liberties in Northern Ireland, London: Pluto

McCann, E. (1981) War and an Irish Town, London: Pluto

McGuffin, J. (1973) Internment, Tralee: Anvil

McGuffin, J. (1974) The Guineapigs, Harmondsworth: Penguin

McKittrick, D. and McVea, D. (2000) Making Sense of the Troubles, Belfast: Blackstaff

Murray, R. (1998) State Violence: Northern Ireland 1969-1997, Cork: Mercier Press

Newbery, S., Brecher, B., Sands, P. And Stewart, B. (2009): "Interrogation, Intelligence and the Issue of Human Rights" Intelligence and National Security vol 24, No.5 October pp.631-643

Ní Aoláin, F. (2000) The Politics of Force: Conflict Management and State Politics in Northern Ireland, Belfast: Blackstaff Press

O'Boyle, M. (1977) "Torture and Emergency Powers Under the European Convention on Human Rights: Ireland v The United Kingdom", The American Journal of International Law, vol 71, No.4 October pp.674-706

O'Dochartaigh, N. (2005) From Civil Rights to Armalites: Derry and the Birth of the Irish Troubles, Basingstoke: Macmillan

O'Doherty, M. (1998) The Trouble With Guns: Republican Strategy and the Provisional IRA, Belfast: Blackstaff

Peirce, G. (2010) Dispatches from the Dark Side: On Torture and the Death of Justice, London: Verso

Smith, M.L.R. (1995) Fighting for Ireland? The Military Strategy of the Irish Republican Movement, London: Routledge

Spjut, R. (1986) "Internment and detention without trial in Northern Ireland 1971-75: Ministerial Policy and Practice" *Modern Law Review* vol 49, November pp.712-40

Swan, S. (2008) "Why Internment Failed" Prospect Issue 142, 20 Jan
Taylor, P. (1980) *Beating the Terrorists? Interrogation in Omagh, Gough and Castlereagh,* Penguin

Taylor, P. (1998) *Provos, the IRA and Sinn Fein,* London: Bloomsbury

Walsh, D. (2000) *Bloody Sunday and the Rule of Law in Northern Ireland,* Dublin: Gill and Macmillan

Weitzer, R. (1987) "Contested Order: The Struggle over British Security Policy in Northern Ireland" *Comparative Politics* vol 19 No.3 April pp.281-298

White, R. and Falkenberg White, T. (1995) "Repression and the Liberal State: The Case of Northern Ireland 1969-1972" *The Journal of Conflict Resolution* vol 39 No.2 June pp.330-352

Wilson, D. (1997) *Democracy Denied,* Dublin: Mercier Press

Winchester, S. (1974) *In Holy Terror,* London: Faber and Faber

Interviews with author
Micky Donnelly 16 September 2010
Paddy Joe McClean 17 September 2010

8.

RESTRUCTURING GOVERNMENT'S EXPERTISE ON VIOLENCE AND DELINQUENCY IN FRANCE

Konstantinos Delimitsos

In the late nineties, a new group of people appeared in the French public debate on crime. Enjoying an important media exposure and in spite of their very different personal and professional backgrounds, they rapidly established themselves as security experts specializing in "urban violences and security". A major role to this achievement of the actors henceforth called the *"new security experts"* was the undertaking of a significant publishing effort concerning the "urban violences". Following an analysis of contents operated on this corpus of published works[1] in the frame of a sociology thesis, this paper is a contribution to the analysis of the rhetoric, the means of reasoning and the representations that these *new security experts* convey. However, a brief introduction of the authors in question is necessary, as well as a reconstitution summary of the principal sociopolitical conditions that seem to have made it easier for them to emerge.

1. The "new security experts"

1.1 The socio-political context

In order to do so, we need to go back to the late eighties when France was marked by several sociopolitical evolutions that cannot be satisfactorily displayed here. Some of them are important enough, however, to point out briefly. In regard to the political elite, the call into question of their social and counter crime policies, lead the French Socialistic Party to a gradual withdrawal to postures mostly adopted up to then by right wing commentators. Concurrently to this relative neutralization of the political controversy on crime in the main national political arena, and in the aftermath of the large decentralization operated from the early 80's, the mayors across the country saw local security matters fall more and

---

[1] For an overall view of the textbooks in cosideration : The new security experts' bibliography

more within their competence. Lacking experienced and competent staff and struggling to live up to what they interpreted as a growing massive popular demand for security, they found themselves compelled to seek advice within the private sector (Bonelli, 2008). Meanwhile, the Institute of High Studies in Internal Security (IHSIS- our traduction)[2] was found under the auspices of the Ministry of the Interior. Generously granted in order to promote security related research and training, the institute will eventually impose itself as a major meeting spot for scholars, techno-crats and public and private security agents, forging an apolitical interior security spirit (Rimbert, 2001). Last, but not least, the mass media standpoint towards popular suburbs has also altered, as related reports on turbulent incidents have slowly but steadily disappeared from the social or political columns to join the crime related ones (Collovald, 2001).

In other words, during the nineties, a radical modification took place in France in the way in which they were apprehended by several and quite important public opinion and decision makers, on both a na-tional and local level, the questions of violence and delinquency, espe-cially in their juvenile forms. Caught in what could be defined as a *paradigm* change, the elite were now facing a new social reality and their theoretical and methodological tools appear as obsolete. It was at this stage that a new category of social actors came out to bring an an-swer to what could be described as a conceptual and operational vac-uum. We are referring here to numerous private agencies offering their services on "security expertise".

1.2 The "new security experts"

One of those agencies, soon to join the leaders of this newfound market, was AB Associates whose founder, president and sole employee is Alain Bauer. A quick glance at his rather unusual career is quite important. Member of the Socialist Party since his high school years, after studying law and political science and been awarded a Professional Master in management, Alain Bauer participated in the creation of the IHSIS in 1989, as a prime-ministers' counselor. In 1993, he became the European Vice-president of the Science Application International Company before creating in 1994 AB Associates. In 1996-1997 he participated in the 7th annual session of the IHSIS and managed to undertake in a few years'

---

[2] Actually National Institute of High Studies in Security and Justice (NIHSSJ - our traduc-tion).

time dozens of contracts, providing "security consulting services" to numerous local public authorities and semi-public and private companies. This quite noteworthy performance assorted with an important media exposure, procured him a remarkable national visibility, leading him to occupy numerous posts of consultancy and theoretical training in various institutions, both in France and abroad. Today, he is notably the president of the French National Observatory of Delinquency and Penal Responses (NODPR, since 2003), while chairing, among others, the High Council of Strategic Research (since 2009), the Parliamentary Working Group on Customs Files (since 2009), the National Crime Commission (since 2003), the National CCTV Commission (since 2007), the Police Files Control Group (since 2006). In regard to his teaching activities, Alain Bauer has occupied since 2009 the very controversial (Mucchieli, 2010), newly founded and unique in France, chair of criminology at the National Conservatory of Arts and Crafts while teaching at the Universities of Paris 1, Paris 2, Paris 6, at the National Police and the Gendarmerie Academies, in the United States and in China[3].

Throughout his entire career, Alain Bauer has written and published an important amount of textbooks. Nevertheless, the publication that seems to have really boosted his career was a 1998 manual titled "Urban violence and insecurity" in collaboration with Christian de Bongain, alias Xavier Raufer., Xavier Raufer begun his career as an extreme right-wing activist and journalist during the sixties, before joining mainstream right-wing movements during the seventies. Working as a journalist and a writer on security issues, he manages to get in touch with a part of the military and police elite. From the early eighties, he has produced dozens of manuals and articles on national and international delinquency and terrorism. Although rather recently awarded with a PhD in geography (2009), Xavier Raufer has been teaching at the Paris Criminology Institute hosted by the University of Paris2 since 1987, where he evolves within the Department of Research on Contemporary Criminal Threats while also teaching in several other higher education institutions, both in France and abroad. At the same time, Xavier Raufer is the director of the "International Criminality" collection with the PUF[4] and "Arès" with CNRS-Éditions[5].

---

[3] For an overall view of Alain Bauer's activities: [online] Available at:
<http://www.alainbauer.com/gb/public-tasks.html> [Accessed 22 February 2011]
[4] Presses Universitaires de France.

Since 1998, Alain Bauer and Xavier Raufer have presented intense literary work on delinquency in general and "urban violences" in particular. Partly signed exclusively by them, either individually or in partnership, this publication activity also contains a number of synergies with several other authors mostly acquainted in the corridors of the NIHSSJ. Among them, notably Christophe Soullez, criminologist, chief of department with the NODPR within the NIHSSJ, Richard Bousquet, former National Police Commissioner and member of the Direction Committee of the National Police Commissionaires and Higher Officials Syndicate (NPCHOS - our traduction), and André Michel Ventre, National Police Commissioner, former Secretary General of the NPCHOS and president of the NIHSSJ since 2009.

Reproducing an overall homogeneous speech on crime and delinquency, all these authors are hereby referred to as "new security experts". Before developing our reasoning behind this choice, let us point out that if we have drawn attention to the trajectories of the "experts", it was only to emphasize the neutralization of the public debate on crime that these public figures express and serve. As for the term "new security experts", the adjective "new" is chosen not as an allusion to a new approach of the criminal phenomenon but rather as a reference to their unusual professional background which is, when it comes to the two principal actors, the private sector and not, for instance, some "traditional" milieu like the public security enforcement forces, the penal justice system or the academy. And the word "experts" seemed suitable as on the one hand they adopt what Catherine Paradeise (1985) calls the "classic expert rhetoric", jugulating the "necessity rhetoric" (they claim to meet a social need) and the "monopole rhetoric" (they present themselves as the only people capable of bringing appropriate answers to this social need). And on the other, "experts" as they are undeniably integrated into public decision making processes and they therefore meet the famous expert's definition proposed by Theys and Calaora (1991:190)[6].

---

[5] For an overall view of Xavier Raufer's activities: [online] Available at: <http://www.xavier-raufer.com/> [Accessed 22 February 2011]
[6] The understanding of a particular subject turns into an expertise « *then and only then it is articulated to a decision making process and it is precisely that process that confers to this understanding the value of expertise* » (our traduction)

2. The "new security experts'" discourse

Whilst their published work mostly treats juvenile violence and delinquency, the *new security experts* choose to approach it in terms of "urban violences", a recently invented, police originated, technocratic term
used to describe "*collective and provocative juvenile acts taking place in
public and thus creating a strong feeling of insecurity in the general
population*" (Bauer & Soullez, 2007:10). This crucial vocabulary choice
is to be taken under serious consideration. In fact, defined as previous,
the term "urban violences" permits a rather questionable amalgam between a impressively large amount of acts and events, perpetrated by
groups (gathering from a fistful to some hundreds of youngsters), taking
place in different circumstances (among others school violence, political
rallies, sports events, opposite gangs settling accounts, etc), sparked off
by different motives (money-spinner violence, ludic violence, expressive
violence, political violence, etc.) and carried out in various ways (physical violence, psychological violence, armed or naked hands violence,
etc). Nevertheless, all this problematic around the dubious character of
the "urban violences" concept is not really examined in the "new security experts". On the contrary, the term is rather taken for granted in their
reasoning. Let us now examine this reasoning, as displayed in their published works, which seems to follow a pattern of exposing crime's current state and an etiological diagnosis before suggesting potential treatments.

2.1. Reconstructing the crime reality

The *new security experts* seem to set their sights above all on the display
of a rather obscure picture of actual criminal activity. In order to do so,
they develop a quite alarming statistical picture, especially in the works
published before the presidential elections of 2002. The figures published, sometimes lacking any specific references or sources, are mostly
public security forces statistics. Though quite often described as "partial
and compartmental", the official data is taken as granted, without calling
into question its numerous weaknesses. In addition to the official accounting system, the *new security experts* refer to statistic tools measuring the evolution of "urban violences" such as the very controversial
"Bui-Trong scale". Established in reference to a "single criterion, that of
the open and provocative questioning of public order and institutions",

the "Bui-Trong scale" ensures *mainly* the presentation of a reality far more alarming than the one illustrated by the official data, when it qualifies for instance as an aggression the simple presence of young people in the halls of social housing buildings.

Besides the official statistical apparatus, the new experts also refer to victimization, self-reporting and insecurity feeling surveys. While the victimization surveys serve in reflecting a social reality more violent than that depicted by the official statistics, self-reporting surveys come in support to quite crucial reasoning for the *new security experts'* double argument. On the one hand, the hypothesis of a rejuvenation and hardening of today's delinquent minors. This idea emerges regularly under the standardized phrase "law offenders getting younger and younger, more and more violent, more and more reiterating". And on the other hand, the so-called "5% theory" postulating the existence of small cores of supposedly super-active extra-violent young criminals tyrannizing the popular suburbs. As for the surveys measuring the feeling of insecurity, used without questioning the social conditions of their development, they should be circumscribed in a context of omnipresence of the concept of insecurity in the *new security experts'* work. Objectified and supposed in growth following the proliferation of "urban violence", insecurity is a basic legitimating element of the on-going securitairian public debate, as well as of the actors participating in it.

In addition to all this largely fragmentary statistical data, the reconstruction of the field's reality is marked out from the very start by the reference at various, rather isolated violent facts; in fact, stories of violent confrontations between opposite gangs, aggressions on public security agents or extraordinary criminal careers often resurface. Described as "evocative examples reported by the press", they are however reconstituted with no further clarification of their supposedly representative nature. Summarizing the common features of these "evocative examples" we identified a pattern related to the profile of the authors, presumed or confirmed, most commonly living in popular neighborhoods and bearing names with foreign consonance, the relative absence of political implications, as well as their important media repercussion ensuring them a place in the collective memory in the long run. These events are from time to time corroborated by the quotation of remarks allotted to public security agents. Described as "testimonies from the field of action" and therefore allegedly giving us an "inside glance", advanced anonymously and lacking to justify their trustworthiness, these quotations usually sum up to a rather shocking reconstruction of the criminal reality.

2.2. Proposing an "etiologic diagnosis"

After illustrating an overwhelming picture of the "urban violences'" growth, the *new security experts* develop an etiologic diagnosis articulated around two central explanatory registers. The first puts forward a number of hypotheses concerning the motives of the youngsters implicated in "urban violences". The first hypothesis is that of a more or less well structured effort of turning certain urban zones into criminal "no man's lands", where all kinds of illegal activities could be protected from both the police, the local community and potential competitors. Some authors would even go as far as to describe a "true war declared against the police", or even more an "intifada à la française". It is however interesting to note that the same explanatory hypothesis, namely the protection of underground economy networks, is also used regarding some popular suburbs not having exhibited any "urban violence" for a certain amount of time. The second hypothesis leans onto the ethnic origin of the authors of violence. More precisely, the *new security experts* are to affirm unanimously, that the "urban violences" are in its great majority perpetrated by young immigrants failing integration into the French society for cultural reasons. Finally, a third hypothesis, more rarely considered underlines the psychological dysfunctions from which would be allegedly suffering the young actors of "urban violence" who would thus be predisposed to senseless violence.

The second explanatory register advanced by the *new security experts* focuses on the supposedly depleted mobilization of the social reaction mechanism. In fact, a number of social regulation institutions are allegedly taken into a vicious circle of blindness and amateurism, refusing or exporting the problem and thus resulting in an inappropriate social reaction; the "lazy" penal justice system, the "outgoing" family guidance, the "retiring" national education system or the political leadership subjugated to a rightwing, sociological, excuse-seeking ideology. In other words, with the exception of "struggling but hands tied, outnumbered police", the entire formal and informal social control system would fail to bring an adequate answer to a severe social problem.

2.3. Formulating recommendations

The *new security experts* then predict the time of disillusions while preaching a pragmatic approach. Numerous proposals are then formulated, pointing out an appropriate course of action in order to face violence and delinquency. A number of means and actions is therefore advanced as technical solutions and thus supposedly external to political or social antagonisms. Drawing the outlines of a typology, we propose a classification in five categories. It goes without saying that the axes of the typology hereby displayed are far from rigid, the same suggested action often being a subject of multiple categorizations at the same time.

First of all, the *new security experts* make a unanimous call for the overall intensification of formal social control, starting from the penal code itself. Here, the reinforcement of existing coercive legislation is strongly claimed, combined with a large scale incrimination of acts and especially the penalization of *"incivilities"*, those minor everyday acts of naughtiness that allegedly lead up to heavy crime. As for the penal justice system, the need for a more strict and automatic application of the existing legislation is brought forth, in particular in terms of the increase of immediate hearings and imprisonment, both before and after the verdict. As for the public forces, a constant reinforcement of their technical equipment is highly considered, while the central idea remains to "put some blue back in the street", in other words to assure a massive presence of public security agents in urban zones identified as risky or as "no man's land" territories.

The second big set of actions suggested by the *new security experts* concerns a number of spatial interventions aligning with the "situational crime prevention theory" and aiming at reducing the opportunities for law offenders to commit a crime. Reportedly combining the "rational choice", the "opportunities" and the "defendable space" theories, the idea consists in posing multiple obstacles between the object at risk and the potential contravener in order to dissuade him from passing to the act. A series of technical provisions is therefore advanced, seeking to secure public and semi-public spaces, especially by the means of CCTV and other crowd control or target neutralization dispositions.

Looking closely to the importance accorded to the "situational crime prevention", we realize how it is used as a "Trojan horse", legitimating the demand for the amplification of synergies between the state and private security operators, the demand framing the third axe of our typology. Whether it is about supplying council services or technical equipment or quite simply assisting the maintenance of public order, the private security sector is regarded as a natural, well qualified partner of the formal social control system that cannot and should not be ignored. On this subject, it is very interesting to point out the fact that in every enumeration of the main law enforcement agencies serving currently in France, the *new security experts* enlist the so called "private police" along with the Gendarmerie, the National and the Municipal police.

The fourth ground of action to which the *new security experts* appeal is that of the social action. More particularly, a series of proposals referring, implicitly or explicitly, to the installation of a partnership between the social action institutions and the penal law system. Set out to make both deviating minors and their legal guardians aware of their responsibility, the new authorities resulting from this partnership would be equipped with a wide range of coercive administrative measures. Placing under quarantine or even banning a young offender's entire family from the social welfare system are some of the measures suggested.

Up to here, the criterion retained for the categorization of the *new security experts'* recommendations is that of the various fields of action likely to be invested - or reinvested - by the formal social control system. Nevertheless, a certain amount of recommendations escape this categorization because of their miscellaneous nature. This is the case when the word is, for instance, about enlarging the autonomy of the public forces from their political officials, or softening the legal constraints and boundaries regulating their activities or even extending the policing role reserved to mayors. This is why we delimited a fifth *ad hoc* category, which we propose to name "course of actions aiming at the promotion of personal or corporatist interests". This methodological choice appeared convenient to us since in a very great majority of cases, the actors in question exert either as "security consultants" within various public, semi-public or private structures, or as high graded union official public security agents. Within this framework, we believe that a subset of wishes expressed by the *new security experts* is to be considered as aiming to the consolidation of their status and the amplification of their influence.

References

The "new security experts" bibliography

Bauer, A. (2007). Bilan annuel de la délinquance et de la criminalité enregistrées en 2006, Paris: OND.

Bauer, A., Busson, J.-L. and Quere, St. (2006). *Géographie de la France criminelle*, Paris: O. Jacob.

Bauer, A. and Freynet, Fr. (2008). *Vidéosurveillance et vidéoprotection*, Paris: PUF.

Bauer, A. and Perez, E. (2000). *L'Amérique, la violence, le crime. Les réalités et les mythes*, Paris: PUF.

Bauer, A. and Perez, E. (2003). *Le crime aux Etats-Unis*, Paris: PUF.

Bauer, A. and Perez, E. (2003). *Les polices aux Etats-Unis*, Paris: PUF.

Bauer, A. and Perez, E. (2009). *Les 100 mots de la police et du crime*, Paris: PUF.

Bauer, A. and Raufer, X. (1998). *Violences et insécurité urbaines*, Paris: PUF.

Bauer, A. and Raufer, X. (2002). *La guerre ne fait que commencer*, Paris: J.-C. Lattès.

Bauer, A. and Raufer, X. (2007). *Le nouveau chaos mondial. Penser la sécurité dans un monde chaotique : principes et perspectives*, Paris: Les Editions des Riaux,.

Bauer, A. and Soullez, Chr. (2007). *Violences et insécurité urbaines*, Paris: PUF.

Bauer, A. and Ventre, A.-M. (2002). *Les Polices en France : sécurité publique et opérateurs privés*, Paris: PUF.

Bousquet, R. (1998). *Insécurité. Nouveaux enjeux. Les quartiers de tous les dangers*, Paris: L'Harmattan,.

Bousquet, R. (1999). *Insécurité. Nouveaux enjeux. L'expertise et les propositions policières*, Paris: L'Harmattan.

Bousquet, R. (2002). *Insécurité. Sortir de l'impasse*, Paris: LPM.

Bousquet, R. and Lenoir, E. (2009). *La prévention de la délinquance*, Paris: PUF.

Raufer, X. (2002). *L'explosion criminelle. Les réponses*, Paris: Valmonde et cie.

Raufer, X. and Quere, St. (2005). *Le crime organisé*, Paris: PUF.

Rudolph, L. and Soullez, Chr. (2000). *La police en France*, Toulouse: Milan.

Rudolph, L. and Soullez, Chr. (2002). *Insécurité. La vérité*, Paris: J.-C. Lattès.

Rudolph, L. and Soullez, Chr. (2007). *Les stratégies de la sécurité 2002-2007. Avec 150 propositions pour aller plus loin*, Paris: PUF.

Soullez, Chr. (2006). *Les violences Urbaines*, Toulouse: Milan.

General bibliography

Bonelli, L. (2008). *La France a peur. Une histoire sociale de l'« insécurité»*, Paris: La Découverte.

Collovald, A. (2001). Des désordres sociaux à la violence urbaine, *Actes de la recherche en sciences sociales*, 136-137, pp. 104-113.

Mucchielli, L. (2010). Vers une criminologie d'État en France ? Instituions, acteurs et doctrines d'une nouvelle science policière, *Politix*, n° 89, pp. 195-214.

Paradeise, C. (1985). Rhétorique professionnelle et expertise, *Sociologie du travail*, 1, pp. 17-31.

Rimbert, P. (2001). Envahissants experts de la tolérance zéro. *Le Monde Diplomatique,* février, pp. 20-21

Theys, J. and Kalaora, B. (1991). *La Terre outragée*, Paris: Autrement.

9.

THE EDUCATIVE AND EMANCIPATORY POTENTIAL OF HUMAN RIGHTS IN PRISONS: LESSONS FROM ENGLISH & DUTCH PRISONS

Anastasia Karamalidou

Introduction

At United Nations (UN) and Council of Europe (CoE) level post war have seen the legalisation of human rights. As a result, a multitude of human rights legal instruments have been developed with direct and indirect applicability to prison conditions and prisoner treatment. In particular, the CoE via its Convention on Human Rights has ushered in the prisoner as a legitimate rights holder like any other human agent. By virtue of *Golder v. UK* 1978 was the year that the tide began to turn for prisoners, marking a shift in the CoE judicial attitude that had hitherto been rather unsympathetic to prisoners (Livingstone et al, 2003).

Long and painstaking as the process of recognition of their human rights has been for prisoners, it has equally proven painfully slow for governments to implement human rights in prison. To use as an indicative example the current Western European leader in incarceration tables (Walmsley, 2008) – England & Wales – six years of procrastination on the part of the UK government have elapsed since its blanket ban on prisoner voting was found in contravention of the European Convention on Human Rights in *Hirst v. UK* (2005). In defiance of the latest European Court's condemnatory ruling in *Greens & M.T. v. UK* (2010), in February 2011 the British Parliament voted for the continuation of the blanket disenfranchisement of prisoners (BBC News Online, MPs reject prisoner votes plan, 11 February 2011).

The chapter draws on the author's comparative research on human rights in English and Dutch prisons. Data were gathered from 63 English and Dutch prisoners through semi-structured interviews and questionnaires. The research objective which is the focus here was to unravel the potentiality of human rights in prisons and its implications for imprisonment as a state punishment.

The chapter is divided into 4 sections. Section 1 maps the legalisation of prisoners' human rights from a European angle, drawing when necessary on relevant English and Dutch case law. Section 2 introduces the concept of the proactive potential of human rights in prison and outlines its four strands. Section 3 elucidates the educative and emancipatory potential in terms of their meaning, rights and implementation strategies involved. Section 4 offers some concluding thoughts.

An Introduction to the Legalisation of Prisoners' Human Rights: a European enterprise

As indicated above, the Council of Europe has shown great zeal in promoting human rights in prisons to the point that it has surpassed the taken for granted leadership of the United Nations. It has created a league of its own founded on a two tier-strategy which strikes a balance between theory and practice to a significant degree.

Its treaty and body that opened the way for the legalisation of prisoners' human rights are the 1950 Convention for the Protection of Human Rights & Fundamental Freedoms (ECHR) and the European Court of Human Rights (ECtHR). The Convention is the spine of European human rights law which subsequent treaties and non-mandatory legal instruments are inspired from. It established the Court as an enforcement mechanism and, although it is not a bona fide prisoner treaty, it has become one due to a substantial body of successful prison related cases. Through the establishment of the Court (the only permanent and fully-fledged judicial tribunal of its kind) victims of human rights violations have now not only a voice but also access to a legal remedy both internationally and nationally. Countries signatories to the Convention are legally bound by its provisions.

There are five principles that govern the judicial interpretation of the Convention[1]. Amongst them the positive duty of care merits particular attention.

In human rights theory and practice, the positive duty of care is pitted against negative interference. Whilst negative interference regards limited state intervention in citizens public and private affairs as the only necessary way for the protection of their human rights, the positive duty of care prescribes as essential that the state also ought to interfere by tak-

---

[1] The other four are: legality, proportionality, legitimate aims, and the margin of appreciation (Wadham & Mountfield, 2001).

ing proactive steps (Wadham & Mountfield, 2001:6, 24). A proactive approach typically entails the amendment of laws and the alteration of policies with a view to a) institute procedures that are b) robust in terms of staff professionalism and accountability as well as c) effective in terms of regularity, authority and power to instigate preventive action and to redress the balance when needed. What is noteworthy about the positive duty of care is that in its application it does not distinguish between negative and positive rights, hence invalidating its long-held (though partial and restrictive in its effects) association only with the positive cluster of human rights[2].

The Convention lists 13 civil and political rights and freedoms that are supplemented with additional ones in a series of protocols. Within the ECHR framework and based on ECtHR prison case law, inmates (and by association their relatives in some instances) have the following positively entrenched human rights.

- Article 2 – the right to life

The right to life has inbuilt negative and positive obligations and a procedural aspect. Prison authorities must refrain from actions which potentially endanger prisoners' physical well being. At the same time, they are required to implement procedures that effectively safeguard prisoners against risks to their life and limb even if the latter are likely to be self-incurred such as self harm and suicide (*Keenan v. UK*, 2001). Prisoner on prisoner homicide (*Edwards v. UK*, 2002; cited in Livingstone et al, 2003:63-4) that is the result of lapses in inter-agency communication on prisoners' medical history and of ineffective screening procedures for the purposes of cell sharing is a pertinent example. The procedural element requires the existence of a prompt, thorough and impartial investigation procedure into deaths in custody (*McCann & Others v. UK*, 1996; cited in Starmer, 1999:456).

---

[2] There has been a misconception that the positive duty of care only applies to the so-called new generation of rights, namely social, economic and cultural rights. The misconception has resulted from contemporary human rights philosophy which distinguishes between negative (freedom from) and positive (freedom to) human rights. Freedom of action occupies a central stage in the writings of negative human rights theorists. Positive human rights theorists, on the other hand, call for negative and positive rights to be on the same footing on the grounds of the similar structures needed for their realisation and of an equal need of them. In the 2005 World Summit, the UN Commissioner on Human Rights endorsed the application of the positive duty of care to both categories of human rights, laying particular emphasis on its applicability to the civil rights to life and freedom from torture (UN Commissioner on Human Rights, The Rights of Others, 16 February 2006, LSE).

- Article 3 – the prohibition formula of torture

In a descending order of gravity, it is distinguished into a) torture, b) inhuman treatment or punishment, and c) degrading treatment or punishment. The prohibition impacts on a diversity of situations ranging from conditions of detention, to treatment (e.g. strip-searches, solitary confinement) and medical care (Starmer, 1999:456-68).

- Article 5 – the right to liberty and security

Article 5 contains fundamental procedural safeguards for arrestees and detainees. It is the lex specialis for indeterminate detention on grounds of mental disorder and its associated risk of danger to the public. The Dutch entrustment order known as TBS and English life sentences are two examples of indeterminate sentencing that fall within the remit of Article 5 and whose modus operandi has raised considerations of compliance with its stipulations[3]. Under Article 5 are justiciable a) the lawfulness of the continuation of one' s detention once considerations of dangerousness cease to exist, b) the promptness and efficiency of relevant review processes, c) the availability of effective means to challenge the continuation of one' s detention, and d) the power of the review organ to order release.

- Article 6 – the right to a fair trial

Prisoners have the rights to a) access the courts, b) to legal aid and representation for an appeal against their sentence, in disciplinary adjudications and reviews of the prolongation of their sentence, c) to have the all important issues of their guilt/innocence and punishment determined in circumstances that are not prejudicial to the outcome of their case, and d) to have the equally important aspects of the length of their sentence and ultimate release decided by a judge (*T & V v. UK*, 2000; cited in Livingstone et al, 2003:505-6).

- Articles 8-10 & 12

Under them prisoners have the rights to respect for their private and family life, to freedom of thought, conscience, religion, and expression, and to marry. Freedom of expression recognises the rights to enter into

---

[3] See *Weeks v. UK* (1988); *Thynne, Wilson & Gunnel v. UK* (1991); *T & V v. UK* (2000); *Erkalo v. The Netherlands* (1998); *Rutten v. The Netherlands* (2001); *Hirst v. UK* (2001); *Benjamin & Wilson v. UK* (2002); *Stafford v. UK (2002)*; *von Bulow v. UK* (2004); *Wynne v. UK* (2004); *Hill v. UK* (2004); *Morsink v. The Netherlands* (2004); *Brand v. The Netherlands* (2004); *Nakach v. The Netherlands* (2005); *Schenkel v. The Netherlands* (2006)

private correspondence, to subscribe to periodicals, to access writing materials and, crucially, to have contact with the media[4].

- Article 13 – the right to an effective remedy:

The contribution of Article 13 to human rights protection in general is immense because in a clear cut fashion it creates on the part of states the additional positive obligation to devise and implement legal channels through which the validity of arguable human rights claims can be determined (Wadham & Mountfield, 2001:121-2). It has proven valuable not only for prisoners but also for their families. In *Keenan v. UK* (2001) and *McGlinchey & Others v. UK* (2003), the English coronial system that a) did not allow for relatives' active participation in the inquest into the deaths of their children and parents and b) its lack of powers to return a verdict of negligence and to direct the prosecution of those found responsible for the deaths, compounded by the absence of alternative legal avenues, contravened Article 13.

- Article 3 of Protocol 1 – the right to free elections:

Last but not least, even behind bars those who would have been otherwise eligible to vote in local, national and European parliamentary elections retain their right to do so. *Hirst v. UK* (2005) and *Greens & M.T.* (2010) are the latest cases to turn the notion of 'civic death'[5] on its head and to reaffirm the legitimacy and proportionality of a partial enfranchisement of convicted prisoners based on the seriousness and individual circumstances of their offences along with the duration and nature of their sentence.

The Proactive Potential of Human Rights in Prison

As stated in the introduction, the research that the chapter draws upon endeavoured to shed light on whether human rights have exhausted their possibilities for contribution in prison sixty – three years after their entrenchment in international law.

The driving force in this endeavour – English and Dutch prisoners – concluded in the negative. They attached great importance to human rights the recognition and protection of which they unfailingly associ-

---

[4] On prisoners' right to contact the media see *Hirst v. UK* (2002)

[5] The Edwardian notion of 'civic death' signifies the withdrawal of civic membership as punishment for the wrong done to the victim and, by association, to society at large (*Hirst v. UK*, 2005, para.21-4).

ated with the values of a democratic state. In their opinion, the legitimacy of the prison as punishment is dependent upon them because they encourage the optimum normalisation of the carceral environment. For them, the optimum normalisation of their conditions of detention and treatment is vital to the facilitation of their resocialisation and reintegration which are taken to be the only legitimate aims of imprisonment in a democracy.

In this context, human rights acquire a *proactive* function that is supplementary to their existing *reactive* one that is sprung from their legalisation. Of enormous significance as the latter has proved for many and, in particular, prisoners, one cannot pass over the fact that the Court's remedy of compensation cannot undo the victims' suffering. They are consequent upon it; hence the Court's reactive function. Although it has an inbuilt preventative function, this is at group level – not at individual level. Legal and policy changes as a result of positive findings of human rights violations strengthen the protection of those who may or are likely to be in similar situation to that of the present victim in the future.

In contrast, the *proactive* function of human rights has an instrumentality that is of constant relevance to prisoners' needs and can be beneficial to all of them. It displays four potentialities: a *psychotherapeutic*, a *humanizing*, an *educative*, and an *emancipatory* one. The *psychotherapeutic* potential promotes prisoners' self-awareness and empowers them to become self-assured, spurring them on to develop and take control of their lives. The *humanizing* potential restores their self-respect, worth and dignity through meaningful interaction with others and harness their communication, interpersonal and team-working skills. The *educative* potential opens the door to prisoner awareness of human rights and, crucially, helps them appreciate the close intertwining of human rights with 'human' responsibilities. The *emancipatory* potential provides them with strength and determination to return to society, willing to participate fully in its life.

Before we look into the educative and emancipatory potential in more detail, it must be stated that none of the four potentials takes precedence over the other. Instead, they carry an equal weight and are inextricably linked, forming a unitary contribution to the realisation of what in prisoners' eyes are the only defensible aims of their imprisonment.

The Educative and Emancipatory potential of Human Rights in Prison
a) The educative potential

The educative potential is credited with developing prisoners' awareness of their human rights while in and post custody and their appreciation of the duality of the concept in the sense that it implies responsibilities (personal, social and civic) on the part of human rights holders and expects of the latter to honour the former. It was informed by two findings.

English and Dutch inmates stated that they had received no information on human rights by the prison authorities. Human rights did not feature in any discussion either amongst themselves or with staff. It was only customary to be informed of their rights and duties under the prison rules. They were also uncertain on the aspect of legalisation; that is whether they could bring a human rights claim before the courts and what human rights were protected by law.

Moreover, the great majority on either side had serious difficulties in envisioning whether their status as human rights holders created any meaningful responsibilities on their part. While they recognised at once the reciprocity between rights and duties as evidently necessary for the purposes of an ordered life, they failed to do so in relation to human rights. They were also unwilling to acknowledge that their crimes had potentially violated other people's human rights to the point of being openly hostile to the idea. The English opted for silence while for the Dutch such a claim was only valid in the case of violent offences that resulted directly in physical injury or death.

The above speak of an old truth that tends to slip somehow into oblivion. Knowledge by itself does not translate into a critical understanding of the implications that are either intrinsic to or consequent upon its object. The abilities of reflection and perception are require intellectual stimulation, confrontation and exercise.

For the educative potential to get off the ground, prisoners identified as instrumental the rights

- to freedom of expression without the fear of penalisation (espoused by both national samples)
- to participation in cultural and prison life (espoused by both national samples; only that the English interpreted its benefits in terms of independence and autonomy whilst the Dutch in terms of acquiring a sense of belonging through their contribution to

common affairs)
- to vote (valued dearly by almost half of the Dutch sample and English lifers)

In their view, their transgressions did not take away their ability to hold and express opinions. Nor was it perverse to argue that they had rightfully a say in how society, which they had been and would again be living in, was governed. They had also a vested interest in its governance by way of association and interaction with others who as participating members themselves were affected by developments around them. Voting was important because it sensitized the individual that they were part of a common body that shared a common present and future. If they were disillusioned with their present and aspired to a better future, they had to initiate individual action and to be mobilised as a body for change to be effected.

- to respect for private and family life (echoed across the board)

Family held an enormous significance. It connoted that they were normal and normalised the artificiality of their prison lives to some extent. It did so in two ways. By acting in their capacities as somebody's children, parents and partners and performing their respective role duties, they escaped momentarily the label of the drug-addict, the killer or of the slightly disturbed to join their relatives in being the *normal other*. Secondly, their inclusion in family affairs was amongst the strongest gestures confirming that they were normal.

On these grounds family was credited with enabling them to counteract the alienating effects of imprisonment and with rekindling consequently their determination to rid of their deviant persona. For both the English and the Dutch family had a reintegrative shaming effect[6] that had an educative potency in terms of developing a sense of personal responsibility. For the English the reintegrative value of the family stemmed mostly from their capacity to name and shame them that induced feelings of guilt whilst for the Dutch it was derived from the integral element of reciprocal trust.

For example, in the English setting a connection was made between mothering with independent agency and prudent lifestyle post release. A number of imprisoned mothers argued that to be given the opportunity to meet their parental responsibilities not only enabled them to forge and maintain a bond with their children and protect the latter's right to moral

---

[6] To borrow the term from Braithwaite (1989)

and emotional development, but also functioned as a wake up call for what their priorities as parents should be.

- to education

It is worth noting that only Dutch inmates put an emphasis on education and did so strongly. They identified its benefits as humanistic (instructional value) and economic (instrumental value) and viewed both vital for the learner's development, associating the former with the educative potential and the latter with the emancipatory one.

In an Aristotelian vein, they saw the accumulation of knowledge as an intellectually bankrupt enterprise if it failed to instil an ethos of personal and social responsibility which was implicit in each other and indispensable for a self-determinate life. By association, an educator who fails to impress this on their students' memory fails in their duty to them.

On this note, the Dutch shifted the focus of attention from the tutee (prisoner) to the tutor (the authorities), exhorting them to take cognizance of the added responsibilities emanated from their position of power. They reminded them that learning is an interactive activity that requires as such the instructor's engagement with their subjects. Moreover, from a pedagogic standpoint, it necessitates student encouragement which as a technique and action recognises that they can do well. So, showing confidence in inmates' potential provides them with support which they can use as a springboard to personal independence.

The instructional value of education highlights the primacy of social interaction for the educative potential, influencing the strategies employed for its realisation. Sociability as a human instinct and socialisation as a fundamental human need are pretty old news (Midgley, 1978). But, what tends to be forgotten is that they bring consistency in the development of one's personal and social identity. They bond *the personal* and *the social* together.

- to work

Like education, work has an instructional and instrumental value for inmates. English lifers and Dutch prisoners focused equally on both while the rest of the English participants advocated the latter. As above, the instructional value of work was seen as pertinent to the educative potential, with its instrumental force applied to the emancipatory one. The former was couched in the following terms.

The average prisoner had not been in regular employment due to a lack of qualifications, interest or both. So, they were not habituated to the idea of work. To get into the habit of working, they needed to feel confident about and proud of their abilities. Based on common sense labour that required no mental effort and/or was financially unrewarding (like prison work) was de-motivating and demoralising. To the person responsible for that kind of work it signalled that the optimum of what they could be trusted to do was the minimum, dealing a blow to their appreciation of the worthiness of employment and, most crucially, of its legal forms.

The strategies that prisoners mentioned as conducive to the educative potential are:

- longer, more frequent and private visits (shared across the board)
- the reinstatement of weekend visits

This was called for by Dutch inmates who identified their rescheduling to weekdays as one of the aspects indicative of the harshening of their penal system. They considered it utterly thoughtless and heartless and listed a number of newly generated complications which the former arrangement demonstrated their tractability. Visits on weekdays were highly disruptive of visitors' lives. For example, for those who worked, they entailed work absences and potential losses of earnings which were bound to be longer and more difficult to sustain when they had to travel far. Travelling incurred more expenses that discouraged them from the weekly journey to prison. Children were also affected. They would miss school and extra curriculum activities that would disrupt their learning experience and increase the negative impact of their parents' absence on their development.

- the reintroduction of evening socialisation

This was again a Dutch suggestion and amongst the cited indicators of the repressiveness of Dutch penal regimes[7]. According to interviewees with previous prison experience the last 15 years have seen the drastic downsizing of guards between 5pm and 8am when a standard full shift comes on duty again[8]. During these 15 hours the number of officers in the whole of the establishment stands in single figures, inmates are

---

[7] Dutch participants identified a number of things as indicative of a regressive penal climate. The most widely referred to were: double cells, lock down at 5pm and the consequent loss of evening socialisation, the change of visits from weekends to weekdays, cutbacks in resettlement opportunities, and life-long imprisonment.

[8] Cells open four hours in the morning (8am – 12pm) and another four in the afternoon (1pm – 5pm) in the course of which prisoners can socialise in each other's cells or common areas if they are not at work. In the one hour between 12pm and 1pm, they are locked up for lunch. In the summer lockdown is at 6pm.

locked in cells, and there is no recreational period in the evening. In the past, lockdown was at 9pm, allowing for recreation.

Alluding to the primacy of social interaction for the educative potential, for the Dutch its educative potency was not restricted to the classroom or the workshop. It laid beyond them in everyday conversation. They believed that socialising created constant opportunities for holistic learning; holistic in the sense that it could contribute to one's personal and social development.

To socialise, they had to exercise their volition and interact with others. This meant that they had to learn how to approach one another and engage in conversation. By holding a conversation, they gradually became skilful in expressing their views with clarity, listening patiently and debating respectfully.

Decision-making gave one a feeling of accomplishment which provided them with a sense of self-respect and worth and made them resilient and resolute as a result. While these attributes were found within the person, they derived their strength from its surroundings. The better they were able to overcome the challenges of human interaction, the stronger they became. In prison, decision-making and communication acquired an added urgency. Dutch inmates felt that they received no mental stimulus worthy to respond to or to provoke a radical shift in their thinking. They were reduced to pawns and internalised their passive role. While some admitted that this was a less painful stance to adopt in order to survive the pains of incarceration, all acknowledged that passivity compromised their chances of resocialisation. They would enter the real world as handicapped as when they left it; that is with no personal resolve, reliable plans, and adequate interpersonal skills which was overwhelmingly the case post release.

In this respect, productive communication with officers was credited as empowering and educational. Those with previous experience of imprisonment remarked that reductions in officers' numbers and working shifts impacted negatively on the quantity and quality of time that they spent with inmates. They highlighted that among the benefits of recreation was guards' personal contact with prisoners. In the past, when resources allowed for recreation, the interaction between them was more regular and closer. Contrary to the popular saying their familiarity did not breed contempt but willingness to try to understand their respective positions, priorities and concerns. It brought about the realisation that they shared the same problems, interests and struggles, for example as parents.

This realisation may not have fostered a spirit of solidarity among them but it certainly led to more openness, appreciation and trust which gave prisoners a sense of purpose and belonging. As officers were more *social* and made efforts to help them, inmates were more likely to abandon their passivity and intransigence. Guards' engagement with them and belief in some goodness in them were a powerful incentive for their mobilization. They were more willing, for example, to co-operate and to act as informal mediators in disputes between themselves or with guards. Leaving aside the institution's collateral gain in terms of control maintenance, their thinking and interpersonal skills were enhanced; they learnt how to negotiate, find solutions to problems and to compromise. Moreover, by getting involved in communal affairs, they began to appreciate the value and meaning of being part of a community which was vital to their reintegration.

- provision and access to further/higher education (a Dutch recommendation)
- enfranchisement
- prisoner executive committees and discussion fora:

These were recommended by the English. In their proposal of prisoner executive committees they sought freedom from the authorities' arbitrary decision-making instances of which were found in the form of unclear prison regulations, lack of feedback to inquiries and of information on changes in the institution's daily schedule, and poor communication. Prisoner committees would offer them the opportunity to air their views freely and to actively participate in executive decisions which was a great learning and empowering exercise. They would provide them with a model of behaviour that they could apply later to their private and social sphere, teaching them how to prioritise, manage their finances, negotiate with social institutions and tailor ends to means. Should they be allowed to exercise their agency than continue to be condemned to dependence, they would feel less insecure and powerless against the reality that awaited them outside. Infantilisation and dependence hindered their resocialisation because they left the skills necessary for its realisation underdeveloped.

In addition, the introduction of regular discussion fora composed of inmates and officers would help in dispelling feelings of antagonism and mistrust between them to some extent. They would be a stimulus to both to discover the person behind the mutually derogatory labels and the differing impact the reality of prison life had on them. This would create more receptive attitudes on both sides for, as the foreign would become familiar, they would be more inclined to consider the causes of one's actions and not just their actions.

b) The emancipatory potential

The emancipatory potential is credited with instilling strength and determination in prisoners to return to society and equipping them with the necessary tools to reintegrate. For their successful resocialisation and re-integration, prisoners singled out as important the rights
- to respect for private and family life that as stated before held wide currency

Maintenance of contact with family did not only help them survive incarceration but also eased their transition from the enclosed sphere of the prison to the open space of the community. Oppressive and infantilising as the claws of institutionalisation were, they offered them that unparalleled embryonic security in the womb. They were shielded as much from outside dangers as from those within them. Support from their family was empowering. Through its capacity for reintegrative shaming, itself legitimised by its attribute of trust, it encouraged them to embark and persist on changing their lives and alerted them to the reciprocity of human relations.
- to education, vocational guidance and training

As mentioned earlier, only the Dutch invoked this right. Here, the focus is on instrumental value as evidenced by the proposed strategies that will be seen shortly.
- to social security and assistance (raised only by the Dutch)
- to work and fair remuneration (shared across the board)

Here, like in the case of education, the emphasis is on the instrumental value of work.
- to equal treatment that both national samples passionately called for

The strategies that prisoners regarded as conducive to the emancipatory potential are:
- the implementation of consistent sentence planning

All interviewees were of the opinion that the process of their socialisation should be gradual. It has to be guided by an individual sentencing plan which sets out goals matched to the different stages of their sentence and is regularly reviewed. Its objective should be to prepare them on a step by step basis for their eventual return to society. To be allowed near their release date to experience small waves of freedom through visits to their family and work in the community would enable them to re-adjust gradually to the pace of the outside world. It would also provide them with time to arrange important issues such as accommodation and social security assistance which are typically the most pressing concerns once outside the prison gate.

- provision and access to academic and vocational education:

The Dutch argued that the aim of resocialisation may still have had a presence in policy papers, but that its project on the ground was a joke. They complained as much about inequality of educational provision as of opportunities. Across the board the level of academic education was basic, failing particularly the ones who were bright and were serving long sentences. Their progress was brought to a halt as the authorities did not have the responsibility to encourage academic excellence or to fund it, for that matter. Vocational training suffered from similar problems. The skills that were taught did not correspond to the contemporary demands of the employment market or bore little value per se.

Gaining access to schemes, especially of one's choice, was identified as a major obstacle to prisoners' personal and professional development. Rises in prisoner numbers did not tally with increases in the provision of courses. The adversity of this structural disadvantage was worsened by a selection procedure which inmates felt that it sabotaged the very purpose of its role; namely to identify people who take an interest in their future, demonstrate an ability to work with others and urgently need a chance to mark a new beginning in their lives.

In their view, the management and operation of the late initiative of penitentiary programmes[9] illuminated this clearly. It was conceived as

---

[9] Penitentiary programmes were introduced by the 1999 (Dutch) Penitentiary Principles Act (PPA). There are different kinds of penitentiary programmes focusing upon three broad areas of concern that influence prisoners' resocialisation and reintegration prospects – education, employment and mental health (DJI, 2000, Penitentiary Programmes). Each programme consists of a minimum of 26 hours per week spent on related activities which take place in a community setting and are tailored to the individual needs of participants (DJI, 2000:.3). At the end of their daily schedule, participants spend the remainder of the day at home. Electronic tagging is always applied in the first instance; for at least the first 16 weeks for those from closed establishments and 12 weeks for those from semi-open institutions. Inmates from open facilities are electronically monitored only if they engage in work (DJI, 2000:5-6). Penitentiary programmes are not compulsory and not accessible to all. Participation to them is

spur to positive action; that is to sensitize them to the personal and wider impact of their lifestyle and to empower them to take responsibility for their actions. The most immediate and tangible benefit was that they regained their freedom since participation in the programmes entailed early release. However, the design of its implementation (its community based character) nullified two important selection criteria and spurred them into deceitful action instead. Successful candidates' institutional record had to testify to their reliability and willingness to reform. So, dangling the reward of freedom before prisoners quickly created a long queue in which everyone professed to be ready to change their ways.

By virtue of these two conditions, the age group that was more prone to recidivism – mostly offenders in their twenties – was unfairly disadvantaged. Older prisoners witnessed many talented and intelligent ones missing out on opportunities because of their tempestuous youthfulness. Instead, it was them who were offered a place in a programme which most times were unsuitable to their station in life. Neither young nor older prisoners gained in the long term.

- provision and access to work

On both sides, prisoners were furious with their governments regarding prison work. Swarmed as they were with detainees, English jails had insufficient places. Genuine willingness to work was not a guarantee of a placement. Then, when an opportunity came, the job usually offered no real employability skills and was always underpaid. Dutch prison work was characterised along the same lines, although no complaints were made about the availability of work places as such. According to Dutch inmates in reality there were shortages that were tackled by the operation of two 4 hour shifts – one in the morning and one in the afternoon. In this way, more people could work.

- extension of the legally minimum wage to working prisoners

The Dutch demanded for the legally minimum wage to be extended to prisoners. Both sides raised rhetorically the question of how they were to espouse a strongly defined ethic when the nature of and payment for their work devalued them from the start. The argument went that criminal lifestyles could be prevented and cut short when their actors felt valued. To feel valued, they had to be entrusted with responsibilities. To this end, not only were they in need of skills, which corresponded to current labour market demands, but also of a fair chance.

---

governed by a selection procedure that shortlists candidates against specific eligibility criteria (Tak, 2003).

- legal duty on employers to include in their workforce a certain quota of (newly) released prisoners

For the Dutch, this fair chance translated into the introduction of a legal duty placed on employers to employ a certain number of ex-prisoners.

Conclusion

The elemental function of punishment in general is to communicate a message. This is its symbolic value. In the case of criminal punishment, the message expresses censure on a behaviour considered by the majority as harmful as well as on the agent's disobedience to state laws and indifference to society's welfare (Walker, 1991). The symbolic value of punishment along with the very need for it has no purpose of existence if it does not also have an instrumental value. With regard to the punishment of offenders, the instrumental value is to educate them about their personal and social responsibilities as individuals and members of society. The aim is to dissuade them from engaging in similar actions in the future. Failure to attempt to educate and to actively involve the punished in this process compromises a priori the objective of punishment. Even worse, deliberate failure to do so run contrary to democratic ideals. It seriously undermines social and political emancipation, thereby permanently excluding offenders from participating in their own lives. The state's right to punish them for their crimes does not imply the right to hold them perennially hostages to their past actions.

On these grounds, decisions to manage (rather than combat) offending behaviour through harsher punishment, intermittent incapacitation and permanent exclusion of its actors from the mainstream society is wilful. It smacks of delusional superiority, unfairness, discrimination, personal and social injustice. It is in nobody's long-term interests to incapacitate an increasingly growing number of people socially, economically and politically. From a functionalist angle, and based on past experience, lest society and state crumble away, they need full-time citizens and in full numbers.

Human rights can play an important role in this respect. But, only when the depth of their meaning and the breadth of their contribution are not publicly belittled in the joined interests of electoral profiteering and an offensive criminal law policy (Jareborg, 1995) that is obsessed with the actuarial management of the risks of offending behaviour and deviant/foreign lifestyles (Blad, 2003; Downes & Morgan, 2007). As Dutch

inmates put it very succinctly, they cannot wake up to their responsibilities by proxy, but they need help from the state and that society understands in order to do this. With their proactive and reactive functions entwined, human rights can assist this as they confirm time and again
 a) the duality involved in their protection (negative and positive interference) and
 b) break down old frontiers that separated negative from positive rights in terms of importance and way of protection

References

Arbour, L. (2006). *Protecting Human Rights in an Age of Uncertainty.* Available at: www2.lse.ac.uk/humanRights/events/Louise_Arbour.aspx (Accessed May 2006).

Arnott, H. and Creighton, S. (1999). Developments in Prison Law. *Legal Action*, January Issue, pp. 18-21.

Arnott, H. Collins, N. and Creighton, S. (2002). Recent Developments in Prison Law. *Legal Action*, June Issue, pp.10-4.

BBC News, (2011). *MPs reject prisoner votes plan.* [online] Available at: www.bbc.co.uk/news/uk-politics-12409426 [Accessed 12 February 2011].

Beccaria, C. (1963). [1764] *On Crimes and Punishments.* Indianapolis: Bobbs-Merrill.

Bedau, H.A. (1983). Why Do We Have The Rights We Do?. *Social Philosophy & Policy*, 1(2), pp.56-72.

Benjamin & Wilson v. The United Kingdom Judgment, (2002). Available at: www.echr.coe.int/ECHR/EN/Header/Case-Law/HUDOC.

Blad, J. (2003). Against Penal Instrumentalism. In: IIRP (International Institute for Restorative Practices) *4th International Conference on Conferencing, Circles and Other Restorative Practices.* Veldhoven, The Netherlands, 28-30 August 2003, Available at:www.iirp.org/library [Accessed 6 August 2007].

Bloed, A. and van Hoof, F. (1985). Some aspects of the Socialist view of Human Rights (1). In: A. Bloed and P.van Dijk, eds. *Essays on Human Rights in the Helsinki Process*, The Hague: Martinus Nijhoff Publishers.

Blom-Cooper, S. (1998). *The Penalty of Imprisonment.* Utah: University of Utah Press.

Boerefijn, I. and Goldschmidt, J. (eds) (2007). *Human Rights in the Polder.* Antwerpen – Oxford: Intersentia.

Boin, R.A. James, O. and Lodge, M. (2005). New Public Management and Political Control Comparing three European correctional systems. In: SCANCOR (Scandinavian Consortium on Organisational Research), *Workshop "Autonomization of the State: From integrated administrative models to single purpose organisations"* Stanford University, 1- 2 April 2005, Available at: www.sorgrc27.org/Paper/Scancor/boin_stanford_paper.doc [Accessed 30 June 2008].

Braithwaite, J. (1989). *Crime, Shame and Reintegration.* Cambridge: Cambridge University Press.

Brand v. The Netherlands Judgment, (2004). Available at: www.echr.coe.int/ECHR/EN/Header/Case-Law/HUDOC.

Brugger, W. (1996). The Image of the Person in the Human Rights Concept. *Human Rights Quarterly,* 18(3), pp.594-611.

Carter, P. (2003). *Managing Offenders, Reducing Crime.* London: HMSO.

Cassesse, A. (1996). *Inhuman states: imprisonment, detention and torture in Europe today.* Oxford: Polity.

Cheliotis, L. (2006). How iron is the iron cage of new penology? The role of human agency in the implementation of criminal justice policy. *Punishment & Society,* 8(3), pp.313-40.

Coroners Service Reform Briefing Note, (2006). London: Department of Constitutional Affairs

Coroners and Justice Act (2009). London: HMSO.

Cranston, M. (1973). *What Are Human Rights?.* New York: Taplinger Publishing.

Creighton, S. and King, V. (1996). *Prisoners and the Law.* London: Butterworths.

Creighton, S. (1998). Developments in Prison Law. *Legal Action,* February Issue, pp.19-22.

Dershowitz, A. (2004). *Rights from Wrongs: a secular theory of the origins of rights.* New York: Basic Books.

Donnelly, J. (1982). Human Rights and Human Dignity: An Analytical Critique of Non-Western Conceptions of Human Rights. *American Political Science Review,* 76(2), pp.303-16.

Downes, D. and Morgan, R. (1997). Dumping the 'Hostages to Fortune'? The Politics of Law and Order in Post-War Britain. In: M.Maguire, R.Morgan and Reiner, R.eds. *The Oxford Handbook of Criminology.* 2nd ed. Oxford: Oxford University Press, Ch. 3.

Downes, D. and Morgan, R. (2002). The British General Election 2001: The centre right consensus *Punishment & Society,* 4(1), pp.81-96.

Downes, D. and Morgan, R. (2007). No turning back: The politics of law and order into the new Millennium. In: M.Maguire, R.Morgan and Reiner, R. eds. *The Oxford Handbook of Criminology.* 4th ed. Oxford: Oxford University Press, Ch. 9.

Dworkin, R. (2005). *Taking Rights Seriously.* London: Duckworth.

Erkalo v. The Netherlands Judgment, (1998). Available at: www.echr.coe.int/ECHR/EN/Header/Case-Law/HUDOC.

Faugeron, C. (1998). Prison: Between the Law and Social Action. In: V.Ruggiero, N.South and I.Taylor, eds. *The New European Criminology: Crime and Social Order in Europe*. London: Routledge, Ch. 6.

Faulkner, D. (2007). Prospects for progress in penal reform. *Criminology & Criminal Justice*, 7(2) pp.135-52.

Garland, D. (2001). *The Culture of Control: Crime and Social Order in Contemporary Society*. Oxford: Oxford University Press.

Gerwith, A. (1983). The Epistemology of Human Rights. *Social Philosophy & Policy*, 1(2), pp.1-24.

Goffman, E. (1991) [1961] *Asylums: Essays on the Social Situation of Mental Patients and Other Inmates*. London: Penguin Books.

Goodhart, M. (2003). Origins and Universality in the Human Rights Debates: Cultural Essentialism and the Challenge of Globalisation. *Human Rights Quarterly*, 25(4), pp.935-64.

Green, M. (2001). What We Talk About When We Talk About Indicators: Current Approaches to Human Rights Measurement. *Human Rights Quarterly*, 23(4), pp.1062-97.

Greens & M.T. v. The United Kingdom Judgment, (2010). Available at: www.echr.coe.int/ECHR/EN/Header/Case-Law/HUDOC.

Hart, H.L.A. (1955). Are there any natural rights? *Philosophical Review*, 64(2), pp.175-91.

Hart, H.L.A. (1977). Positivism and the separation of law and morals. In: R.M.Dworkin, ed. 1977. *The Philosophy of Law*. Oxford: Oxford University Press.

Hill v. The United Kingdom Judgment, (2004). Available at: www.echr.coe.int/ECHR/EN/Header/Case-Law/HUDOC.

Hirst v. The United Kingdom Judgment, (2001). Available at: www.echr.coe.int/ECHR/EN/Header/Case-Law/HUDOC.

Hirst v. The United Kingdom Judgment, (2002). Available at: www.echr.coe.int/ECHR/EN/Header/Case-Law/HUDOC.

Hirst v. The United Kingdom Judgment, (2005). Available at: www.echr.coe.int/ECHR/EN/Header/Case-Law/HUDOC.

Hobbes, T. (1981) [1651]. *Leviathan.* London: Penguin Classics.

Holloway, R. (1999). *Godless Morality.* Edinburgh: Canongate.

Howard, R.E. and Donnelly, J. (1986). Human Dignity, Human Rights, and Political Regimes. *American Political Science Review*, 80(3), pp.801-17.

Human Rights in Prison, (1986). Strasbourg: Council of Europe.

Human Rights in International Law, (2000). Strasbourg: Council of Europe.

Ignatieff, M. (2001). *Human Rights as Politics and Idolatry.* Princeton: Princeton University Press.

Jareborg, N. (1995). What Kind of Criminal Law Do We Want? In A.Snare, ed. *Beware of Punishment: on the Utility and Futility of Criminal Law, Scandinavian Studies in Criminology.* Oslo: The Scandinavian Research Council, Pax Forlag, A/S.

Junger-Tas, J. (2006). Introduction: The Respect of Human Rights of Prisoners in Europe. *European Journal on Criminal Policy and Research*, 12, pp.79-83.

Keenan v. The United Kingdom Judgment, (2001). Available at: www.echr.coe.int/ECHR/EN/Header/Case-Law/HUDOC.

Kocis, R.A. (1980). Reason, Development, and the Conflicts of Human Ends: Sir Isaiah Berlin's Vision of Politics. *American Political Science Review*, 74(1), pp.38-52.

La Torre, M. (1998). Citizenship and Social Rights: a European perspective. *EUI Working Papers, EUF No. 98/2,* Italy: European University Institute.

Lacey, N. (2008). *The Prisoners' Dilemma: Political Economy and Punishment in Contemporary Democracies.* Cambridge: Cambridge University Press.

Lauterpacht, H. (1945). *An International Bill of the Rights of Man.* New York: Columbia University Press.

Leach, P. (1999). Recent developments in European Convention Law. *Legal Action,* July Issue, pp. 15-9.

Liebling, A. (2001). Whose side are we on? Theory, Practice and Allegiances in Prison Research. *British Journal of Criminology,* 41(3), pp.472-84.

Liebling, A. Elliot, C. and Arnold, H. (2001). Transforming the prison: Romantic optimism or appreciative realism?. *Criminal Justice: International Journal of Policy and Practice,* 1(2), pp.161-80.

Liebling, A. (2004). *Prisons and their Moral Performance.* Oxford: Oxford University Press.

Livingstone, S. (1997). International Human Rights Law and Prisons. *INTERIGHTS Bulletin: Prisoners' Rights,* 11(4), pp.135-7.

Livingstone, S. Owen, T. and Macdonald, A. (2003). *Prison Law.* 3rd ed. Oxford: Oxford University Press.

Locke, J. (1980) [1690] *Second Treatise on Government.* Indianapolis: Hackett Publishing.

Locke, J. (2004) [1689] *An Essay Concerning Human Understanding.* London: Penguin Classics.

Matravers, A. and Maruna, S. (2004). Contemporary Penality and Psychoanalysis. *Critical Review of International Social and Political Philosophy*, 7(2), pp.118-144.

McCloskey, H.J. (1965). Rights. *Philosophical Quarterly*, 15(59), pp.115-27.

McGlinchey & Others v. The United Kingdom, (2003). Available at: www.echr.coe.int/ECHR/EN/Header/Case-Law/HUDOC.

McLaughlin, E. Muncie, J. and Hughes, G. (2001). The permanent revolution: New Labour, New Public Management and the Modernization of Criminal Justice. *Criminology and Criminal Justice*, 1(3), pp.301-18.

Midgley, M. (1978). *Beast and Man: The Roots of Human Nature*. Sussex: The Harvester Press.

Morgan, R. (1997). Preventing Torture and Protecting Prisoners. *INTERIGHTS Bulletin: Prisoners' Rights*, II(4), pp.178-81.

Morgan, R. and Liebling, A. (2007). Imprisonment: An Expanding Scene. In: M.Maguire, R.Morgan and R.Reiner, eds. *The Oxford Handbook of Criminology*. 4th ed. Oxford: Oxford University Press, Ch. 32.

Morsink v. The Netherlands Judgment, (2004). Available at: www.echr.coe.int/ECHR/EN/Header/Case-Law/HUDOC.

Murphy, T. and Whitty, N. (2007). Risk and Human Rights in UK Prison Governance. *British Journal of Criminology*, 47(5), pp.798-816.

Murray, J. (2007). The cycle of punishment: social exclusion of prisoners and their children. *Criminology and Criminal Justice*, 7(1), pp.55-81.

Nakach v. The Netherlands Judgment, (2005). Available at: www.echr.coe.int/ECHR/EN/Header/Case-Law/HUDOC.

Nelissen, P. (1998). The Re-integration Process from the Perspective of Prisoners: opinions, perceived value and participation. *European Journal on Criminal Policy and Research*, 6, pp.211-34.

O' Manique, J. (1990). Universal and Inalienable Rights: A Search for Foundations. *Human Rights Quarterly*, 12(4), pp.465-85.

Owers, A. (2006). The Protection of Prisoners' Rights in England & Wales. *European Journal on Criminal Policy and Research*, 12(2), pp.85-91.

Paine, T. (1996) [1791] *Rights of Man*. Hertfordshire: Wordsworth.

Paine, T. (2004) [1776] *Common Sense*. London: Penguin Books.

Pakes, F. (2000). League Tables in Mid-Table: On the Major Changes in Dutch Prison Policy. *Howard Journal of Criminal Justice*, 39(1): 30-39.

Pakes, F. (2004). The Politics of Discontent: The Emergence of a New Criminal Justice Discourse in The Netherlands. *Howard Journal of Criminal Justice*, 43(3), pp.284-98.

Pakes, F. (2005). Penalisation and retreat: The changing face of Dutch criminal justice. *Howard Journal of Criminal Justice*, 5(2), pp.145-61.

Penitentiary Principles Act (1998), The Hague: Ministry of Justice.

Penitentiary Programmes: phase by phase return to society, (2000). The Hague: DJI.

Peukert, W. (1999). The European Convention for the Prevention of Torture and the European Convention on Human Rights. In: R. Morgan and M.D. Evans, eds. *Protecting Prisoners:The Standards of the European Committee for the Prevention of Torture in Context*. Oxford: Oxford University Press, Ch. 3.

Prisons, (1999). The Hague: DJI

Prison Brief for the United Kingdom: England & Wales, (2011). Available at:
www.kcl.ac.uk/depsta/law/research/icps/worldbrief/wpb_country.php?country=169 [Accessed 11 January 2011].

Reiner, R. (2007). Media made criminality: the representation of crime in the mass media. In: M. Maguire, R.Morgan and R.Reiner, eds. *The Oxford Handbook of Criminology*. 4th ed. Oxford: Oxford University Press, Ch.11.

Rodley, N. (2000). *The treatment of prisoners under international law*. Oxford: Oxford University Press.

Rousseau, J. (1999) [1762] *The Social Contract*. Oxford: Oxford University Press.

Ruggiero, V. (2003). *Crime in Literature*. London: Verso.

Rutten v. The Netherlands Judgment, (2001). Available at: www.echr.coe.int/ECHR/EN/Header/Case-Law/HUDOC.

Ryder, R. (2001). *Painism: a modern morality*. London: Open Gate Press.

Schenkel v. The Netherlands Judgment, (2005). Available at: www.echr.coe.int/ECHR/EN/Header/Case-Law/HUDOC.

Schinkel, W. (2003). Discipline or Punishment? The Case of the Dutch Prison System in Innovation *European Journal of Social Science Research*, 16(3), pp.211-26.

Schone, J.M. (2001). The Short Life and Painful Death of Prisoners' Rights. *Howard Journal of Criminal Justice*, 40(1), pp.70-90.

Shestack, J.J. (1998). The Philosophic Foundations of Human Rights. *Human Rights Quarterly*, 20(2) pp.201-34.

Stafford v. The United Kingdom Judgment, (2002). Available at: www.echr.coe.int/ECHR/EN/Header/Case-Law/HUDOC.

Starmer, K. (1999). *European Human Rights Law*. London: Legal Action Group.

Stern, V. (2003). Prisoners as enemies or prisoners as citizens? - the responsibility of the state. In: ICCPPC (International Commission of Catholic Prison Pastoral Care) *XI World Congress on Responsibility, Rehabilitation and Restoration.* Dublin, 5-12 September 2003, Available at:
www.iccppc.org/congress_2003/talks_prisoners_as_enemies_citizens.ht m[Accessed 15 June 2006].

T. & V. v. The United Kingdom Judgment, (2000). Available at:
www.echr.coe.int/ECHR/EN/Header/Case-Law/HUDOC.

Tak, P.J.P. (2003). *The Dutch Criminal Justice System.* 2nd ed. The Hague: Wetenschappelijk Onderzoek-en Documentatiecentrum.

TBS: Placement under a hospital order, (2007). The Hague: DJI.
Thynne, Wilson & Gunnel v. The United Kingdom Judgment, (1991). Available at: www.echr.coe.int/ECHR/EN/Header/Case-Law/HUDOC.

Tonry, M. (2001). Symbol, Substance and Severity in Western Penal Policies. *Punishment and Society,* 3(4), pp.517-36.

Treverton-Jones, G.D. (1989). The Legal Status and Rights of Prisoners. London: Sweet & Maxwell.

Vagg, J. (1994). *Prisons Systems: a comparative study of accountability in England, France, Germany, and the Netherlands.* Oxford: Clarendon Press.

Valier, C. (2000). Looking daggers: a psychoanalytical reading of the scene of punishment. *Punishment and Society,* 2(4), pp.379-94.

Van Dijk, P. (1995). A Common Standard of Achievement: About Universal Validity and Uniform Interpretation of International Human Rights. *Netherlands Quarterly of Human Rights,* (13(2) pp.105-21.

Van Swaaningen, R. and de Jonge, G. (1995). The Dutch Prison System and Penal Policy in the 1990s: from humanitarian paternalism to penal business management. In: M.Ryan, J.Sim and V.Ruggiero, eds. *Western European Penal Systems: a critical anatomy.* London: Sage.

Van Zyl Smit, D. and Dunkel, F. eds. (2001). *Imprisonment Today and Tomorrow*. The Netherlands: Kluwer Law International.

Van Zyl Smit, D. (2006). Humanising Imprisonment: A European Project?. *European Journal on Criminal Policy and Research,* 12, pp.107-20.

Van Zyl Smit, D. (2008). Long-term imprisonment at home and abroad, Available at: *www.rsj.nl/Images/Van_Zyl_compleet_tcm60-104805.pdf* [Accessed 15 September 2009].

von Bulow v. The United Kingdom Judgment, (2004). Available at: www.echr.coe.int/ECHR/EN/Header/Case-Law/HUDOC.

Wadham, J. and Mountfield, H. (2001). *Blackstone's Guide to Human Rights Act*. 2nd ed. London: Blackstone Press.

Walker, N. (1991). *Why punish? Theories of punishment reassessed*. Oxford: Oxford University Press.

Wallace, S. (2002). Requesting computers for prisoners. *New Law Journal*, 152(7039), pp.1038-39.

Walmsley, R. (2009). *World Prison Population List*. 8th ed., Available at: www.kcl.ac.uk/depsta/law/research/icps/downloads [Accessed 5 January 2010].

Weeks v. The United Kingdom Judgment, (1988). Available at: www.echr.coe.int/ECHR/EN/Header/Case-Law/HUDOC.

Wilson, C. (1993). Going Europe: Prisoners' rights and the effectiveness of European Standards. *International Journal of the Sociology of Law*, 21, pp.245-64.

Wynne v. The United Kingdom Judgment, (2004). Available at: www.echr.coe.int/ECHR/EN/Header/Case-Law/HUDOC.

Zedner, L. (2002). Dangers and Dystopias in Penal Theories. *Oxford Journal of Legal Studies*, 22(2), pp.341-66.

10.

POOR CRIMINALS IN PRISON. VIOLATION OF THEIR FUNDAMENTAL HUMAN RIGHTS

Demetra Fr. Sorvatzioti

"Prison is the darkest side of the criminal justice system"
Michel Foucault

Introduction

Within the years 2006-2009, a qualitative research was carried out in order to define whether the economic situation of an arrested person or an accused one could affect his treatment in the criminal judicial system and in which particular way. For study purposes, we clarify that the Greek Criminal Justice System as a Continental one, belongs to the inquisitory systems of justice. For research purposes, we separated the stages of the criminal justice system according to the rules of the Greek Code of Criminal Procedure for a closer approach of possible violation of human rights in each one.

The primary sources of the research were the criminal files I handled as a defense counsel during the last 20 years of practicing law and 43 interviews in total, from judges, public prosecutors, clerks of criminal courts, policemen, correction officers, prisoners and lawyers. Two important researches were the cornerstones of our study. One is the research that was conducted in Canada regarding the Justice and the Poor (Canada Welfare Council 2000). The report, issued in 2000, brought in light the fact that there is discriminatory treatment towards the poor in the criminal justice system. The research concluded that "Canada's criminal justice system is anything but just" (Canada Welfare Council 2000:120). while discrimination against the poor accused and offender is more than obvious. The other document was a quantitative research that took place in Greece by the N.C.S.R (EKKE) and was published in 1983 in relation to Greek Criminal Justice. In this research it's well proven that society strongly believes that the Greek Criminal Justice discriminates against the poor.

Regarding the stages of the criminal justice system, we can briefly mention that in our research, we separated them as following: in the police stage, the stage before the investigating judge, the one before the court including the sentencing and the final stage in prison.

While we found that discrimination is well proven during all the stages prior to imprisonment, we were wondering how it could be possible for those who are imprisoned to have an unfair treatment while the place, the food and the facilities in general are common for every prisoner. Even the guards, the correction officers, are the same for all. Our interviews, from prisoners and correction officers proved that the discrimination in treatment towards the prisoner is driven by his economic status. The more money the more power, but not only this, the more money the more the law is applied.

We tried to determine to what extent discrimination appears and we found that it concerns the leaves, the disciplinary offences and the conditional releases of poor prisoners.

Leaves, Disciplinary Offences, Conditional Releases

Leaves

Among the interviews we took from young prisoners, one young boy says: "I am 19 years old and my parents are divorced. I do not know where my father is, but my mother lives in Rhodes island. She needs 18 hours by boat to come to Piraeus port and then she needs to take the bus to come here. She needs 4-5 hours more to come to prison to visit me. She works in a bakery. She can't take a two days' leave to come to see me and it's so expensive to pay tickets and hotel. To take an airplane is just an imagination……".

The same period we found a news release saying that: "Another dead prisoner was added to the long list of dead prisoners. Lusi Ismet, 34 years old, from Albania, who had been imprisoned since 2001, was found struggled in the toilet of his cell. The letter he sent to his parents explained the reasons of his death. Desperate, without anyone to visit him during all these years of imprisonment and without getting any leave, even if he had fulfilled all the necessary legal prerequisites, without affording any longer his life in prison he could not but commit suicide"(www.keli.gr 4/6/2009).

Section 54&4 of the Greek Correctional Code, (Law 2776/1999), provides that: "Only the status of the prisoner as immigrant or homeless or without family does not preclude him from granting prison leave". The immediate legal consequence of this article is that a negative answer from the prison council regarding a prisoner's leave can't include the homeless or immigrant or the non family status of the prisoner in its reasoning because this would lead to straight and obvious discrimination against him. Instead, the prison council decisions, as the practice usually proves, have as ratio that the personality of the prisoner does not guarantee that he will use well his leave and it is possible for him to escape. This reasoning is founded on section 55 of the code, which provides that the estimation of the prison council that the prisoner will not commit new crimes during his leave must be based on a reasonable expectation that he will use his leave the proper way and that there is no possibility that he escapes. For these estimations the council evaluates the prisoner's personality, his behavior during imprisonment, his personal, professional and social status and his family situation. The council must also take into account from one side the benefit the leave will have for the prisoner and his family and on the other hand the importance the leave will have to his future rehabilitation. It is obvious that the estimations must be reasonable in order to grant someone the prison leave. But how reasonable can these estimations be for a poor prisoner when he is homeless or has a broken family or he is immigrant with no permanent stay in the host country? Although section 54&5, demands a specific justification by the prison council in order to refuse the leave of a prisoner, this doesn't happen. After a rejection the prisoner has the legal right to appeal in front of a court arguing that there is no justification for the negative decision. In case a prisoner wants to appeal the prison's decision, he needs to hire the services of a good lawyer, expert in the execution of sentences and able to write down specifically the legal points of the non justification of the prison decision. This of course leads to the major problem that the poor prisoner who does not have money cannot hire an expert of the kind. Legal aid is not permitted according to law for such services and as a result the prison secretary completes a typical form of appeal, where no real legal arguments are presented. What usually happens in such cases is that in order to decide, the judge relies, upon the opinion of the prison council, considering it as the most appropriate one since in prison they are those who know better the prisoner's personality and behavior. And so, one rejection follows the other. We can easily realize how discrimination is applied in this level. The decision of the prison council remains capital because no one can find which the reasons of the rejection were. Phrases like "the personality of the prisoner in general does not assure good use of his leave" are so "general" that seem indefinite and vague. By this way we can't have real legal control from a higher court. We realize that although the judges have both the knowledge and the potential to reject the negative decision of the prison council they silently and fatally decide to approve of the prison council decision based on the alleged supposition that the prison authorities know the prisoner better. We must notice that no higher judicial review is provided by law against the court decision. So the court reviews the prison council decision but no one reviews its own decision. During our research in criminal files we found a decision of a court in 2009, regarding a prisoner's appeal for his leave. The court approved the prison council decision for no granting prison leave and added that the prisoner applied for his leave immediately after he reached the time limit needed by the law, and this fact indicates danger of escaping. We also found another decision of the same year that had the following additional reasoning for rejection: "although the prisoner, who was an immigrant, would stay in his cousin's home and his relatives from Pakistan would visit him, this does not preclude the danger of his escaping". In this particular case, the prisoner was 60 years old, life sentenced and less than two years remained, according to the law, to be conditionally released from prison. The Greek Penal Code states that the conditional release is granted if someone has completed the 3/5 of his sentence (over 5years till life sentence) with no disciplinary offences.

We can easily conclude that in a negative decision for a five or eight-day leave from prison, based on the legal justification of the danger of escaping, is common and suits those with no family and social standards better than those who are not immigrants and/or poor with broken families. In addition to our observation, the Special Report of the Greek Ombudsman (2009) regarding the prisoners' leaves indicates that the data shows that immigrant prisoners don't take prison leaves because of not having stable family bonds in the host country. As for Greek prisoners who have relatives far away from prison they can't see their families due to the very long distances.

Disciplinary Offences, Conditional Releases

"As for the poor, we have them for several services, they wash the clothes, they cook, they carry things such as bread, food, ice, coffee, we call them "taxi drivers", and they are those who run from the ground floor to the 3rd floor of the prison. Some of them are those who carry drugs on behalf of others. Some are forced to do so. They can't refuse it to the powerful ones; otherwise they regret it very quickly the hard way. It's like in real society. Some of us belong to a different economic class from others. We have the power, they are poor."(From a prisoner's interview). And a correction officer adds that "for any illegal thing that happens in prison, behind the poor are those of the prisoners who have money and they are the invisible parties to crime, because the poor are previously forced not to speak in case of arrest". He continues by revealing that his monthly salary is not enough and he might easily feel weak and get bribed by a wealthy prisoner. He also says that wealthy prisoners stay for a short period of time in prison, they work in order to minimize the length of their imprisonment, take leaves, have connections and they spend their time in prison as painlessly as possible.

A prisoner says: "in prison when you have money you own illegal things as cell phones, drugs, generally you can have a better time when you own money It's exactly like in open society, the high class, the middle and the lower one. Those who have money in prison are together, those who don't are "finished", they beg for cigarettes they can be tortured, they wash the clothes of others with something in return or you beat them up and they do it. That's it". While at the same time a correction officer assures that "...the prisoner who has money can bribe the correction officers to import drugs and other illegal things which are forbidden by the prison rules".

What can be easily understood from the above interviews is that not only is every day life in prison different among those who have money and those who don't, but also the poor are vulnerable enough to break the law in prison, not only the Correctional one but the Criminal as well. Therefore, when poor prisoners are forced to carry drugs or they do it in return of some money for their leaving, or for their drug dose, they face two consequences. If they are caught, they have one disciplinary offence and a criminal one. The first according to the Correctional Code is punished with a ten-day imprisonment in an isolation cell but also a written record appears in the prisoner's file showing that he didn't rehabilitate in prison; instead, he continued his criminal activities by possessing and carrying drugs, if not selling them. This, consequently, means that he will not take any leave and if he is close, time speaking, to applying for his conditional release, he will definitely get rejected. Additionally, a new criminal offence is supposed to have been committed and the prisoner will face an accusation bringing an imprisonment lasting from ten years to life. If now he does not have money to hire a lawyer or if he has a legal aid of someone who doesn't know what to do as an expert in drug cases, the problem is really serious. Explaining this we mean that a drug addict prisoner who might not apply for a medical report regarding his addiction will be judged without the privilege of the addiction and the recidivism will lead him straight forward to life sentence even if the quantity of the drug was less than a gram although not for personal use. A lot of criminal cases ended up with life sentences against poor prisoners, who had no money to hire expert lawyers. Of course in such cases the poor prisoner is the vulnerable victim who will continue to commit similar crimes in prison either forced by others or forced even by his own need for his daily dose of drugs. In order to find if this means discrimination we have to give an answer to the following reasonable questions: Would this prisoner commit the same crime if he had money and would he face such a sentence of imprisonment if he had a quality defense lawyer? If the answer is no, this leads to discrimination.

Finally, the so desired conditional release never comes for all those who break either the Correctional Code or the Criminal one. Although the Correctional Code in the article 69&4 sets that the disciplinary offences are prescribed two years after being committed and they are not considered for the leaves and the conditional releases, in reality no one says that they disappear from the prisoners' personal records in the prison file, and no one stops the prison clerks from mentioning that a disciplinary offence has been committed but is barred according to the law. This of course doesn't let the judge free to decide in favour of a prisoner's leave or conditional release when the prison council insists that, especially in his case, his personality does not guarantee that while in society, he will use his leave or his release in a good and legal way.

Conclusion

The great importance of leaves during imprisonment and their role regarding prisoner's rehabilitation has been explained and analysed many times. The prisoner can come back to society in a smooth way but also he has the possibility to be closer to his family while in prison. The Correctional Code didn't discriminate against prisoners but didn't also mention anything in favour of the poor ones because this would probably lead to discrimination. If we want to help the poor it's in our hands and if we don't want, we have the power to do so. It's not easy for a weak prisoner, poor, drug addict, with no family to find a way in the light of the law. No special recommendations are needed to overcome this obvious discrimination. Poor people are vulnerable in all levels. Poverty is like a permanent obvious characteristic which reminds us of its existence everywhere. In our research we didn't choose to use the word inmate instead of the word prisoner. We believe that such a word suits better to those who serve sentences in institutions in a civil way. Public prison never changed its character to something better, at least in Greece. So we believe that there is no reason not to call the prisoners with their name, especially when they are poor. The prisoner's identity for them stays close to the poverty one and remains as a stigma for ever in their lives. Our civilized society of 2011 didn't manage to control poverty and probably failed to do so. It would be a great pretence to analyse the benefits of our legal civilization for those who can't exercise even the minimum of what it provides. Perhaps it will be better if we try to find experts to provide their services to the vulnerable ones when they need it. This of course, is the state's responsibility, if we believe that in 2011 the welfare state is part of our social and legal civilization. Moreover, we shouldn't ever forget our personal responsibility not to encourage the discrimination against the vulnerable, poor people. Not encouraging doesn't mean mercy but active participation to stop violations against their fundamental rights. Compromising in such violations means nothing else but acceptance.

References

Beze, L. (1991). Data from the Psychological State of Prisoners, *Chronika*,Vol. 1 pp.55-74, Athens – Komotini: A.N.Sakkoula. (in Greek).

Brakoumatsos, P. (2002). Prisoners Leaves, *Poiniki Dikaiosini*, pp. 1193-1196, Athens Greece : Nomiki Bibliothiki, (in Greek).

Brakoumatsos, P. (1996). Disciplinary Procedure and Correctional Code. Current Law and Suggestions, *Poinika Chronika MΣT'*, pp. 156-160, Athens Greece: P.N. Sakkoulas (in Greek).

Brakoumatsos, P. (2000). Permitted Violence: Use of Force by the Correctional Officers, *Poinika Chronika N'*, pp. 581-586, Athens Greece : P.N. Sakkoulas (in Greek).

Canada Welfare Council (2000). *Justice and the Poor*, National Council of Welfare Publication, Canada.

Demopoulos, Ch. (2005). *Correctional Legislation*, Athens Greece: Nomiki Bibliothiki (in Greek).

Farcedakis, I. (1998). How to Deal with Prisoners' Disciplinary Offences. The French Example, *Poiniki Dikaiosini*, pp. 561-565, Athens Greece: Nomiki Bibliothiki (in Greek).

Foucault, M. (1991). *Discipline and Punish: The Birth of the Prison*, Greece: Kedros (in Greek).

Frantzeskakis, I. (1991) From Prison to Freedom, *Poinika Chronika*, Vol. MA', pp. 116-123, Athens Greece : P.N. Sakkoulas (in Greek)

Katz, J., (1985). Caste, Class, & Counsel for the Poor, *American Bar Foundation Research Journal*, Vol.10, No 2, pp.251-291.

Kenneth, A. (1992). Adjusting to Prison Life, *Crime and Justice*, Vol.16., pp.275-359.

Kosmatos, K. (2005). Disciplinary Rights, Disciplinary Sentences and Conditional Release, *Poiniki Dikaiosini*, pp.463-468, Athens Greece: Nomiki Bibliothiki (in Greek).

Kourakis, N. (1991). Prison and Violence: Parallel Lives, *Poinika Chronika* MA' pp. 129-158 Athens Greece : Sakkoulas (in Greek).

Liebling, A. (1999). Prison Suicide and Prisoner Coping, *Crime and Justice*, Vol.26, Prisons, pp.283-359.

Livos, N. (1993). When the Conditional Release is Mandatory, *Poinika Chornika* ,ΜΓ', pp.922-928, Athens Greece : P.N. Sakkoulas (in Greek).

Maganas, A., Gr., Lazos (1997) *Social Values of Offenders and Non Offenders*, Athens: Panteion University (in Greek).

Maganas , A., Gr., Lazos, D.,Svourdakou (2008). *Criminology Upside Down*, Athens Greece: Nomiki Bibliothiki (in Greek).

Manoledakis, I. (1996). The Protection of the Vulnerable Persons in the Criminal Law, *Yperaspisi,* pp.931-939, Athens Greece : A.N. Sakkoulas (in Greek).

Margaritis L., G., Dimitrainas (1995). *Adults' and Juveniles' Conditional Release*, Athens Greece : Nomiki Bibliothiki (in Greek)

N.C.S.R (EKKE), Daskalakis E. et al., (1986). *Justice in Greece*, Athens: EKKE in (Greek).

Ombudsman Greek, (2009). Special Report (prot.no. 369/07/1.8.2008) *Poiniki Dikaiosini*, Vol.6-7, pp.706-714, Athens Greece: Nomiki Bibliothiki (in Greek).

Panayiotopoulos, M. (2004) The Good Behavior in Prison as a Mitigating Factor for the Penal Treatment of the Prisoner. (Comment on the current and the previous case law of the High Court-Areios Pagos), *Poinika Chronika* ΝΔ', pp.959-960, Athens Greece : P.N. Sakkoulas (in Greek).

Panousis, G. (2004). Who is the Corruptor of our Prisoner? (Corruption and Prison), *Poiniki Dikaiosini*, pp.412-421, Athens Greece : Nomiki Bibliothiki (in Greek).

Panousis, G. (2002). The Crime of the Poor and Poverty as a"Crime" (Under Universalism Conditions), *Poiniki Dikaiosini*, pp.412-421, Athens Greece: Nomiki Bibliothiki (in Greek).

Panousis, G. (1991) Disciplinary Law for Prisoners, *Chronika*, Vol 3, pp.33-47, Athens - Komotini : A.N.Sakkoula. (in Greek)

Poulopoulos, Ch. (1998). Correctional System, Detoxification and Rehabilitation of Drug Addicts, *Poiniki Dikaiosini*,pp.117-119, Athens Greece : Nomiki Bibliothiki (in Greek).

Rubin, S. (1932). Criminal Justice and the Poor, *Journal of Criminal Law and Criminology*,Vol.22, No.5, pp.705-715.

Sisilianos, L.A., G.,Ktistakis, N.,Sitaropoulos (2001). Report and Suggestions of the National Committee for Human Rights. The Imprisonment Conditions in Greece, *Poiniki Dikaiosini*, pp.1058-1063, Athens Greece : Nomiki Bibliothiki (in Greek).

Spinelli, K., K.,Kourakis (1992). *Correctional Legislation*, 2nd ed., Athens : Nomiki Bibliothiki (in Greek).

Spohn, C., D., Holleran (2002). The effects of Imprisonment on Recidivism Rates of Felony Offenders: A Focus on Drug Offenders, *Criminology* Vol.40, pp.329-358.

Statheas, G. (2000). The Prisoner's Prerequisites for Conditional Release, *Poinika Chronika*, MZ', pp.1563-1565, Athens Greece : P.N. Sakkoulas (in Greek).

Stefanidou, B.S. (2000). Alternative Measures Instead of Imprisonment and Especially the Control Surveillance, *Poiniki Dikaiosini*, pp.544-552, Athens: Nomiki Bibliothiki (in Greek).

Sorvatzioti, D. (2008) ....And the Poor Will Be Prisoners, *Poiniki Dikaiosini*, pp.977, Athens Greece : Nomiki Bibliothiki (in Greek).

Themelis, O. (1999). Suicide in Prison –Technical Specifications in Prison as a Major Preventive Way, *Poinika Chronika*, ΜΘ΄, pp.622-624, Athens Greece : P.N. Sakkoulas (in Greek).

Themelis, O. (2005). Violent Deaths in Prison: The Coming Back of the Punitive Character of Imprisonment. *Poiniki Dikaiosini*, pp.1330-1335, Athens: Nomiki Bibliothiki (in Greek).

Tzanetaki, T.(1993). Private Prisons and the Challenge of the Limits of State Operation, *Poinika Chronika*, Vol. ΜΓ΄, pp. 5-32, Athens Greece : P.N. Sakkoulas (in Greek).

Wacquant, L. (2003). Toward a Dictatorship over the Poor? *Punishment & Society*, Vol.5, No.2, pp.197-205.

Zimianitis, D. (1999). Prisoners' Leaves as a Relief from the Negative Consequences of Imprisonment, *Yperaspisi*, pp. 1357-1376, Athens : A.N. Sakkoulas (in Greek).

http://www.keli.gr/2009/06/blog-post.html

11.

THE CRIMINALIZATION OF THE MIGRATION POLICY
AND THE NEW EUROPEAN TERRITORIALITIES OF
SOCIAL CONTROL

George P. Nikolopoulos

A. The political management of the migration into Europe is related to the wider process of european integration and, more specifically, to the way in which it is (re)creating new frontiers and territorialities for the exercise of social control over crime and deviance, implicating multiple actors coming from different jurisdictions (administratives, penals) and from various levels of governance (regionals, nationals, inter-nationals, supra-nationals and universals). From this point of view, the criminological analysis of the migratory movements follows the epistemological trend of the *"sociology of globalisation"* (Sasen 2007), in which it has been proposed the construction of a *"criminology beyond the nation state"* (Hogg 1997), of a *"transnational and comparative criminology"* (Sheptycki and Wardak 2005) or of a *"criminology of mobilities"*(Aas 2007).

Following this perspective, the process of european integration could be emerged as a distinct subject for criminological investigation[1]. However, the prospect of european integration is still for the time being an evolving process, with its institutional characteristics still unshaped and with continual contradictions and setbacks that undermine its future and, specially, its democratic legitimation. Therefore, I think that the long period of retrenchment and the procrastination into which the european integration process seems to have fallen, essentially reflect the difficult politicization of an initially economic undertaking.

But, in any case, it is evident that the issue of migratory movements have become central to current european social control policies, following the currently dominant trend of interpreting the social phenomena by focusing on the criminogenic potential assumed in various

---

[1] I believe that at present we can indeed speak about the *"resurgence of a distinctively European criminology"*, as A. Edwards and G. Hughes noted in the Editorial of the special issue of *Theoretical Criminology* on *"The Governance of Safety in Europe"* (2005:259-263). See also the criminological agenda proposed by I. Taylor (1999: 333-346).

social groups and subjects (*"criminalization of the social policy"*) (Garland 2001, Papathéodorou and Mary 2006) and usually referred to in the bibliography as *"the securitization of migration"* (Cesari 2009, Huysmans 2000, Imbrahim 2005, Pallida 2009, Tsoukala 2005), so that the political management of the migration into Europe constitute, according to D. Melossi (1997:70), *"a sort of acid-test for social control in the Europe"*: *"In the same way* (this author continues) *that the social control of crime is a dependent variable of the much broader issue of social control, so in Europe today the social control of immigration is strictly related to the concept of social control that is going to prevail in Europe – that is, to the kind of social and political constitution that will ultimately obtain."*

Therefore, I will propose to shift the focus of the debate about the social control of immigrants away from the measurement of their criminality, to the criminalizaton of the immigration policy itself, i.e. to the study of the institutional and social conditions which drive the immigrants into the realm of the penal system. By following this line of investigation, I will try to avoid the limitations of the quantitative data supplied by the police and judicial registration systems, and to restore the macrosocial dynamics at play in the "grey area" before the penal reporting. Therefore, my goal is to examine all the relevant discourses and practices, the formal and informal norms, the attitudes and representations, in short, the complete social apparatus which sets into motion the social reactions, spontaneous or officials, towards immigrants. With the implementation of the above research tools I am hoping to prove that the over-representation of immigrants among the "clients" of the penal system is nothing else but a self-fulfilling prophecy about their criminality.

B. I will begin therefore by putting forward three working hypotheses which, I believe, reflect recent developments in the area:

First Hypothesis: As a result of the "Treaty of Amsterdam" (1996) and the decisions of the European Council in Tampere (1999), for the establishment of an *"area of freedom, security and justice,"* a new European territoriality of social control is gradually emerging. Its main features are the formation of a complicated nexus of agencies and networks through which various strategies of policing circulate and transfer crossnationally, aiming, notably, at the management of the entry and the movement of persons within the EU territory.

The increasing development of this repressive component of european integration is producing profound changes in the morphology of social control in present day Europe. Notably, these changes call into question the idea that the state constitutes the most important boundary for the exercise of social control of crime and deviance.

Second Hypothesis: Movements of non-european citizens intending to reach the territory of the member states are seen as a matter of criminal risk, a viewpoint that has resulted in a connotation between criminality and non european citizenship. The logic of social control has thus prevailed on the issue of international mobility of persons, whereas other, more beneficial effects, are neglected, such as economic development and demographic increase. It is well known, of course, that later on, a policy reversal was noted from "zero immigration" to quotas and selections of foreigners with professional qualifications. In this way, although the establishment of an effective policy on illegal migration remains a top priority for the EU, nevertheless, it seems to be a gradual move towards addressing development goals through legal migration instruments. However the predominant viewpoint of "inclusio/exclusio" was not abandoned nor was the taking of proactive and repressive measures against third countries nationals.

In this way, a new form of government is being adopted, known - as well put by D.Bigo (1995, 1998) - as *"governmentality through fear"*. This one is implemented by applying strategies of *"policing at a distance"* from the borders of the state - witness, for example, the process for granting a "Schengen visa" or the cases where the so-called "integration tests" are not only required of persons who have already been accepted as immigrants in this country, but also from those who seek to became immigrants in the future (Guild 2006).

In these cases the logic of the proactive policing of the consulates and embassies abroad prevails, which aims primarily to hold foreigners *"at a distance"*, to keep 'undesirables' away, by hindering their movements; as D. Bigo and E. Guild (2005:9) note very aptly: *"The surveillance and similar controls are now at a distance, by remote control, by international collaboration, by anticipation of crime before it happens"*. This is particularly true with regard to the latter method of control (that is *"by anticipation of crime before it happens"*); in a very insidious way, the excessive reactions of the "professionals of security" dominated, based much more on symbolism and stereotypes, to the detriment of any convincing piece of evidence about the *"corpus delicti"*, even if this one was still embryonic – as they put it, something which of course can only increase our suspicions

Third Hypothesis: These developments are branded by their unilateral criminal policy function and democratic deficit, to the detriment of the guarantees provided by human rights and the protecting guarantees of penal procedure. Indeed, these politics of policing "*at a distance*" are profoundly distinguished from the traditional preventive politics, if not for other reasons, at least because they are not limited to the taking of general and impersonal measures against criminal possibilities but, rather, because policing "*at a distance*" is oriented towards repressive tactics, against predefined groups, so that it seems much more as a sort of sanction which replaces the criminal and the crime with the suspicious and the suspect.

C. The previous hypotheses emerge in essence from a common assumption about the crisis through which the normative hegemony of the nation-state has been passing. Of course, this crisis has not leaded either states or the diversity of social norms to disappear – quite the opposite! But, clearly, the position and the role of states in the regulation of social relations must be reexamined today (Robert and van Outrive 1993:7-8), in light of the wider process that we usually call "*globalization*".

The interest of social scientists and more specifically of criminologists in these developments is due to the weakening that these developments bring to the redistributive capacity of states and, by extension, to the increasing of social inequalities, which lead to a multiplication of the processes of social marginalization and polarization. It is also well known that the nation-state, in reaction, is turning more and more to the field of penal policy, looking for new sources of legitimation, in order to replace those that it lost with its gradual withdrawal from the socio-economic field.

However, even this preferential investment of the state in the field of penal policy is not developing without the influence of external constraints. Indeed, the predominance of the viewpoint about the internationalization of criminal activity – consequently to the internationalization of the legal economic activities – constituted the justification for the detachment of the issue of security from the exclusive competence of the state and its preferential transfer to an inter-national and trans-national level. From then on, the social control of crime imposes a reaching out and a coordination of the state with agencies and networks "over" and "above" it, without of course in this way bypassing the serious issues of the democratic accountability of the policies so produced.

A typical example of this development is, of course, the process of european integration. In this case, the premise of security proved to be the primary subject to be worked out within the framework of the "*euro-peanization*" of control and justice, in expectation of the creation of a "*large European market without borders*". In this way, the liberalization of the movement of capital, products and services, led in counterbalance, to the redefinition of the borders as points of social control for persons, in order for the European labor market to be protected from undesirable immigration inflows. Thus, what E. Balibar (1997:23) termed a "*multi-valency*" of the borders (in french: "*polysémie*") has come about, that is to say, that the importance of the borders controls change according to the national identity of those who attempt to cross them.

These developments express, in essence, the paradox faced in the implementation of the liberal premise of the free circulation of persons in the european territory. Indeed, while the removal of border controls was established initially to serve the economic goals of the european in-tegration, it was however at the same time considered a source of risk, due to the fears of cross-border criminality. The latter, however, could not be confronted effectively through the self-regulating rules of the market and, for this reason, the normative convergence of different na-tional strategies of policing was chosen. In other words, on the issue of the movement of persons was not followed a liberalization correspond-ing to that of the movement of capital, products and services. Rather, a criminogenic approach concerning the non-european origin of the threats was adopted, which led to the taking of proactive measures against "third" countries' citizens.

Furthermore, as we know, in response to the increased european concerns about security in the aftermath of 11/9, there has been an over-zealous application of security measures in relation to free movement of persons, immigration and asylum seeking. In this respect, the concerns about the securing of the E.U. territory are also generating an external relations strategy, which has been developed in non european and even in cross-Atlantic dimensions[2].

---

[2] Witness, for example, the increased cooperation of the EU with the USA and other "third countries", notably regarding the management of migratory pressures, the readmission of ille-gal migrants and the "*war against terrorism*", as in the cases of agreements signed between EU-USA on extradition and mutual legal assistance and the processing and transfer of per-sonal data (the so-called "*Passenger Name Record Data*") of europeans traveling to the US.

D. The result of the policies mentioned above was the creation of a new european territoriality for the exercising of the social control, initially within the framework of the project "*european judicial area*" of the Single European Act of 1987, which was enlarged later - after the review of the Treaties in Amsterdam (1996) - in an "*area of freedom, security and justice*". Of course, we must always keep in mind that, in the EU rhetoric, the content of the meanings "*freedom*", "*security*" and "*justice*" do not cover the entire interpretive field that corresponds to each of these, but rather is focused on very specific aims. Thus, "*freedom*" is limited to the free movement and residence of persons within the territory of the member states, "*security*" to the taking of appropriate measures for the control of movement (primarily through the availability of information between the various agents of security and the interoperability between different systems and databases); finally, the meaning of "*justice*" is limited to the convergence of national penal legislations and the cooperation of the competent authorities of the member states and the respective agencies of the EU as well.

Thus, we can see that at the starting point of the construction of a european field of social control, a double reassessment of the borders of the member states as "*internal*" and "*external*" can be found; consider, for example, the case of international airports, which function either as "*internal*" or "*external*" borders of the EU depending on the origin or the destination of each flight. In this respect, the external borders of the state are increasingly located in the interior, not at the geographical "edges" of the state; in other words, as W.Walters and J.H.Haahr (2005:103-4) point out: "*a disjuncture has occurred between the space of border controls and the political-territorial borders of the polity. They no longer neatly coincide. The space of border control is now partly configured around a network of airports*" – that is to say, "*in the interior*" of the state.

Moreover, the borders are "opened" or "closed" depending on the person's citizenship and the particular regimes that govern the various areas that make up this new field of european social control – as for example the "Schengen area", which, as is well known, does not coincide with the entire territory of the E.U. These developments indicate that the creation of a transnational "european citizenship" has contributed to the alteration of the traditional link between the nationals and the territory of a state. But, on the other hand, considering that the right to move and reside freely throughout the E.U. territory is a precondition for the exercise of most of the other basic rights conferred by european laws, it follows that the crucial question is who may be included or excluded from that privilege. In this respect, we must note that the difficulty of penetration of the "internal" and "external" borders for "third" country nationals and their residence in a member state, does not depend only on the attention given to crime control but also on the political decisions that regulate the conditions in the european labor market, the unremunerated training and voluntary services, the family reunification, the studies and the scientific research.

Paradoxically, the regulations of the labor market concern not only the free movement of "third" countries citizens but also "european citizens", who come from the states that joined the E.U. after its enlargement of 2004. Specifically, it is typical of the *"new spatialization"* of the control regimes which are in place today in the EU that for all of our new "european co-citizens" – other than those from Cyprus and Malta – the absolute exercise of their right of free movement and residence in the "older" 15 member states has been restricted until 2011. On the other hand, some "older" member states – such as the United Kingdom, Ireland, Sweden and Greece - are already proceeding to a gradual removal of that restriction (Adinolfi 2005, Carrera 2005, Plümper and Schneider 2007).

E. I believe that these current examples may bring once again to mind the old criminological hypothesis of Georg Rusche and Otto Kirchheimer (1937), concerning the effects of the labor market conditions on the patterns and the intensity of social control. Indeed, I think that this theoretical perspective - specially as it was reworked   by D.Melossi (1985, 1989:311) through the notion of *"vocabularies of punitive motives"* - can provide us an adequate analytical framework for analysing the penalizing effects of the current policies of labor market deregulation – especially the 'moral panic' that the free circulation of workers provoke among the european employees, which ends up in the marginalization and criminalization of the "third" countries residents. Thus, we can understand that the changing concepts of frontiers and territotialities being put in place within the framework of European integration are traversed *"by a series of different social relations"*, which - as we are reminded by D. Garland and P.Young (1983:21) - *"do not merely 'influence' or 'shape' or 'put pressure upon' penality* (instead of penality we could put here: "upon the european field of social control"), but these social relations *"operate through it"* (that is to say "through the european field of social control") *"and are materially inscribed in its practices"*.

In this way, a new *"european archipelago of policing"* is created - as D.Bigo (2005:13) quite accurately calls it - referring to the greater and greater enlargement of the numerous specialized services that undertake policing within the area of Europe. In fact, the setting up of "institutional frontiers" inside and outside the member states is aimed at keeping newly arrived immigrants in a status of irregularity, at confining them to the margin of citizenship. Certainly, these institutional frontiers are sometimes "opened", as can be seen in the results of the successive procedures of regularization of immigrants that have taken place in some member states. But, even these procedures, confirm - at least - the predominant logic of social control and its "inclusio/exclusio" implications, since - with the exception of those who successfully achieve these procedures - a significant number of illegal immigrants always remain out of them, in the realm of the underground economy and the undeclared work, so that they become vulnerable to all kinds of exploitations and abuses of power. In total, as S. Carrera (2006:2) points out, *"The notion of integration does not seem to involve a process of social inclusion of immigrants, but has rather become a juridical and policy mechanism of control by which the state may better manage who enters and who is included inside its territory"*. From this point of view, we can think that the criminalization of migrants arises as the outcome of an *"ambiguous treatment – 'formally administrative' and 'concretely penal'"* (De Giorgi 2006:133), which constitutes the crucial point for the definition of their social status (i.e. as "regular" or "irregular" residents), leading, at last, to the *"immigration as an 'ontological crime"* (De Giorgi 2006:124).

F. Coming to a conclusion, I think that the question definitely focuses upon the reversal of the current emphatic dedication of the EU to security policies and upon the significant disproportion that those policies display in relation to the respective policies for the protection of individual rights and freedoms. From this perspective, I think that we must focus our interest at the level of social control practices, that is to say, where the most significant diversions from the human rights' premises occur. Moreover, the issue of the protection of human rights is not so much a case of establishing abstract rules, as the setting of the necessary preconditions for them to be exercised.

Particularly with regard to the creation of an *"area of freedom, security and justice"*, what is certain is that security continues to function as the center of gravity for its overall equilibrium, limiting respectively the range of the other two values: enough freedom so that security is not violated and enough justice so that security is served first and foremost. In this way however, the intentions of crime control surpass the rule of law's mandatory limits and, more generally, all of the premises that we assemble under the umbrella of "human rights". On the contrary, as I.Manoledakis (1989:39) notes in a characteristic way, human rights may constitute the starting point for a drastic *"demystification of the effectiveness of penal suppression at all levels"* or - as A. Pires (1991:71) neatly turns the question around - instead of wondering *"how to use penal law to strengthen human rights"*, it is more worthwhile to think about *"how human rights can constitute a tool in the rethinking of penal law and its relationship with other legal systems."*

Following this perspective, I think that we could mitigate the democratic deficit which is created by the new field of social control that is emerging in the process of the european integration; moreover, we can eliminate all the well known tragic consequences provoked by the intensive policing of human mobilities...

References

Aas, K.F. (2007) Analysing a world in motion. Global flows meet 'criminology of the other', *Theoretical criminology*, 11:2, pp. 283-303.

Adinolfi, A. (2005) Free movement and access to work of citizens of the new member states: the transitional measures, *Common Market Law Review*, 42, pp. 469-498.

Balibar, E. (1997) Frontières et violence, *Transeuropéennes*, n. 9, pp. 23-28.

Bigo, D. (1995) Les États face aux flux transfrontières de personnes : enjeux et perspectives, *Les cahiers de la sécurité intérieure*, n.19, pp.115-125.

Bigo, D. (1998) Sécurité et immigration : vers une gouvernementalité par l'inquiétude? *Cultures et Conflits*, n.31/32, pp.13-38.

Bigo, D., Guild, E. (2005) La logique du visa Schengen: police à distance, *www.libertysecurity.org/article260.html*.

Bigo, D. (2005) La mondialisation de l' (in)sécurité ? Réflexions sur le champ des professionnels de la gestion des inquiétudes et analytique de la transnationalisation des processus d' (in)sécurisation, *Cultures et Conflits*, n. 58, pp. 53-100.

Bigo, D., Guild, E. (2005) Introduction: Policing in the Name of Freedom, in Bigo, D., Guild, E. (eds.), *Controlling frontiers Free Movement Into and Within Europe,* Aldershot: Ashgate, pp.1-13.

Carrera, S. (2005) What does free movement mean in theory and practice in an enlarged EU? *European Law Journal*, 11:6, pp. 699-721.

Carrera, S. (2006) Towards an EU framework on the integration of immigrants, in Carrera, S. (ed.), *The nexus between immigration, integration and citizenship in the EU*, Collective Conference Volume, Center for European Policy Studies, April, www.ceps.be.

Cesari, J. (2009) *The securitization of Islam in Europe*, Challenge – Liberty and Security, Research Paper n.15, 2009, www.ceps.eu.

De Giorgi, A. (2006) *Re-thinking the political economy of punishment. Perspectives on post-fordism and penal politics*, Aldershot: Ashgate.

Edwards, A., Hughes, G. (2005) Editorial - The Governance of Safety in Europe, *Theoretical Criminology*, 9:3, pp.259-263.

Garland, D. (2001) *The culture of control. Crime and social order in contemporary society*, Oxford - N. York: Oxford University Press.

Garland, D., Young, P. (1983) Towards a social analysis of penality', in Garland, D., Young, P. (eds.), *The power to punish. Contemporary penality and social analysis*, London, New Jersey: Heinemann Educational Books, pp. 1-36.

Guild, E. (2006) Conclusions: Where is the nexus? Some final considerations on immigration, integraton and citizenship, in S.Carrera (ed.), *The nexus between immigration, integration and citizenship in the EU*, Collective Conference Volume, Center for European Policy Studies, April, www.ceps.be .

Hogg, R. (1997) Criminology beyond the nation state: global conflicts, human rights and the 'new world disorder', in R. van Swaaningen, *Critical criminology. Visions from Europe*, London: Sage, pp. 185-217.

Huysmans, J. (2000) The European Union and the securitization of migration, *Journal of Common Market studies*, 38:5, pp.751-777

Imbrahim, M. (2005) The securitization of migration: A racial discourse, *International migration*, 43:5, pp.163-187

Manoledakis, I. (1989) The abuse of penal repression, *Hellenic Review of Criminology*, n.3-4, pp.39-57, in Greek.

Melossi, D. (1985) Punishment and social action: changing vocabularies of punitive motive within a political business cycle, *Current Perspectives in Social Theory*, 6, pp.169-197.

Melossi, D. (1989) An introduction: Fifty years later. "Punishment and Social Structure" in comparative analysis, Contemporary Crises, 13:4.

Melossi, D. (1997) State and social control *à la fin de siècle*: from the new world to the constitution of the new Europe, in R.Bergalli, C.Sumner (dir.), *Social control and political order. European perspectives at the end of the century*, London: Sage, pp. 52-74.

Pallida, S. (2009) Criminalization and victimization of immigrants in Europe, *Crimprev info*,22bis, http://lodel.irevues.inist.fr/crimprev/index.php?id=229

Papathéodorou, Th., Mary, Ph. (dir.) (2006) *Mutations des politiques criminelles en Europe,* Athènes: Papazissis.

Pires, A. (1991) Éthiques et réforme du droit criminel: au-delà des philosophies de la peine, *Ethica*, vol.3, n.2, pp.47-78.

Plümper, T., Schneider, C. (2007) Discriminatory European Union membership and the redistribution of enlargement gains, *Journal of Conflict Resolution*, 51:4, pp. 568-587.

Robert, Ph., van Outrive, L. (1993) Introduction:Un bilan européen, in Robert, Ph., van Outrive, L. (dir.), *Crime et justice en Europe. Etat des recherches, évaluations et recommandations*, Paris : L' Harmattan

Rusche, G., Kirchheimer, O. (1937/1968) *Punishment and Social Structure,* Morningside Heights/N.York: Columbia University Press/ Russell & Russell Co.

Sasen, S. (2007) A Sociology of Globalization, New York : W.W. Norton & Company.

Sheptycki, J., Wardak, A. (ed.) (2005) *Transnational and comparative criminology*, London: GlassHouse Press.

Taylor, I. (1999) Criminology post – Maastricht, *Crime, Law and Social Change*, 30:4, pp. 333-346.

Tsoukala, A. (2005) Looking at Migrants as Enemies, in D. Bigo, E. Guild (ed.), *Controlling Frontiers. Free Movement into and within Europe*, Aldershot: Ashgate, pp. 161-192.

Walters, W., Haahr, J. H. (2005) *Governing Europe. Discourse, governmentality and European integration*, London-New York: Routledge, pp.103-104.

12.

PROGRAMMES FOR ABUSIVE MEN – RESULTS FROM A SWEDISH EVALUATION STUDY

Christina Ericson

Introduction

Programmes for men who use violence in intimate relationships have been the subject of many discussions, research projects etc., in the western world since the 1980s (for example, see Gondolf, 2002; Edleson and Tolman, 1992; Dobash and Dobash et al, 2000). The first programmes for abusive men were developed in the United States at the end of the 1970s. Today there are approximately 2,500 programmes in the United States, even though the Domestic Abuse Intervention Project (DAIP) is the model that has probably had the greatest impact (WHO, 2003; Saunders, 2008). Most of the programmes work with skills training based on Cognitive Behavioural Therapy (CBT) principles. There are also those which are psychodynamically oriented or which are using dialectical counselling and partner therapy etc. (Gondolf, 2004). There are a number of international evaluations of programmes for abusive men, showing varying results. For example, the World Health Organization (WHO) has stated that the programmes at least show "modest effects", while other evaluations are barely able to detect any effects at all (WHO, 2003). According to Gondolf (2004) over 40 published programmes have attempted to address the effectiveness of "batterer programmes" in preventing reassaults. Summaries and meta-analysis of these evaluations suggest little or no programme effect (Gondolf, 2004).

In Sweden, there are few evaluations of programmes for abusive men and the ones that do exist are qualitatively oriented, such as interview studies with the staff or men taking part in the programmes. It has not been without controversy to invest in treatments and interventions for men who use violence in intimate relationships. Especially in the 1990's criticism of treatment for individual men came from advocates of the radical feminist perspective on domestic violence in Sweden. These advocates were of the opinion that domestic violence are caused by structural rather than individual factors, and therefore requires changes in the structure of society to end (Ericson, 2005). Concerns have also been expressed that such programmes take up resources that could have been spent on the support of women and children affected by the violence. Now, however, there seems to be a greater consensus regarding the need for such efforts, and this is also reflected in policy decisions. In recent years, politicians, practitioners and researchers in Sweden have showed a greater interest in treatment for abusive men and the outcomes of these treatments.

Purpose

In 2007, the National Board for Health and Welfare, where I work, was commissioned by the Government to evaluate Swedish interventions within the social services for men who use violence against their partners. The purpose of the study was to find out if the programmes/interventions within the social services were effective in ending the violence.[1] The report containing the results was delivered to the Swedish Government in July 2010. So far no quantitative evaluation of this size has been performed in Sweden.

In this chapter I will present some background information to the study and also some of the results.

The programmes

Eight programmes situated in different parts of Sweden, mostly larger cities, were included in the study. From the beginning these eight programmes were categorised into three groups. The categorisation was based on the similarities and differences we found in the existing material about the treatments that were used, and also on information we received from the therapists that worked with the men. The differences we found in the rather sparse material about the treatments were, unfortunately, overestimated at the outset of the study. Our later documentation of the programmes, which was carried out at the same time as the data collection from the men in treatment, showed great similarities between all of the programmes and few differences. The comparisons between the three groups of programmes turned out to be fruitless. The purpose of categorising them into three groups was partly to be able to compare

---

[1] A manual-based programme also exists for abusive men within the correctional system (Integrated Domestic Abuse Programme - IDAP), but it was not included in the study.

results from different types of programmes with each other (quasi-experimental study) and partly to prevent getting too small samples per programme which would have prevented us from being able to detect a statistical significant effect.

The length of the eight programmes varied for each individual, from three individual sessions to more than 20 individual/group sessions. All of the programmes offered both individual and group sessions, even though most of the therapists preferred the men to take part in group sessions. The programmes included themes such as responsibility for the violence, consequences of the violence for women and children, gender and violence theory, alternatives to violence, communication, problem solving, sexuality and alcohol etc. A whole range of treatment theories, such as learning psychology, psychodynamic theory, systems theory and cognitive behaviour therapy etc., had inspired the therapists while putting the programmes together. Overall, the programmes included in the study were very dynamic and flexible in their character and none of them were manual based.

Study design

A quasi-experimental design with pre- and post-measures of the men and their female partners was used. Only female partners who took part in a so-called "Women's Safety Worker Programme" could be questioned for the study.[2] The assessment instruments consisted of questionnaires which the men and women completed separately in the presence of a research officer. The questionnaire took approximately one hour to complete and all of the included assessment instruments were validated. The violence was measured with Conflict Tactics Scale 2, which is a scale that has been used widely since the 1980s (Straus, Hamby and Warren, 2003). It has, among other things, been criticised for not taking into account the context surrounding the relationships, but it gives quite a good picture of the kind of violence that is used (physical, psychological, sexual, injurious, material). We also measured mental health, alcohol and drug abuse, sense of coherence and the client's satisfaction with the treatment etc.

---

[2] A Women's Safety Worker, among other things, provides information to the partner about the offender's attendance at the programme and asks her (if she still has contact with him) about his behaviour outside the treatment. Only three of the eight programmes had a Women's Safety Worker organization connected to them. For ethical reasons, we could not contact women who did not have this kind of support.

The pre-measurement was carried out very close to the start of the treatment and the post-measurement 12 months later. The men were asked to take part in the study by the therapists and the women were asked to take part by their Safety Worker. The women's answers were supposed to validate the men's answers. No randomisation was performed and it was not possible to get an untreated control group. The sample of men was based on self-selection, which means the men started treatment at the programme they had chosen to turn to in the first place. Most of the men in the study took part voluntarily in the programmes without being under police suspicion or convicted of a violent crime (the man had not been reported to the police by his partner). Nevertheless, some of the men included in the study had been referred to the programmes by the criminal justice system.

The participants

Every man who contacted one of the included programmes during the one-year inclusion period was asked if he would participate in the study. At the end of the 12 months, 228 men had been asked to take part. There were, however, 40 men who declined to participate, for reasons such as "I will not talk to the authorities", "I haven't got the time" etc., which resulted in 188 men who completed the pre-measurements. The attrition level, compared with the post-measurements, one year later, was 48 men (25.5 per cent), which gives a sample of 140 men in the follow-up study.

We were only able to get 16 out of a total of 63[3] women to complete the pre-measurement questionnaires. One reason was probably that some of the Safety Workers did not telephone the women or book a personal meeting to inform them about the Safety Worker Programme and the study, but instead sent them a letter asking them to participate. Another reason could be that the women did not want to have anything to do with their ex-partner and therefore did not contact the Safety Worker. Two women decided not to take part in the post-measurements, which makes 14 women one year later. Because of the large loss of women in the study we didn't compare the answers from the women with the answers from the men. Therefore, below I will mostly refer to the men's results.

---

[3] As mentioned earlier, only three programmes had a Women's Safety Worker organisation connected to them and that is why the numbers differ from the original 188 men that agreed to participate in the study.

The men's background and family relations

The study included 188 men aged 19 to 68 years. The average baseline age was 38 years. Approximately half (53 per cent) had attended secondary school as their highest level of education, and most of the men (68 per cent) were employed. More background variables are reported in Table 1.

Table 1. Socio-demographic background, men (N=188).

Average age	38 years
Not born in Sweden	20%
University	28%
Secondary school	53%
Primary school	20%
Employed	68%
Students	8%
Long-term sick/unemployed	16%
Retired	4%

When the men began their treatment the majority (69 per cent) were in relationships with the women they had abused. Just over half (55 per cent) also had children with the women. A year later, half of the participants in the survey (49 per cent) were still in a relationship with the woman they had abused and 22 per cent were in a new relationship. The men started treatment because they had used violence against their partners. Yet, a fifth (22 per cent) had recently used violence against someone outside the family too during the years before the start of the treatment. The men also answered questions about whether they had been subject to violence by their parents when they grew up. More than half (58 per cent) of the men said they had been exposed to physical violence and just under half (45 per cent) said that they had experienced psychological violence. More than half (56 percent) of the men had also experienced one parent exposing the other parent to psychological violence, and one third (33 percent) reported the same about physical violence.

Results

The men's treatment

One year after the treatment started, 38 per cent of the men had completed their treatment according to the therapists. In total, 43 per cent had dropped out and 19 per cent were still in treatment (N = 170, data missing for 18 men).

Violence

To measure the men's violence a self-assessment instrument called CTS2 (The Revised Conflict Tactics Scale) was used. The instrument consists of 78 questions which can be divided into 10 different scales, including six scales measuring the presence of various types of violence in the relationship and two scales measuring injuries caused by the violence (for the sake of simplicity, injuries caused by violence are also called violence from now on). It is these eight scales that will be analysed here. The different scales consist of questions of how many times a number of concrete actions or events have happened in the previous 12 months. [4]

Before treatment

Table 2, below, shows the percentage of men who had engaged in various types of violence according to their answers in the questionnaire.

---

[4] For example: "I pushed or shoved my partner", "I used a knife or gun on my partner", "I called my partner fat or ugly", "I slammed my partner against a wall", "My partner needed to see a doctor because of a fight with me, but didn't", "I destroyed something belonging to my partner", " I insisted on sex when my partner did not want to (but did not use physical force)", "I threatened to hit or throw something at my partner" etc.

Table 2. Percentage of men who had engaged in various types of violence. Pre-measurements, (N = 188).

Minor psychological violence	98%
Severe psychological violence	59%
Minor physical violence	78%
Severe physical violence	51%
Minor injuries	61%
Severe injuries	30%
Minor sexual violence	23%
Severe sexual violence	2%

The most common type of violence was minor psychological violence. As many as 98 per cent of the men said they had exercised this type of violence at some point in the past 12 months. A significant proportion, 78 per cent, had also used minor physical violence. Even the serious forms of violence were common. Severe psychological violence was perpetrated by 59 per cent and serious physical violence by 51 per cent. However, severe sexual violence was reported by only 2 per cent (four men).

Change in the use of violence

Table 3 shows the change in use of different types of violence for the total number of men (188) who were included in the study. The 48 men who did not participate in the follow-up measurement are also included in the analysis. This means that the figures in the table are based on the assumption that their behaviour did not change from pre- to post-measurements, a so-called "intention to treat" analysis. In the analysis presented here, the men received one of two values on the scales: "used" and "not used" in relation to which type of violence that was under question. The focus of the analysis will be on whether the men reported that they had ceased or continued to use various types of violence, that is, any change between pre- and post-measurements. The word "cease" in this context means that the man stated that he had not exercised the type of violence at any time in the past 12 months – in contrast, during the 12 months preceding the survey he had replied that he had exercised violence. No analysis for the category severe sexual violence will be performed as only four men stated that they were engaged in such violence and therefore any calculations based on such a small sample would be unreliable.[5]

Table 3. Changes in use of violence in the follow-up period, shown as percentages, (N = 188).

	Ceased	Con-tinued	Begun	Never used	
Minor psychological violence	17*	81	2	0	100
Severe psychological violence	23*	36	3	38	100
Minor physical violence	36*	43	0	21	100
Severe physical violence	30*	21	2	47	100
Minor injuries	31*	30	3	36	100
Severe injuries	21*	9	2	68	100
Minor sexual violence	14*	9	2	75	100

*All of the changes in the column "ceased" are statistically significant (McNemar, $p < 0.05$).

The table shows that the category minor physical violence had the largest decrease: 36 per cent stated that they had ceased using this kind of violence. Slightly fewer had ceased using severe physical violence (30 per cent) and severe psychological violence (23 per cent).

Even though some of the men had ceased using violence, it is clear that substantial proportions of men had continued to use different types of violence. Most had continued to use minor psychological violence (81 per cent). One fifth had continued using severe physical violence and more than one third had continued using severe psychological violence. For many types of violence the results also show that substantial proportions of men either at pre- or post-measurements reported they had used them. 75 per cent said they had never exercised minor sexual violence, 68 per cent said they had never caused severe injuries to their partner and nearly half (47 per cent) answered that they had never used severe physical violence.

---

[5] Of the four men who had used severe sexual violence three reported that they had ceased using this kind of violence.

Mental health

The men's mental health was examined via self-assessment scale Symptom Checklist-90 (SCL-90), which consists of 90 questions measuring a person's experience of various psychiatric symptoms. At the pre-measurement stage, the self-perceived mental health of the men was significantly worse than for an average group of Swedish men. The average values of 10 of the 12 indexes and sub-scales of the SCL-90 ended up at a level similar to a group of male patients who participated in a study when the Swedish version of the SCL-90 was standardised (Armelius et al., 2010). The patient group in the standardisation study consisted of patients with neurosis, borderline and psychosis diagnoses and patients with a heavy drug use. Their average value was 1.02 in an index which indicates the general level of psychological difficulties, called global difficulty index. The corresponding value for men in the present study was the same as for the patient group, 1.02. For the men in the "average group" the mean value was 0.32.The two sub-scales in which the abusive men differed from the patient group was a sub-scale for hostility, where the mean for the abusive men was significantly higher, and a sub-scale of phobic anxiety, were the abusive men had a substantially lower value than the patient group. Yet, the value for phobic anxiety was still higher for the abusive men than for the "average men".

Changes in mental health

At post-measurement, the men's mental health had improved. The average values of all indexes and sub-scales were significantly lower, although still higher than the group of "average men". The mean global index of difficulty was 0.76. Here too, the 48 men who were lost in the follow-up are included in the analysis and are seen as unchanged.

Alcohol

Alcohol use was examined using the screening instrument Audit. Audit measures the alcohol habits, hazardous drinking and signs of addiction and alcohol abuse (Armelius et al, 2010). Of the men included in the study, 5 per cent reported no alcohol consumption at all at the time of the pre-measurements. The proportion of men with hazardous drinking levels was 30 per cent, while the proportion of men with signs of addiction and alcohol abuse was 7 per cent. These proportions can be compared with men in Sweden's general population, where 10 per cent of the men did not consume any alcohol, 18 per cent were in the hazardous drinking group and only a few men had signs of addiction and alcohol abuse (Bergman, 2000).

Changes in alcohol abuse

For all of the men in the study, the alcohol problems had decreased 12 months after they were included in the study. The decrease was significant. The change could have been explained by the fact that some men (14) also participated in drug treatment at the same time as the treatment for their violent behaviour. Still, the difference between pre- and post-measurements remains when this fact is taken into consideration.

The men's opinion of the treatment

One year after the men started their treatment, they also got the opportunity to express what they thought about the treatment. Approximately 90 per cent answered that they were satisfied with the treatment and thought it was of a high quality. Over half (54 per cent) considered the treatment had given them great help in handling their problems in a better way and another 40 per cent said they had received some help with their problems. The men were also given the opportunity to comment, in their own words, on some of the questions. More than half took advantage of this opportunity, and some expressed very clearly that the treatment had been a great change for them. Below are quotes from two different men:
"To contact the programme voluntarily – that I had to make the decision on my own – was probably important. It was probably the best thing that could have happened. All the punishment in the world would not have worked as well as this. I am very happy that this was possible and I cannot describe how grateful I am for this. This has positively changed my whole view of myself and those I live with."
"...it feels like there is more love, they [the children] come to me and say 'daddy, daddy'."
Several men commented on how they had been changed by the treatment, for example: "I have become better at dealing with conflicts", "I have become safer", "I have become calmer", "I have gained a greater self-awareness", "I have gained more understanding of what triggers

psychological violence" and "I have realised that jealousy should not exist in a relationship".

Several men also pointed out that they had gained an insight into their alcohol and substance abuse problems and had done something about them thanks to the treatment. One man wrote that the programme was great because "it showed me the way to another treatment, at the alcohol clinic".

Women's views on the men's treatment and the Women's Safety Worker Programme

The few women who participated in the study were of the opinion that the men had changed for the better after the treatment. Of the 12 who still had contact with the men at the time of the post-measurements, only one woman responded that her husband still used the same level of violence as he did prior to the treatment. Nine women responded that the men avoided the use of violence in situations where they previously used to exercise it, and two women replied that the men never ended up in situations like that anymore. One woman said:

"They have taught my husband that a discussion does not have to end in violence. They have taught him how to discuss."

Ten of the 14 women were satisfied with the Women's Safety Worker Programmes. These ten women had all been in regular contact with the Safety Workers. The four women who were less satisfied with the programme stated that they had only been contacted a few times and that they would have preferred a more frequent level of contact.

Discussion and conclusion

The results indicate that the violence decreased in the short term. The men's mental health also improved and alcohol use decreased. A primary conclusion is that the treatment doesn't seem to be harmful, a conclusion that has not been ruled out by a North American research review (Feder, Wilsson and Austin, 2008).

Another conclusion is that the reduction in violence already occurred during treatment. Although the follow-up measurements, in most cases, were carried out after the men had finished their treatment, the questions in The Revised Conflict Tactics Scale (CTS2) address what happened in the past year, and that period largely coincided with the treatment period. During the follow-up study, in many cases the men referred to the period when they were still in treatment when answering the CTS2 questions. Maybe this fact underestimated the results, since it might be possible that the treatment needed more time to have a full effect. With only one follow-up at 12 months, it is also impossible to know the treatment's more long-term effect.

In order to deal with these shortcomings, follow-ups must continue over a longer period. The use of data other than the men's own answers, such as police records, would also give a more solid result. In this case, it will be possible to analyse data on violent crime from the police. Hopefully such data will be available at the end of 2011.

As the men themselves reported on their use of violence, it is likely that they underestimated it, but the decrease in the reported violence probably corresponds to a real decrease anyway. Their underestimation was most likely greater at the pre-measurement stage than at the follow-up, because, among other things, the main focus in the treatment programmes was responsibility for violence. Therefore, the real decrease may be even larger than reported. The analyses are also based on the conservative assumption that the men that were lost to the follow up did not change their behaviour, which may have led to an underestimation rather than an overestimation of the results.

The improvements affected all three types of programmes. This makes it difficult to determine whether improvements were due to treatment or not. In order to determine this, a control group which did not receive any treatment is called for. But such a research approach was not possible in this case.

Other reasons for the decrease in violence could be a firm decision by the men to stop using violence, which led to the results regardless of the treatment. Or it could be self-healing or a passage of time that led to the solving of a crisis. The latter could, for example, explain the improvement in mental health. On the other hand, most men claimed that it was the treatment that helped them to change their behaviour and make them feel better. Nonetheless, the question could only be given a more certain answer if it would have been possible to use an untreated control group as a comparison.

The fact that the results did not clearly differ between the three groups of programmes is consistent with international research, which has rarely found any significant differences in outcomes between different treatments against violence (Saunders, 2008). One reason may be that the actual differences between the treatment programmes for this group are small. Our own efforts in trying to describe the programmes indicate this.

With a more comprehensive documentation and regular follow-ups of men over longer periods, the therapists working with the men should be able to systematise their experiences and evaluate and develop their own approaches to treatment in a clearer way. Such local follow-up would be easier if the programmes were given access to a simple monitoring/evaluation instrument.

In summary, the results of this evaluation are promising, even though it is a fact that most of the men did not change their behaviour. We must, however, bear in mind that men using violence in intimate relationships presumably need more than one course of treatment to change their behaviour. There is a need for studies over longer periods and studies that can better determine what the active factors in the treatment are. Nevertheless, the results indicate that treatment can reduce male violence against women in intimate relationships. The programmes need to develop their documentation and amend their methods of follow-up to improve their progress. Finally, this study shows that it is quite possible to get men who have used violence in intimate relationships to participate in evaluation studies, which is a positive result in itself.

References

Armelius, B-Å., et. al. (2010) *BiB 2010. Bedömningsinstrument inom behandling och forskning för missbruks- och beroendevården.* Stockholm: Statens institutionsstyrelse (SIS).

Bergman, H. and Källmen, H. (2000) Befolkningens alkoholvanor enligt AUDIT-testet. *Läkartidningen* , 97(17), pp.2078-2084.

Dobash Emerson, R., Dobash, R. P., Cavanagh, K. and Lewis, R. (2000) *Changing violent men.* Thousand Oaks: Sage Publications.

Edleson, J. L. and Tolman, R. M. (1992) *Intervention for men who batter. An ecological approach.* Newbury Park: Sage Publications.

Ericson, Christina. (2005) *Kvinnor och män i kriminalpolitiska motioner 1971-2000. En analys i ljuset av tre feministiska perspektiv.* Stockholm: Kriminologiska institutionen.

Feder, L., Wilsson, D. B. and Austin, S. (2008) *Court-Mandated Interventions for Individuals Convicted of Domestic Violence.* Campbell Systematic Reviews, 2008:12, DOI: 10.4073/csr.2008.12.

Gondolf, E. W. (2002) *Batterer intervention systems. Issues, outcomes and recommendations.* Thousand Oaks: Sage Publications.

Gondolf, E. W. (2004) Evaluating batterer counseling programs: A difficult task showing some effects and implications. *Aggression and Violent Behaviour*, 9(6), pp.695–713.

Saunders, D. G. (2008) Group Interventions for Men Who Batter: A Summary of Program Descriptions and Research. *Violence and Victims*, 23(2), pp.156–172.

Straus, M. A., Hamby, S. L. and Warren, W. L. (2003) *The Conflict Tactics Scale Handbook.* Los Angeles: Western Psychological Services.

WHO, 2003 (2003) *Perspectives with Perpetrators of Intimate Partner Violence: A Global Perspective.*

13.

GENDER, VIOLENCE AND LAW IN THE POST-FEMINIST AND QUEER DEBATE IN ITALY.

Caterina Peroni

The Italian post feminist debate: a genealogy

The aim of this article is to analyse the post-feminist point of view on gender violence and criminal law in Italy. The topic and the analysis approach I have chosen set in a crucial place within the Italian political and public debate, where feminisms have had a central role in defining gender violence as a security and control device whose goal is to shape and to discipline gender relations.

While the theoretical basis where Italian post-feminist movements are grounded is post-modern and radical feminism, it is not possible to forget the genealogy of the feminist movements in Italy. This genealogy speaks about the epistemological revolution fostered by the development of the feminist perspective since the half of the 70s. This revolution is based on two fundamental aspects.

On the one hand we found the criticism of the so-called neutrality of science (Harding, 2004), whose universal subject is typically male, white, and owner: such paradigm doesn't consider sexuality, unbalanced and control relations and the real social and economical position of flesh and blood people within society.

On the other hand, and consequently, feminist epistemology is based on a scientific research approach which is necessarily partial and politically orientated. Therefore it develops methodologies and research practices focused on the concept of *experience* (Butler and Scott 1992). As De Lauretis (1984) states:

"Experience is the process by which, for all social beings, subjectivity is constructed. Through that process one places oneself or is placed in social reality and so perceives and comprehends as subjective (referring to, originating in oneself) those relations – material, economic, and interpersonal – which are in fact social, and, in a larger perspective, historical" (De Lauretis, 1984, quoted in Butler and Scott, 1992).

In fact, "starting from us" is the synthesis of the feminist perspective on scientific research and its social role, that is defining and analyzing the social problems detected through the key analytic category of experience (Terragni, 1998; Scott, 1992). Thus we can identify the deep intersection between subject and object of the research, whose goals are at least political.

The critical feminist movements of the 70s built a structural link between scientific research and social analysis during a historical period of radical social and cultural change, especially in Italy, where we still suffer the strong political influence of the Vatican.

Criticizing heteronormative society. From gender to violence: the use of criminal law on gender violence and the feminist point of view

The most difficult conflict has developed concerning the institution of the traditional family, seen as the place where exploitation, subordination and control of women happens, and regarding the regressive law that supported this model. Examples are abortion, divorce, and sexual abuse (Libreria delle donne, 2005). A new law against sexual abuse was approved only in 1996 after 20 years of public debate.

All these topics concerned the structure of the hierarchical order of relationships between genders, women's self-determination, and sexual independence. It was a political, social, and cultural revolution which involved not only women, but the entire society. Feminist movements denounced the role which laws played in shaping the family, sexuality, and reproduction: the norms fixed the gender roles which trap women in the reproductive function (Pitch, 1998). They defined what "normal" female sexuality is, limiting sexual freedom.

The focus of this article is on the debate regarding the law of sexual abuse which has been developed during the 80's and 90's. The debate introduces 2 closely related aspects that make up the genealogy of the actual feminist debate. These aspects are the bio-political function of sexuality devices, and the criticism of the use of criminal law.

These two items were grounded on a hard theoretical confrontation within the feminist perspective itself about the function of the criminal law as the most useful instrument to discipline relationship conflicts (Libreria delle donne, 2005; Pitch, 1998). This debate is still open.

On one side it was considered strategically useful recurring to criminal justice to make private violence a public matter: this perspective was grounded on the idea that feminist issues needed a legal and symbolic recognition. Today we can see it translated in the equal opportunities movement, represented by leftwing party women.

On the other side, the critical radical feminisms aimed to produce a "light" law on every issue concerning self-determination in the field of sexuality and relationships, for example about abortion and reproduction's choices. The state's intervention through the laws was seen as an improper and violent imposition of ethic criteria which would violate women's freedom.

Concerning the law on sexual violence, the main debate developed around its symbolic function and about the biopolitical consequences it would have produced.

The normative acknowledge of women victim of violence as person (I remind that until 1996 rape was considered a crime against public moral), paid a very high cost. First, the simplification of sexual relationship, whose complexity was reduced to the couple "norm" and "deviance"; second, the equivalence of the women's subjectivity as weak and victimized; third, the representation of sexuality itself like a intrinsically dangerous field of life where it is necessary a repressive intervention by the state, excluding women's voice and their chances to transform the power differentials between genders; fourth, the emergency on violence, seen as an extraordinary event even if it's a structural phenomenon in the unbalanced gender relation; at least, the production and governance of normal and deviant sexualities.

Indeed, sexual violence has a so deep symbolic impact on society that some feminist sociologists define it a total social fact. It is a paradigm which represents women's body as naturally weak, needing state's protection; that is the basis of the emergency speech and, through it, of the security laws. At the same time, the production of normal and deviant sexualities is a biopolitical control device whose aim is to regulate reproduction and govern the whole society.

The use of gender violence as a identity device: the murder of ms Reggiani and the law against the immigration (2007)

Today in the security frame, gender violence has become a device as well: it is exploited to produce a public speech on a public enemy threat circulating in our cities, that now are dangerous, degraded, insecure. The first victims of insecurity are white and native women, who are the object of state's protection, meaning repressive and police control of the cities (Simone, 2010; Pitch, 1998).

In the October 2007 ms Giovanna Reggiani was brutally murdered by a romani immigrant and a great relevance was given to this event by the mass media. Giovanna Reggiani was a middle-class woman, married with a respected navy admiral, and the violence she suffered had a big effect in the public opinion.

The problem of security and its link to immigration was the main topic in the public and political debate, while a new law on security was being discussed in parliament. After the murder of ms Reggiani, the government proposed a very repressive and prohibitionist law against irregular immigration, that was harshly criticized by the left-wing parties and the immigrant and antiracist associations: that episode become immediately the pretext to step over all the oppositions, approving in 24 hours the most questionable norm of the law, the one that provided the immediate expulsion of communitarian citizens (as romani are) if considered guilty of very heavy crimes. At the same time, the murder of Giovanna Reggiani opened another argument strictly interconnected to the topic of security: the exploitation of Italian women's body as a symbol of Italian identity and ethnicity defense.

In this way, the frame of violence against (white, wealthy, respectable) women was linked to the criminalization of immigrant men, defined as an objective dangerous social category for women and consequently for every honest citizen. That's nothing new.

"Not in my name!": Post feminist movements and the critique to the security laws

One month later, in concomitance with the world day against violence on women promoted by the United Nations, feminist movements organized a big demonstration whose name was "Not in my name", with a clear reference to the opposition to the anti constitutional law approved in parliament. Evidently the title of the demonstration was referred to the war declared by the government to irregular immigrant people, and to the improper use of the violence against women to increase the social alarm on immigration. Some parliamentary women went to the demonstration, but they have been chased away by the demonstrators.

Furthermore, there was a conflict between feminist groups, around the possibility or not for men to be present at the parade. On one side there were separatist feminists, on the other new feminist groups whose political aim was the opposition to violence against women by men and women.

On the grounds of this interior conflict there were two different approaches on gender violence: an essentialist approach, derived from the feminism of difference developed in the 70s, and a deconstructive or postmodernist vision of gender itself, seen as the (production) device of differences and inequality. For these movements, the consequence of the heterosexual norm is the submission and victimization of women.

It wasn't possible to overcome this conflict: on the streets of Rome there was a parade of "women for women", but the movements interior debate, and over all the younger ones, has prosecuted later on.

    a) The theoretical background of the younger feminists: nomadism, deconstructionism, situated knowledge.

The gap between the two feminist perspectives turns around the meaning given to the gender identity and depends on the activists' composition, considering how the younger have often lived other movements' experience, not only with reference to feminism and other gender issues, and most of them are working in gender and women's studies.

The post-feminist criticism is directed to the normative gender categories, seen as the grounds of social hierachization and control.

This approach is grounded on the intersection between postmodernism and feminism, critical and postcolonial studies and queer theory.

Crucial to this approach is the concept of nomadism, meaning situated and embodied knowledge elaborated by Braidotti, Harding and Haraway: in this approach it is possible and necessary to build a self-reflexive knowledge grounded in experience of real and multiple-becoming bodies that are moving in the communication, physic and political spaces.

In other terms the question posed by nomadism is on one hand how we can identify the subjectivity and normative devices?, and, on the other hand, where subjectivity could get free into nomadism and build dynamic non- hierarchical relation with other subjectivities? This theory employs

"A self-reflexive mode of analysis, aimed at articulating the critique of power in discourse with the affirmation of alternative forms of subjectivity... at the articulation of questions of individual gendered identity with issues related to political subjectivity"

The nomadic category, in its disassembling identity, takes distance from both naturalization and culturalization of genders: multiple sexual subjectivities disrupt in the post-feminist scenario, overcoming the binary code of gender, thus becoming an expression of desire and no more a matter of destiny.

This approach enlarges the speech on the (hetero)-sexual norm and the subjectivity devices, that are now marked by the multiple tools of control on our bodies and at least on our lives.

As Braidotti (2005) said: "The project on nomadic subjects emerges from feminist philosophies, post-colonial philosophies and anti-racist philosophies, critical theory, social theory. [...] We have to think about the multiple forms of belonging of subjects and map out different configurations of nomadism, different ways in which a subject can have multiple belongings, multiple ways in which ethnicity, nationality and citizenship can actually be combined, even within the same nation state"

b) The ambivalence of security in the postmodern age: precarity, gender, sexuality, social control

In Italy, together with the alarm on security, there has developed a debate on de facto couples and on the artificial insemination technologies. These are two items deeply interconnected to the discipline of legitimate reproduction and of the definition of sexualities and genders. In both cases, the point was that all the different subjectivities not involved in the hetero-sexual norm were excluded from the legal horizon and especially in the case of artificial insemination this happens even to not married hetero-sexual couples.

The result of these normative categories means that many sections of the population are excluded from the welfare state, and I think that this point in the world economic crisis is not insignificant at all.

That's why the categories of "precarization", "welfare crisis", security, immigration, and so on are intersected within the post-feminist political debate: all these aspects contribute to the subjectivation of everyone in an articulate and complex way. As Fantone (2007) argues:

"In the late 1990s, political activists reclaimed the term *precario* in an attempt to raise consciousness and dissent over increasing temporary work contracts. The use of the word *precario* became common, and was used with increasing pride by the year 2000. This change was inspired by the similar successes of reclaiming words like "gay" and "queer", based on a strategic use of political irony and *detournement*, borrowed from situationism and other politically savvy forms of communication.

(...) at the same time, some young feminists were discussing their own precarious work conditions. They soon developed a critique not only of precariousness in relation to a flexible market but also of other less flexible societal structures affecting their lives, such as heterosexual marriage, maternity, care-work and corporate brand loyalty".

In the Italian post-feminist speech there is a deep relation between the gender issues, the control of sexuality, the economic and social role of men and women, and the concept of security.

The reflection on violence as a device through which it is built the frame of security law is situated in the context of a raising uncertainty rooted into the economical and social crises which, in Bauman's perspective intensify the insecurity and solitude perception.

In this context the equivalence immigration = urban blight = fear is necessary to designate immigrant men as the scapegoat for all evils of society. This category is moreover useful if we want to understand why in the mass media and in the public debate it is often represented the outdoor violence and not the intimate one: linking violence to a man coming from abroad permits us not to face to our hetero-sexual reality: in Italy one-third of women in their life has been raped or hit, and almost the 60% of them have been raped or hit by their partner or ex partner.

Pretending that this is not the crucial problem of gender violence is like affirming and confirming the existence of natural sexual roles, that is to say that the unbalanced relation between genders is not modifiable. This is the deepest reason of the hetero-sexual norm which stands beyond the biopolitical social order.

Moreover, the identities placed aside from the hetero-sexual norm are removed from the public space: gay lesbians, bisex, intersex and transgender, meaning all the different kind of sexuality deriving from the free expression of desire.

In this norm the feminine gender is "naturalized" as weak and the masculine as strong: the consequence of this speech identity is that there will always be someone to defend, and this requires a response.

Focusing on gender violence in this way uphold the communities of belonging to defend against an unknown and dangerous stranger. This is the area where security laws have been growing.

Post-feminist movements against gender violence and social control: the "Transgender" campaign (2010)

Coming back to the post-feminist movements, in Italy they still have no name and organization, while they are composed by many groups that meet up for national campaigns. Since the roman demonstration "Not in my name" there is continuity exactly on the issues of security, social control and main speech on the hetero-sexual norm: the security paradigm was exploiting the (stranger) violence against (Italian) women to consolidate the hetero-sexual social order.

Moreover, the identities exceeding the hetero-sexual norm are excluded from the public space: gay lesbians, bisex, intersex and transgender, meaning all the different kind of sexuality deriving from the free expression of desire. This is the main topic for queer movements to transform the social hetero order.

The first of May of last year the Mayday parade crossed the streets of Milano. Since 2000 it has been the most important (somehow the only) demonstration against precariousness in Italy: it gathers all the movements which are fighting against generational precariousness, temporary work, migrant labor and job insecurity.

At the end of the parade an Egyptian citizen ropes a girl. The matter immediately becomes political and the organizers take the responsibility upon themselves to face this problem. Their main question is: "how could it be possible that it happens in our parade?". The answer was that in 10 years it has never been politically considered a gender connotation of the parade, as if "gender stuff" were less important than the strong matters of the labor market configuration. After the revelation it's not less important, but it crosses all the matters they were facing, the organization called all the feminist, gender and glbt movements and groups to make gender mainstream for the next parade. The idea was that the Mayday parade of 2010 would have been characterized by the presence of "gender stuff", after a deep and involving discussion about violence, exploitation and sexuality.

This project is called "Transgender", to underline the necessary overcoming of sexual and gender identity to open new free spaces of movement.

We think that the movement needs to work above thoughts and practices that fight sexism, such as it has taken on the anti-racist and antifascist struggles. Mayday organization is fighting precarization and ex-

ploitation, against the commercialization of our lives, but there's no possibility for liberation without facing the gender matters.

We want to contribute to build up together a safe Mayday parade without security practices, and developing communicating tools to react against violence.

We need to work with imaginaries and cultural models who produce gender violence, without reproduce the stereotype of women as victim. Our aim is to communicate anti-sexist thoughts and practices also in our politic worlds and movements.

I personally attended all the Transgender meetings, following step by step the development of the campaign. There were all the movements which attend to gender and sexuality, most of which define themselves queer.

The first point of the discussion concerned security: the question was "how can we make the parade safe for all?". Although the call underlined clearly the necessity to overcome the "security paradigm" the first answer was quite paradoxical, because it proposed to make up a security service which should have watched on the parade.

But this proposal was considered alarmist and related to the mainstream speeches on security by the majority of the groups present at the meeting. It also would have increased the insecurity perception by an exclusively repressive point of view. Thus it wouldn't be affirmed the aim to face in a political and critical way the problem of gender violence, starting from our political point of view.

Infact, if our analysis on security paradigm were directed to deconstruct the security and violence concept itself through a strong criticism on gender model and stereotypes, it was necessary to analyze more deeply the sexual identities and use them to reverse the gender unbalanced model.

At the same time another problem was to make clear the contrast between the security imaginary and the one we wanted to oppose as alternative: instead of control and repression, sociality, solidarity and attention to what was happening around us during the parade. The idea was that everyone had to be responsible not only of the safety of the others, but also of the political involving of every one present at the parade.

After this briefing, we had the name of the campaign: "Let's re-gender places, imaginaries, culture. I don't delegate responsibility – I care who's around me"[1].

This name is a play on words on the term gender: on one side it means to regenerate places etc, on the other to use the lens of gender to read the world around us, for it's not neutral but always gendered. The suffix ri- indicates the repetition that overcomes the dualist vision of genders and makes it excessive. In other words, gender in this way become an empty box in which we can put all our infinite desires, inclinations, and potentialities. The object – places, imaginaries and culture – are the three main fields in which, for the activists, the problem of security by a gendered point of view is more meaningful.

In fact, the real and metaphorical places they wanted to "regenderate" are the cities in which we live, the imaginaries which build up gender stereotypes, and the culture of diversity.

The second point was: how can we communicate our positive and strong feeling about security and gender to the participants at the parade? The idea was to deal some double-sided printing cards with texts and pictures: cards are very easy to hand out, and people can bring them home. Furthermore, the communication factor of pictures is very important for its immediate impact, and a short text beyond will explain the message.

The three items of the campaign – places, imaginaries and culture – become as many cards, added to a general explanation of the reason of the campaign and a little sticker-badge everyone will dress like security staff always do: thus everyone becomes part of the staff, responsible of what's happening during the parade.

The FIRST CARD is the general one. The picture is divided in two parts and represents on one side the repressive, dark, grey, desert and full of cameras and tanks city, on and the other the colored, lively, and joyful one, the one we prefer of course. There are a girl and a boy crossing the border through a gate that represents the general brand of the campaign: the masculine and feminine symbol composing a circle, giving the idea of the continuity between genders.

Close up in our favorite city a drag queen is dancing, which symbolizes the crossing of genders as a liberation act from control and repression. The text states:

---

[1] http://rigeneriamo.noblogs.org/archives/, http://italy.euromayday.org/generi/laboratorio-trans-generi/.

Let's re-gender us! During last year a network of women and men, groups and individuals has reflected over the episode of male violence against a girl happened last year during the mayday parade.

Have you got it? Our spaces are not free by violence and machismo!

Precarity, exploitation and blackmailing are exceeding job's dimension and invade life, affects and relations. Mayday claims it since 10 years. The card you're handling now is a bet to re-gendering actual masculine and feminine models which are trapping our desires, our freedom and self-determination. We are betting on a Mayday where violence has no citizenship, and on a future without fear! We want to crash the schemes which are reproducing injustice, abuses and violence. Only starting from us we can refuse and subvertize normative identity roles and stereotypic models of femininity and masculinity. To crash those rules which want us to be macho men and weak women? To give voice to our desires, our bodies and to meet the other's. (?) To be free to express freely and fearless, in this parade and in our daily life.

Against the gender violence (any physical, sexual or psychological violence based on intolerance and discrimination related to gender and sexual orientation) it is necessary to re-gender cultural models.

The SECOND CARD, the place's one, shows on the background the dichotomy "security city-favorite city we prefer" and here the accent is on the contrast between pervasive control of grey desert and scaring city from which boys escape to go to a city where there's a party, with dancing people.

The reference is to the repressive bylaws promulgated by many local municipalities, which exploiting the security speech have closed to people the historical centers of the towns, providing the anticipated closing of bars, pubs and meeting places. The aim of those bylaws was to prevent young people from disturbing the public peace, seen as the cause of deterioration of public spaces.

As maybe you had the occasion to see, the result of these policies is quite depressing: the squares and the streets of many towns are desert, and this increases the perception of fear more than it reduces it. Living the city, having fun and socializing is the reply proposed as one of the solutions to the perception of fear exploited by the municipalities.

The THIRD CARD represents the famous scene of Hitchcock's Psycho: but instead of Norman and the girl we can see on the curtain the threatening shadow of a man brandishing a big phallus on his hand and a terrified boy in the shower. The symbolism is very clear, isn't it? The picture is explained by a sentence: "I don't hate gay people so long as they don't try it on me!". This is a word game that hint at the hypocrisy of the tolerance classic speech ("I do tolerate as long as it doesn't concern me").

The text on the back if possible is even clearer:

Even if you didn't realize it, thanks to feminist, lesbian, homosexual, transgender and queer movements, since 30 years it's no more obligatory getting married, making sex to procreate, keeping the same anatomic sex from your birth, being heterosexuals! But in 7 countries homosexuality is still punished with death by law and in 80 with jail.

Self-determination of women, gay, lesbians, trans, queer is not a thread but an opportunity of freedom for all! Relax: you can also stop in hide yourself when you see a transgender! And tablets of soap have been substituted by handy bubble baths. Just try to manage your ass hole more quietly: you can use it also in heterosexual intercourses! If a gay, a lesbian, a trans or an ambiguousness sex person tries it on you don't worry! The free circulation of desire is a commons! (?) If your friends laugh at your sexual diversity, you can always shirk or change your friends!

Let's refuse the intolerance against homosexuals, lesbians, trans and who increases it.

Against hate and prejudice we want free and ri-gendered desires

The FOURTH CARD is dedicated to the gender stereotypes in the heterosexual norm. Also this background is divided in two parts but this time it's characterized by colors: one side is pink and the other is blue, the gendered colors of feminine and masculine *par excellance*. Figures are a woman and a man, which exaggerate their respective stereotypic social roles: she is a housewife, with her Hoover, a rolling pin, baby and shopping bags; he is super macho man, with a cigar, dollars, football ball and a macho book. All these elements are drawn as if they were stickers, and suggesting the idea that the construction of gendered social roles is a game for children. The element which unites the two halves of the background, like two parallel worlds, is a painting hung to the wall which says: "home sweet home" over a couple of crossed knives, reminding us that the home is the more dangerous place for women. But what the two features say in the bubbles is in contrast with the whole pictures: she says "we are fed up with these roles that taste mouldy!" And he answers: "we want to be free to be what we want to be!".

On the back the text says:

We were born female or masculine... or this is the legend we are told. Just to be fussy, there's who born with both the sexes or who feels ill at ease with his natural sex and looks for another identity which makes him feel better. We don't born men and women: we become it! It doesn't matter if you're born with a willie or two tits, but how you want to live with your willie or your tits... or why not? With both of them! It's clear it's not easy, because we are persecuted by stereotypes and cultural models. If you're a man and you have relations with a lot of women you're cool. If you're a woman and also have relations with a lot of men you're a bitch. If you're a sensible guy and you're a man you won't have a simple life. If you're a women and you don't want to make children (?) you're not regular. Men like a hunt, women like a prey; women at home, men at work.

Aren't we fed up with these roles that taste mouldy? Are we still believing that there is an only right way to be men and women and that there's not anything in the between? How better would be the world if people could play with their identities defying all the borders? Gender is a desire, not a destiny!

We want to be free to be who we want to be.

Let's re-gender the roles. Against closed identity and stereotypes, to rigender relations!

Let's re-gender imaginaries.

Finally, the sticker of the "security staff":

I don't delegate responsibilities – I care who's around me

Let's re-gender places, imaginary and culture

We don't want to live in prohibitionist cities under siege by army, we want to cross streets full of people who look after the others, not empty by patrol – we want to live in warm towns for all, natives and migrants, women-trans-men. Let's look around us to not look beyond us.

To be continued...

After all that, I propose a short reflection on the importance of the link between situated knowledge, definition of social problems and research that I mentioned in the beginning. The experience of this campaign demonstrates that this link is necessary to formulate practicable answers starting from the real needs of subjects involved. I think that the most important result in this case has not been the solution of the problem but the subjectivation process it has started. This is one of the most interesting aspects of the feminist methodology that in its different branches puts at the center of its speech the person, her desires, her experience and above all the conflicts in which she is situated.

A lot of questions are still open in my research: the distance between the juridical control of sexuality and social change, the effects of the policies against violence, the introduction of gender issue into movements' practices and theories.

References

AA.VV., (2006). *Lessico di biopolitica*. Roma: Manifestolibri.

Adami, C., Basaglia, A., Bimbi, F., Tola, V. (eds.) (2000). *Libertà femminile e violenza sulle donne*, Milano: FrancoAngeli.

Baratta, A. (1982). *Criminologia critica e critica del diritto penale*. Bologna: il Mulino.

Braidotti, R. (2003). Il pensiero femminista nomade. *Posse*, Apr. 2003. Manifestolibri, pp. 93-106.

Braidotti, R. (2005). A critical cartography of feminist post-postmodernism, *Australian Feminist Studies*, Vol. 20, no. 47, pp. 1-15.

Butler, J. (2004). *Scambi di genere. Identità, sesso e desiderio*. Milano: Sansoni.

Butler, J. (2006). *La disfatta del genere*. Roma: Meltemi

Dal Lago, A. (1999). *Nonpersone*. Milano: Feltrinelli.

Duden, B. (2007). *Il corpo della donna come luogo pubblico*. Bologna: Bollati Boringheri

Fantone, L. (2007). Precarious changes: gender and generational politics in contemporary Italy, *Feminist Review*, 87, pp 5-21.

Ferrari, V. (1997). *Lineamenti di sociologia del diritto. I. Azione e società*. Bari: Laterza

Ferrari, V. (2009). *Diritto e Società*. Roma: Laterza

Foucault, M. (1977). *Microfisica del potere*. Torino: Einaudi

Foucault, M. (2004). *Nascita della biopolitica*. Milano: Feltrinelli

Foucault, M. (2004). *Sicurezza, territorio, popolazione*. Milano: Feltrinelli

Foucault, M. (2008). *La volontà di sapere*. Milano: Feltrinelli

Garland, D. (2007). *La cultura del controllo. Crimine e ordine sociale nel mondo contemporaneo*. Milano: Il saggiatore.

Girard, R. (1987). *Il capro espiatorio*. Milano: Adelphi.

Harding, S. (2004). *The feminist standpoint theory reader*. London: Routledge.

ISTAT, *La violenza e i maltrattamenti contro le donne dentro e fuori la famiglia* Anno 2006: www.istat.it/salastampa/comunicati/non_calendario/20070221_00/testoi ntegrale.pdf.

Libreria delle Donne, (2005). *Non credere di avere diritti*. Torino: Rosenberg & Sellier.

Mosconi, G. (2000). *Criminalità, sicurezza e opinione pubblica in Veneto*. Padova: Cleup.

Naletto, G. (2009). *Razzismo democratico*. Roma: Manifestolibri.

Pitch, T. (1989). *Responsabilità Limitate. Attori, conflitti, giustizia penale*. Milano: Feltrinelli.

Pitch, T. (1998). *Un diritto per due. La costruzione giuridica di sesso, genere e sessualità*. Milano: Il Saggiatore

Pitch, T. (2000). Introduzione, in *Quaderni di città sicure*, Bologna, 6 (19).

Pitch, T. (2008). *La società della prevenzione*. Roma: Carocci.

Pitch, T., Ventimiglia, C. (2001). *Che genere di sicurezza. Donne e uomini in città*. Milano: Franco Angeli.

Romito, P. (2008). *Un silenzio assordante. La violenza occultata su donne e minori*. Milano: FrancoAngeli.

Sabbadini, L. L. (2002). *La sicurezza dei cittadini : un approccio di genere*. Sistema Statistico Nazionale, Roma: Istituto Nazionale di Statistica.

Scott, J. W. (1992). *Experience*, in Butler, J., Scott, J. W. eds., *Feminists theorize the political*. London: Routledge.

Simondi, Mario, Pavarini M., R. Grandi (eds). (1985). *I segni di Caino*. Napoli: Edizioni scientifiche napoletane.

Simone, A. (2010). *I corpi del reato. Sessualità e sicurezza nelle società del rischio*. Milano: Mimesis.

Terragni, L. (1998). *La ricerca di genere,* in Melucci, A., *Verso una sociologia riflessiva. Ricerca qualitativa e cultura*. Bologna: Il Mulino.

14.

'LITTLE INNOCENTS NO MORE': CRIMINALISING
CHILDHOOD SEXUALITY IN THE UK.'

Jane Harris

In May 2010 three children aged 8 and ten were involved in a rape trial at the Old Bailey in London. This paper offers some critical reflections on the dilemmas faced by children who are in law, both conferred responsibility yet denied agency. It is an attempt to draw together some rather exploratory thoughts on the broader concerns about sexual offences and the shifting discourse on children and sexual agency. It is hoped it will also provide an opportunity for us to think about the construction and regulation of childhood, sexuality and the potential for an ethical discussion about children and sex. To avert any misconceptions it is important to emphasise that the argument is not to deny that children harm others; in particular it is not suggested that sexual assault did not occur in the case discussed. Rather it is intended to raise questions about appropriate state responses and your responses and discussion are welcomed.

The Case

The case concerns three very young children, boys A and B, aged ten at the time and a known playmate of theirs, an 8 year old girl. On October 22nd 2009, while playing with the boys on local playing fields, the girl alleged she had been forced to touch the boys' genitals and that they had 'penetrated' her. The girl's mother called the police who arranged for a specially trained female PC to interview the girl and the police continued with the inquiry (Jones 2010).

The Crown Prosecution Service (CPS) prosecuted the young boys on two counts of rape and two counts of attempted rape each under the Sexual Offences Act 2003. The public trial lasted two weeks and was widely reported in the national press and television news. The crown court room was 'adapted' to be more child friendly, in as much as the symbolic clothing of courtroom theatre and seating arrangements altered. Even with modifications this must surely have been a most intimidating and bewildering environment for all three children. Artist impressions depicted the two boys sat at their mothers' side.

It was alleged that boys A and B, playmates of the girl, had taken it in turn to assault her during the afternoon in October 2009. The jury was shown a video of the girl's account, throughout which she clutched a teddy bear for comfort. As the trial progressed the jury witnessed the cross-examination of the eight year old girl via video link; during which the young girl admitted a false allegation of rape. She said she had been worried that her mother would not buy her sweets if she found out that she had been "naughty" (Pidd and Jones, 2010). Notwithstanding this the presiding Judge Saunders continued with the trial1. In the absence of any DNA evidence to link the boys to the rape allegation the girl's testimony was pivotal. After instructions from the judge to reach a majority decision the jury (6 women, 6 men) returned a majority verdict (10-2) of guilty of attempted rape but acquitted the boys of rape. Both boys were instructed by the judge to sign the Sex Offenders Register (1997). Legal representatives for both boys lodged an appeal against the conviction on the basis that the case should not have continued after the girl admitted the false allegation (Pidd and Jones 2010). The Appeal was unsuccessful with the judges supporting the trial judge's decision to continue with the trial even though the girl admitted lying. Lord Justice Hughes did however express 'dismay' that the case had ended up in an adult court, suggesting that the youth court had adequate powers to deal with the case and asserted the principle that cases involving children should always be heard in the youth court (Camber 2010). According to the Lords commentary, the Crown Prosecution Service had erred in its decision to use the 'grave crime' test for referral to the crown court

On 18th August 2010 boys A and B were given a (non –custodial) three year Supervision Order and required to stay on the Sex Offenders Register for two and a half years. The mothers were each given a 12 month Parenting Order.

On sentencing the Judge is reported to have told the boys, that he did not believe that the boys understood the seriousness of what they did (Pidd and Jones 2010) and that a custodial sentence would have been counter-productive. In response to Judge Saunders concerns Justice Secretary Kenneth Clarke has ordered a review on how children are treated in criminal courts.

---

[1] Judge Saunders expressed concern about the cross-examination but said that it was for the jury to decide on the reliability of the young witness.

Discussion

Two key areas relevant to the discussion are legislative change pertaining to criminal responsibility and sexual consent. Regarding the former, academics, lawyers, children's charities and penal reform groups are among the those publicly critical of the UK for its low age of criminal responsibility. At ten in England and Wales it is unusually low, the lowest in the European Union and one of the lowest in the world (NACRO 2002, Muncie 2009). For many years it was assumed in law that children under 14 were also incapable of criminal intent. In 1998 the Labour administration removed the rebuttal presumption of doli incapax in the Crime and Disorder Act 1998s.34, as part of its 'tough on crime' agenda. The United Nations Committee on the Rights of the Child, which monitors the implementation on the United Nations Convention, regularly urges the UK to raise the age of criminal responsibility and expresses 'particular concern' that very young children can be brought into the criminal justice system. The joint committee on human rights has also criticised the low age, in particular since the removal of doli incapax. In a rather perverse response to the criticism the government insists that early intervention is in the best interests of the child (Muncie 2009). More recently, the Independent Commission on Youth Crime called for a 'Fresh Start' yet defended the low age of criminal responsibility, suggesting it was consistent with early preventative intervention.

Children are in a contradictory position in that criminal responsibility is conferred to children in their early years yet they are without legal power to consent to sexual activity. Boys A and B were prosecuted under the Sexual Offences Act 2003 which provides that a child under 13 will not be capable in law of giving consent to any form of sexual activity. The record of the parliamentary debates shows the primary intention of the act was to clarify the definition of rape and protect children from abusive adults. It was not the intention of the law to criminalise children for early childhood errors; indeed Lord Falconer of Thoroton urged the CPS to view the public interest in the context of alternatives for children:

Even where the sexual activity is abusive, the Crown Prosecution Service may consider that it was not in the public interest to prosecute someone under 16 if other courses of action were likely to be more effective. The CPS has discretion about whether or not to prosecute in such cases. We would expect it to continue to use that discretion wisely. (Lord Falconer of Thoroton)

Crown Prosecutors in the UK have been criticised for the low conviction rate for rape and the consequences for under-reporting and women's confidence in the Criminal Justice System (Kelly, Lovatt and Regan 2005). In 2009 the Director of Public Prosecutions encouraged the CPS to take an 'active lead in improving rape conviction rates'. In an independent review of how public authorities respond to rape cases Stern records the inconsistent application of the recently adopted (2009) Police/CPS protocol for Investigating and Prosecuting Rape Cases. There is considerable pressure for public authorities to reduce the ongoing decline in conviction rates and improve the 'justice gap' (Kelly et al, 2005). It is the contention here that the decision to prosecute boys A & B cannot be removed from the current climate of criticism and the need to improve conviction rates.

The new CPS/Police protocol recognises a child rape victim poses particular challenges that does not make any special consideration for age and stresses that the serious nature of the crime should always presume prosecution if the evidence suggests a realistic prospect of conviction is satisfied (para 4.5). The CPS Chief prosecutor Alison Saunders, considered the girls statement of evidence as a 'clear and compelling' account and pointed out that she deserved, 'justice' (Camber 2010). The detail and the consistency of the girls initial account and interviews with a specially trained police officer, was clearly a factor in prosecuting the boys. In addition, the most difficult issue in rape cases is that of consent, to claim consent is the most likely and successful defence (Kelly et al, 2005). The girl's age meant the thorny issue of consent was not of legal concern, thus removing this particular burden from the decision to prosecute.

Regarding the public interest element the CPS guidance to prosecutors (Feb 2010) states that rape is so serious that a prosecution will be required in the public interest (para 4.5). Importantly the guidance instructs prosecutors to consider factors against as well as for prosecution. The Sexual Offences Act 2003, Code for Crown prosecutors states, where the accused is a child the over-riding public concern is to protect children, indeed it may not be in the 'best interests of a child or in the public interest to pursue a prosecution. This begs the question, in whose interest was the prosecution secured?

The 'clear and compelling' evidence account offered by the young girl in the early stages of the investigation (unsurprisingly) crumbled during cross-examination. Under the instructions of the judge the trial continued to the jury majority verdict, not guilty of two charges of rape but guilty of two charges of attempted rape. The boys were ordered to sign the sex offenders register and became the youngest sex offenders in Britain and subject to notification requirements for a period determined according to the length of their sentence.

Public protection is the 'driver' for notification, based on deterrent notions and assessment of 'risk'. Notification applies to all offenders without distinction for children, blurring the regulatory boundaries between children and adults. The requirement is intended to be both preventative and deterrent. Deterrence, used as a principle for sentencing adults relies on a maturity to understand the consequences of ones actions (Stone 2009). Judge Saunders raised his concerns about how the register applies to children, particularly given that there was no indication that the young boys posed a threat to other children or had previously been known to the police. Indeed the Appeal judge noted that all children involved were of impeccable character

Stone (2009) suggests that the notification requirement reflects popular and entrenched views of the sex offender as un-reformable and an enduring threat. In this regard children barely above the age of criminal responsibility who offend sexually are treated as adults and flaunting the principles of youth justice that might assist in a positive maturation.2 Examples of the children abusing others children are rare but in the last decade there have been numerous attempts to convict very young children of serious sexual offences and a rise in the criminal statistics on sexual offences committed by those under 18 years. Youth Justice Board data show 1,869 sexual offences recorded for 08/09 including 17 offences by 10 year olds and 49 offences by 11 year olds (YJB Annual workload data, May 2010). Are we witness to the 'emergence of a new social problem' of the young sexual offender? The Youth Justice Board appears to think so. In their 2006 publication, 'Young People Who Sexually Abuse' it is argued that this distinct but heterogeneous group are

---

[2] The Court of Appeal has recently concluded (2009) that 'no purpose is served by keeping on the Sex Offender's Register a person of whom it may confidently be said that there is no risk that he will commit a sexual offence' The court concluded that the case of a declaration of incompatibility with article 8 of the ECHR was even stronger with young offenders that is in the case of adult offenders (see Stone 2009)

now a 'public policy issue'. It appears the knowledge base of this new social problem draws uncritically on cognitive work with adult sex offenders, which indicates that their sexually abusive behaviour started from a much younger age. It is one matter to identify past experience but quite another matter to predict offending from what is often transitory youthful behaviour. Furthermore, Brownlie (2001) highlights a worrying development in that she suggests that since the 1990s there has been a shift away from seeing sex offences as a response/reaction to previous abuse to viewing ever younger children as 'very young children who abuse' and child perpetrators' in psychotherapeutic setting. If we place such constructions in the context of legislative change such as the removal of the presumption of innocence, the removal of the presumption that boys aged 10-13 are incapable of rape and the dominance of the at risk paradigm I suggest we are seeing the construction of children who exhibit their sexual agency as a distinct 'risky' group requiring legal and technical regulation. We must challenge adjudicators and 'knowing adults' to engage in an ethical dialogue with children about the relevance of childhood sexuality to a healthy, affirmative childhood. It appears that by erasing child sexuality from discourses of (early) childhood, (in an attempt, quite rightly, to protect children from adult abuse) evidence of its embodiment is constructed as threatening and outside childhood or defined as play (Angelides, 2004). Indeed the dominant discourse on children and sexuality is one of fear of child sex abuse by adults, where children are perceived to be without knowledge or power over their sexuality and adults with knowledge and power over theirs (Scraton and Corteen, 1997).

Concluding remarks

The decision to hold a public trial, whilst flaunting international legislation and exposing the children to criminalising, intimidating and exacting judicial processes, demonstrates that the criminal law is a blunt and inappropriate response to early childhood errors. The low age of criminal responsibility, the decision to prosecute and the current concerns and sanctions for rape and sexual abusers all provide evidence of the necessity for a child first approach. In addition, to give primary concern to the best interests of children and their welfare requires 'knowing adults' to facilitate a discussion with children about learning to manage their sexual desires and the risks this may pose to themselves and others. To assist the maturation to adulthood children require safe spaces to explore both risks and pleasure. When children's sexuality is constructed as absent, or a present danger, with predictive power, we deny children the opportunity to become knowledgeable actors. The case discussed here demonstrates an urgent need to provide spaces for an ethical discussion of child sexuality if we are to resist, as we should, criminalising early sexual experiences.

References

Angelides, S. (2004) 'Feminism, child Sexual Abuse, and the erasure of child sexuality' *GLQ a Journal of Lesbian and Gay Studies*, 10:2 pp141-177

Brownlie, J. (2001) The 'Being Risky Child' Governing childhood and Sexual Risk. *Sociology* Vol.35(2) pp519-537

Camber, R (2010) 'Appeal Court judge condemns decision to try two 10-year-old boys for rape at Old Bailey'
http://www.dailymail.co.uk/news/article-1298124/High-Court-judge-condemns-decision-try-10-year-old-boys-rape-Old-Bailey.html

Cipriani, D. (2009) *Children's Rights and the Minimum age of Criminal Responsibility: a Global Perspective*. Ashgate: London.

Camber, R. (2010) "Why were children forced to go through rape trial?" *Daily mail* 25th May 2010 (accessed 07/06/2010).

Corteen, K & Scraton, P (1997) 'Prolonging 'childhood' manufacturing innocence and regulating sexuality' in Scraton, P (ed) (1997) *Childhood in Crisis*. Routledge

Foucault, M (1988) The Danger of Child Sexuality – an interview available at http://www.ipce.info/ipceweb/Library/danger.htm

Grimshaw, R (2008) *Young People who Sexually Abuse*. Youth Justice Board.

Independent Commission on Youth Crime and Antisocial Behaviour (2010) *Time for a Fresh Start: The Independent Commission on Youth Crime and Antisocial Behaviour*. London: The Police Federation.

Jones, S. (2010) "Boys, aged 10 and 11, guilty of attempted rape" *Guardian* June 2010.

Pidd, H. and Jones, S. (2010) 'Supervision order for 11-year-old boys convicted of attempting to rape girl, 8' *Guardian* 18th August

Kelly Liz, Lovett Jo, Regan Linda (2005) *A Gap or a Chasm: attrition in rape cases*. Home Office Studies

Muncie, J. (2009) *Youth and Crime*. Sage:London.

NACRO (2002) Children's rights - recommendations for youth justice. Available at,www.nacro.org.uk/publications/YouthBriefings.htm

Sexual Offences Act 2003

Stern, V. (2010*) The Stern Review. How rape complaints are handled by public authorities in England and Wales*. HMSO

Stone, N. (2007) 'Youthful Sex: Experimentation, Expression of Affection or Exploitation?' *Youth Justice* Vol.7, No.1 pp52-63

Stone, N. (2009) 'Children on the Sex Offenders Register: Proportionality, Prospect of change and Article 8 Rights' in *Youth Justice* Vol.9, No.3 pp286-294

PART 3

INTRODUCING CRITICAL CRIMINOLOGICAL RESEARCH OF LAB "EKNEXA" – UNIVERSITY OF THE AEGEAN

15.

REVOLT OR DEVIANCE?
GREEK INTELLECTUALS AND THE DECEMBER 2008
REVOLT OF THE GREEK YOUTH

Panagiotis Sotiris

Introduction[1]

The December 2008 explosion of the Greek Youth was one of the most important recent examples of social mobilization. However, it has been analysed by a large segment of mainstream Greek intellectuals and social theorists in terms of deviance, persistent culture of violence, lack of civility and evidence of a deficient political culture. Contrary to this position, we are going to offer an alternative interpretation of the December revolt as a highly original social movement. Consequently, we are going to treat the reactions of these intellectuals as symptomatic of an inability of main-stream social and political theorists to come in terms with the social and political causes of social explosions of such magnitude. Finally we are going to interpret these reactions as evidence of a theoretical crisis, which is an aspect of a crisis of hegemony in a conjuncture of economic crisis and rising class conflicts.

1. Greek intellectuals and their reaction to the December 2008 revolt

In this section, we attempt an overview of the reactions of mainstream Greek intellectuals to the December 2008 revolt. By 'mainstream' we refer to theorists situated in political positions closer to the political centre, something that in the Greek political landscape can be translated to those with opinions closer to the two main power parties in Greece, the more conservative centre-right New Democracy and the social-democratic cen-tre-left PASOK. In addition, we include theorists situated in the 'moderniz-ing' Left that represents the right wing of the Greek post-communist Left. The classification is based on the different discoursive modalities em-

---

[1] The writer wishes to thank Stathis Kouvélakis, Spyros Sakellaropoulos, Sevasti Trubeta and Aimilia Voulvouli for their comments and suggestions on an earlier version of this paper.

ployed in the reactions against the December 2008 and not necessarily on the political positioning of each intellectual.[2]

1.1 December 2008 as social delinquency

The first reaction of many intellectuals was to discredit the December revolt as a movement, in line with the neoconservative attitude to treat social movements as sporadic irrational reactions to neoliberal orthodoxy. Stathis Kalyvas and Nicos Marantzidis have been the most obstinate supporters of the view that whatever happened in December 2008 was not a social movement. According to them it was not an insurrection of the Greek youth, it had no central idea or demand and was not a result of social tensions aggravated by the international economic crisis (Kalyvas and Marantzidis 2008; Kalyvas 2009a; Kalyvas 2009b). It was only the result of a culture of violence and disrespect for authority (Kalyvas 2008). Kalyvas exhibits the same reluctance to seek social and political causal mechanisms for political violence in his book on civil war violence (Kalyvas 2006). The only explanations they offer are the failure of necessary reforms, because of the resistance of organized minorities, ineffective policing, and a general incapacity to deal with a culture of violence (Kalyvas 2009; Marantzidis 2009a). For them this culture of violence is a heritage of the 'Metapolitefsi'[3] political culture, which treats the demands of any social group as a noble right, justifies all forms of social mobilization, including violence against authority (Kalyvas 2008a), and treats the smooth functioning of institutions as anomaly (Marantzidis 2009). For Marantzidis Greece is the last country in Europe where a 'popular democracy' ideology still prevails in the form of left-wing populism that leads the forces of the anti-systemic Left to support political violence (Marantzidis 2009b; Marantzidis 2010; Marantzidis 2010a). Similarly, Manos Matsaganis (2009) cites as possible causes of violent protests the indifference of the Greek population towards terrorist groups, the support for totalitarian regimes in the name of their anti-imperialism and a general lack of civility. Others have seen not a movement but only violent 'hooded youths' (Someritis 2008) and anarchists (Papangelis 2008), and have lamented the lack of goals or values (Papangelis 2009), and the malfunctioning of institutions (Konidaris 2008).

---

[2] For a more extensive statistical approach to the reactions of intellectuals to the December revolt see Costopoulos 2010.

[3] We use the Greek term that refers to the period that followed the 1974 fall of the dictatorship and the full establishment of parliamentary democracy. Especially its first phase (1974-1981) was characterized by social and political radicalization.

1.2. Misreading December 2008 as political nihilism

Criticism of the 'negative' discourse of the movement has been a basic tenet of mainstream theorists. For them the anti-authoritarian position of the movement is evidence of a more general crisis of politics (Papadimitropoulos 2009). For Papatheodorou (2009; 2009a) the individualistic character of most insurrectionary practices during the December movement will enhance, despite the anarchist and leftist rhetoric, an egocentric imaginary in line with neoliberal ideology (Papatheodorou 2009, 2009a). Others attribute violence to the fact that the 'prevailing values in the society are those of distrust, lack of solidarity, indifference to common interest issues, and contempt of the law' (Zeri 2009). In an open letter, seven university professors (with left or centre-left orientation) lamented the culture of nihilism, resentment and envy exemplified in anarchist violence and demanded zero tolerance to all forms of violence and abuse (Georgiadou *et al.* 2008). The same accusation of nihilism, attributed to the excessive rationalism of the Age of Enlightenment, is the main point of Stelios Ramfos (2008), who champions the alignment of Orthodox Christianity and capitalist modernization. Others have attributed this nihilism to a general climate of political and moral crisis (Tsoukas 2008), an inability to deal with a period of crisis (Veremis 2008), sense of impunity that fuelled violence (Gousetis 2008), attributed to a widespread culture of permissiveness and anomie (Pagoulatos 2008). In its more eloquent version this criticism does not deny that there are political references in the discourse and the imagery of the December explosion, but considers them a political mythology originating in the post-1968 radicalism (Kanellis 2009). Treating the movement as anomic led others to consider protests, such as the interruption of theatrical performances, as an attack on the freedom of expression (Doxiadis *et al.* 2008).

1.3 December 2008 as crisis of civil society and its institutions
Nicos Mouzelis (2008a, 2009) has insisted on the lack of adjustment to the exigencies of postmodern societies that led to widespread feelings of youth insecurity and attributes the mobilization to an underdevelopment of civil society. Although he refers to rising inequalities and new forms of pauperization (Mouzelis 2008), he attributes the same importance to the disorganization of the police force due to the political clientelism! It is a combination between an earlier Marxist emphasis on social inequalities and the emphasis on institutions as facilitators of social rationalization associated with mainstream post-Weberian and post-functionalist social theorizing. However, the unease at dealing with the movement is made evident by

Mouzelis' reference to an underdevelopment of civil society despite the fact that in December 2008 we witnessed a flourishing of grassroots initiatives. The underestimation of social inequalities and class polarization is evident in interventions by intellectuals of the 'modernizing' Left. For Giannis Voulgaris (2008) December 2008 exemplified a crisis of authority regarding social and political institutions with youths facing the collapse of the compromise between generations and the inability of family protection to help them cope with the difficulties of working life. For Pantelis Mpasakos (2008) the danger is the undermining of the institutions of post-1974 democracy, whereas Giannis Papatheodorou (2008) treats the turn towards state authoritarianism as the result of the decay of democracy. For Nicos Alivizatos (2009) the eruption of violence during the December movement is the result neither of the economic crisis nor of worsening prospects for youths, but of the lack of credibility of the political system and of the crisis of education and the inability of the educational apparatus to adjust itself to the changing environment. For Alexis Kalokerinos the movement was the result of a crisis of institutions, especially education, that create 'structural distortions' (Kalokerinos 2009: 24).

1.4 Attempts at coming in terms with the dynamics of the movement
It would have been unfair to suggest that there have not been attempts to understand the dynamics of the movement. An enduring radicalism, along with a tradition of radical critical perspectives that is still vibrant in parts of the Greek academy have produced valuable and inspired readings of the movement. The Contentious Politics Circle, a network of academics and researchers based in Panteion University, has attempted a very interesting reading of the events of December 2008, organizing an important Conference in December 2009.[4] There have been interventions in the public debate, right from the beginning, stressing the need to come in terms with the causes of the explosion and to express solidarity with struggling youths (Seferiadis 2008; Kouvélakis 2008; Psimitis 2009; Serntedakis 2009; Sevastakis 2009; Douzinas 2009.). Theoretical reviews such as *Synchrona Themata*, *Theseis*, and Αλήθεια have been the venue for theoretical interventions in the debate and the same goes for the pages of the daily and weekly newspapers of the Left such as *Avgi*, *Epohi*, *Prin*.

---

[4] See http://contentiouspoliticscircle.blogspot.com. See also Seferiadis 2009.

2. The social movement mainstream intellectuals failed to see[5]

2.1. The limits of thinking in terms of deviance and anomie

Events such as the December movement 'test the interpretative ability and the analytical clear-sightedness of political and social scientists' (Douzinas 2009: 107) and bring forward the need to 'reconnect research on social movements and social conflict with the analysis of the broader structural changes caused by processes of the neoliberal globalization' (Serdedakis 2010). One could expect that social unrest of this extent, duration and magnitude would have been treated as a social phenomenon demanding explanation and search for underlying social conflicts and trends. On the contrary, one can discern a quick turn from the descriptive towards the prescriptive, with a strong sense of ideological bias. By this, we do not suggest that a neutral reaction to the December revolt would have been possible. What we see is that kind of ideological bias that obstructs the analysis of social phenomena and leads to a form of 'begging the question'. References to violent insurrectionary practices being the symptom of inadequately functioning institutions, lack of values, endemic political violence, crisis of political representation are not the result of actually examining the dynamics (and contradictions) of the movement, but of mainly preconceived opinions.

Treating social movements and political contention as forms of deviance and anomie has a long history in social theory. Beginning with LeBon (2002) the behavior of the 'crowd' has been treated as evidence of the political pathology of the subordinate classes. In the long tradition of sociological positivism, from Durkheim to Parsons and Merton, social unrest has been treated as evidence of social pathology and dysfunction, despite the attempt to incorporate rebellion into the paradigm (Durkheim 2004; Thompson (ed.) 2004; Parsons 1991; Merton 1938). In the positivist tradition consensus has always been seen as a more natural societal condition than conflict and contention (Taylor, Walton and Young 1973).

Consequently, the December movement is being read as mainly deviance, both in the 'narrow' sense of activist delinquency and in the 'broad' sense of Greek society moving away from the ideal types expected in a fully modernized (or post-modern) society. In this reading, December 2008 was not a movement that social institutions must try to cope with, listen to its demands, enter in dialogue and negotiation with, but something pathogenic, 'a chain of irrational or openly anomic practices' (Sevastakis 2009: 304) and 'the condensation of chronic degeneration of the networks

---

[5] For an earlier version of the argument presented in sections 2 and 3, see Sotiris 2010.

and subsystems of Greek life' (Sevastakis 2010: 288). This can explain why some intellectuals opt for a disciplinary attitude calling for the adjustment of Greek society to the social and political norms associated with projects of capitalist modernization.

2.2. Why December 2008 was a highly original social movement

December was a unique example of mass mobilization: mass demonstrations took place in almost every city and town in Greece; in hundreds of high schools some form of strike kept on for two weeks; the majority of university campuses was occupied; tens of police stations all over Greece became the target of student rallies; tens of local radio stations were occupied in order for messages of solidarity to be broadcast; the studios of the National Television Company were briefly occupied in prime time; Town Halls were occupied and housed mass assemblies; theatrical shows, including a premier at the National Theatre, were interrupted by protesting drama students; more than 180 bank branches were attacked, hundreds of stores, ATMs and traffic lights were smashed, with the total cost of damages estimated to have exceeded 1,5 billion euros.

As Michalis Psimitis (2009) has shown, the emergence of a collective identity, the anti-systemic confrontational attitude and the refusal to negotiate, provide ample evidence of the emergence of a social movement. We were dealing with a form of collective action that involved solidarity, engagement in conflict and breaking the limits of compatibility of a system, in line with Alberto Melucci's definition of a social movement (Melucci 1989; Melucci 1996). We could discern in the December movement the 'informal networks based on [...] shared beliefs and solidarity, which mobilize about [...] conflictual issues, through [...] the frequent use of various forms of protest' suggested by Della Porta and Diani as characteristics of a social movement (Della Porta and Diani 1999: 16). We could witness the synthesis of a 'sustained, organized public effort making collective claims on target authorities; [...] employment [...] [of] forms of political action [...] participants' concerted public representations of [...] worthiness, unity, numbers, and commitment on the part of themselves' suggested by Charles Tilly (Tilly 2004: 3-4). Therefore, one should try and understand the motivation and rationality behind this highly original form of 'collective insurrectionary action' (Seferiadis 2008; Seferiadis 2009).

For the first time it was not just the student movement, but also the whole *youth movement* that dominated the social scene. The December movement united high school students and youths from vocational training centres, university students and young workers, middle-class youths and youths facing social exclusion, Greeks and immigrants. The participation of immigrant youths was massive, marking a widespread demand for active political participation, but not in the name of a particular identity (Kalyvas A. 2010). It was neither a classical student movement nor an explosion of disenfranchised socially excluded youth, like the 2005 *banlieu* riots in France. Both the deterioration of employment prospects and the restructuring of the educational system provided the material basis for this unity. The movement accelerated the re-articulation of a collective identity in the Greek youth that comprises struggle, solidarity, hostility towards authority and the traditional political scene, and an anti-systemic demand for radical change. The movement was based on various forms of coordination, often informal, and self-organization (Kotronáki 2009), and used extensively the Internet and new communication technologies, something, following the pattern observed in other recent youth movements (Tsimitakis 2009; Bindix and Park 2008). It also attracted various segments of the workforce, including young workers and unemployed youths, teachers and professors, people working in precarious posts of intellectual labour. It acted as a catalyst for all forms of social and political activism, the best example being the movement of solidarity to Konstantina Kuneva, a Bulgarian janitor who was attacked and nearly died because of her union activity against precarious labour.

Moreover, we must try to discern the particular logic behind the violence in December 2008. Treating collective violence as simply irrational and pathogenic runs contrary to much of current critical social theorizing that insists on discerning the particular logic of collective violence (Tilly 2003) and considers an analytical mistake to treat political violence as another form of common criminal violence (Ruggiero 2006). The mass destruction of banks and retail stores in the centre of Athens on December 8th 2008, was directed mainly against symbols of economic power, and even youths that opted for more 'peaceful' ways to demonstrate experienced rioting as a necessary aspect of a collective effort to 'make themselves heard'. Therefore, it is possible to treat violence as aspect of a repertoire of protest (Koronáki 2009; Papanikolopoulos 2009). Treating the violent aspects of youth protest as a form of social deviance or anomie would simply reproduce the neoconservative and neoliberal trend towards a disciplinary, punitive and penal treatment of social problems (Wacquant 1999; 2008).

The political dynamic of the movement represented a profound demand for radical social change. The rage expressed by youths against what they called the 'policies that kill our dreams' and the popularity of slogans such as 'down with the government of murderers' provides evidence of its anti-systemic orientation. However, treating the movement as the expression of a post-proletarian 'precariat' (Xydakis 2008), or as the rising of the 'Multitude' (Gavriilidis 2009) following Negri's theorization (Hardt and Negri 2000) can be misleading. Concerns about working conditions, education, and collective goods, combined with a deep distrust of the political establishment, make this movement much less a 'nomadic multitude' and much more a view in advance of a potential counter-hegemonic bloc of the subaltern classes.

3. A condensation of social tensions and systemic contradictions

One cannot explain the extent of the revolt without reference to the social tensions and systemic contradictions related to dominant policies of neoliberalism and capitalist restructuring.

3.1.Deterioration of working protests and the emergence of a common youth identity

Despite high growth rates from the mid 1990s up to 2007 (INE GSEE – ADEDY 2008), Greece has experienced high rates of youth unemployment and underemployment. According to Eurostat estimates the unemployment rate of young people (15-24) in Greece in 2008 was at 22.1% with the EU-27 average being at 15.4% and in the end of 2009 it had reached 27.5% with the EU-27 being at 20.3% (*Eurostat* 2009; *Eurostat* 2010). According to Karamesini (2009: 21) six years after graduation one out of three Higher Education graduates, two out of three secondary education graduates and one out of three compulsory education graduates have not found some form of stable employment. Those who manage to enter the labour market have to put up with low wages, part-time posts, working 'off the books', harassment by employers. Better qualifications do not necessarily lead to better employment prospects. In the 20-24 and 25-29 age groups unemployment rates are higher among those with better educational qualifications, such as university degrees (Karamesini 2009:21), following a trend observed across Southern Europe where leavers from upper secondary education and even higher education have at least equal unemployment rates with the least qualified (Gangl *et al.* 2003: 282). A large survey of the employment prospects of Greek university graduates (Karamesini 2008) has shown that many of them face flexible work forms and / or are obliged to accept positions different from their formal qualifications. Despite the differences in employment and social status between the different segments of youth (especially between those that leave school at the end of compulsory or secondary education, opting for vocational training and early entry into the workforce, and those continuing to Higher Education), they all face the deterioration of employment prospects. This is one of the reasons for the reproduction of a rather unitary identity for youths in Greece, a 'unity in difference' (Karamesini 2009: 21).

3.2 Education as social battleground

From the 1990s reforms have aimed at increasing access at post-secondary education and at the same time making sure that university degrees do not lead to guaranteed work prospects, bringing Higher Education closer to business interests and disciplining the student movement, in line with the so-called 'Bologna Process' (Katsikas and Sotiris 2003). In the 2000s the combination of a highly competitive system of entry exams for Higher Education –that requires tremendous amounts of studying and many extra hours of expensive tutorial courses– with the prospect of obtaining a university degree that will not lead to secure employment has produced a widespread feeling of growing insecurity as regards young people's prospects. In 2006-2007 a wave of reforms that included changes in the status of university degrees that would de-link them from professional qualifications, harsher disciplinary measures, intensified study schedules, and the continuing attempt to legalize Private Higher Education in Greece, despite an explicit constitutional ban on private universities, led to an impressive movement by university student and professors.

University reform is part of a broader process of capitalist restructuring. Commodification and entrepreneuralization of higher education (Ovetz 1996; Slaughter and Lelslie 1997; Harvie 2000; edu-factory collective 2006) are important aspects, but equally important are changes in the role of education in social reproduction. Educational reforms tend to 'internalize' the changes in the labour market and the capitalist labour process within the educational apparatus. This subsumption of education to the imperatives of capitalist accumulation, is not limited to changes in university funding. It takes the form of changes not only in the relative value of university degrees but to the very notion of the degree, leading to new fragmentations, educational hierarchies, processes of individualization that respond to the new realities of the workplace. It can also account for the emphasis on training instead of education, for changes in curricula, for the emergence of an entrepreneurial culture in Higher Education. Consequently, youths in the educational apparatus have a stronger than before perception of the realities of the workplace. As with the French student movement against the CPE (Contract of First Employment), students tend more easily to associate with the labour movement. Student movements are not just a reaction to the devaluation of degrees but are a part of greater social mobilization against the neoliberal 'restructuring of the totality of capital – labour relations' (Kouvélakis 2007: 279).

3.3. Capitalist Crisis and social tensions

The economic crisis was surely a contributing factor to a general feeling of discontent. In 2008 the Greek economy was already sliding into recession (Bank of Greece 2009) in sharp contrast to high growth rates and intense capitalist restructuring attested from the mid-1990s. Households were facing stagnant wages, job insecurity and rising indebtedness, compounded by a policy of strict fiscal austerity. Rising social inequality became an integral aspect of the Greek social landscape (Kouvélakis 2008). All these accentuated feelings of growing insecurity and a widespread sense that things were going to get worse in the next months. A few months after the December revolt a special Eurobarometer survey captured these negative expectations for the future (*Eurostat* 2010a: 43-57).

3.4. Police violence in perspective

Police violence was a contributing factor to the revolt. However, a tendency to focus on the inability of the police to deal with youth protest or on the rituals of youth collective delinquency misses the point. It is not enough to link hostility to the police to the historic association of the police force in Greece with state authoritarianism and constant persecution of left-wing and communist militants. Police violence acted as a metonymy for the systemic social violence of capitalist restructuring and neoliberalism (Belantis 2006; Kouvélakis 2010). An extreme case of police aggression, such as the murder, in cold blood, of 15-year-old Alexis Grigoropoulos, was perceived as the 'tip of the iceberg' of all forms of social inequality, insecurity and oppression.

3.5 Legitimization crisis

On the political level, rising social discontent was condensed in a wider sense of legitimization crisis of the Greek State (Bratsis 2009). The apprehension of widespread political corruption and direct links between business and the political system intensified these tendencies, and the same goes for the inability of the Greek State to deal with emergencies such as the devastating forest fires of 2007. Despite the fact that this did not take the form of an open 'systemic' political crisis, it surely contributed to the extent of the anger and protest in the streets of Athens in December 2008.

The humiliating defeat of New Democracy in the 2009 general election exemplified the extent of the discontent.

4. Beyond a simple *'trahison des clercs'*: the inability of mainstream intellectuals to understand the movement

The inability of mainstream theorists to grasp the significance of the December 2008 explosion is a symptom of underlying ideological displacements, the attachement of mainstream intellectuals to projects of modernization and the ideological crisis of mainstream social theory in Greece as part a broader tendency towards hegemonic instability after the exhaustion of the neoliberal paradigm.

4.1 Left-wing Intellectuals and projects of modernization

Modernization has been a key word in the evolution of Greek political culture in the past 4 decades. In the theoretical plane, it was the theorization of tendencies of underdevelopment and / or distorted development in Greek society (Tsoukalas1977, 1983, 1986; Mouzelis 1978, 1986) that offered the necessary justification for the need for modernization. From the 1960s to the 1980s, a basic tenet of the Greek Left has been the inability of the Greek bourgeoisie, because of its backwardness and dependence on foreign imperialism, to lead the process of modernization of Greek Society. It was up to the people's movement to lead the way of both social modernization and social emancipation. This facilitated a certain duality from the part of intellectuals in the 1970s and 1980s. One the one hand it helped them to be in touch with a climate of social and political radicalization, exemplified in the demand for 'Change'. On the other hand, it facilitated their role as 'organic intellectuals' of state. It allowed them to make more articulate a historical transition already in motion, namely the transition of Greece to an advanced capitalist economy, to a European-style parliamentary democracy, to the establishment of welfare state institutions.

4.2 'Modernization' as a break with the aspirations of the subaltern classes

The 1980s and early 1990s marked a turning point for Greek intellectuals and their commitment to projects of modernization. The gradual right-wing turn of PASOK, the austerity program of 1985, and the beginning of the distancing between social demands and government measures evolved into a conflict between the social aspirations of the lower classes and projects of modernization. The project of modernization started to incorporate elements of the emerging neoliberal policy consensus. However, large segments of the subordinate classes remained faithful to aspects of the 'Metapolitefsi' ideology. Consequently, the appeals of public intellectuals towards the modernization of Greek society started to incorporate the element of break with the ideological, social and political practices of the subordinate classes. The accusation of populism became commonplace, referring to the attitudes and practices by the working class and large segments of traditional petty bourgeois strata that insisted on secure employment, income redistribution, state intervention. The enemy of the modernizing project became the subordinate classes themselves.

Nikiforos Diamantouros (1994) epitomized this position. He reformulated the cultural dualism thesis that had been commonplace in the discussion of Greek political culture. While adhering to the description of two cultures, one originating in the experience of Ottoman rule and the other on the encounter with European Enlightenment, he suggested that after 1974 an 'underdog' political culture emerged. It comprised a 'levelling egalitarianism [...] a compensatory sense of justice [...] a profound diffidence towards capitalism and the market operation' (Diamantouros 1994: 38). We are dealing here with a semantic and ideological shift, where instead of referring to pre-modern traditionalism the problem is located in the anticapitalist political and social reflexes of the subordinate classes and their endorsement of social justice.

The momentum of the demand for modernization was not only theoretical but also political. Costas Simitis, a self-proclaimed modernizer in PASOK, and himself a theorist of 'modernization' (Simitis 1989, 1992, 1992a, 1995), was the winner of the succession race that followed the resignation of A. Papandreou in 1995. The appeal to 'modernization', in the sense of complying with capitalist norms expressed in the process of European integration, became dominant. The participation of intellectuals in the development of specific policy initiatives, the growing importance of research programs funded by the European Union, and the need to ideologically legitimize capitalist restructuring, all these facilitated the emergence of a new consensus among Greek mainstream intellectuals. In this consensus, modernization implied the identification of democracy with parliamentarism, the distrust against radical social movements, the viewing as essentially conservative of all demands that were in contrast to neoliberal economic orthodoxy, the acceptance of the market as a vector of social rationality. However, the demand for modernization, although dominant in the public sphere and discourse, especially when coupled with the appeal to Europeanization, was never fully hegemonic in the collective self representation of the lower classes, leading to dualisms and contradictions in Greek political culture (Voulgaris 2008a).

If we want to understand why mainstream theorists had such a difficulty in dealing with December 2008 as a social movement, we must pay particular attention to these theoretical and ideological displacements. The identification of modernization with neoliberal orthodoxy led to social movements being considered as inherently parochial, representing interests and practices that can impede progress. This is in sharp contrast even to the positivist tradition that reluctantly left room for the 'functional rebel' (Durkheim) or 'rebellion' (Parsons, Merton) or openly admitted the importance of conflict (Dahrendorf). Treating social contention and conflict as obstacles to an inescapable road to progress, leaves no room for analysis, assessment of dynamics and search for underlying causal mechanisms.

4.3. Crisis of hegemony and the impasse of mainstream intellectuals
The inability to comprehend December 2008 as a social movement is an expression of the exhaustion of the hegemonic potential of the dominant discourse on modernization and 'reform' in a conjuncture of rising social tensions and conflicts and consequently hegemonic instability.

In the second half of the 2000s, after the end of the artificial euphoria orchestrated around the Olympic Games, Greek society witnessed rising social inequalities, tensions, and confrontations. Greece was becoming a more unequal and socially polarized country. In 2007, the 'at risk of poverty' rate was at 20%, higher than the EU average, the top 20% of the population (in terms of disposable income) received 6 times as much of the total income of the bottom 20%, and the Gini coefficient of income inequality distribution was at 34, higher than the EU-27 average at 31 (*Eurostat* 2010a). There was the gradual exhaustion of the Greek 'developmental paradigm'. This was based upon capitalist restructuring, cheap labour, constant flow of EU funds and the growth of sectors sensitive to the tendencies of the general economic conjuncture, such as tourism, shipping and construction and experienced, without ever successfully solving a problem of competitiveness that was accentuated by the monetary and financial architecture of the Eurozone.

The growing distrust of large segments of the electorate against the political establishment reflected a more general inability of the neoliberal project to be hegemonic in the positive sense of actually gaining active consent from the subaltern classes. The political scene was becoming more alienated from the working class and large segments of the 'middle class', leading to a political cycle where the party that came to power was gaining more from the discontent against the policies of its predecessor than from the positive appeal of its program. The erosion of the hegemonic and integrating ability of the State in most advanced capitalist social formations can explain the rise of the 'Security State', which aims at disarming the subordinates from any possibility to comprehend the reasons for their discontent and at directing their anger against stigmatized minorities (Kouvélakis 2010). We are a strategic impasse from the part of the political and economic elites. It is obvious that ahead of us lie more social tensions and even explosions. However, there is an almost complete inability of the political system to think of an alternative other than successive 'shock and awe' waves of reforms aiming at complete demoralization of the subordinate classes, a bet far from safe. This can also explain inability of mainstream intellectuals and theorists to comprehend the dynamics of the December 2008 movement. It is not that they are not aware of the possibility of social explosions. They are unable to treat them as social phenomena that require comprehension, because this will also mean articulating possible policy changes and class compromises, something precluded in advance in the dominant discourse. Thus, this whole conception of these movements as dangerous obstructions, that entail the danger of generalized anomie, a conception that necessarily implies that the only way to deal with them is though disciplinary practices and technologies. Therefore, the ideological displacement of mainstream Greek intellectuals is also an aspect of a more general crisis of capitalist strategy (and consequently 'prosystemic' social theory) in a period of hegemonic instability.

Conclusion

The December 2008 explosion of the Greek Youth presents a very important challenge for radical social theory. It belongs to a cycle of protest and discontent against dominant neoliberal policies, which is far form over. The inability of mainstream Greek intellectuals and social theorists to comprehend its dynamics and their insistence on treating as some form of deviance can be explained through their historical attachment to projects of capitalist modernization and a more general a crisis of dominant strategy with repercussions in mainstream social theory. Radical social theory must answer this challenge, and attempt to come in terms with the theoretical and political exigencies of such movements.

References

Alivizatos, N., (2009). The challenge of violence: a defeat of the reformers. (in Greek). *Nea Estia,* 1819, pp 196-201.

Bank of Greece, (2009). *Governor's report for 2000* (in Greek). Athens: Bank of Greece.

Belantis, D., (2006). On the crisis of the modern representative democracy. (in Greek). *Diaplous* 25, pp. 45-48.

Biddix, P.J. and H.W Park., (2008). Online networks of student protest: the case of the living wage campaign. *New Media and Society* 10(6), pp. 871–891.

Bratsis, P.,(2009). Legitimization Crisis and the Greek Explosion. *International Journal of Urban and Regional Research* 34(1), pp. 190-6.

Costopoulos, C., (2010). Intellectuals and the December Revolt. (In Greek). *Avgi* 3 January 2010. Available at <http://www.avgi.gr/ArticleActionshow.action?articleID=514972> [Accessed on 20 August 2010]

Della Porta, D. and Diani M., (1999). *Social Movements. An Introduction.* Oxford: Blackwell.

Diamantouros, N., (1994). *Cultural Dualism and Political Change in Postauthoritarian Greece.* Estudio/Working Paper. Madrid: Center for Advanced Study in the Social Sciences, Fundación Juan March.

Douzinas, C., (2009). What We Can Learn from the Greek Riots. *The Guardian* 9 January 2009 Available at <http://www.guardian.co.uk/commentisfree/2009/jan/09/greece-riots> [Accesed 1 August 2010].

Doxiadis, A., T.s Theodorópoulos and P. Márkaris, (2008). An attack on the freedom of expression. (In Greek). *Eleftherotypía* 24 December 2008. Available at <http://archive.enet.gr/online/online_text/c=113,id=23827372,29554988> [Accessed 1 August 2010]

Durkheim, E., (2004). *Suicide. A Study in Sociology.* London and New York: Routledge.

edu-factory collective, (2006). Manifesto. Available at <http://www.edu-fac-tory.org/index.php?option=com_content&task=view&id=5&>[Accessed 10 May 2009].

Eurostat, (2009). *Labour Market Statistics.* Luxembourg: Publications Office of the European Union.

Eurostat, (2010). Euro Area Unemployment at 10.0%. *Eurostat Newsrelease* 46/2010.

Eurostat, (2010a). *The Social Situation in the European Union 2009.* Luxembourg: Publications Office of the European Union.

Gangl, M., W. Müller and D. Raffe, (2003). Conclusions: explaining cross-national differences in school-to-work transitions. in W. Müller and M. Gangl eds. 2003. *Transitions from Education to Work in Europe. The Integration of Youth into Labour Markets.* Oxford: Oxford University Press.

Gavriilidis, A., (2009) [Greek Riots 2008:] – A Mobile Tiananmen. In: Economides and Monastiriotis, eds. *The Return of Street Politics? Essays on the December Riots in Greece.* London: The Hellenic Observatory, LSE.

Georgiadou V. *et al.,* (2008). Neither Democracy Nor Anarchy, Democracy! (In Greek). *Kathimerini* 14 December 2008. Available at <http://news.kathimerini.gr/4dcgi/_w_articles_politics_2_14/12/2008_296 051> [Accessed 2 August 2010].

Gousétis, D., (2008). Bullying and rage equal backwardness. (in Greek). *Avgi* 13 December 2008. Available at <http://www.ananeotiki.gr/el/readArchives.asp?catID=1&subCatID=5&tex tID=3033> [Accessed 5 August 2010].

Hardt, M. and T. Negri, (2000). *Empire.* Cambridge, Mass. and London, England: Harvard University Press.

Harvie, D., (2000). Alienation, Class and Enclosure in UK Universities. *Capital and Class,* 71, pp. 103-132.

INE GSEE – ADEDY, (2008). *Greek Economy and Employment.* (In Greek). Athens: INE GSEE – ADEDY.

Kalokerinos, A., (2009). Warped Institutions, Political Failure and Social Guilt. In: Economides and Monastiriotis eds. *The Return of Street Politics? Essays on the December Riots in Greece.* London: The Hellenic Observatory, LSE.

Kalyvas, A., (2010). An Anomaly? Some Reflections on the Greek December 2008. *Constellations,* 17(2), pp. 351-365.

Kalyvas, S., (2006). *The Logic of Violence in Civil Wars.* Cambridge: Cambridge University Press.

Kalyvas, S., (2008). Why Athens is burning. Available at <http://www.nytimes.com/2008/12/11/opinion/11iht-edkalyvas.1.18595110.html> [Accessed 30 August 2010]

Kalyvas, S., (2008a). The culture of the metapolitefsi. (In Greek). *Kathimerini* 14 December 2008. Available at <http://news.kathimerini.gr/4dcgi/_w_articles_politics_2_14/12/2008_296 059> [Accessed 3 August 2010.

Kalyvas, S., (2009). Stagnation and Retreat. (In Greek). *To Vima* 17 May 2009. Available at <http://www.tovima.gr/default.asp?pid=2&ct=114&artid=268596&dt=17/ 05/2009> [Accessed 3 August 2010.

Kalyvas, S., (2009a) …and what it was not. In Greek. *To Vima* 6 December 2009. Available at <http://www.tovima.gr/default.asp?pid=2&ct=114&artid=303459&dt=06/ 12/2009> [Accessed 3 August 2010].

Kalyvas, S., (2009b). The 'December insurrection' as a symptom of the 'Metapolítefsi culture. (In Greek). *Athens Review of Books* 2, Available at <http://www.booksreview.gr/index.php?option=com_content&view=articl

e&id=60:-l-r-l-r&catid=38:-2-2009&Itemid=55> [Accessed 3 August 2010].

Kalyvas, S. and Marantzidis, N., (2008). The December events as farce. (In Greek). *To Vima* 21 December 2008. Available at <http://www.tovima.gr/default.asp?pid=46&ct=72&artId=241058&dt=21/12/2008> [Accessed 3 August 2010].

Kanellis, I., (2009). The December culture. (In Greek). *Athens Review of Books* 3. Available at <http://www.booksreview.gr/index.php?option=com_content&view=articl e&id=66:2009-12-23-12-57-03&catid=39:-3-2009-&Itemid=55> [Accessed 4 August 2010].

Karamesini, M., (2008). *The entry of university degree holders in the labour market.* (In Greek). Athens: Dionikos.

Karamesini, M., (2009). Difficulties of youth employment in Greece. (In Greek). *Epochí* 18 January 2009. Available at <http://www.epohi.gr/index.php?option=com_content&task=view&id=204 3> [Accessed 30 July 2010].

Katsikas, C. and Sotiris P., (2003). *The Restructuring of Greek University.* (In Greek) Athens: Savalas.

Konidáris, I.M., (2008). Shop closed due to end of season. (In Greek). *To Vima* 21 December 2008. Available at <http://www.tovima.gr/default.asp?pid=46&ct=72&artId=241060&dt=21/12/2008> [Accessed 5 August 2010].

Kotronaki, L., (2009). When mourning revolts. (In Greek). *Epohi* 09 January 2009.

Kouvélakis, S., (2007). *La France en révolte. Luttes Sociales et cycles politiques*. Paris: Textuel:.

Kouvélakis, S., (2008). La Grèce en révolte. Available at <http://www.contretemps.eu/interventions/stathis-kouvelakis-grece-en-revolte> [Accessed 5 Augsut 2010].

Kouvélakis, S., (2010). Pour une politique de l'insurrection. Réflexions à partir du décembre grec. Notes sur la stratégie 1'. Unpublished manuscript.

Le Bon, G., [1896] (2002). *The Crowd. A Study of the Popular Mind.* Mineola NY: Dover.

Marantzídis, N., (2009). Smooth functioning as anomaly. (In Greek). *To Vima* 18 January 2009. Available at <http://www.tovima.gr/default.asp?pid=2&ct=6&artid=251168&dt=18/01/2009> [Accessed 8 August 2010].

Marantzídis, N., (2009a). Everything was reminiscent of a forgotten past. (In Greek). *To Vima* 6 December 2009. Available at <http://www.tovima.gr/default.asp?pid=2&artid=303460&ct=114&dt=06/12/2009> [Accessed 6 August 2010]

Marantzidis, N., (2009b). La farce grecque : bilan d'une fausse révolte. *Le Monde* 28 April 2009.
Available at <http://lexandcity.blogspot.com/2009/04/2008-monde.html> [Accessed 10 August 2010].

Marantzidis, N., (2010). The deafening silence of the antisystemic Left. (In Greek). *To Vima* 18 April 2010. Available at <http://www.tovima.gr/default.asp?pid=2&ct=6&artid=326531&dt=18/04/2010> [Accessed 10 August 2010].

Marantzídis, N., (2010a). The fundamentalism of the Bible Left. (In Greek). *To Vima* 6 June 2010. Available at <http://www.tovima.gr/default.asp?pid=2&ct=114&artid=335916&dt=06/06/2010> [Accessed 10 August 2010].

Matsaganis, M., (2009). Facing up to the culture of violence. in Economides and Monastiriotis eds. 2009. *The Return of Street Politics? Essays on the December Riots in Greece.* London: The Hellenic Observatory, LSE.

Melucci, A., (1989). *Nomads of the Present. Social Movements and individual needs in contemporary society.* Philadelphia: Temple University Press.

Melucci, A., (1996). *Challenging Codes. Collective Action in the Information Age*. Cambridge: Cambridge University Press.

Merton, R.K., (1938). Social Structure and Anomie. *American Sociological Review*, 3(5), pp. 672-682.

Mouzelis, N., (1978). *Greek Society. Aspects of underdevelopment*. (In Greek), Athens: Exantas.

Mouzelis , N., (1986). *Parliamentarism and industrialization in the semi-periphery. Greece, Balkans, Latin America.* (In Greek), Athens: Themelio.

Mouzelis, N., (2008). Explosive mixture of luxury and pauperization. (in Greek), *Imerisia* 13 December 2008. Available at <http://www.ananeotiki.gr/el/readArchives.asp?catID=1&subCatID=1&textID=3041> [Accessed 10 August 2010].

Mouzelis, N., (2008a). Social explosion and civil society. (In Greek). *To Vima* 21 December 2008. Available at <http://www.tovima.gr/default.asp?pid=46&ct=72&artId=241057&dt=21/12/2008> [Accessed 10 August 2010].

Mouzelis, N., (2009). On the December Events, in Economidis and Monastiriotis eds. 2009 *The Return of Street Politics? Essays on the December Riots in Greece*. London: The Hellenic Observatory, LSE.

Mpasakos, P., (2008). The voice and the violence. (in Greek). *Kathimerini* 28 December 2008. Available at <http://news.kathimerini.gr/4dcgi/_w_articles_columns_2_28/12/2008_29 7518> [Accessed 9 August 2010].

Ovetz, R., (1996). Turning Resistance into Rebellion: Student Movements and the Entrepreneuralization of the Universities. *Capital and Class, 58*, pp. 113-152.

Pagoulatos, G., (2008). The vision of the hooded ones. (In Greek). *Kathimerini* 21 December 2008. Available at <http://news.kathimerini.gr/4dcgi/_w_articles_columns_2_21/12/2008_29 6910> [Accessed 11 August 2010].

Papadimitropoulos, D., (2009). The cry of silence and the silence of politics. (In Greek). *Nea Estia,* 1819, pp. 275-284.

Papangelis, T., (2008). The asylum is in the streets. (In Greek). *To Vima* 14 December 2008. Available at <http://www.tovima.gr/default.asp?pid=46&ct=6&artId=240217&dt=14/1 2/2008> [Accessed 6 August 2010].

Papangelis, T., (2009). No rumble without its benefits. (in Greek). *To Vima* 6 December 2009. Available at <http://www.tovima.gr/default.asp?pid=2&ct=114&artId=303461&dt=06/ 12/2009> [Accessed 5 August 2010].

Papanikolópoulos, D., (2009). Organization, discourse and repertoire of the revolt. Advantages and disadvantages. (in Greek). *Avgi* 11 January 2009. Available at <http://www.avgi.gr/NavigateActiongo.action?articleID=427650> [Accessed 10 August 2010].

Papatheodorou G., (2008). Deep Blue, almost Black. (In Greek). *Avgi* 14 December 2008. Available at <http://www.ananeotiki.gr/el/readArchives.asp?catID=1&subCatID=7&tex tID=3048> [Accessed 10 August 2010].

Papatheodorou, G., (2009). The symptom and the crisis. (In Greek). *Nea Estia,* 1819, pp. 285-293.

Papatheodorou, G., (2009a). The invisible December. (In Greek). *Sýnchrona Thémata,* 103, pp. 112-113.

Parsons, T. (1991). *The Social System.* London: Routledge.

Psimitis, M., (2009). Confronting a new youth social movement. (In Greek). *Epohi* 4 January 2009, pp. 30-31.

Ramphos, S., (2008). Zero as a long death rattle. (In Greek). *Kathimerini* 14 December 2008. Available at <http://news.kathimerini.gr/4dcgi/_w_articles_politics_2_14/12/2008_296 056> [Accessed 2 August 2010].

Ruggiero, V., (2006). *Understanding Political Violence. A Criminological Analysis*, Maidenhead: Open University Press.

Seferiadis, S., (2008). What is the cause of violence? (In Greek). *To Vima* 21 December 2008. Available at <http://www.tovima.gr/default.asp?pid=46&ct=72&artId=241059&dt=21/12/2008> [Accessed 1 August 2010].

Seferiadis, S., (2009). Le 'décembre grec' comme action insurrectionnelle. Available at <http://www.contretemps.eu/interviews/decembre-grec-comme-action-insurrectionnelle> [Accessed 1 August 2010].

Serdedakis, N., (2009). The crisis of theory as opportunity. (In Greek). Avgi 11 January 2009. Available at <http://www.avgi.gr/NavigateActiongo.action?articleID=427670> [Accessed 2 August 2010].

Sevastakis, N., (2009). Thoughts about the management of a revolt. (In Greek). *Nea Estia,* 1819, pp. 300-315.

Sevastakis, N., (2010). Matter everywhere, Love nowhere. (In Greek). Αλη*th*εια, 4-5, pp. 287-290.

Simitis, C., (1989). *Development and modernization of Greek society.* (In Greek). Athens: Gnosi.

Simitis, C., (1992). *Proposals for another policy strategy.* (In Greek). Athens: Gnosi.

Simitis. C., (1992a). *Nationalist populism or national strategy.* (In Greek). Athens: Gnosi.

Simitis, C., (1995). *For a strong society. For a strong Greece.* (In Greek).Athens: Plethro.

Slaughter, S.A. and Leslie L.L., (1997). *Academic Capitalism. Politics, Policies and the Entrepreneurial University.* Baltimore and London: The John Hopkins University Press.

Somerítis, R., (2008). Hooded youths, students and neonazis. (In Greek). *To Vima* 14 December 2008. Available at <http://www.tovima.gr/default.asp?pid=46&ct=6&artId=240212&dt=14/1 2/2008> [Accessed 6 August 2010].

Sotiris, P., (2010). Rebels with a Cause. The December 2008 Greek Youth Movement as the Condensation of Deeper Social and Political Contradictions. *International Journal of Urban and Regional Research*, 34 (1), pp. pp. 203-209.

Taylor, I., Walton, P. and Young, J., (1973). *The New Criminology: For a Social Theory of Deviance*, London: Routledge and Kegan Paul.

Thompson, K. ed.. (2004). *Readings from Emile Durkheim*. London and New York: Routledge.

Tilly, C., (2003). *The Politics of Collective Violence*.Cambridge: Cambridge University Press.

Tilly, C., (2004). *Social Movements. 1768-2004*. Boulder and London: Paradigm Publishers.

Tsimitakis, M., (2009). Revolt and the internet. (In Greek). *Sýnchrona Thémata*, 103, pp. 29-33.

Tsoukalas, C., (1977). *Dependence and Reproduction*. (In Greek). Athens: Themelio.

Tsoukalas, C., (1983). *Social development and the State. The constitution of public space in Greece*. (In Greek). Athens: Themelio.

Tsoukalas, C., (1986). *State, Society, Labour in post-war Greece*. (In Greek). Athens: Themelio.

Tsoukas, C., (2008). Murder and outbreak. (In Greek). *Kathimerini* 28 December 2008. Available at <http://news.kathimerini.gr/4dcgi/_w_articles_columns_2_28/12/2008_29 7481> [Accessed 2 August 2010].

Veremis, T., (2008). Individual and collective responsibility. (In Greek). *Kathimerini* 14 December 2008. Available at <http://news.kathimerini.gr/4dcgi/_w_articles_politics_2_14/12/2008_296 061> [Accessed 2 August 2010].

Voulgaris, G., (2008). The rage of impotence. (In Greek). *Ta Nea* 11 December 2008. Available at <http://www.tanea.gr/default.asp?pid=10&ct=13&artID=4491662> [Accessed 3 August 2010].

Voulgaris, G., (2008a). *Greece from the Metapolitefsi to Globalization.* (In Greek), Athens: Polis.

Wacquant, L., (1999). *Les prisons de la misère*, Paris: Raisons d'agir Editions / Editions du Seuil.

Wacquant. L., (2008). Ordering Insecurity: Social Polarization and the Punitive Upsurge. *Radical Philosophy Review.* 11(1), pp. 9-27.

Xydakis, N., (2008). Smoke signals. (In Greek). *Kathimerini* 28 December 2008. Available at <http://news.kathimerini.gr/4dcgi/_w_articles_columns_158_28/12/2008_ 297491> [Accessed 2 August 2010].

Zeri, P., (2009). The Riots of December: A Spontaneous Social Phenomenon or a Social Movement? In: Economidis and Monastiriotis eds. *The Return of Street Politics? Essays on the December Riots in Greece.* London: The Hellenic Observatory, LSE.

16.

LGBT MOVEMENTS, BIOPOLITICS AND NEW CRIMINOLOGY: A PRELIMINARY RESEARCH IN THE EASTERN MEDITERRANEAN REGION

Aimilia Voulvouli

Introduction

Even though sexuality emerges as a strictly personal, individual attribute of one's identity, it surely involves socio-political aspects. Especially when sexual preferences appear as manifested responses to policy-making (Lesbian, Gay, Bisexual, Transgender - *LGBT* movements), the latter is quite apparent. This paper aims at discussing the suppression of gay identity in countries of the Eastern Mediterranean - where at first glance, sexual repression stems from religious-oriented cultures – as a result of the uneven contact with the West (Drucker 1996). In addition, the pages that follow will attempt to exemplify, using the case of Greece and Cyprus, that *LGBT* movements in former colonies and cryptocolonies (see below) resist not only to sexual but also to general social repression. As Drucker (*ibid*) claims, along with economic came the sexual domination of the colonisers, in terms of what is 'normal' and what is 'unnatural' in sexual behaviour. On the contrary in countries like Turkey which the orientalist mind would classify as more prejudiced against homosexuality, as far as legislation is concerned, anti-gay laws had been abolished a long before the Christian West. That is not to suggest, that in predominantly Muslim countries homosexual behaviour is not being repressed. It is just to claim that anti-gay prejudice and legislation is mostly related to geopolitics and economic hierarchies rather than to tradition (religious or not).

The question arising from the above is why sexuality is being subject of social control? A question that has been answered very convincingly – according to my opinion – by Michel Foucault in his usage of biopolitics; that is "the explosion of numerous and diverse techniques by modern states for achieving the subjugations of bodies and the control of populations" (Green 2010:317). According to Foucault (1977; 1980) disciplinary power transforms 'docile bodies' into discipline subjects of the state and medicine, working in the service of domination and formal social control.

Following this, I will attempt to initiate a discussion based on the assumption that the suppression of gay identity and particularly of *LGBT* movements aims at not only sexual orientation but also and probably most importantly at the repression of a series of demands that accompany such movements and gay identity in general. As Weeks (1989) very well put it

"it is not homosexuality in itself that poses the real threat. [...] In many societies around the Mediterranean littoral, for example, and in Latin America, a form of easy-going male homosexuality co-exists with highly traditional family values. And this undermines neither masculinity nor heterosexuality. The real threat comes when lesbian and gay activities become part of an alternative way of life. For when people endorse the idea of sexual pluralism they are also implicitly endorsing social and political pluralism. When they affirm their lesbian or gay identities, when they assert their sense of belonging to social movements and communities organized around their sexual preferences they are making a political statement. Homosexuality then becomes more than an individual quirk or private choice. It becomes a challenge to absolute' values of all types [...] authoritarian and not only (my emphasis) *regimes don't like that".*

Reccep, Europe and 'us'

My interest on this subject was triggered during a journey from Istanbul to Athens by bus, when I was conducting fieldwork in Turkey on environmental activism. During the long hours that such a journey lasts I met a young man who confessed that although his family and friends knew that he was going to Greece for professional reasons, he was actually going to Athens to meet his Greek boyfriend. In, what seemed to me, an attempt to justify his dishonesty to his family and circle of acquaintances, he asked me what was my opinion about his 'deviant' sexual behaviour and when I told him that as far as I was concerned there was nothing deviant about it, our conversation became even more vivid. Having believed that I had gained his trust – as much as this is possible during a twelve-hour journey – I turned the discussion in more interesting for me topics. One of them was his opinion about the current government of the pro-Islamist Justice and Development Party (in Turkish Adalet ve Kalkınma Partisi – *AKP*) and his reply was very disorienting for my orientalist mind.

> I am very satisfied by Reccep[1] and his administration. He is very liberal, Euro-friendly and he is the only one who can make Turkey's accession a reality. If this happens many things will change for us (homosexuals).

As I have already mentioned above his comment surprised me because in my mind, homosexuals belong to the progressive part of society and Islam according to my preconceptions of it was not at all progressive, a fact constantly reminded to me by my secularist informants during my fieldwork. How could a homosexual individual support such a party? Trying to answer this question, I turned to what in such cases seems helpful: the literature and particular the one dealing with homosexuality in non-western settings. I came across a brilliant article written by Peter Drucker, published in the *New Left Review* (1996) in which he claims that homosexuality as an identity and consequently a deviant one in non-Western countries, has its roots in the uneven contact with the West.

According to him the developing world has been influenced by a 'commodified transgenderal' sexuality that arose in late medieval and early modern Europe and has been replaced by another type of sexuality as late as in the twentieth century that first appeared in Europe, namely reciprocal gay and lesbian sexuality. Developing nations have followed this shift once businesses catering to same-sex networks are established. "Once such networks grow, it becomes more likely for a broad group, including transgenderal people, to spend more time in an emergent gay community and to begin to identify with it" (*ibid*: 90). He uses Turkey as an example claiming that, "with a level of economic development higher than the average in the Middle East, gay subcultures, virtually unique in the Islamic world, have grown up in the big cities Ankara, Istanbul and Izmir" (*ibid*: 90).

---

[1] Reccep Tayyip Erdoğan, the current prime minister of Turkey.

In light of his argument I have started to research on the legislation of ex-colonies Muslim dominated countries. It turned out that the eastern Mediterranean is a region that fulfils the above criteria. In addition, as Matthew Waits claims (2010:64) in an article about sexuality as a central issue in the culture war between Islam and the West: "We live in a shadow of war. [...] [There is] a context of culture wars between 'Islam' and 'the West' which have a long standing history [...] but became heightened in focus from 2001 after the events of 9/11. These global culture wars are centrally focused on issues of gender and sexuality". Eastern Mediterranean is in the middle of this war and it is indeed a region where gender and sexuality issues are in the midst of the conflicts that take place.

Homosexuality in the West

In the West, as sexuality became a distinct element of identity since the 17th century onwards, homosexuality also "became for the first time in late nineteenth-century Europe the domain of a specifically and systematically identified set of people which included not just transgenderal people but *all* those engaging in same-sex activity" (Drucker 1996:83). Similarly, Boswell (1989:20) informs us that "what we call 'homosexuality' (in the sense of the distinguishing traits of 'homosexuals'), for example, was not considered a unified set of acts, much less a set of qualities defining particular persons, in pre-capitalist societies.... Heterosexuals and homosexuals are involved in social 'roles' and attitudes which pertain to a particular society, modern capitalism".

Ever since, homosexuality has been treated either as disease or as deviance (Foucault 1980; Wolf 2004). In one of history's darkest hours, during WWII, homosexual individuals have been exterminated by Nazi Germany (Wolf 2004). In almost all the western world, there has been reported targeting and discrimination over homosexuals until very late as for example during the MacCarthy era in the USA (Wolf 2004). However, *LGBT* groups created new gay subcultures mostly urban and this in turn gave rise to new theories of homosexual behavior as inherent in a person and thus not possible to change. These theories altered the ways gay people perceived themselves; that is, different from the rest of society a view shared by the non-gay community (*ibid*). For example, as Wolf (*ibid*:http://www.isreview.org/issues/37/gay_oppression.shtml) mentions in 1950 "the U.S. Senate launched an investigation into allegations of homosexuals "and other perverts" in federal government jobs. According to the Senate report, gays "lack the emotional stability of normal persons"; "sex perversion weakens the individual"; and "espionage agents could blackmail them".

In the socialist world even if the Soviet State abolished penal restrictions on homosexual activities as soon as it was created, in 1934 "homosexuality once again became a criminal offence in the USSR and the Communist movements of the rest of the world soon followed suit in labeling   homosexuality as 'unsocialist' " (Wolf 2004: www.isreview.org/issues/37/gay_oppression.shtml).

Nevertheless homosexual activism has been identified with the Left (Weeks 1989; Wolf 2004) and in the Western world this association was a fact during some periods (Weeks 1989). A similar association between gay activism and other groups such as the Black Power Movement (Wolf 2004) indicates that *LGBT* movements do not limit their agenda to the pure sexual liberation demand. A more recent example from Massachusetts exemplifies this claim: In 2004, "the Massachusetts Teachers Association, Service Employees International Union Locals 509 and 2020, the Massachusetts Nurses Association, the National Association of Government Employees, International Brotherhood of Electrical Workers Local 1505, and the Massachusetts United Auto Workers (UAW) union all passed resolutions defending gay marriage" (*ibid*). This fact suggests that *LGBT* movements identify with labour movements and that repression either, sexual, gender, work or class is the main issue around which such movements mobilise[2]. In other words, this chapter aims at initiating a discussion concerning the repression of gay-identity as an identity carrying with it a lot more than the pure sexual liberation demand.

Homosexuality in non -Western settings

According to Massad (2009) outside the western world
> *"men who engage in sex with men (and women who engage in sex with women, though there is less interest in the literature in the latter) do not identify or name themselves in accordance with these*

---

[2] As June Nash (2005:13) claims for example, 'feminism is a movement against sexism that has expanded to include men and gays as well as women. The goals of many feminist groups are the liberation of society from behaviours that constrict the humanity of any one group".

intimate practices anymore than those men who have sex with women identify themselves in accordance with their practices. While there is a small number of upper class and upper middle class westernized Arabs who are seduced by gayness and the American example of it, they are not representative of, nor can speak for the majority of men and women who engage in same sex practices and do not identify themselves in accordance with these practices".

As Drucker (1996) discusses, "same-sex eroticism or other kinds of indigenous sexuality such as transgenderal sexuality was very common in pre-class, non-western societies as well as in class-based and slave-based economies where the lowest class "was torn apart from kinship and community ties" (*ibid*:81). He goes on to say that "the prohibition of certain indigenous sexual practices was part of a far-reaching process of making colonized societies serve their conquerors' needs, just as the disintegration of kinship structures facilitated the establishment of exploitative forced or waged labour. [...] The existence of same-sex eroticism among the indigenous peoples of the Americas was even used as a pretext by the Spanish for exterminating them or, at the very least, for conquering, dispossessing and converting them. The same pretext was used in other colonised areas" (Drucker 1996:85).

However, indigenous sexualities have been persistent especially in areas that have not been Christianized. Thus we have the survival of male to male eroticism in the Arab-Islamic world even if legislation in most of the case in the Eastern Mediterranean for example, doesn't support such behaviour[3]. In addition, as Altman (1996:87-88) argues "The significant aspect of the contemporary globalization of capitalism is the growth of affluence in many countries and the corresponding greater freedom for individual choice it makes possible. Affluence, education, and awareness of other possibilities are all prerequisites for the adoption of new forms of identity, and the spread of these conditions will increase the extent to which gay identities develop beyond their base in liberal Western societies".

---

[3] In Syria according to the Article 520 of the Penal Code of 1949 "unnatural" sexual intercourse is prohibited and a maximum sentence of three years imprisonment is provided; in Lebanon homosexuality is also illegal; the Palestinian territories have a more complicated legislation: in the Gaza Strip it is illegal for men but legal for women; in the West Bank homosexuality is legal since 1951; Similarly, in Israel it is legal since 1963.

LGBT Movements: Greece, Turkey, Cyprus

In spite of gay oppression, organized resistance of it emerged early on. The first gay organisation named the Scientific – Humanitarian Committee was founded in Germany in 1897 (Wolf 2004). Such organisations flourished during the period 1919 – 1923, but the modern *LGBT* movement was born out of the famous Stonewall riots[4]. As Drucker (1996:83) reminds us "beginning in the 1890s, lesbians and gay men influenced by feminism or other radical ideologies organized politically, giving rise by the 1970s to demands for the abolition of the social categories of gender and of 'homosexuality' and 'heterosexuality'". Today, both in the West and in the developing world *LGBT* resistance movements are very much present, active and "caught up in global economic and social developments" (*ibid*). The present chapter is based on data and literature from Greece, Turkey and Cyprus. The reason for choosing these countries as examples lies on the interesting fact that in Turkey private homosexual conduct has never been subject to penal restrictions since it is legal - even before Turkey became a nation state in 1923 (since 1858). In addition, all legal restrictions have been short-lived and do not seem to be associated with religious traditions. On the contrary in Greece and Cyprus penal restrictions on private homosexual conduct have been removed in 1951 and as late as 1998 respectively (http://en.wikipedia.org/wiki/*LGBT*_Rights) and especially in Cyprus it seems that the Cypriot Orthodox Church and the colonial legacy of the island are very much involved in this delay. In addition, although Greece and Turkey have never been officially colonized, I take Michael Herzfeld's notion of crypto-colonialism[5] very seriously.

---

[4] The Stonewall riots took their name form a drag-queen bar in New York's Greenwhich Village, call the Stonewall Inn. On June 28 1969 a riot against police forces burst and for three days 2,000 gays, lesbians, and their supporters fought police in the streets of lower Manhattan. The activists demanded the termination of anti-gay legislation, police harassement and public respect (http://en.wikipedia.org/wiki/Stonewall_riots). Today the riots are being commemorated every June in many big cities around the globe in the form of the Gay Pride marches.
[5] According to Herzfeld (2003: 213) 'crypto-colonialism' is a situation in which, as the price of freedom from colonial rule, some countries accepted the tutelary control of Western nations, especially in the adoption of a bureaucratically conceived, fundamentally positivistic understanding of the territorial nation-state. In the Greek case, this entailed a particularly ruthless "cleansing" of indigenous cultural forms.

Greece

In Greece *LGBT* rights are limited to the non-penalization of same-sex sexual activity. Other than that, there is no legal provision for same-sex marriage and for same-sex couples' adoption rights. In addition, even though during the last decade, there has been a legislative effort to offer several rights to unmarried couple, this effort does not concern same-sex couples. Major controversy was caused in 2008 when the, at the time, mayor of Tilos Anastasios Aliferis married two homosexual couples citing that the 1982 law that legalized civil marriage between two individuals, does not specify the gender of the individuals, thus leaving room for interpretation (www.lesbian.gr/scene.php?t=politics&id=94). His initiative was strongly opposed by the Church of Greece and the - at the time - Minister of Justice Sotiris Hatzigakis did not accept the unions as valid (www.tovima.gr/relatedarticles/article/?aid=23).

Nevertheless, the Archbishop of the Greek Church Ieronymos II, has later on stated that "should be more open-minded and less moralistic" (www.pinknews.co.uk/news/articles/2005-7284.html) and even if he has never specified if this view applied to same-sex civil marriages, many have interpreted his view as such. In this climate the current minister of Justice, Transparency and Human Rights has declared that the Ministry's proposition is to modernize Family Law and this will include provisions of same-sex couples. In addition, legislative efforts have prohibited gender discrimination in the workplace, except armed forces.

As far as society is concerned homosexuality is not widely accepted in Greece. Indicative of this climate are the cases of fines issued by the Greek National Council for Radio and Television to various TV channels and radio frequencies for having exposed scenes of affection between homosexual individuals on the grounds of insult of moral values. In 2007 Eurobarometer published a survey in which was mentioned that 77% of Greeks believed that homosexuality is a disadvantage. (http://en.wikipedia.org/wiki/LGBT_rights_in_Greece).

The gay and lesbian movement in Greece was formed in the aftermath of the seven year dictatorship. In such a context gender inequalities were seen as a result of the authoritarian regime the country had just come out from as well as a result of the economic inequalities of capitalism (Michopoulou 2006). Feminism has also been an ideological vantage-point for this movement as it was for the movements formed in western Europe and north America during the 1960s and the 1970s where gay movements have flourished hand in hand with feminist, black people's as well as marginalised and oppressed groups (Kantsa 2009).

In 1975 we have the foundation of the "Women's Liberation Movement" and in 1977 the foundation of Hellenic Homosexual Liberation Movement (in Greek *AKOE*) while in 1978 we have the foundation of the "Autonomous Group of Homosexual Women" (*ibid*). The meeting point (literally and ideologically) of such groups was the Women of Athens House (*Spiti Gynaikon*) which was constituted by feminist, political and gay groups (Michopoulou 2006).

Today Greece and especially Athens has a large number of *LGBT* groups. Since 2005, an Athens Pride is taking place every year as well as a Gay and Lesbian film festival. This scene seems disassociated from the political atmosphere of the 1970s but it still seems influenced by the kind of *LGBT* activism that flourishes in Western Europe and North America.

Turkey

In Turkey, *LGBT* rights are also limited to non-penalization of gay sexual conduct between consenting adults in private. Nevertheless, *LGBT* discrimination is not legally prohibited and same-sex marriages and civil unions are not recognised. *LGBT* groups claim that homophobia is common in contemporary Turkey, a fact suggested by the various attempts to abolish *LGBT* groups. As far as society is concerned, the incident mentioned above between me and my gay friend indicates that there is indeed a sense of discrimination among homosexuals in Turkey, something which is also declared by *LBGT* groups in their numerous allegations of homophobic incidents. Nevertheless, today, Turkey's *LGBT* movement consists of various organizations based on Ankara, Istanbul, Antalya and Diyarbakır. The first Gay Pride took place in 2003 in Istanbul where the gay scene is quite large and open. The !F Independent Film Festival, held every year in Istanbul has an *LGBT* section.

Cyprus

In Cyprus same-sex relationships were legalized as late as 1998 by a law which replaced the 1889 British law against "buggery" (Jelatis-Hoke 2006). Similarly as in Greece and Turkey same-sex marriage and civil unions is not recognized by law. Nevertheless, anti-discrimination law is implemented except from the armed forces on the grounds that homosexuality is a mental illness. In the Turkish Republic of Northern Cyprus which is the part of the island occupied since the Turkish invasion of Cyprus in 1974 male homosexuality is still illegal while female homosexuality does not exist as a legal category. The Cypriot Orthodox Church whose political and social influence is quite large states that homosexuality is immoral and the public is very skeptical as legal liberalization proceeds a fact shown in a survey published in 2006 and mentioned that 75% of Cypriots think of homosexuality as an illness. The first gay group of the country – the *Cypriot Gay Liberation Movement* – was founded in 1987 and in 2010, *Accept – Cyprus* an *LGBT* rights movement was formed. In Northern Cyprus, the *Initiative Against Homophobia* was founded in 2007 and in 2008 the *Shortbus Movement* was created. The Cypriot gay scene is weak but gradually growing especially since the decriminalization act in 1998. Similarly, the gay movement is also weak and it seems to have been enacted from outside of the country by gay men who have studied or worked abroad and imported ideas from Europe and North America (Jelatis – Hoke 2006).

Discussion: The Suppression of Gay Movements within the New Criminology theoretical framework

New Criminology (1973) set the basis for an analysis of crime not as a pathology but as a phenomenon inherent in capitalist society. Accordingly, deviance - which is a notion often used to describe homosexuality -should be studied sociologically taking into account the whole social context as shaped by inequalities in wealth and power stemming from class relations (Georgoulas in this volume). Such a study should revolve around social structure and the interactions between people and structures of power in the context of which deviance as a process takes places (*ibid*). In addition, the contradictions of crime as an inherent part of the whole phenomenon is studied under the viewpoint of conflict which analyses crime as the product of criminalisation of those in power and hence winners of the social conflicts at the expense of the weak and hence losers. Social conflicts take part in all sorts of social realms and gender conflict is a much discussed example of such a conflict. It is in this context that the effort to penalize homosexuality with a bill that was introduced to the Greek parliament in 1977 should be studied. The bill mentioned among other things that "anyone that walks in meeting points and looked suspicious could be arrested" even if it came to the attention of the police based on anonymous complaint (Koukoutsaki 2002). As Altman (2001:88) claims, 'modern' ways of being homosexual threaten not only the custodians of 'traditional' morality but also political establishments. This brings us to the second point I would like to raise which is that 'gay' or gay-like social formations continue to emerge in countries around the world as a vehicle for claiming free space and asserting alternative ways of relationship formation (Bereket and Adam 2006). As has already been mentioned above, gay-identity is an identity carrying with it a lot more than the pure sexual liberation demand and this is why biopolitical discipline focuses not only on the control of individual but also on the political body[6]. In this sense, it is fair to say that the suppression of *LGBT* movements aims at not only sexual orientation but also and probably most importantly at the repression of a series of demands that accompany gay-rights movements and gay identity in general. For example, in Turkey homosexual activism has been discussed in relation to other kinds of activism such as environmental, which is also associated with wider claims such as respect for human rights and democratization (Voulvouli 2009;2010). As Kandiyoti (2002) claims in Turkey, gay groups have been involved also in environmental and transnational human rights activism and similarly, Arat (1994:223) argues that the aftermath of the 1980s coup d' etat resulted in "environment, nuclear proliferation and gay rights awareness". Therefore, I believe that the discussion on *LGBT* movements and the ways they are being dealt with by state power outside Western Europe and North America should historically investigate sexuality following the work of Foucault (1977;1980) and others who have claimed that sexuality is constructed, cultivated and implanted (Green 2010). In this sense, *indigenous sexualities* should not be seen as elements of states that "lack human rights in relation to sexual orientation and gender identity but they need to be interpreted with reference to critiques of global racism, Orientalism and various cultural hierarchies" (Waites 2008). "Classifications of sex, sexual orientation and

---

[6] Drucker (1996:76) claims that "those who repress [...]lesbians and gay men are one-sidedly selecting from and manipulating indigenous traditions. Anti-gay attitudes do not help to free [...] peoples from outside domination. Rather, they are a single aspect of their more general suffering under the 'New World Order' and the current global economic crisis. Newly arising gay and lesbian movements are an aspect of [...] peoples' efforts to reclaim and redefine their nations and cultures".

race fix bodies, subjectivities and identities in socially constructed categories, which, in turn, form the basis of stratification, social regulation and control" (Green 2010: 320). As Jelatis – Hoke writes about researching gay identity in Cyprus (2006:3): "a lot of background research was required before I would be able to do this sort of in-depth analysis[…] (especially) after becoming aware of the deep colonial legacy left to homosexuals in Cyprus. A discussion based on such an approach could lead in the shaping of a theoretical framework on which scholars dealing with gender suppression in countries of the Eastern Mediterranean could base their research.

References

Altman, D. (2001). *Global sex*. Chicago: The University of Chicago Press.

Altman, D. (1996) Rupture or Continuity: The Internationalization of Gay Identity, *Social Text 48*, 14(3): 77–94.

Arat, Y. (1994) Toward a Democratic Society: The Women's Movement in Turkey in the 1980s. *Women's Studies International Forum.* 17(2-3): 241 – 248.

Bereket, T. and Adam, B.D. (2006) 'The Emergence of Gay Identities in Contemporary Turkey', *Sexualities* 9(2): 131–51.

Boswell, J. (1989) Revolutions, Universals, and Sexual Categories. In Duberman, M., Vicinus, M. and Chauncey, G (eds.), *Hidden From History: Reclaiming the Gay and Lesbian Past.* New York: Meridian.

Drucker, P. (1996) 'In the Tropics There Is No Sin': Sexuality and Gay–Lesbian Movements in the Third World. *New Left Review* I/218: 75-101.

Foucault, M. (1977) *Discipline and Punish: The Birth of the Prison.* New York: Vintage.

Foucault, M. (1980) *The History of Sexuality: An Introduction.* New York: Vintage.

Georgoulas, S. (2011) Radix of radical criminology- Hesiod. In: Georgoulas, S. (ed.) *The Politics of Criminology*. Berlin: LIT Verlag.

Green, A. I. (2010) Remembering Foucault: Queer Theory and Disciplinary Power. *Sexualities* 13(3): 316–337.

Herzfeld, M (2003) *The Body Impolitic: Artisans and Artifice in the Global Hierarchy of Value*. Chicago: The University of Chicago Press.

Jelatis – Hoke, T. (2006) Voices from the Closet: Male Homosexuality and Dual Identity in the Republic of Cyprus. Independent Study Project. SIT: Cyprus.

Kandiyoti, D. (2002) Introduction. In : Kandiyoti, D and A Saktanber (eds.) *Fragments of Culture: The Everyday of Modern Turkey*. London and New York, I.B. Tauris & Co Publishers.

Kantsa, V. (2009) Visible invisible, invisibly visible: Two features of lesbian presence in Greece (in Greek). Paper presented at the one-day conference "Sexualities and Gender: Lesbian, Gay, Bisexual, Transgender and Queer Communities in Greece" Organized by the Athens Pride. May 9th 2009, Panteion University.

Koukoutsaki, A. (2002) *Drug use, Homosexuality: Non-compliance attitudes between penal and medical regulation* (in Greek). Athens: Kritiki.

Michopoulou, A. (2006) Feminist theory and feminist movement in post-dictatorship Greece: Fertile and infertile encounters during 1974 - 1988. Paper presented at the European Meeting "Women Studies/gender studies and women movement: exploring the relationships". May 4th 2006, Panteion University.

Weeks, J. (1989) Sexual Politics: What do Fidel Castro and Margaret Thatcher have in common? *New Internationalist* 201 November 1989.

Life & Society (2009) The West and the Orientalism of sexuality: Interview with Joseph Massad.

Taylor, I.. Walton, P. and Young, J., (1973). *The New Criminology: For a Social Theory of Deviance*. London: Routledge and Kegan Paul.

Voulvouli, A. (2009) *From Environmentalism to Transenvironmentalism: The Ethnography of an Urban Protest in Modern Istanbul*. Oxford: Peter Lang.

Voulvouli, A. (2010) Leftism, Secularism, Transnationalism and Localism: The Identities of an Urban Protest in Contemporary Istanbul. *Ethnologia On-Line (http://www.societyforethnology.gr/site/pdf/TheidentitiesofASG.pdf)*.

Waites, M. (2008) Analysing Sexualities in the Shadow of War: Islam in Iran, the West and the Work of Reimagining Human Rights. *Sexualities* 11(1-2): 64 – 73.

Weeks, J. (1989) *Sex, Politics and Society: The Regulation of Sexuality Since 1800*. London: Longman Limited.

Wolf, S. (2004) The Roots of Gay Oppression. *International Socialist Review*. 37: September – October.

Websites:

http://en.wikipedia.org/wiki/Stonewall_riots (Accessed on 10.03.2011)

http://en.wikipedia.org/wiki/LGBT_Rights (Accessed on 15.03.2011)

http://www.pinknews.co.uk/news/articles/2005-7284.html/ (Accessed on 15.03.2011)

http://en.wikipedia.org/wiki/LGBT_rights_in_Greece (Accessed on 15.03.2011)

http://www.lesbian.gr/scene.php?t=politics&id=94 (Accessed on 18.03.2011) http://www.tovima.gr/relatedarticles/article/?aid=23 (Accessed on 22.03.2011)

17.

GOING THROUGH THE GATES: PRISON AND MOTHERHOOD, ADJUSTMENT AND SOLIDARITY

Toulina Demeli

The present paper is based on the PhD research I completed at the department of Social Anthropology and History, University of the Aegean, on imprisoned mothers: how do they speak of motherhood and their own experiences of being mothers behind bars (Demeli 2007). I conducted qualitative field research at the *Closed Central Women's Prison of Korydallos* in Athens[1], for about one year and a half, from September 2001 till January 2003. We won't to mention here the numerous difficulties of conducting such a research, mainly due to prison's totalitarian closed character and the ways this affects inmates[2].

At the time of the research the women's prison was overcrowded[3]: there were about 370 to 400 women imprisoned in an institution with a capacity to receive maximum 270[4]. Three out of four women in prison are mothers and motherhood is obviously reflected in the way they speak about their imprisonment. Women in prison find themselves accused by society because they committed a crime according to the court's decision, but moreover because they committed a crime although they had underage children to protect and look after. They are stigmatized as "criminals" but also as "bad mothers"[5].

The fact they are mothers, on the other hand, gives them strength and courage to face the 'Pains of Imprisonment' (Sykes 1958), provides

---

[1] Structural, administrative, organizational and other information about the Women's Prison of Koridallos can also be found in the works of Dimopoulos 1998, Thanopoulou, Fronimou, Tsilimigaki 1997, Kourakis, Milioni 1999.
[2] About the practical, ethical, methodological etc difficulties of conducting research in prison and their possible solutions see Lundström 1987, Rhodes 2001: 76-77.
[3] According to Acoca, because women are correctly considered to be less violent than men it is more likely for them to be imprisoned by the competent authorities in small spaces (1998: 63). In Greek correctional institutions however, both women and men's prisons are overcrowded.
[4] On September 2006 the number had risen to 560 inmates.
[5] See also Dobash, Dobash, Gutteridge 1986: 193, Watterson: 1996, Enos 2001, Dodge, Pogrebin 2001: 52 etc.

them with hope and focus for their future[6], that is for their release, their return to their children and society at large. Through the impersonal and dominantly indisputable ideal of 'motherhood' they try to overcome their personally stigmatized penal and maternal identity.

Through this paper I would like to refer to their efforts to adjust to prison life and constitute solidarity networks based on 'motherhood'.

Mothers I spoke with describe their prison experience, from their first efforts to adjust and socialize till the living present in prison and the perspective of their release, through the prism of their maternal identity. According to their ethnic and socioeconomic status, their previous and present relationship with their children and their families of origin, the sentence for the crime they did or did not commit and their unique personal characteristics, they redefine and identify themselves as "mothers" to the researcher.

Strategies of maternal performance

Performing motherhood in the domestic milieu seems to be dominated by the services mothers offer to their children[7]. While in prison, though, ipso facto, there is a very limited capability to provide for the children[8]. Mothers I spoke with manage maybe to speak with their children and give them advice through the phone, during the visiting hours or by mail, but they can not feed them, put them to bed, play with them or protect them on a daily basis. Confronted with their weakness to offer maternal services to their children they have to invent new ways of expressing their presence and interest for them, each one according to her financial and personal status and her choices[9]. Behind prison walls, women's maternal performance is more or less restricted. They try to construct presents by the means they have, to communicate during the visiting hours, through the telephone[10] or mail[11], as already mentioned[12].

---

[6] In a similar way, many mothers of handicapped children claim to be stronger, different and better mothers because of their child's disability that gives them a new goal and focus in their lives (Landsman 2000: 178).

[7] See Dubisch 2000, Paxson 2004, Christea-Doumani 1989 etc.

[8] See Young, Jefferson Smith 2000: 134.

[9] For imprisoned mother's efforts to prove that their capable mothers see also Garcia Coll et all 1998.

[10] For many researchers communication through the telephone is the best way to maintain contact with the children Caddle, Crisp 1997: 31., 43.

[11] Inmate psychiatrist Forest (1980), estimating that her communication with her children through mail is very important, writes to them form Madrit's Prison Yeserias one letter per

Women in prison emphasize on their will to be and behave as mothers to their children. By adopting and performing specific maternal strategies the try to prove that although they are in prison they can be "good" mothers, corresponding in the best possible way to the relevant dominant social demands. We are actually speaking of a "different", "restricted" motherhood, which, in contrast to the motherhood in free society, is performed, mainly from a distance and under special circumstances defined by their imprisonment. Sometimes the children might even not be the direct recipients of this performance.

Solidarity relations based on maternal identities

As far as solidarity relations are concerned, they should not be taken for granted inside the prison environment. Just like in the "free" world, there is hierarchy and authoritarian relations among people, codes of conduct and unwritten rules that have to be followed, mean feelings, jealously, arguments and fights. Prison is a representation of society in the micro level, where conflicts and power relations multiply and emerge more obviously and clearly. But, also just like in "free" society strong friendships, sympathy and solidarity relationships emerge[13].

Women in prison are "in-mates", a word that implies in English, at least theoretically, similar personal situation and companionship. Besides the fact of their common imprisonment, they are also bind by the common experiences of the past and the present, by their common misfortunes and by the fact that they are mothers away from their children. All these bonds are likely to formulate unspoken informal solidarity networks among them.

Motherhood, as a culturally recognized moral value connected to women, articulates an objective common reference for all imprisoned mothers, "good" or "bad" ones.

The painful facts of conviction and imprisonment, the cohabitation in the same totalitarian environment with the same daily schedule, occa-

---

week, letters witch, along with her five days diary in solitude, are published in the book: Diary and letters from prison. Athens: Themelio.
[12] For problems related to the visits of the children and the phone / mail communication see Easteal 2001: 104, Young, Jefferson Smith 2000: 133-134, Morris 1987: 116, Voglis 2004: 181. Besides the problems, maintaining that kind of bonds with the children and their family is very important for their post release and rehabilitation period (Finney Hairston 1988).
[13] Greer stresses the temporary character of friendships emerging behind prison walls (2000: 449).

sionally connect women and produce solidarity relations. Solidarity among prisoners, male of female, is expressed also against people and actions relevant to the prison institution and the official power of the state. At this paper though, we are interested in solidarity relations based on the common experiences and the maternal identity of imprisoned women.

Many women in prison, realising the common pain of the forced separation from the children that binds them with their inmates, often reinforce and encourage one another, regardless of being already intimate on not. Parallel to the typical declarations of sympathy among women, true and essential solidarity actions take place and can make a prisoner feel better. There are too many hard moments encountered by women in prison that make their need for encouragement urgent. When a prisoner has to face a difficult family situation, sympathy and solidarity from her fellow inmates give her courage and strength to continue. Besides tension and arguments in prison there is also sympathy and comfort.

Electra, a woman that serves a 20 years sentence for the murder of her husband, more or less declares to be very much frustrated from her fellow prisoners. She admits though that when she was shattered to be informed about the sudden severe aggravation of the health of her mother, her inmates pleasantly surprised her with their attitude and the respect they dealt with her problem (I am quoting Electra):

> …Well.. The other day I was in the prison kitchen and they told me that my mother had fallen in a comma, I nearly sank into a comma myself. I sat in the kitchen with my hands on my head, I was crying, I didn't know what to do. I went crazy. One or two women came there to comfort me. These days, when I was very much upset about the situation of my mother and until she got better, until she reopened her eyes, the rest of the women didn't even listen to the radio. I couldn't expect that kind of attitude. I told that to one woman working there with me: "I feel as if you were my own intimate people". This is what I told her. Because at that time I didn't know what to do, I felt trapped. Furthermore, it was weekend and not even the prosecutor was on duty. Because you can only leave prison if the prosecutor allows it and orders so.

While Electra had to go through these tough moments, women in solidarity stood by her. By a symbolic non action, women didn't listen to any music for 3 days, silently expressing by this gesture that they were on her side supporting her as a daughter whose mother's life is in danger. Electra almost lost her mother at that time. Her fellow inmates with their supportive attitude wanted to express their respect for the maternal relationship in general, especially behind prison walls and no matter what the part of the prisoner is in this relation (mother of child).

Especially when motherhood in prison is at stake in any way, the rest of the mothers often express their solidarity placing symbolically themselves in the position of the mother that is facing the problem. While I was visiting the women prison of Korydallos, many women spoke to me in sympathy and pain about the story of "giagia Froso" that lost her son because of drugs. Lina, who was convicted in a life sentence of the murder of her husband, referred to the drama of giagia Froso in deep sorrow, absolute understanding and intense skepticism concerning her own life. She would rate this incident (the loss of gigia Froso's son) as one of the worse moments she went through while being for about 9 years already in prison:

All of our moments are ugly here. Every minute...

Yesterday that giagia Froso's son died, he was a drug addict, they found him frozen in the backyard of a church.

It is the pain of the other person next to you, that you can do nothing about it.

You can never forget the reason you are in here.

We are going through the same thoughts. Every day.

I met giagia Froso myself by accident in a prison corridor just after she received the tragic news. My meeting with giagia Froso and her story was one of the most emotional moments and shocking experiences of my field research. I would like to share with you some notes I kept in my personal ethnographic diary about giagia Froso:

..Lina talked to me about her pain, the pain of the other women, the pain of giagia Froso that lost her son.

I met giagia Froso in a prison's corridor. The guards were carrying her. They were carrying her because she could not walk by herself.

She was crying, weeping and shouting. When she looked at me she caressed me on the chick and started calling me "My Kassandra. My Alki". She thought I was her daughter. And continued to weep and shout even more. The guards took her away to the social service's office. I left. I will never forget her face.

Two days later. I was waiting at the social service's office when Ms Olga, a giagia Froso's fellow inmate entered. She wanted to make an order: wheat, sugarplum, sugar. "The poor lady" she explained "she is so sad, crying all the time. At least we should organize a death ceremony for her (enniamera). It will be a nice ceremony, you 'll see. It will please her a lot".

Giagia Froso suffers because she lost her son and because being in prison she can not be a proper mother for him, not even in his death, "to sooth his soul". And to sooth her own soul. She feels as if she is loosing hem for the second time.

Even the ultimate, painful maternal performance, mother's ceremonial care for her dead child is not possible for giagia Froso, and for every imprisoned mother that looses her child. In addition to the pain of the loss of the child, a woman has to cope with the accusation against herself that she is incompetent to take care of the proper death ceremonies, her last chance to perform maternally, to "be a mother to her child". In an action of solidarity and in an effort to sooth the pain and the self accusation of giagia Froso, her fellow inmates take the initiative to perform, even inside prison walls the proper death ceremonies (mnimosina) "to please her" as Olga said, soothing the torturous thought of not being a good enough mother towards her dead son.

In the case of giagia Froso the solidarity demonstrations among women in the prison community, at least of those that have children, is based mainly on the common pain of imprisonment and on motherhood. When one of the socially recognized "positive female characteristics" such as "motherhood" or one of the common elements that constitute the prison community is disputed in the face of one prisoner, the rest of the women often express their solidarity explicitly, because the insult expands to them all. And the most crucial bonds among them that create and reinforce solidarity relations are motherhood and pain.

The story of giagia Froso that unexpectedly lost her son while she was trapped in prison brought together almost all of the women. By mourning all together with Froso for her dead son they expressed their own grief and personal drama in relation to their children, realizing in despair that they are far away from them and totally unable to protect them if and when needed. As Anna, a woman from Ydra convicted for fraud, remembers when I saw her a few weeks after the death: "When Giagia Froso's son died we all felt as if it was our own child that died. We organized a death ceremony for Alki.".

Following the personal grief of the biological mother, the death ceremony takes place in a way of collective maternal mourning. Many women share the pain of loss seeking redemption. Not only giagia Froso's redemption but everybody's redemption. Alki's death reminds and brings them face to face with their inadequate fulfilling of their maternal duties because of their imprisonment, it brings into surface their personal tragedy, their own worries, guilt and self reproof. Solidarity to giagia Froso and participation to the collective mourning is transformed into a collective maternal performance, into a massive public apology for the "collective responsibility" of imprisoned mothers towards their children.

References

Acoca, L. (1998) Defusing the Time Bomb: Understanding and Meeting the Growing Health Care Needs of Incarcerated Women in America. *Crime and Delinquency* 44(1):4969.

Caddle, D., Crisp, D. (1997) Imprisoned Women and Mothers: A Research and Statistics Directorate Report. London: Home Office Research and Statistics Directorate. *Research Study* 162.

Christea-Doumani, M. (1989) *The Greek Mother Formerly and Nowadays.* Athens: Human Relations Research Laboratory, Kedros (in Greek).

Demeli, P. (2007). *Mothers under Confinement: Maternal representations in a greek women's prison.* Lesvos: University of the Aegean. (unpublished PhD).

Dimopoulos, Ch. (1998) *The Crisis of the Prison Institution and the non Confinemental Penalties.* Athens-Komotini: Sakkoulas (in Greek).

Dobash, P. R., Dobash, R. E., Gutteridge, S. (1986) *The Imprisonment of Women. Oxford.* UK: Basil Blackwell. New York, USA: Basil Blackwell.

Dodge, M., Pogrebin, R. M. (2001) Collateral Costs of Imprisonment for Women: Complications of Reintegration. *The Prison Journal* 81(1): 42-54.

Dubisch, J. (2000) *The Religious Pilgrimage in Modern Greece: An ethnographic approach.* Athens: Alexandria (in Greek).

Easteal, P. (2001) Women in Australian Prisons: The Cycle of Abuse and Dysfunctional Environments. *The Prison Journal* 81(1): 87-112.

Enos, S. (2001) *Mothering from the Inside: Parenting in a Women's Prison.* New York: State University of New York Press.

Finney Hairston, C. (1988) Family Ties During Imprisonment: Do They Influence Future Criminal Activity? *Federal Probation* 52: 48-52.

Forest, E. (1980) *Diary and Letters from Prison.* Athens: Themelio. (in Greek).

Garcia Coll, C., Surrey, L. J., Buccio-Notaro, P., Molla, B. (1998) Incarcerated Mothers: Crimes and punishments. In: C. Garcia Coll, J. L. Surrey, K. Weingarten (eds). *Mothering Against the Odds: Diverse voices of contemporary mothers.* New York, London: The Guilford Press.

Greer, R. K. (2000) The Changing Nature of Interpersonal Relationships in a Women's Prison. *The Prison Journal* 80(4): 442-468.

Kourakis, N., Milioni, F. (1999) *Research in the Greek Prisons: B. The Women Prison of Koridallos.* Athens: Univeristy of Athens (not published) (in Greek).

Landsman, G. (2000) Real Motherhood, Class, and Children with Disabilities. In: H. Ragoné, F. W. Twine (eds): *Ideologies and Technologies of Motherhood: Race, Class, Sexuality, Nationalism.* New York and London: Routledge: 169-187.

Lundström, F. (1987) Research Design in Total Institutions: Problems, Pitfalls, and Possible Solutions. *Quality and Quantity 21*: 209-218.

Morris, A. (1987) *Women, Crime and Criminal Justice.* Oxford, New York: Basil Blackwell.

Paxson, H. (2004) *Making Modern Mothers: Ethics and Family Planning in Urban Greece.* Berkley, Los Angeles, London: University of California Press.

Rhodes, A. L. (2001) Toward an Anthropology of Prisons. *Annual Review of Anthropology* 30: 65-83.

Sykes, G. (1958) *The Society of Captives.* Princeton: Princeton University Press.

Thanopoulou, M., Fronimou, E., Tsilimigaki, V. (1997) *Imprisoned Women Released: The right to professional rehabilitation.* Athens-Komotini: Sakkoulas (in Greek).

Voglis, P. (2004) *Prison and Exile Experience: Political Prisoners in the Civil War.* Athens: Alexandria (in Greek).

Watterson, K. (1996) [1973]. *Women in Prison: Inside the Concrete Womb.* Boston: Northeastern University Press.

Young, S. D., Jefferson Smith, C. (2000) When Moms are Incarcerated: The Needs of Children, Mothers and Caregivers. Families in Society: *The Journal of Contemporary Human Services* 81(2): 130-141.

18.

FOCUS GROUP, A RESEARCH METHOD TO ANALYZE FREE SOFTWARE MOVEMENT AND SOCIAL CONSTRUCTION OF CRIME

Angeliki Kitsiou

Introduction

Every social phenomenon taking place in the complex of social relations reflects a part of social reality, according to the signification assigned to it by each social subject. Social reality is defined by the interaction of individual and social acting, that is, the interaction of individuals and society within the framework of these actions. Each phenomenon which is integral part of the social reality constitutes a social action. Crime as a social phenomenon is a form of social action of individual as well as collective character. Its evaluation and signification as a meaning and action, is formed in relation to the current social and cultural conditions and the legal framework in force.

In this paper, an effort is made to present that the construction of the meaning of crime constitutes a social product, that is, a result of sociopolitical and economic relations, through the study of the free software movement actions. Crime has constituted and still constitutes a social action, which, through the activities of social movements, has been redefined, resignified and reinterpreted, according to social movements' influence on society and on current institutional dictates.

The reasons for choosing the free software movement

The presence of the information technologies and especially the expansion of internet within the organization of modern western societies regarding the financial sector, the political decision-making centres as well as the citizens' everyday social life, affecting some forms of its social and cultural aspects, is dominant in the last decades. A major feature of the information technology regarding its functionality for the formation of modern social life is that its use sets the terms for its commercialisation, leading to many changes in economic, political and thus social level.

The use of information technology, however, is not enough by itself to bring about social changes. "It is about a technology that in its interior the dominant social standards and the power relations generating them are registered and inhered". (Naxakis, 1998:63-64). For social changes to come about, the element of conflict is required, which strongly characterises western societies. So, new structural conflicts are created between social groups aiming at the acquisition of new forms of control, such as the use of information technology with emphasis to information, being at stake.

So it is clear that conflicts do not only concern the material conditions of the society, but they are mainly associated with conditions of cultural character, of which the newly appeared social movements are considered main advocates and especially those related to the use of information technology, the free software movements.

Free software movement appeared in the early '80s, when Richard Stallman, computer programmer, founded the GNU community, the objective of which was the development and dissemination of free software as information technology. (Hess, 2005). The concept of use of the particular information technology was developed in parallel to the free software community.

According to the GNU Manifesto, free software is the software that respects the freedom of the user and is characterised by four fundamental freedoms of its user. These four freedoms are the following:

Freedom 0: the freedom of the user to run the programme for any purpose.

Freedom 1: the freedom of the user to study how the source code of the programme works, and change it at will.

Freedom 2: the freedom to redistribute copies of the programme at will.

Freedom 3: the freedom to release copies of the modified versions whenever the user wishes to.

This movement was broadly followed by other groups of programmers, developing different free software programmes which always are governed by the fundamental principles of free redistribution, of knowing the source code and the free modification of this code (Hemphill, 2005). These groups of activists, gathered around the principles of free software demanding the establishment, dissemination and preservation of these freedoms, constitute the free software movement (Stallman, 2004). The movement's goal is the computer users' liberation from the enslavement of the proprietary software (software with restrictions regarding its use, copy and modification, imposed by the owner) (Stallman, 2004).

According to A.Giddens (2002:665), social movement is defined as "a collective attempt to further a common interest or secure a common goal outside the sphere of established institutions". These freedoms promoted by the free software movement are vital. They are necessary not only for the user's benefit, but also because they promote social solidarity—which is about distribution and cooperation. These freedoms become even more significant since culture and actions of social life become more digitised. In a world of digital sounds, images and words, free software increases in order to be counterbalanced with freedom in general". For free software movements, free software is a moral command, since only free software respects the user's freedom. This freedom is in contrast to the established socio-economic conditions, having as a result, the state authorities to highly penalise behaviours connected to the promotion of this kind of freedom.

Criminal behaviour within this field is a clearly political issue, affected by the movement's actions. "The change of legal framework mainly of the procedures of criminalization of new behaviours or decriminalization, the changes in practices of the justice system and the anti-criminal policy, in general, the new trends of prevention and treatment of crime" (Artinopoulou, 2000:24) constitute issues in which the free software movement is engaged actively and plays a definite part in their formulation. In many cases, its actions have restructured the legal framework. Typical example is the issue of patents.

Patent is a person's right to monopolise an invention. The inventor applies to the respective public service, which evaluates the invention in order to examine whether this invention is real, innovative, non obvious, and industrially applicable, and grants the inventor the exclusive rights for 20 years. (source: www.wikipedia.org)

In Europe, the fundamental legislation on patents is the European Patent Convention, 1973. In article 52, the Convention clearly states that discoveries, scientific theories and mathematical methods, rules and methods for performing mental acts and programmes for computers are not inventions; therefore they cannot be bound by patents. The legislator had reasons for this decision: while typically patents concerned physical constructions, software patents cover abstract meanings. Instead of patenting a particular kind of mouse-trap, any "method of capturing mammals", or "data capture method in simulated environment" is patented.

In 1986, the European Patent Office (EPO), violating article 52 of the Convention, started granting patents for computer programmes. Today, the number of such patents is estimated to more than 30 thousands, being increased by 3 thousands per year. (source: www.wikipedia.org) .

The free software movement is opposed to this kind of patents, since fundamental freedoms, promoted by the movement and constituting its fundamental philosophy, are violated. In Greece, the main representative of the opposition against patents is the activist group of epatents, (epatents.hellug.gr), under the auspices of the Hellenic Linux User Group (www.hellug.gr). The activist group of epatents today has about 10 active members, while 40 more are enrolled in its mailing list, watching closely its progress. This particular group constitutes the research object of this paper, so that through the observation of its actions, the social construction of crime to emerge.

For the success of the social movements regarding the achievement of their goals, always in this particular social-political framework in which they develop and act, Schumaker and Burstein[1] define five basic criteria which determine the success of this achievement. These criteria are the access to institutions, placing the demands on the political agenda, policy making, output, impact and changes on the institutions of a society, on attitudes and social values. In order for social movements to be able to satisfy these criteria and fulfill their goals, leading to structural and cultural changes to society by affecting public policy, it is necessary to be fully recognised by the society and develop political alliances. New social movements' support by powerful mediators such as the public opinion and by social forces holding institutional authority is one of the factors playing a dominant role in the achievement of their goals. At the same time, new social movements try to use political opportunities in respect to their efficiency. So they create political alliances without the intervention of public opinion, mainly through their institutionalised bodies, the non-governmental organisations.

---

[1] Schumaker, PD. Policy responsiveness to protest-group demands. J. Polit. 37: 488-521, 1975 In V. Artinopoulou, 2002, Burstein P, Rachel L., Einwohner and Jocelyn A. Hollander. The success of Political Movements: A bargaining Perspective. In the Politics of Social Protest, edited by J. Craig Jenkins and Bert Klandernmans, 275-295. Mineapolis: University of Minessota Press. 1995 In V. Artinopoulou, 2002

It is clear from all the above that the change of policies for the determination of criminal behaviour, "is the result of a procedure of interaction including the social movements, the state, the political parties and the public opinion[2]". At this point, the interaction developed between the social subjects is obvious, indicating, through the collective procedures of the social movements, "the active participation of the subjects of social action in the determination of conditions" (Tatsis, 1997:236) of social reality in connection to other social actors.

From the above, it is clear that the theoretical origin of the research for the study of the actions of the activist group of epatents of the Greek free software movement, apart from the conflict theories, is based on the theory of symbolic interaction. Group action is the assembly of individual forms of action. Each person aligns his/her action with the action of others. The common definitions of conditions, structured in the past, allow the individuals to act similarly. These common definitions leading to common actions can lead to social changes, that is, the appearance of new conditions that invite the individuals to take new forms of action. These changes pass through action units which interpret the encountered conditions. So it is understood that crime constitutes a behaviour that is determined by the penal legislation, if and since this is exercised within specific social and political commands. By serving specific interests a social action can be defined as criminal or not, presenting thus that the definition of this behaviour can only be the result of impositions within the framework of a politically organized social system. The free software movement, through its whole spectrum of expression, also interacting with other social powers within this framework, contribute to the establishment of the approach that crime is a socially constructed concept, signified acording to the interests of social reality it serves.

Within the framework of these theoretical principles and according to the actions of the activist group of epatents in Greece which refer to: a) writing and translation of information material regarding the evils of software patents, b) distribution of this material and coordination of actions through the site http://epatents.hellug.gr, c) promotion of this issue to printed and online newspapers, d) collection of signatures to protest against software patents by academic and research bodies, e) associations and computer companies, as well as individuals, f) informing members of the parliament and the European parliament and politics, g)

---

[2] Constain AN. Majstorovic S. Congress, social movements and public opinion: multiple origins of women's rights legislation. Polit. Res.Q. 47:111-35, 1994 In V. Artinopoulou, 2000

coordination with the respective bodies (mainly the Foundation for a Free Information Infrastructure, FFII) in European level and support of the international actions, h) promotion of the pan European protest against software patents, the subject under study will be examined.

Methodology of research

Based on the above mentioned theoretical approaches it is necessary for this research to be qualitative and use a semi-structured interview. According to Blee and Taylor (2002) the semi-structured interview as a method is of special significance in regard to the research on social movements, since it provides great breadth and depth of information about the participants' motivations as well as the activities of the movements' networks and organisations. In order to raise the issue of the social construction of crime through the action of the free software movement, the use of this method is necessary to present the particular actions of the movement that have brought about changes to the present legal European and Greek framework, and at the same time to study the movement members' motivations regarding the procedures of criminalization and decriminilisation in respect to the use and operation of free software.

In addition, the semi structured interview leads to the success of access to more specialized groups of the movement. Thompson (1988:125) reports that usually the ideas of the movement are expressed by the leaders of the movement's bodies and these can be filtered. With access to the base of the movement a great variety of motivations and aspects emerge, which could not otherwise appear. This methodological feature is of major importance for this research, since the actions of the epatents activists are studied, that is of a specialised group of the free software movement in Greece.

Blee and Taylor (2002) summarise the advantages of the use of this particular method regarding the research of social movements as follows: primarily the interview is very helpful for subject matters that have not been thoroughly studied, or respectively specific dynamics have not been studied. It is equally typical that in respect to the Greek reality at least, free software movement actions and dynamics have not been studied in depth, having as a result Greek bibliography to be limited regarding this issue. So, it is clear that the use of semi-structured interview would allow the researcher to highlight particular issues which until then had not been thoroughly examined.

Secondly, the semi-structured interview provides access to the understanding of the meaning and the definition of actors, in their individual and collective identity, the recording of hope and expectations by critisising the present and making plans for the future, giving the opportunity to comprehend the longitudinal course of the movement. These issues concerning the Greek activist group of epatents have not been deeply clarified. Finally, the particular method allows the research of emotional issues emerging, while there is the opportunity to observe the ways in which the movement's messages are received by the members themselves, the devoted public but also the external recipients (Gampson, 1998). This fact is very important for this paper, since it is necessary to understand the ways in which the Greek activist group of epatents succeed their goals, based on the criteria by Schumaker and Burstein (1975).

As it is referred by Ragin (1994) qualitative method is an "open window" in the activists' world, which generalises what they represent by including the voice of the subject and minimizing the voice of the researcher.

Type of semi structured interview

Equally important information for this paper is to determine the type of semi structured interview which will be used for the outcome of the research on the Greek activist group of epatents. In this case, the type of focus groups is used.

There are many definitions concerning focus groups in bibliography. Kitzinger (1994) refers to this method as organized discussions, and (1995) is focused on interaction, Powell et al (1996) define focus groups as a collective activity while Goss and Leinbach (1996) as social events.

In other words, focus group is a method of group interview, "a tool of extraction of qualitative data, elements and information, through a procedure of direct interaction of the group members about a specific and clearly defined object" (Iosifidis, 2003:58). According to Krueger (1994:6) a focus group can be described as "a carefully planned discussion designed to obtain perceptions on a defined area of interest in a permissive non-threatening environment". Groups "are focused" in the sense that they involve some kind of collective activity around a small number of issues and are interactive in that the group "forces" and dynamics are of outmost importance. (Litosseliti, 2003).

The method of focus groups is applied in cases of research of the operation of organised social groups, the operation of institutions and frameworks of production and policy implementation, research of social conditions where the element of individual and group interaction and the need of coordination prevail (Iosifidis, 2003).

So, based on the above mentioned theoretical approaches and studying the interaction of the participants of the free software movement within the group, as well as with the current sociopolitical framework for criminalisation or decriminalisation of behaviours or actions regarding the use of free software, this particular method is considered more suitable. Besides, Morgan (1997:12) characteristically refers that focus group is based on the interaction within the group based on topics supplied by the researcher.

Furthermore, the suitability of the method is based on the fact that, in this case, the under study subject does not concern all the actions of the free software movement in respect to criminalisation or decriminalisation of behaviours or actions, but specifically the issue of patents, and especially concerning the activist group that is engaged in this particular subject, and not all of the members of the free software movement in Greece.

In addition to the use of this particular method the researcher can observe the way with which individuals construct their own reality, and produce meanings through their own operation as a group, which shares common ideas and behaviours about the way they perceive themselves and the world (Munday, 2006:101) but as Gamson (1992) underlines it provides the means to study the cultural expression of the movement, that is, the way with which people perceive, incorporate the ideas, the targets, the practices as well as the identities of the activist group of the movement. Both these elements are necessary for the conduct of this research, since there is the need to study the way in which the Greek group of activists manages to create its alliances by externalizing its ideas and targets highlighting its identity is required.

The action of the free software movement, for an independent concept construction ceases to exist anymore in an internal framework in which a culture has been already developed and it is now taken in a public level, being in contrast to political authority. It is necessary for this culture to be studied and for this reason the particular method is considered more suitable, since the focus group allows the researcher to collect information to find out why an issue is salient, as well as what is salient about it (Morgan, 1988).

Moreover, the focus group is used when there is an interest in the everyday use of language and culture of a group, or when the researcher wishes to discover the degree of consensus of the group on a given topic (Krueger, 1993). So in regard to the actions of free software after their publication, the issue of naming emerges. "The procedure of naming and meaning construction that take place on the level of individuals and the underground networks of everyday life is the most significant aspect of the modern social movements". (Melucci, 2002:111). Bearing in mind that naming reflect the cultural framework from which they come, essentially this conflict is clearly of cultural character between established order and social movements (Melucci, 2002). Through these procedures of the free software movement where the languages and grammars of change are produced, it is possible for their public action to be established and a plural speech to be developed, which is direct and receptive in contrast to the speech that excludes, and which can be expressed by this type of interview.

Advantages of the focus group

Although focus group is a relatively new method in respect to the research of social movements, it presents several advantages. Its main advantage in relation to other interview approaches is based on the fact that the researcher is provided with instruments to analyse not only what it is said during the discussion, but also its framework and the process itself. (Munday, 2006:102)

An equally fundamental advantage, compared to individual interviews, is that they allow to the researcher to observe the interactions for the under discussion topic which can provide insightful information about the ways in which activists of the movement collectively produce the action fields and the ways in which they create and develop solidarity. (Blee, Taylor, 2002:107). Furthermore, the fact that the participants are found in a setting similar to their natural one, since Krueger (1994:19) reports that "participants are influencing and influenced by others just as they are in real life" gives the researcher the opportunity to comprehend in-depth the primary objective of the selection of this type of interview, that is the interaction among participants.

Moreover, it must be noted that while the individual interviews focus on individual beliefs and attitudes, and can be more easily controlled by the interviewer, the method of focus group aims to obtain multiple views and attitudes and often requires complex negotiation of the ongoing interaction processes among participants (Litosseliti, 2003:2).

In parallel, compared to individual interviews, focus groups, apart from eliciting a multiplicity of views, they can also elicit emotional processes within a group context. So, if multiple meanings and explanations are revealed by participants, multiple explanations of their behaviour and attitudes will be more readily articulated. (Gibbs, 1997).

According to Morgan (1997) this type of interview can provide an outcome between participant observation and in-depth interview, since like individual interviews, it allows to the researcher to study the meaning of interpretation, as it is expressed in words by the personal point of view, opinion and experience of each participant. A focus group is based on the "interaction" among participants (Gibbs, 1997) and contrary to observation it allows to collect a larger amount of information "in a shorter period of time.

In parallel, this particular method provides the researcher with the insight of understanding how the movement's targets are interpreted by the members themselves. This fact is very important since the free software movement consists of a great number of members in all of the western counties, with the most active of them staying in America. So it is clear that the movements' goals or the concepts constructed by its source may not be understandable or not interpreted in the same way by the movement's members who experience a different socio-cultural status, for example the one of the Greek activist group in relation to that of the activist group in America.

According to Morgan (1997) a focus group provides the means to understand the participant's thoughts and expression by recording a real discussion and interaction, offering the special advantage of the creation of a dynamic procedure of sharing and comparing among participants. This point is equally interesting in respect to the present research since the Greek activist group of epatents is under the auspices of the Hellenic Linux User Group.

The use of focus group methodology facilitate not only the data collection in relation to the collective identity of the under study group, but also the collection of data for the interaction, negotiation and confirmation procedure, through which the identity is produced and "maintained" (Munday, 2006:100). Bryman (2001) characteristically reports that focus groups provide the opportunity to the researcher to study how individuals collectively structure and assign meaning to phenomena. This particular feature is the one that distinguishes focus groups from other types of group interviews. It is the emphasis given on the interaction and the explicit use of such interaction as research data (Kitzinger, 1994)

Although focus groups can help to explore or generate hypotheses (Powell & Single 1996), "they are quite demanding to organize conduct moderate and analyze successfully although they may often appear easier to use or less structured than other research methods" Litosseliti, (2003:9).

The moderator's part

Focus groups are facilitated by a moderator who guides the discussion using a number of predetermined and carefully developed open-ended questions with minimal intervention. According to Litosseliti, (2003:5) a moderator has to ensure that the key questions are discussed the discussion develops and the participants do not shift away from the topic of discussion. To moderate a group successfully requires a moderator with good communication managing and interpersonal skills so that for example to keep the discussion on track without inhibiting the flow of ideas and avoid leading or "closed" questions.

Type of focus group

This particular type of focus group is the interpersonal full focus group, that is, a group of six to ten people (MacIntosh 1993). A focus group can be conducted in a familiar setting, where the participants' meetings already occurred, if they are a pre-exisiting group. (Gibbs, 1997). For this reason the focus group of the Greek activist group of epatents is planned to be conducted with the ten members that constitute the group in the place where they had their meetings so far, that is, in a classroom of Athens Polytechnic. This place is selected in order for the participants to feel at ease among themselves, since, according to Morgan (1988), if the participants share a common way of thinking or a similar level of understanding of the given topic the outcome would be more appealing. "The understanding of the factors influencing the collective attitude and dynamics, such as individual, interindividual and socio-intergroup factors, being a prerequisite for the interpretation, evaluation and presentation of the obtained qualitative data" is (Iosiphedes, 2003:58) a main target.

Focus group guide

According to Krueger and Casey (2002) the first few moments in a focus group discussion are critical. The moderator must prepare the ground for discussion, creating an insightful and at the same time permissive atmosphere, provide the ground rules and set the tone of the discussion. For this reason the introduction pattern has to be well planned from the beginning. In this paper the introduction is as follows:
Introduction
"Good evening and welcome to our today's discussion. My name is Aggeliki and I am working on my doctoral thesis in the Department of Sociology of the University of the Aegean. Thank you for spending some of your time to discuss the development of the actions of your group and the changes they have brought about to the present socio-political framework. You are invited to participate in this discussion, since you are the main representatives of the group of activists of epatents, the free software movement in Greece. Please understand that in the following discussion there are no right or wrong answers, only different views. Feel free to share all of your perspectives about the discussion topics, even if your approaches are different from those of your fellow participants. Obviously, all of you have noticed the tape recorder on the table. This discussion has to be recorded, since I don't want to miss any of your comments and it is not possible for me to write them all down. Be sure that for this research the rules of ethics and confidentiality will be followed. Let's begin by giving some information about yourself according to how you are seated. So, tell us what is your name and where do you live …."
Index of topics
1. free software movement and philosophy
2. free software movement in Greece
3. activists group against patents in European level
4. Greek activists group against patents
5. Greek activists group against patents and language code
6. Greek activists group against patents and public
7. activists group against patents and legislation

8. Greek activists group and legislation
9. actions of the Greek activists group against patents
10. successes of activists group against patents in European and Greek level
11. free software and crime
12. patents and crime
13. future targets

References

Artinopoulou, V. (2000) *New Social Movements- A criminological perspective*. Athens: Nomiki Bibliothiki Publications (in Greek).

Blee, K., Taylor V. (2002) Semi-structured Interviewing in Social Movement Research, in B. Klandermans and S. Staggenborg (eds) *Methods of Social Movement Research*, pp. 92–117. Minneapolis: University of Minnesota Press.

Blumer, H. (1995) *Social Movements*, in Lyman, M., "Social Movements, Critiques, Concepts, Case-studies", Macmillan press ltd

Bryman, A. (2001) *Social Research Methods*. Oxford: Oxford University Press.

Flores J.G., Alonso C.G. (1995) Using focus groups in educational research, *Evaluation Review* 19 (1): 84-101.

Giddens, A. (1989) Sociology. Cambridge: Polity Press, 659-716.

Giugni, M., McAdam, D., Tilly, C. (1999) *How Social Movements Matter*, Minneapolis- London: University of Minnesota Press.

Gordenker, L., Weiss Th. (1996) NGOs, *The UN and Global Governance*, pp.17-47 Boulder, Co: Lynne Rienner Publishers.

Goss J.D., Leinbach T.R. (1996) focus groups as alternative research practice, *Area* 28 (2): 115-23.

Hemphill, B. (2005) *Top 10 Tips for Managing E-Mail More Effectively* Business Credit.

Hess, D. (2005) *Object conflicts in the movement for organic agriculture. Science as Culture.* New York: Routledge.

Holbrook B., Jackson P. (1996) Shopping around: focus group research in North London, *Area* 28 (2): 136-42.

Homan R. (1991) *Ethics in Social Research.* Harlow: Longman.

Hoppe M.J., Wells E.A., Morrison D.M., Gilmore M.R., Wilsdon A. (1995) Using focus groups to discuss sensitive topics with children, *Evaluation Review* 19 (1): 102-14.

Munday J. (2006) Identity in Focus Groups: "The Use of Focus Groups to Study the Construction of Collective Identity", Sociology, *vol.* 40: 89-105

Kitzinger J. (1994). The methodology of focus groups: the importance of interaction between research participants, *Sociology of Health* 16 (1): 103-21.

Kitzinger J. (1995) Introducing focus groups, *British Medical Journal* 311: 299-302.

Kreuger R.A. (1988) *Focus groups: a practical guide for applied research.* London: Sage.

Krueger, R. (2000) *Focus Groups: A Practical Guide for Applied Research*, 3rd edn. London: Sage.

Lankshear A.J. (1993) The use of focus groups in a study of attitudes to student nurse assessment', *Journal of Advanced Nursing* 18: 1986-89.

MacIntosh J. (1981) Focus groups in distance nursing education, *Journal of Advanced Nursing* 18: 1981-85.

Merton R.K., Kendall P.L. (1946) The Focused Interview, *American Journal of Sociology* 51: 541-557.

Morgan D.L. (1997) *Focus groups as qualitative research*. 2nd Edition. London:Sage.

Morgan D.L. and Kreuger R.A. (1993) When to use focus group groups and why, in Morgan D.L. (Ed.) *Successful focus Groups*. London: Sage.

Morgan D.L. and Spanish M.T. (1984) Focus groups: a new tool for qualitative research, *Qualitative Sociology* 7: 253-70.

Morgan D.L. (1988) *focus groups as qualitative research*. London: Sage.

Morgan, D. (1993) *Successful Focus Groups: Advancing the State of the Art*. Newbury Park, CA: Sage

Morgan, D. (1998) *The Focus Group Guidebook*. Thousand Oaks, CA: Sage.

Munodawafa D., Gwede C., Mubayira C. (1995) Using focus groups to develop HIV education among adolescent females in Zimbabwe, *Health Promotion* 10 (2): 85-92.

Naxakis, H. (1998) *Growth-technological Change and Unemployment, Unemployment: Fables and Reality*, Athens: Alternative Publications, (in Greek).

Powell R.A. and Single H.M. (1996) focus groups, *International Journal of Quality in Health Care* 8 (5): 499-504.

Powell R.A., Single H.M., Lloyd K.R. (1996) Focus group groups in mental health research: enhancing the validity of user and provider questionnaires', *International Journal of Social Psychology* 42 (3): 193-206.

See, E. (2004) *Criminological Theories: Introduction, Evaluation, and Applications*, Los Angeles, California: Roxbury Publishing Company.

Stallman, R. (2004) *The free software community after 20 years: With great but incomplete success, what now?* http://www.gnu.org/philosophy/use-free-software.html.

Tarrow S. (1994) *Power In Movement*, New York : Cambridge University Press

Tatsis, N. (1999) *The teaching of sociological theory*. Athens: Gutenberg, Library of Social Science and Social Policy (in Greek).

Touraine, A. (1995) Beyond Social Movements? in Lyman, M.(ed) *Social Movements, Critiques, Concepts, Case-studies*, Macmillan press ltd

Vold G., Bernard T., Snipes J. (2002) *Theoretical Criminology*, New York: Oxford University Press.

19.

A PARTICIPANT OBSERVATION ON POLICE CULTURE IN GREECE

Dimos Sarantidis

Introduction

The term police culture originates some 45 years ago with Michael Banton (1964) and Jerome Skolnick (1966), who suggested that certain problems inherently associated with the nature of policing generated a shared sub-culture among the police rank and file which facilitated the resolution of these difficulties. Particularly, the notion derives from the discovery that the uncertainties inherent within the legal rules relating to stop, search, arrest and charge powers cannot determine practical policing and thus allow for an extensive exercise of discretion by police officers in how they enforce the law; that discretion and many other routine police practices are thought to rely upon the taken for granted beliefs and values shared by the police generally, and particularly by the lower ranks, who are most likely to encounter members of the public in conditions of low visibility. As J. Chan (1996) observes, 'cop-culture' has become a convenient label for a range of negative values, attitudes and practices among police officers, which are largely underlined by concepts such as authority, sense of danger (the real work), demand for deference, and need to produce results. Similarly Reiner (1992: 111-129) identifies certain features of the police culture as being a cynical view of the world, a machismo and racist attitude, a strong sense of solidarity with other officers, and a conservative political attitude. Although a great many of researchers have associated the notion of 'cop-culture' exclusively with the above mentioned negative values and characteristics, it has also been recognised that police culture is not primarily negative. According to Chan (1996: 111) it is seen to be functional to the survival of police officers in an occupation considered to be dangerous, unpredictable, and alienating." Goldsmith (1990: 93-94) suggests that the bond of solidarity between officers "offers its members reassurance that the other officers will 'pull their weight' in police work, that they will defend, back up and assist their colleagues when confronted by external threats, and that they will maintain secrecy in the face of external investigations."

In recent years, qualitative work has become an increasingly popular approach to social research. The popularity, and indeed in some areas dominance, of qualitative research stems partly from the growing disillusionment with quantitative methods which had long been the dominant method of social research (Marshall & Rossman, 1999). It is widely recognised that quantitative methodology is incapable of adequately reflecting and providing an insight in people's experiences, life histories and everyday behaviour (Silverman, 2000). Qualitative research is a powerful tool enabling the exploration of social life, cultures and people's experiences, motivations, behaviour, desires and needs. It goes beyond, 'who' is doing 'what', to the 'how' and 'why' behind the 'what'. It is an invaluable tool for addressing social problems and influencing policy making (Bloor, 1997). Central within the qualitative research tradition is participant observation research, i.e. the observation *of* and participation *in* processes, activities or everyday events, aiming at the acquisition of an in-depth understanding of that process, activity or event and the identification of patterns of contextual behaviour and meaning.

The aim of this paper is to describe how the method of participant observation proved to be an extremely helpful research tool in examining some basic aspects of police culture in Greece. An analysis will also be made concerning the difficulties I faced during my participant observation such as ethical issues, the adoption of roles by the researcher, the problem of reactivity, objectivity matters etc. I regarded that, in a first instance, a paper on all the above had priority and, consequently, in the present article I am not making reference to the substance of my research, meaning the identification and analysis of specific cultural characteristics of the police, which came into light during my participant observation.

Participant Observation: A Definitional Approach

Participant observation or ethnographic research is one of the most common and simultaneously most demanding methods of qualitative data collection. It requires that the researcher becomes a participant in the culture or context being observed, and has routinely been regarded as the foundation of cultural anthropology (e.g. Silverman, 2000:37). The term itself clarifies amply the purposes of this method. *Participant* implies getting close to the intended subjects and making them comfortable enough with the presence of the researcher so that information and logic about the subject may be recorded (Hammersley & Atkinson, 1995). However, as the purpose of the researcher is ultimately limited and distinctly objectifying, *observer* is an appropriate adjective. Very often the ethnographer has to replicate the daily lives of his subjects, sometimes for a considerable length of time 'in order to eventually replicate some of the subjective knowledge of the world under view' (Rock, 2001:32).

The Current Research

This current research started on the 8th of April 2009 and finished on the 15th of December 2009. It took place in an immigrants and asylum seekers detention centre[1] on Lesvos (Mytilene) island, guarded by the police. In addition, I was making almost daily visits to the central police department of Mytilene in order to observe, listen, chat, interview and examine aspects of police culture. My initial role was to provide legal assistance and counselling to migrants as a member of an NGO (Ecumenical Refugee Program). This role was the reason why I had obtained permission by the Ministry for the Protection of Citizen for an everyday access to this detention centre and the police station.

The Field

Pagani detention center is located almost 1 kilometer out of the town of Mytilene. This "Reception Centre" is in a complex of buildings, which used to be a warehouse. All new-comers migrants without papers were taken into a so-called administrative detention there for registration from the Greek state. Officially the place was planned for detaining a total of 250 people to go through this process but in summer and autumn 2009 the number of people detained there reached and in some cases exceeded the number of 1000. The detention period varied from some days to three months. Every day newcomers were arriving and, at the same time, people were also released. There were seven cells, which all presented

---

[1] The formal name is E.X.Π.A. meaning special place for the reception of migrants. This name is not quite descriptive of the real nature of this "reception center". According to reports it is a detention center for immigrants and asylum seekers. During the visit of the vice minister (21st October 2009) of the Ministry for the Protection of Citizen Mr. S. Vougias he officially referred to this detention center as being worst than Dante's inferno.

the same picture: Around 150 detainees were locked up and crowded. One of the cells was for women and another one for unaccompanied minors. There was only one toilet and one shower in each cell. The yarding of the detainees was not taking place on an everyday basis and its duration was almost no more than 45 minutes. All the above mentioned bad detention conditions were a basic reason for demonstrations taking place, revolts, hunger strikes etc. The police were responsible for arresting the migrants when they entered the Greek territory, guarding the inside and outside of Pagani, taking fingerprints and photos, issuing deportation orders, and making the interviews of those seeking asylum. I had access to the detention center on an everyday basis. I was visiting the place around 9.00 in the morning and staying there until afternoon. In cases there were revolts etc. I was visiting Pagani even during the night hours.

I was also visiting the Mytilene police department almost 4-5 times per week. It was located in the town of Mytilene and my visits included talks with personnel from the aliens' office, the administration of the security department and very often with the administration of the Mytilene police department.

The Subjects

The subjects of my participant observation included policemen both in the detention centre and the police station at Mytilene including lower and higher ranks. Inside the detention centre there was personnel who were guards, police officers who were taking fingerprints and photos of the detainees, personnel from the security department, port policemen and special forces of the police –squads. The squads were present inside and outside the detention centre on an everyday basis after August 2009, since demonstrations, riots and hunger strikes had then started been an almost everyday phenomenon. Because of the fact that, during summer 2009, the situation in the detention centre was very problematic there was also presence of higher ranks of the police inside Pagani.

Regarding my participant observation at Mytilene police station my visits included conversations with personnel from the alien's office, the security police and mainly the constabulary and the management police officers there. In some occasions I came in touch with the headquarters in Athens and the political leadership of the police, in order to discuss about crucial issues concerning the detention centre.

Research Tools

In order to observe and examine the aspects of police culture in the field I used, in brief, the following methods:

a. An everyday diary of events as they occurred chronologically in the field. After a period of 15-20 days a more systematic organization of this material was taking place.
b. Notes concerning my dialogues with policemen in the detention center.
c. Notes concerning my dialogues with policemen in Mytilene police department.
d. Notes concerning the dialogues among policemen and detainees.
e. Notes concerning the dialogues among policemen.
f. Notes concerning the criticism raised by lower ranks policemen on the strategies followed by their administration.
g. Letters exchanged between the NGO I was working for and the police.
h. Reports of national and European organizations concerning the situation in Pagani.
i. Written evidence of allegations against Mytilene police, the outcomes of those allegations and the police response.

Participant Observation v. Direct or Plain Observation

It appears crucial at this point to distinguish between participant observation research and 'plain' or 'direct' observation since not all fieldwork is participant observation. As mentioned earlier participant observation requires that the researcher *becomes a participant in the culture or context being observed*, and may indeed require months or years of intensive work before the researcher becomes accepted as a natural part of that culture or context. 'Plain' or 'direct' observation is distinguished from participant observation in numerous ways. Direct observation suggests a more detached perspective than participant observation. A direct observer does not try to become a participant in the context; the researcher is watching rather than taking part, and typically strives to be as inconspicuous as possible so as not to bias the observations. Furthermore, direct observation inclines to be more focused than participant observation since the researcher is usually observing certain sampled situations or people rather than endeavouring to engross himself or herself in the entire context. As a result, direct observation tends to take much less time than participant observation.[2]

It should be noted, however, that despite the differences distinguishing between participant observation and direct participant, the dividing line between the two is a rather thin one. So, regardless of the fact that a researcher is not acting as part of the context / culture, s/he might *participate* in the everyday life of it as an *observer*.

During my participant observation somebody could probably argue that a direct observation and not a participant observation took place. As a matter of fact I never intended and I did not become a part of the police everyday life and culture. However, I had an active role concerning the everyday procedures the police were following in trying to enforce the law in the detention center. During conversations I had with the higher ranks of Mytilene police my opinion was always being asked, about finding solutions in problematic situations taking place in the detention center. They were telling me that they regard me us a police associate and not as an obstacle for their work. In many cases of revolts the police were asking me to go and talk with the detainees in order to find a solution for their problems and demands. In addition, I was acting on an everyday basis as an intervener in order to transfer demands of the detainees to the police.

I spent hundreds of hours with lower and higher ranks police officers and this led in having a relationship of confidentiality and respect with many of those. My initial role in the detention center was the provision of legal aid and counseling to the detained migrants. This role was allowing me to be present in the detention center and the police station on an everyday basis at any time. So I could make interventions, chat with the police and observe. This role gave me the opportunity to be in a continuous touch with the way of thinking of the police and police culture in general. Practice showed that my role as a lawyer in the detention center was extremely beneficial in trying to observe police culture. In case I was present there only as a researcher I have many doubts that I would be able to gain such an amount of information.

It is also worth to mention that even if the detainees knew that I was a lawyer and not a policeman the way they were facing me, in some occasions, looked like the way they were facing the policemen. I was

---

[2] For a rather different and more detailed distinction between observation research see: Friedrichs & Lüdtke, 1975:5-6.

always outside their cells (it was not allowed for me to get into) and, consequently, they were facing me as somebody who was free and had the power to intervene, in order for some of those to be released. Sometimes they were addressing me as ''police'' and were telling me: ''what are you doing for us to be released? You are one of those...(the policemen)''. As a result, could understand, in a way, how the policemen working in the detention center were feeling and better understand and interpret more efficiently attitudes and practices of the police. I was also present during many protests that took place by demonstrators and activists. During those incidents I was inside the detention center and I could see the reactions of the police. This was very helpful in identifying several cultural characteristics of the police.

By taking into account all the above I strongly believe that my research in Pagani and the police station of Mytilene was mainly a participant and not a direct observation. In addition, the fact that through written reports addressed to the police I was making comments on their practices and, almost immediately I was receiving written or oral answers, shows that there was a continuous interaction and dialogue with the police, meaning that the police were perceiving me as being a part of their work concerning the detention center.

Overt v. Covert Participant Observation – Adoption of Roles by the Researcher

Participant observation involves an array of data collection methods, including observation, natural conversations, various kinds of interviews,[3] checklists, questionnaires, and fieldnotes (Bernard, 1994; Emerson *et al*, 2001). The methods to be utilised depend largely on whether the research takes the shape of *covert* or *overt* participant observation, i.e. whether the subjects are aware of the real identity of the researcher and her or his purposes. Covert participant observation, for example, is almost bound to be restricted to interaction, observation and conversations, leaving no room for detailed questionnaires or the use of notes in the field (Hammersley & Atkinson, 1995).

Similarly, the dichotomy faced by the researcher as to whether to assume an already existing role or to negotiate a new role is partly contingent to the overt or covert nature of the research. If it is covert participant observation, the researcher has little choice but to adopt a pre-

---

[3] e.g. structured, semi-structured, unstructured.

existing role. Aggleton for example, in order to conduct research on the transition of youths from school to work adopted, *inter alia*, the role of a teacher (1987). However, even in overt participant observation, the researcher may find little option but to take on an existing role, though this method usually provides greater options and increased flexibility to adapt and modify roles. There also exists the possibility of being able to negotiate new roles.[4]

As mentioned above, I gained access to the detention centre and the police department of Mytilene because of the fact that I was working as a lawyer for a human rights NGO, specializing in refugee law. An open entry as a researcher could not be negotiated since I had already tried to ask permission to make a participant observation in Mytilene police and the answer was negative. Especially, in the case of Pagani the access was difficult even for people specializing in human rights issues and had permission from the ministry of Public Order to have access. For example, before the beginning of my participant observation there was access, until then, only to one social scientist and one lawyer. The lawyer had access twice a week and the social scientist's access was daily, but, in many occasions the police were denying them to have access for different reasons each time. As a result, the only people who had direct access were policemen and personnel from the Prefecture of Lesbos, who were responsible for medical issues, cleaning, provision of food for the detainees etc. Reports by national and European organisations[5] were talking about a highly problematic detention centre.[5] So, I considered my presence in Pagani detention centre very important firstly because of the political and humanitarian dimension of the problem and, secondly, because I saw it as a useful research tool for my PhD on police culture.

The access inside Pagani was possible only as a lawyer working for a humanitarian organisation. Consequently, my participant observation was initially covert. On the other hand, untypically, almost everybody in the police –lower and higher ranks- knew that I was also doing my research on the police, except working there us a lawyer. In many cases during conversations I had with several police officers I had in-

---

[4] e.g. Sevigny (1981) in relation to art classes in a college (cited in: Hammersley & Atkinson, 1995:109).

[5] For instance see: The Greek Ombudsman, Rights of Children, Unaccompanied minors at Pagani, (Decemer 2006), ProAsyl, (2008), "The situation in Greece is out of control" Research into the situation of asylum seekers in Greece Carried out by Karl Kopp.

A PARTICIPANT OBSERVATION ON POLICE CULTURE 311

formed them about that. Specifically, I was telling them that I am also a PhD student at the University of the Aegean and I am doing a research on the police. It was very interesting that every time I was mentioning that the policemen, mainly those from the higher ranks, were trying to change the conversation immediately. It was like they already knew something but did not want to make any further conversation about it. In one case a police officer from the higher ranks of the Mytilene police told me: ''You are one of the very few people who have access to Pagani detention centre and the only lawyer there... do you think that we do not know who you are, what are you doing and which are your interests? Before giving you access we already knew everything about you...''

By taking into account all the above it could be argued that, on the one hand, my participant observation was typically covert but, on the other hand, there is much circumstantial evidence that it was untypically and substantially overt.

Ethics of Participant Observation

One should also make reference to the ethical considerations and difficulties posed by participant observation, especially in its covert form. Clearly, every research plan must be able to justify itself to the members of the scientific community in terms of 'beneficence' as well as those involved in terms of 'non-maleficence', 'justice' and 'self- determination' of the subjects (Murphy & Dingwall, 2001). Yet, covert participant observation poses particular considerations, due to the concealed identity and purposes of the researcher, the straightforward deception of the subjects involved, and the lack of any consent on their part (Bulmer, 1982). Humphrey's study of homosexual encounters in public lavatories (1975), which involved a series of deceptions not only on the homosexual subjects but also the police, represents a notorious case of participant observation research which has been subjected to sharp criticism (see Warwick, 1982, for discussion).

Given these ethical complications relating to covert participant observation, it appears essential that the ends for any given covert participant observation research must justify and outweigh the means (Reynolds, 1982). Anonymity and confidentiality are necessary but not sufficient safeguards for the subjects of research, whose personality and privacy should not, as far as possible, be sacrificed in the name of science.

One should also keep in mind that the need for covert methods of research may be considerably exaggerated and that 'open entry may more often been negotiated than is commonly supposed' (Bulmer, 1982:250).

Concerning this last point my access to the field, as mentioned above, was extremely difficult for anyone. Pagani was a place where mainly policemen had access and practice had shown that access for anybody else was almost inevitable. In addition, I strongly believe that my participant observation in Pagani in a covert form, by being present there as a lawyer and not as a researcher was of crucial importance for my research, because it helped me to have an active participation in the everyday police activities, make interventions, discussions and chat on issues concerning practical issues and problems that had to be directly resolved.

Regarding the straightforward deception of the subjects involved I have to highlight that it was never in my intentions to observe specific characteristics of one – individual policeman. Although individualistic approaches (Maguire M. et all., (1997: 1015) can explain why police discretion operates as it does my intention was to focus on cultural accounts affecting police discretion. As a result, I was focusing on specific individual attitudes and practices that seemed to be affected by a broader ideology and culture within the police mentality. So, my goal was not to condemn individual attitudes and practices but rather to correlate those with the notion of police culture.

My research was concerning, in a broader view, a critical analysis of the enforcement of the rule of law by the police and in such a case any argument concerning deception of the subjects involved is not strong enough, since this particular research relates to the lawful working of an organization and the public weal. In addition, the amount and sort of information collected could not have easily been collected by any other qualitative method. Interviews with police officers, for example, would have clearly not revealed the information necessary for the study, not only because police officers would not be willing to disclose illegal conduct on their behalf, but also because the subjects would have been 'too much involved in the context to see the obvious' (Friedrichs & Lüdtke, 1975:85). As Bronfenbrenner (1952:453) states "the only safe way for somebody not to turn against his professional ethics is to totally abandon any kind of research activity."

The problem of 'reactivity'

I have already claimed above that on the one hand my participant observation was typically covert but, on the other hand, there is much circumstantial evidence that it was substantially overt. In that case although it
could be argued that the overt presence of the researcher might have had
comparable effects on the conduct of the subjects, one should keep in
mind that the intensive rapport building by the researcher and the extensive interaction and familiarisation between the subjects and the researcher had significantly mitigated any such effects (Westmarland,
2001:524).

This latter point is closely related to the problem of 'reactivity', i.e.
the alteration of the subjects' behaviour as a result of their awareness of
the fact that they are being studied (Hammersley & Atkinson, 1995).
This is particularly problematic with certain other types of qualitative
methods such as interviewing (Miller & Glassner, 1997), where not only
the knowledge of the subjects that they are being studied might have an
effect on their attitudes, but also the personal characteristics of the researcher might have an impact on the answers given. Nevertheless, due
to the rapport developed and the long-term interaction in overt participant observation any such effect is drastically reduced, as can also be the
case in relation to focus group research (Morgan, 1998).

In fact, the 'reactivity' problem is non-existent in covert participant observation, where the subjects are ignorant of the fact that they are
being studied. An illustrative example of a covert participant observation
study where no reactivity effect can be identified is Simon Holdaway's
police research which was conducted while the researcher was still employed by the British Police as a constable (1982).

If we take for granted that my research at Pagani and the police
station of Mytilene was typically covert there was not really any kind of
'reactivity' problem. However, the fact that I was present there as a lawyer could be problematic, since the police were might trying to 'hide' in
some cases aspects of their ideology and their practices. Many of their
attitudes or practices, against the detainees could lead to allegations or
reports to national – European organizations. Of course the expression of
the notion of police culture does not necessarily mean that a police officer has to commit a criminal or disciplinary offence in order to bring this
culture into light. Police culture does not only involve unlawful acts by
police officers. Its meaning has a much broader sense. Even in that case,

it must be mentioned that even when I was not present during unlawful acts and behaviours by the police the next day the detainees or other people working in the detention center were informing me about those incidents. So, it was almost inevitable for me not to be aware or at least to have a general view of what was going on in the detention center.

The most important indicator, concerning the absence of the problem of reactivity, was the fact that from August 2009 until October 2009 the situation in Pagani was in many cases out of control. As I have already mentioned demonstrations were taking place on an almost every day basis by activists. Revolts and hunger strikes by migrants were also very common. Mytilene police had to face a difficult and unprecedented situation and at a small town, like Mytilene, such incidents had never before taken place. Consequently, the police were mainly focusing in managing and controlling this situation and my presence there as a lawyer or as a researcher seemed to be the last thing they had to focus their attention on. It is not a coincidence that during that period the police –lower and higher ranks- were expressing their thoughts and beliefs in front of me, asking in many cases, in a desperate way, my opinion on what should be done.

During the above mentioned period, because of the crisis in the detention center, there was presence of both lower and higher ranks. In addition there were special squads (MAT). So, it was very interesting to observe a special cultural characteristic of the police, namely the management V Street distrust. Police solidarity and police isolation were also quite intense.

Lack of Objectivity

Despite the reduced 'reactivity' problems involved in participant observation research, there is always the danger of lack of objectivity and the operation of researcher bias. This obstacle is more predominant in participant observation research than any other qualitative research method, due to the very nature of this method. Participant observation involves the subjective experience of a setting, event or culture. The researcher perceives and experiences the object of his or her study in light of his or her personal experiences, values and beliefs and reports them accordingly (Bernard, 1994). The researcher 'reflects' on his or her 'sociohistorical locations, including the values and interests that these locations confer upon' him or her (Hammersley & Atkinson, 1995:16). Furthermore, the more or longer the researcher interacts with the subjects of his or her field, the more he or she is likely to take on, at least to a certain degree, the values and semantics of the observed. As Friedrichs and Lüdtke nicely put it, 'the higher the degree of involvement of the observer in the actions of the others, the lower his impartiality towards them and to the incidents which he is to observe. The observations become inexact and biased, leading to insufficient data recordings' (1975:35).

This is not to say that other qualitative methods are bias-free or that social research can ever be entirely objective. Similar difficulties can be identified in most qualitative methods of research such as the analysis and interpretation of tapes, videos, and transcripts (see Heath, 1997; Peräkylä, 1997), and qualitative interviews (see Sherman-Heyl, 2001). This is directly connected with the *ontological* assumptions under which qualitative research operates.   Each person experiences reality from a different point of view and therefore experiences a different reality. Accordingly, it is difficult, if not impossible, to have value-free research; all research is essentially biased by the researcher's individual perceptions (Trochim, 1999). However, it seems that in participant observation research the researchers should be more vigilant in 'taking stock of their actions and their role in the research process, and subject these to the same critical scrutiny as the rest of their data' (Mason, 1996:67).

But for the general ethical considerations raised by participant observation research which were discussed earlier on in this paper, reference should also be made to the ethical dilemmas and difficulties faced by the researchers in the field. Due to the fact that, contrary to any other method of qualitative research, researchers actually experience and participate in the lives or their subjects they may often come across unforeseen incidents and situations which might be contrary to their morals and beliefs. As a result, the researchers might find themselves in the dilemma of whether some action on their behalf should be taken. Vivid indications of such dilemmas can be found in Westmarland's research, which entailed the observation of numerous illegal violent incidents between the police and suspects. As Westmarland graphically reports, she was often placed in an ambiguous position leading uncomfortable decisions about whether to jeopardise her access and trust relationship with the subjects or collude with illegal and violent behaviour through inaction (2001:527-531).

During my research there were many cases when detainees informally told me about racist and brutal police behavior. However, they almost never wanted to formally bring this into light through allegations or reports, because they were afraid police would make reprisals. In one occasion, on the 22nd of October 2009 a case concerning the ill treatment of a 17 year old unaccompanied minor took place and many detainees were willing to give testimonies. So, allegations were made against the police and the case gained much publicity. I supported those people as a lawyer. The period this incident took place was near the ending of my participant observation and consequently did not negatively affect my research. However, I saw in practice that after those allegations confidentiality that was built during the past months between the police and me had started being vanishing.

Conclusion

In this paper I mainly focused on some theoretical and methodological issues concerning my research on police culture. However, it is important to say that my participant observation led to the identification of several cultural characteristics of the Greek police: isolation, police solidarity and the "code of secrecy", the bad mentality of public servants, (which seems to be a special characteristic of the Greek police), conservatism, cynicism, racism etc. Positive characteristics of police culture were also identified, which seemed to be helpful for police officers to deal with the extremely problematic and full of gaps situation surrounding the Greek refugee law and the incapacity of the Greek State to build a coherent and fair migration policy. Those findings, about the cultural characteristics of the police, constitute the substance of this research and hopefully will be the main issue for a next paper on police culture in Greece.

References

Aggleton, P. (1987) *Rebels without a Cause: Middle-Class Youth and the Transition from School to Work.* London: Faber.

Banton. M. (1964) *The Policeman in the Community*, London: Tavistock.

Bernard, H. R. (1994) *Research Methods in Anthropology* (2nd ed.). Thousand Oaks: SAGE.

Bernard, H. R. (1987) Sponge Fishing and Technological Change in Greece. In H. R. Bernard and P. J. Pelto (Eds.), *Technology and Social Change* (2nd ed.), (167-206). Prospect Heights: Waveland Press.

Bloor, M. (1997) Addressing Social Problems through Qualitative Research. In D. Silverman (Ed.), *Qualitative Research: Theory, Method and Practice* (221-238). London: SAGE.

Bronfenbrenner, U. (1952) "Principles of Professional ethics: Cornell studies in social growth", *American Psychologist*, vol., 7 ch. 8

Bulmer, M. (1982) The Merits and Demerits of Covert Participant Observation. In M. Bulmer (Ed.), *Social Research Ethics: An Examination of the Merits of Covert Participant Observation* (217-251). New York: Holmes and Meier.

Chan, J. (Winter 1996) Changing Police Culture, *The British Journal of Criminology,* Vol.36, No.1.

Emerson, R. M., Fretz, R. I., and Shaw, L. L. (2001) Participant Observation and Fieldnotes. P. Atkinson, A. Coffey, S. Delamont, J. Lofland, and L. Lofland (Eds.), *Handbook of Ethnography* (352-368). London: SAGE.

Fleisher, M. S. (1989). *Waterhousing Violence*. Newbury Park: SAGE.

Friedrichs, J. and Lüdtke, H. (1975) *Participant Observation: Theory and Practice*. Farnborough: Saxon House.

Goldsmith, A. (1990) Taking Police Culture Seriously: Police Discretion and the Limits of Law, *Policing and Society*, Volume 1, number 2.

Hammersley, M. (1992) *What's Wrong with Ethnography? Methodological Explorations*. London: Routledge.

Hammersley, M. and Atkinson, P. (1995) *Ethnography: Principles in Practice* (2nd ed.). London: Routledge.

Heath, C. (1997). The Analysis of Activities in Face to Face Interaction Using Video. In D. Silverman (ed), *Qualitative Research: Theory, Method and Practice* (183-200). London: SAGE.

Holdaway, S. (1982) 'An Inside Job': A Case Study of Covert Research on the Police. In M. Bulmer (Ed.), *Social Research Ethics: An Examination of the Merits of Covert Participant Observation* (59-79). New York: Holmes and Meier.

Humphreys, L. (1975) *Tearoom Trade: Impersonal Sex in Public Places* (rev. ed.). Chicago: Aldine.

Maguire M., Morgan R., Reiner R. (1997) *The Oxford Handbook of Criminology*, second edition, Oxford University Press.

Malinowski, B. (1978) *Argonauts of the Western Pacific: An Account of Native Enterprise and Adventure in the Archipelagoes of Melanesian New Guinea*. London: Routledge.

Marshall, C. and Rossman, G. (1999) *Designing Qualitative Research* (3rd ed.). Thousand Oaks: SAGE.

Mason, J. (1996) *Qualitative Researching*. London: SAGE.

Miller, J. and Glassner, B. (1997) The 'Inside' and the 'Outside': Finding Realities in Interviews. In D. Silverman, *Qualitative Research: Theory, Method and Practice* (99-112). London: SAGE.

Morgan, D. L. (1998) *The Focus Groups Guidebook – Focus Group Kit*. Thousand Oaks: SAGE.

Murphy, E. and Dingwall, R. (2001) The Ethics of Ethnography. In P. Atkinson, A. Coffey, S. Delamont, J. Lofland, and L. Lofland (Eds.), *Handbook of Ethnography* (339-351). London: SAGE.

Peräkylä, A. (1997) Reliability and Validity in Research Based on Tapes and Transcripts. In D. Silverman, *Qualitative Research: Theory, Method and Practice* (201-220). London: SAGE.

Reiner, R. (1992) *Politics of the Police*, 2nd edn. London:Wheatsheaf.

Reynolds, P. D. (1982) Moral Judgements: Strategies for Analysis with Application to Covert Participant Observation. In M. Bulmer (Ed.), *Social Research Ethics: An Examination of the Merits of Covert Participant Observation* (185-213). New York: Holmes and Meier.

Rock, P. (2001) Symbolic Interactionism and Ethnography. In P. Atkinson, A. Coffey, S. Delamont, J. Lofland, and L. Lofland (Eds.), *Handbook of Ethnography* (26-38). London: SAGE.

Sevigny, M. J. (1981) Triangulated Enquiry – A Methodology for the Analysis of Classroom Interaction. In J. L. Green and C. Wallat (Eds.), *Ethnography and Language in Educational Settings*. Norwood: Ablex.

Sherman Heyl, B. (2001) Ethnographic Interviewing. In P. Atkinson, A. Coffey, S. Delamont, J. Lofland, and L. Lofland (Eds.), *Handbook of Ethnography* (369-383). London: SAGE.

Silverman, D. (2000) *Doing Qualitative Research: A Practical Handbook*. London: SAGE.

Silverman, D. (1993) *Interpreting Qualitative Data: Methods of Analysing Talk, Text and Interaction*. London: SAGE.

Skolnick, J. (1966) *Justice without Trial*, New York.

Trochim, W. (1999) *The Research Methods Knowledge Base*. Cincinnati: Atomic Dog Publishing.

Warwick, D. P. (1982) Tearoom Trade: Means and Ends in Social Research. In M. Bulmer (Ed.), *Social Research Ethics: An Examination of the Merits of Covert Participant Observation* (38-58). New York: Holmes and Meier.

Westmarland, L. (2001) Blowing the Whistle on Police Violence: Gender, Ethnography and Ethics. *British Journal of Criminology*, 41, 523-535.

Electronic Recourses

Medicine San Frontiers
http://www.msf.gr/index.php?option=com_content&task=view&id=209
4&Itemid=242, visited 02/09/10.

The Greek Ombudsman:
http://www.synigoros.gr/allodapoi/pdfs/_autopsia_lesvos_29_01.pdf

UNHCR: http://www.unhcr.gr/Press_Rel/41_2009_Oct25.htm, visited
20/02/10

Human Rights Watch (http://www.huffingtonpost.com/human-rights-watch/greece-hunger-strike-by-1_b_267071.html, visited 20/02/10.

ProAsyl: www.proasyl.de/.../proasyl/fm.../Griechenlandbericht_Engl.pdf
-, visited 17/05/10.

ProAsyl, (2008), "The situation in Greece is out of control" Research into the situation of asylum seekers in Greece Carried out by Karl Kopp. See:
http://www.proasyl.de/fileadmin/proasyl/fm_redakteure/Asyl_in_Europa
/Griechenland/Out_of_contol_Eng_END.pdf, visited 07/07/09

20.

CINEMA CODES AND CRIME. QUALITATIVE ANALYSIS OF THE MOVIE "HOODWINKED"

Nikos Rinis

Our research is about the transfer of the classic fairy tale Little Red Riding Hood in the film "Hoodwinked". We will examine if the film constitutes the reproduction of stereotypical representations of the criminal and crime. Also, we will examine whether criminological theories are revealed by the picture/image and the language used in this particular film.

Presdee argues that "is always necessary to state and restate that crime is, if nothing else, a human activity, a human thing, cultural in nature and the product of the social order in which we live at any particular historical moment. In other words it involves the everyday live experiences and practices of all members of society" (Presdee 2004: 276). According to this argument, cultural criminology "is the placing of crime and its control in the context of culture; that is, viewing both crime and the agencies of control as cultural products—as creative constructs. As such, they must be read in terms of the meanings they carry."(Hayward, Young 2004:259).

A central concern of the cultural criminologists is to examine the many ways that cultural facts are combined with the crime and crime control. The representation of the crime is, in this way, a social phenomenon. Under this examination, researchers and theorists are going deeper in the meaning of crime, as a social phenomenon. Furthermore, they are able to understand and criticize the penal system and the official agencies of social control. They can achieve this by, continuously exploring the everyday meanings of crime and control that can be found in all the cultural products of a contemporary society. The theorists of cultural criminology are trying to explore the "wealth of research on mediated characterizations of crime and crime control, ranging across historical and contemporary texts and investigating images generated in newspaper reporting, popular film, television news and entertainment programming, popular music, comic books, and the cyber-spaces of the Internet."(Ferrel 2003: 583). Through the signs, the symbols and the codes, cultural criminologists examine different social groups and their characteristics. They aim to examine the relations between social groups and crime control agencies.

It is important, in contemporary societies, to examine how different social groups are stigmatized and their behaviours are criminalized by the crime control system. Dominant social groups, in order to establish and maintain their cohesion and their social power condemn actions and behaviours of other not so powerful groups. For example, here we can take a look at the car stereo culture. 'Boom boys', 'audio thugs' and 'sonic terrorists', are some of the pejorative terms used to describe those who modify their car stereo systems to produce music at high volume. For those within the car stereo culture, it is a hobby and a passion, with some spending thousands of dollars to create a system that may win them acclaim in the competition circuit or at least the rush of 'outlaw' sound pressure levels. However, there is a growing grassroots movement across the United States as well as other countries to quell the 'noise', with accusations that the musical assault constitutes an 'acoustical rape.''(Crawford 2006: 85). These not so powerful groups are characterised by the dominant groups as delinquent subcultures. "The basic characteristic of the delinquent subculture, it is argued, is a system of values that represents an inversion of the values held by respectable, law-abiding society. The world of the delinquent is the world of the law-abiding turned upside down and its norms constitute a countervailing force directed against the conforming social order."(Sykes, Matza 2003: 231). Presdee notes (2000:17), that the criminalization process is the way that dominant social groups achieve to define and limit which action or behaviour is legal or illegal. And through this process social groups realise their position in the society.

The criminal groups are standardized and limited in narrow frames of behaviour and appearance, mainly the appearance and the use of harsh language. On the other hand, mass media aims to create discourse around a social group. And, most of the times, this discourse tends to be negative for a social group that is weaker and conflicts with the dominant groups or the crime control agencies, such as police and penal system. For example, rap music in the United States of America. As Schneider refers, "the genre of rap music is among the more controversial and has been highlighted by the media, politicians, and others, who have criticized the dramatic, violent, and often antisocial imagery that rap music sometimes embodies.[...] This contributes to the creation of continued negative perceptions of this music, which, over a period of prolonged time, become anchored in collective memory and consciousness. These perceptions, when couched in the popular consciousness and cultural narrative, favour the interpretation of particular messages as either normal or deviant and thus contribute to the development of a public discourse surrounding rap music." (Schneider 2011:37). Simply put, mass media develops discourse around specific groups for two reasons. First, the dialogue around crime assists crime control agencies to intensify their social control and repression through fear that is perpetuated with ongoing attention of criminal acts. Secondly, this discourse disorientates the social members from other social problems that the dominant groups or the agencies of crime control can not face and/or solve.

Cinema, empowering this discourse, uses several ways to stigmatize and limit actions and behaviors that are not following the rules of a law-biding society. An example is the Hays Code. Hays Code was "a self-regulatory code of ethics created in 1930 by the Motion Picture Producers and Distributors of America (M.P.P.D.A.), under Will H. Hays, and put into strict effect on July 1, 1934, with Joseph I. Breen as director of the Code Administration"[1]. This code prevented screening on several actions such as drug trafficking or on Ministers of religions which could not be represented as comic characters or as villains etc.

The discourse around crime and crime control is becoming dominant through the use of a specific language and images. The use of a specific language and images for the social phenomena, such as crime and crime control from the mass media and more specifically, cinema, does not have a neutral role. The language is the means of communication and reconciliation between the individuals and the groups of a society. The language is what determines and develops the relations of power and sovereignty in a society. Mass Media, beyond their content that can be analyzed from a lot of aspects, also carry out a social operation. They are the main source of information and an important opportunity to exchange opinions and to discuss for all the members of a society. Through the direct transmission of images in movies, messages and information are transferred to society. As a result, individuals get a lot of information every day and can not process them all. Images have always a meaning. They are tanks that produce and reproduce meaning (Curran, Gurevitch, 2007: 98).

---

[1] http://course1.winona.edu/pjohnson/h140/hays_code.htm

Consequently, if a social group is sovereign, then it might impose a sovereign model of language and, furthermore, it will be in a position to control the thoughts and the social behaviours of individuals and groups of society. When the criminals or the delinquents face the official agencies of social control, such as police and the penal system, they do not express their true perception and therefore, represent themselves falsely. They try to express and analyze their experiences and behaviours according to the sovereign model of language and the social rules. Language helps social members to communicate between each other. Social acts are not conceived from the individuals as innate phenomena, but via symbols and codes. "Form is one indispensable component of the linguistic sign. The other essential component is meaning. And because language is the kind of entity it is, both form and meaning function together within a system that is used for human communication."(Lattey 1989: 45).

Cinema, as a dominant means of understanding everyday life and social acts, spreads and transfers symbols and signs around the criminal, the crime and its control. "Shared meanings, social changes and challenges, narrations of human drama and social reality, utopian dreams and dystopian nightmares, our fears and fantasies, have been *projected* (both literally and metaphorically) through the lens of cinematic technology." (Yar 2010:68). Cinema has a central role in understanding and interpreting social life, its actions and behaviours. After all, it is a means that integrates the viewers into a social reality and it promotes a popular culture that the dominant system produces. "Integration assists persons in understanding and regulating conflicts between social groups." (Lambropoulou 1999:159).

The research[2]

Let's begin to examine the movie Little Red Riding Hood which counts more than 70 versions worldwide[3]. Hoodwinked is a modern version of this particular fairy tale[4]. The film was produced in 2005 from American Kanbar Entertainment[5]. Famous actors of Hollywood participate with their voices in the American version, for example, Anne Hathaway

---

[2] The script of the movie is used only for academic and research reasons.
[3] www.cosmo.gr
[4] http://en.wikipedia.org/wiki/Little_Red_Riding_Hood
[5] http://www.imdb.com/title/tt0443536/

(Red), Glenn Close (Grand mother), James Belushi (lumberjack). The direction and the script are from Cory Edwards, Todd Edwards and Tony Leech.

In this specific case study we used the method of *discourse analysis*. Discourse "refers to language actually produced by users of a language and normally implies interaction, that is, involvement of two or more participants."(Sofianou 2001: 1). More important is to understand that the messages and the symbols have to be interpreted.

"To perceive or appropriate the meaning of a text through reading it is, in other words, an *activity,* not simply passively 'receiving' finished meanings. We are served with a plurality of *signifiers* with a plurality of possible signifieds, and we use our acquired knowledge of codes to determine what they are saying (to us)." (Gripsrud 2002: 131).

Let's see how some parts of the film are combined with criminological theories:

Red, after her meeting with the wolf in the forest reports:

Red: "You've gotta admit, a wolf stopping kids in the middle of the forest... "

That's pretty creepy."

Flippers: "Right. Yes, yes. But we don't arrest people for being creepy."

Officer 1: "Yeah, Bruce. You know that guy we got in the tank?"

Officer 2: "The creepy one?"

Officer 1: "Yeah. Better let him go."

The theories of traditional criminology are confirmed in this point. The representation of criminals to the members of a society and the formal agencies of social control is the same. A criminal or a delinquent is a person that acts and behaves because it has inherited specific external characteristics and has abnormal psychology. Social or other factors are not examined. An ugly person is a danger for the public and has to be isolated by the society. The police officers of this film admit that they had arrested a "dangerous" person, just because he looked scary/creepy.

Let's examine another situation:

Head of the police: "Quit playing around, Wolf! You're looking at three-to-five in an old shoe with no windows! So start singing!"

The head of the police undertakes the role of a judge. Using his power, he threatens the suspect with a condemnatory decision and sordid conditions of detention. To achieve, the police officers use a lot of means to control and force the "suspect" to admit his guilt. Characteristically, they use a tape recorder, a microphone, electrical shock and wooden sticks (similar to the batons that the police use).

The lumberjack is represented as a person with enormous external characteristics (Hulk style) and low intelligence. The chief of the police is making comments for his "strange" accent. Here, we observe the state of madness.

Head of the police: "This guy's a loon."

Officer 3: "Watch it, chief. My mama's half-loon."

The lumberjack is actually an actor who, in order to play the role of a lumberjack for an advertisement, goes to the forest to find the lumberjack that hides in himself. At this point he is presented as an individual that does not even know the use of an axe.

Now, the rabbit is the character that plays for a large part of the film a sweet, nice and friendly "person". But, when the others discover his real character, he changes completely. He changes his language and expressions and reveals his plans for the future. He is a sweet person transformed into a "bad" person, which is something that refers once again to a positivist approach about crime and criminal.

Conclusions

This film represents the sovereign and rendered structures and operations of a society. There is not a difference the way the police acts, as a formal agency of social control, and compared to all the other members of society. At coffee breaks, they eat donuts. Also, they use repressive tools and stigmatize individuals and groups with their language and actions.

Looking at this with this point of view, images and language used by the movies are transformed to symbols and codes. The way the heroes are represented in the movies, the way that they speak and behave gives us specific cultural influences.

Consequently, each social activity and behaviour takes a meaning by the symbols and the codes that are included in a process of production and reproduction of symbols and meanings. This cultural practices use the symbols in order to create meanings in a society.

The language is the means of communication between the individuals and the groups of society. The language is the one that determines and develops the relations of sovereignty in society. The language and the images that are used by this particular film does not differ from the sovereign representation that a big part of the society has for criminals, formal agencies of social control and the dangers that exist "outside there".

Moreover, the formal agencies of social control continuously criminalize more and more behaviours that come against the system. For example, in the movie we have Flippers saying:

Flippers: "The only thing your granddaughter is guilty of is flying hummingbirds without a license".

Alternative styles of art, music and entertainment face the sovereignty of official social control and legislation. And, consequently, they are moved outside the mainstream system.

When society feels increasing threat, official institutions of social control protect and defend the legal order and ethics. The increasing invocation of the term "dangerous", aims only to reproduce and maintain a model of a criminal.

Here are two more examples how images and language help influence the way a culture conceives of a criminal:

Grandmother, trying to describe one of the members of the gang:

"The toughest one is the big fella, really mean-looking, with a fat head and a thick skull. Looks like a shaved ape. I mean, he is u-u-u-ugly! Like a big, swollen, overgrown...".

Flippers: "I guess running the cable car's not so bad, you know. It's a great way to see the forest without worrying about all those big, mean, hairy beasts out there.

Red: "Beasts?"

Flippers: "Oh, yeah, you know, beasts. The wolves and the bobcats and the mountain lions and the tigers! But mostly, wolves."

Red: "The forest can be a dangerous place for a little guy like me, with my cute..."

The use of language and picture is a field of study and research. In this particular film, the story with the bad wolf is not confirmed, however promotes the feeling of danger and fear. The words "robber", "dangerous", "scary", "wild", "theft", "police", "inspector of police", "guilty" are repeated. And the meaning of these words becomes continuous and part of the mainstream.

Lastly, the criminal character might change, but the term "criminal" and the functions of the official institutions of social control remain constant, aiming at the cohesion and the maintenance of order in society.

References

Campbell, E.(2010). The future(s) of risk: Barthes and Baudrillard go to Hollywood, in *Crime Media Culture 2010 6:7*

Crawford, C. (2006). Car stereos, culture and criminalization, in *Crime, Media, Culture 2: 85*

Curran, J. & Gurevitch, M. (eds) (2007). *Mass Media and society*, Athens: Pataki (in Greek)

Fernandez Reyes, A. (2005). Criminologia del Cine. Las cosas del crimen en el cine de la "Epoca de Oro", in *Estudios sobre las Culturas Contemporaneas, Epoca II. Vol. XI. Num. 21*, Colima

Ferrel, J. (2003). Cultural criminology, in McLaughlin, E. & Muncie, J. & Hughes, G. (eds), *Criminological perspectives*, London: Sage Publications

Georgoulas, S. (2003). *Juvenile delinquency*, Athens: Ekremmes (in Greek)

Goffman, E. (2001). *Stigma*, Athens: Alexandria (in Greek)

Gripsrud, J. (2002). *Understanding Media culture*, London: Arnold

Hayward, K. & Young, J. (2004). Cultural criminology: Some notes on the script, in *Theoretical Criminology Vol. 8(3): 259–273*, London: Sage

Jewkes, Y. (2004). *Media and Crime*, London: Sage

Lambropoulou, E. (1999). *The construction of the social reality by the Mass Media Means. The case of violence and criminality*, Athens: Ellinika Grammata (in Greek)

Lambrou, A. (2003). *Superman's Punch*, Athens: Sichroni Epoxi (in Greek)

Lattey, E. (1989). On the role of form in going from sign to text and from text to understanding, in Tobin, Y. (ed.). *From sign to text. A semiotic view of communication*, Amsterdam/Philadelphia: John Benjamins Publishing Company

Leitch, T. (2004). *Crime films*, Cambridge: Cambridge University Press

Lindgren, S. (2008). Crime, media, coding: developing a methodological framework for computer-aided analysis, in *Crime Media Culture 2008 4: 95*, London: Sage

Maguire, M. & Morgan, R. & Reiner, R. (2002). *The Oxford Handbook of Criminology*, United States Oxford University Press

Piquero, A. & Weisburd, D. (eds) (2010). *Handbook of quantitative criminology*, London: Springer

Presdee, M. (2004). Cultural criminology. The long and winding road, *Theoretical Criminology Vol. 8(3): 275–285, London: Sage*

Presdee, M. (2000). *Cultural criminology and the carnival of crime*, Oxon: Routledge

Rabinow, P. (1984). *The Foucault reader*, New York: Pantheon Books

Rafter, N. (2007). Crime, film and criminology. Recent sex-crime movies, in *Theoretical Criminology 2007 11: 403*, London: Sage

Schneider, J. C. (2011). Culture, Rap Music, "Bitch," and the Development of the Censorship Frame, in *American Behavioral Scientist 2011 55:36*

Shoham, G. S., Knepper, P. & Kett, M. (eds) (2010). *International Handbook of Criminology*, CRC Press

Sofianou, M. (2001). *Discourse analysis. An introduction*, Athens: Leader Books (in Greek)

Sykes, G. M. & Matza D. (2003). Techniques of neutralization, in McLaughlin, E. & Muncie, J. & Hughes, G. (eds), *Criminological perspectives*, London: Sage Publications

Vold, B. G., Bernard, J. T. & Snipes, B. J. (2002). *Theoretical Criminology*, New York: Oxford University Press Inc

Yar, M. (2010). Screening crime. Cultural criminology goes to the movies, in Hayward & Presdee (eds), *Framing crime. Cultural criminology and the image*, Oxon: Routledge

Yotopoulos-Maragopoulos, A.(1984). *Criminology. Part A' Introduction*, Athens: Nomiki Vivliothiki (in Greek)

Websites:

http://www.cosmo.gr

http://www.imdb.com/title/tt0443536/

http://en.wikipedia.org/wiki/Little_Red_Riding_Hood

http://course1.winona.edu/pjohnson/h140/hays_code.htm

21.
FORENSIC SCIENCE AND CRIMINOLOGY. THE ROLE
OF MEDICAL CORONERS: A PILOT QUALITATIVE
RESEARCH.

Christos Kouroutzas

Theoretical Framework

Forensic science and Criminology. The role of the medical coroners.

The forensic as science in modern societies has specialized its object while new factors, as forensic odontologist[1], forensic pathologist[2], forensic toxicology[3], forensic archeology[4], forensic anthropology[5] etc, have been developed, factors who also strengthen its role in the modern criminal justice system. Forensic science, 'describes the science of associating people, places, and thing involved in criminal activities; these scientific disciplines assist in investigating and adjudicating criminal and civil cases. Forensic science is an appropriate term for the profession which answers scientific questions for the profession which answers scientific questions for the courts'. (Houck 2007: 1-2).

The main aim and object of its applications is the study and examination of the dead and the investigation of the cause and nature of

---

[1] Forensic odonotology, has 'a large number of applications to the forensic sciences. They include identification of human remains in mass disasters (enamel is the hardest material produced by the body and intact teeth are often found), post-mortem x-rays of the teeth can be compared to ante-mortem x-rays, and the comparison of bitemarks'. (Houck, Siegel 2010: 5).
[2] Forensic pathology, is 'conducted by a medical examiner, who is a physician, specially trained in clinical and anatomic pathology, whose function is to determine the cause and manner of death in cases where the death occurred under suspicious or unknown circumstances'. (Houck, Siegel 2010: 4).
[3] Forensic toxicology, is 'the scientific study of poisons – their nature and effects- in relation to the law'. (Jackson & Jackson 2008: 444).
[4] Forensic archeologists, 'concentrate on the analysis of skeletal remains while forensic archeologists focus on the location and excavation of these remains'. (Bell 2008: 22).
[5] Forensic anthropology, is 'the study of the human skeleton, and how it has developed and evolved throughout the history of the human race. Forensic anthropologists are physical anthropologists who specialize in recovering and examining human skeletal remains where legal questions are involved'. (Lee, Harris 2006: 21-22).

death. The role of forensics in the Bodies of Official Social Control starts from the objects of forensic examination. More specifically, it includes the study and examination of violent deaths (homicides), suspicious deaths, sudden or unexpected deaths and deaths of persons who were not under medical supervision. This conceptual definition is linked with the criminal justice system, after reflecting the type of operation, which later, to the downstream analysis of the case; it has a corresponding penalty in the coroner's findings.

As for the forensic investigation, it is to divided into three stages in solving the 'crime'. More specifically, the first stage of the forensic investigation, includes the autopsy at the crime scene[6] and the autopsy – post mortem examination[7], where the objective is the official statement above all the death, the determination of time elapsed since the death, the competent advice about the cause of death, an initial assessment of the type of injury that brings the body and especially the determination of the type of death (homicide, suicide, etc.). Thereafter, the process in the morgue. The coroner at this stage of research makes a detailed examination by order of the machine, the autopsy and sampling for laboratory tests.

In the third stage of the forensic investigation, including the drafting of the forensic report[8] delivered to the investigator - a police officer, who along with other data collected transmits all the information at the Head of the First Instance Court. The forensic report will define the action as 'criminal' or not, but also the kind of the crime. The judge and prosecutor will decide the sentence, depending on the type of the crime.

The main concern for forensic applications in a legal frame is that, 'while internationally they follow a single and uniform medical way, le-

---

[6] Crime scene: 'everything that happens at the crime laboratory concerning the scientific examination of physical evidence begins with the criminal act – at the crime scene. The crime scene therefore is the start of any forensic science investigation. Crime scenes may be indoors or outdoors. They may be expansive or quite small. In the case of a violent crime, the assailant's body is also a crime scene'. (Fisher, Tilstone, Woytowicz 2009:5).

[7] Autopsy or post mortem examination is 'a complete inspection of a corpse. Investigators often rely on an autopsy to help explain a decedent's cause and manner of death. Pathologists are specialized doctors who usually carry out autopsies. An autopsy is required when the cause of death is suspected to be a criminal matter or when the cause of death cannot be determined medically' (Walker, Wood 2010: 1).

[8] The Forensic scientist (s) 'responsible for the analysis of evidential items during a criminal investigation is required to write up his or her findings in the form of a report for use in court. As well as being comprehensive, the contents of such a report should be readily understood by non-scientists within the criminal justice system. In most cases, the forensic scientist's report is all that is seen by the court'. (Jackson & Jackson 2008: 3).

gally they take place with long term variations according to the procedural law of each country' (Michalodimitrakis 2001: 5). It is observed, therefore, that under the prevailing values of each region or country (society), procedural law is different, showing legal long term variations and demarcating the concept of selectivity of the examination and study of operations that will be classified as criminal. The coroner will be required to appoint medical and legal practice as criminal as he consists the main expresser of criminal law. He will also have to defend the dominant values of the country, but again were these values are delimited by the dominant groups and groups who hold power and force, i.e. interest groups.

This diversity and selectivity that distinguishes the various procedural laws of the countries emerge also from the different roles held by coroners. Examples are the U.S. compared to EU countries. More specifically, while the modern American-style system, responsible for examining a violent death is a (Medical Examiner), who is skilled in forensic doctor, in Greece, the coroner has no direct responsibility by law to consider stand-alone events, but he has only a posted impressive power (Medical coroner[9]).

Where it is apparent natural death, the role of police is not inquisitorial, but the police informs that there is no suspicion and perform procedures to licensed landfill. But when it is clearly violent, sudden, suspicious death or termination of life was startling to young people, then the forensic scientist's report[10] for use in court, is necessary.

The coroner at the first stage is usually called by the police. The police has a double functional mission in the criminal justice system, as a vehicle for the exercise of formal social control. On the one hand, the police is responsible for maintaining order and, therefore, in this part of its operation goes back to prevention, and on the other hand, is responsible for studying the crimes, the discovery of the perpetrators so as their arrest and surrender to the mechanisms of criminal justice.

---

[9] Medical coroner in 'a judicial officer who is elected or appointed, whose tasks are mainly administrative. The job of the coroner is to determine the cause of death by using whatever resources are necessary, which can include ordering an autopsy by a pathologist or forensic pathologist'. (Bell 2004: 46).
[10] The forensic scientist's report 'is a very important document, representing, as it does, the culmination of all the labour that haw been expended during the conduct of a criminal investigation. It is often instrumental in persuading a defendant to plead guilty, thus obviating the need for a trial. Many factors must be taken into account when preparing such a report for use in court'. (Jackson & Jackson 2008: 430).

Throughout this process of successive filtering, the coroner is required to deliver the forensic expert, which will include all information and data of forensic investigations, assisting in the promotion of 'presumed criminals' in the next phase. If the findings are complete and identify the items with the alleged offender they lead him to his formal designation as an offender and with the rest institutions of the criminal justice system will deliver to him the social identity of the offender.

In other words, it is one of the special mechanisms of the criminal justice system that will participate in the process of the exercising official social control.

Finally, as seen from above, 'he who is employed by society as criminal and is treated as such by the formal and informal social reaction, he who is also recorded in official statistics and studies by criminologist as an empirical fact, is not the one who passes to the criminal act, but the one who is finally selected and classified as criminal by the mechanisms of formal social reaction, i.e. the criminal justice system' (Daskalakis 1985: 82).

Thus, the result of all this, is to study the construction of 'new social control', as well as building and creating new formal institutions of social control in the context of the globalization of crime in contemporary social systems.

Critical criminology and the role of forensic science in criminal justice system.

Critical criminology 'has naturally problematized and criticized many of the 'normal' notions about crime. The contribution to this form of 'debunking' varies according to the different perspectives of the stream of critical criminology involved. In a certain period, Marxist criminology predominantly took the stand that 'crime' was a product of the capitalist system, and that crime would disappear if a new society took birth'. (Hulsman 2004: 311).

According to the forensic theory of consensus, any human society is characterized by consensual core values. In this sense, the state exists to alleviate conflicts between people and to show common values and interests.

Unlike the consensus forensic theories, theories of conflict have as dominant visual opposition recording to the shaping of society by the dominant values and interests, arguing that societies are formed under the conflicting interests between the people of the society, resulting in the best interests of the socially powerful, covering the entire spectrum of social life. (Craib, 2000). In this process the state defends the interests of powerful groups. The bodies of formal social control, such as forensic, defend the dominant values and interests, as expressers of the criminal laws of the state. From this the behaviors that will be hired as 'criminal'. Will be defined.

Thus, the behaviour is 'product of the interaction terms of the social environment and how the person will engage and interpret them'. (Mead, 1934).

According to the theory of Becker (1963), 'all social groups make rules and attempt, at some times and under some circumstances, to enforce them. Social rules define situations and the kinds of behaviour appropriate to them, specifying some actions as 'right' and forbidding others as be seen as a special kind of person, one who cannot be trusted to live by the rules agreed on by the group. He is regarded as an outsider. But the person who is thus labeled an outsider may have a different view of the matter. He may not accept the rule by which he is being judged and may not regard those who judge him as either competent or legitimately entitled to do so. Hence, a second meaning of the term emerges: the rule - breaker may feel his judges are outsiders. Thus, in relation to delinquent behaviour and the label, 'the deviant is one to whom that label haw successfully been applied, deviant behaviour is behaviour that people so label'. (Becker 2004: 243). In this sense, forensic and other institutions of formal social control, successfully attach the label for specific behaviour to be defined as 'criminal', expressing the substance of the criminal law. Accordingly, 'criminal' is the one, that the official bodies of social control and thus a part of the social system, has been attached to this label.

Point of concern, is the performance of a specific identity even in the same body during the forensic investigation of the 'crime'. As mentioned characteristically, the recognition, discovery and evaluation of various types of 'Tattoo' on a corpse is of significant value in forensic investigation. In addition to information about the physical identity of the unknown dead, they can also give information on other properties of the deceased. Thus; for example 'the crude and simplistic appearance of an image on the skin indicates rough performance as it often happens in prisons, etc. to find a swallow between thumb and forefinger or two birds going in the same flower or the names of the same sex are indicative of homosexuality, while finding images of fish or the number 13 concerns people who are involved in games of chance. They often indicate strong emotional states ('mother' or the name of sexual partner) and also the usual circle of addicts'.(Michalodimitrakis 2001: 65).

According to Jackson & Jackson (2008), 'tattoos are essentially permanent marks on the skin. They are made by pricking the skin and inserting one or more pigments to form the desired design. The nature and location of the tattoo and, in particular, the inclusion of specific names (often the first name of a boy – or girlfriend) may be useful to the police in identifying the decedent. In some cases, the actual design of the tattoo itself may convey useful information about the activities of the deceased during life. Tattoos are especially useful as identifying features as they are relatively persistent and may be clearly seen, even after the outer layer of the epidermis (the stratum corneum) has been lost during the decomposition process'. (Jackson & Jackson 2008: 362).

Main area of concern is the resending of the stigma and label the person, body or corpse through the forensic investigation. Through all this, we see that the forensic investigators label and stigmatize even the dead body, giving particular social identities such as gay, through the external features bearing the body, such as a 'tattoo'. These data contains information about the physical identity of the deceased, while using these data social identities are awarded, identities such as this of a criminal, of a prisoner or of a gay. At the same time, this information that is gathered through the body of the Coroners, throughout the forensic investigation, will be used by other institutions of formal social control to yield a specific label. Moreover, it is understood that the label is not only for alive bodies, but also involves the dead bodies, where forensic experts are centrally positioned to their study and research.

Therefore, the theory of the label is not only to conduct that people or institutions of formal social control will use her, but also concerns all the features that bring the dead body, features that are exclusively investigated by the forensic science.

According to the forensic conflict theories, social structure is the historical record of the results of the victory of some groups over others. Thus, forensic science historically, was asked to define certain behaviours as 'criminal' behaviours, and delimiting groups in different social systems. Furthermore, the control that the body receives is multilevel, and covers all stages of life and not of the individual. The genetic science[11] is used in all stages in order to carry out this. For example, there are prenatal tests, which study the characteristics of the baby, such as gender, there are controls over one's life, such as biometric controls and there are also controls on the dead body, indicating, for example, sexual preferences that the person had.

More precisely as far as the theory of social conflict is concerned, there are three trends reflected in the field of criminology. According to the first point of the theory of social conflict, with its main supporter Marx, 'his theory linked economic development to social, political, and historical change, but did not deal with the problem of crime in any significant way. So, the principle conflict that Marx presented in his theory, and on which the theory is based, was the conflict between the material forces of production and the social relations of production. As a result, Marx argued, capitalist societies would inevitably tend to polarize into two groups, one growing smaller and larger while getting poorer and poorer. These Marxist theories describe criminal behaviours as the rational responses of rational individuals confronted with a situation structured by the social relations of capitalism'. (Vold, Bernard, Snipes 1998: 261-267). Thus, the conflict is based on economic infrastructure and property relations. In this sense, 'crime' is a creation of the capitalist class society as well as economic disparities.

Furthermore, the development of biotechnology[12] in the wider use of new technologies is directly linked to the economy of the country. The production of medicines, vaccines and various other organic materials with the methods of genetic engineering can be achieved depending on the money given to research and ultimately produce them.

Thus, forensic science is the criminal law in social systems, reflecting the interests of the ruling class, defining behaviours as crimes against the interests and the interests of the state.

According to the second trend, the conflict is placed at the cultural structure base. In this theoretical framework, presented a criminology theory focused on the conflict of 'conduct norms'. Conduct norms are cultural rules that require certain types of people to act in certain ways in certain circumstances - eg in simple, homogeneous societies, many of

---

[11] The term 'genetic science' means the science that studies the principles, rules and mechanisms governing the inheritance. (Koutselinis 1999: 208).

[12] The term 'biotechnology' means the application of methods of genetic engineering. This area was created by the need for production of medicines, vaccines and other biological materials of various methods of genetic engineering. (Koutselinis 1999: 210).

these conduct norms are enacted into law and actually represent a consensus in the society. But in more complex societies, there will be over - lap and contradiction between the conduct norms of different cultural groups. In each of these cases law would not represent a consensus of the various members of the society, but would reflect the conduct norms of the dominant culture. (Vold, Bernard, Snipes 1998: 234 - 236). Thus, the crime is the result of a collision of cultural values. The goal of these types of norm is first of all to translate them into laws and secondly the consent of the members of society, aiming to create a homogenized society, particularly in the context of the globalization of crime.

Similarly, based on the theory of Merton (1957), about lawlessness, the Cohen, Cloward and Ohlin, they present crime and criminality as intercultural phenomenon. Thus, intercultural groups appear to be illegal phenomenon in social systems and corresponding behaviours to be defined as 'delinquent' would come from these intercultural groups. In this sense, the forensic science defines the crime and the "criminal" behaviour through the action of intercultural groups, that the state and powerful groups by the dominant values are defined as such.

According to the third trend of the theory of conflict, social conflict is placed at the level of power. This has as a result, according to Dahrendorf (1959), the ruling classes and therefore the groups engaged in formal social control, to have prestige, power and high social (status).

Also, under the theory of criminalization, (Vold, Bernard, Snipes 2002) refers to the concept of restricted activity or behaviour assessed by the authorities. Thus, the forensic along with the other institutions of the criminal justice system will determine the restricted activity and behaviour. This will happen through specific research and theoretical analysis during the forensic investigation of crime.

Thus, the forensic strengthens the social construction of crime that is constructed through the process of criminalization, since it is the criminal law that defines the status of crime in certain behaviours in the forensic investigation and returns the social identity of the offender to certain entities as implementing body of the criminal law. Moreover, through the forensic expert and the definition of an act as 'criminal' objectifies the criteria to define an act as criminal and a person as a criminal.

The forensic theories of conflict consider the crime as a form of interaction between subjects as well as a form of interaction between subjects and social structures. So the crime in conflict theories is not considered as an autonomous subject of action. The ruling authorities, imposed on the society determine the behaviour that would be qualified as criminal. Therefore, crime is a socially constructed concept that is consistent with the interests and the power of the stronger social group.

Research Methodology

In this research, it is appropriate to use qualitative research methods, since the objective is the explanation and analysis of the reasons that cause the appearance of social phenomena associated with the forensic investigation of the 'crime' during the forensic tests.

More specifically, the present pilot study used three techniques for qualitative research, a principal and two as complementary to the first. Thus, the personal interview is uses as the main method and then the participant observation and analysis of content items to complement the first.

More specifically, it was realised a total of two interviews with a semistructured questionnaire- interview guide and a free non- standardized interview to Coroners, Forensic Medicine and Toxicology Service. The purpose was to study the representations of Forensic as institutions of Official Social Control agencies on issues related to forensic investigation of the 'crime' through forensic analysis, methods and techniques.

With regard to participatory observation, the objective is to observe record and study the phenomena associated with conducting forensic analysis of the Forensic Investigation of the crime in a pilot level.

The category of participant observation that was used was the observer as a participant, knowing our identity and we recorded any activity, the behaviours as well as the data from the scene without participating in the group.

As far as the content analysis documents is concerned, the texts studied, were parts of the "Universal Declaration of Human Rights" in relation to man, the prime subject of Fundamental Human Rights in Bioethics, the Ecumenical Declaration of the International Bioethics Committee as the "Universal Declaration on the Human Genome and Human Rights, adopted by the General Assembly of UNESCO on 11/11/1997 and the "Universal Declaration on Human Genetic Data", adopted on 16/10/2003, the Additional Protocols to the Conventions of the Council Europe relating to Medicine and Biology, as the Additional Protocol to the Prohibition of Cloning (Paris 12/01/1998) and the advisory recommendations of the National Bioethics Commission.

This pilot study used the technique of triangulation in order to properly interpret the data. According to Cohen and Manion (1980), in the technique of triangulation, the researcher takes into account except for studying the phenomenon, and other information, such as interviews, participant observation, etc. that give him the possibility to give proper interpretation of the data available through intersections and clarifications.

Regarding to the geographical areas selected, these were:
1. Forensic Service in Athens.
2. Forensic Medicine Service in Aegean.

Also, an interpretive comparative analysis of the results of personal interviews and of all data recorded during participant observation and analysis of content items was realised.

The division of forensic services starting from the Forensic Service of Athens in Athens, which includes and is separated into regional Forensic Services within the jurisdiction of Athens Forensic Service and also the Local Forensic Services which are subject to regional administrative services and which are related to the first . Furthermore, there are forensic services in universities.

The time that this investigation was planed and conducted was from 15/11/2009 to 28/04/10.

The basic assumption of this research is the following:

- **First working hypothesis: The role of the coroner is related to modern optics of "social construction" of crime.**
- **Working hypothesis 2: The applications in forensic science on criminology help build a "new social control" of modern social systems.**

The aim was to study the construction of the 'new social control' as well as build and create new institutions of official social control, in the frame of the 'globalization of crime' in contemporary social systems.

Basic research conclusions

Initially, in a context of comparative analysis and study, the forensic investigation of crime is different in the way of investigating a 'criminal act' in Greece, compared with other countries members of the European Union, as well as in international level.

Coroner's Interview Extract:

'In America, the analysis is done directly and until the autopsy is finished, they have results of toxicology tests which, in our case, may need one month to be realised and after the autopsy is done – we will be able to get the autopsy results of toxicology ... There are no funds from the state, from the Department of Justice to purchase the equipment'.

Therefore, the role held by the forensic, differs internationally, depending on the degree of power and strength that has been attributed by the current criminal justice system, the state and the political power. Moreover, there is also a difference related to the strength that formal social control is realised, since in some countries it is more strict and less in others.

Also, the 'crime' and criminal policy are established in accordance to the authority and the power of each country. This explains why the most 'developed' countries (economically), apply contemporary models for monitoring and forensic investigation through the use of new technologies in laboratory forensic investigation of crime and further in search of formal social control agencies.

At the same time, about the globalization of the crime, as Ass remarks, 'notwithstanding, there exists by now a wealth of criminological investigations of globalization and its impact on issues of crime and crime control - what might be termed criminology of globalization. Furthermore, global transformation undoubtedly change the dynamics between the national, local and the global, yet these transformations have not necessary given primacy to one at the expense of the other. For example, in cases such as cyber crime, the challenges have become translational rather than being simply inter-national, and demand a simultaneous view of global, national and local level'. (Aas 2010: 427 - 446).

Coroner's Interview Extract:

*'Sure. **Especially cyber crime is a global phenomenon** and we see that in cases where the police have caught some of them, we observe that one is from Argentina, the other from Greece, the other from Russia. Obviously there should be **global base** for this thing to **achieve co-operation between the authorities of any state'**.*

Therefore and according to the first hypothesis, the modern construction of crime is directly connected with the globalization of the crime. Also, through research data, we can see differences in the organizational culture of forensic services[13]. More specifically, there are differences in the structure of the services, where the role of power and hierarchy is apparent. Also, there are differences between staff both in the organization and equipment services.

Coroner's Interview Extract:

'There is no Personal qualified and educated and undergoing training,... no money from the state, or the Justice Department to buy equipment. And from what I know the most modern laboratory is the police has at this time'.

At the same time through the results of research it is determined which crimes will be selected to be inserted in the criminal justice system and what will be hired as a social crime, through the above procedures, respectively, they are selected psychological, biological and social characteristics of the 'alleged perpetrators', but also the causes of crime, according to coroners. As noted below, these features are based on consensus forensic theories.

Coroner's Interview Extract:

'No, just have in mind that all this leads men to crime, and women to prostitution. Women these days are more unlikely to commit crimes in comparison with a man »...« Yes, definitely. The environment, education, social level, the humble instincts, in which city spends his life ... "Sure. There is a biological aspect to commit the crime ..." Look to see, first of all the **psychological problems of the offender** *are unaccountable, and he cannot take into consideration what is going on ....« The mental status is something to consider also in the case of suicide. I really believe, speaking as a doctor that plays a very important role ... "Certainly, depression or psychiatric disorders such as schizophrenia, etc. all these are elements that could lead to crime and suicide ... "Definitely it is the coroner who will respond if the death has come as a result of crime or accidentally . 'We will say that according to the examination realised sperm was found in such and such area. Beyond this stage there comes the police. There are some potential perpetrators. If there is any actor we would take a sample from it and compare them'.* Therefore, through the action of an official inspection agency, those who will be awarded the social identity of the of-

---

[13] Public forensic science laboratories are financed and operated by a unit of government. Different jurisdictions have different models for where the laboratory appears in the governmental hierarchy. Federal laboratories have their own positions within the federal system. (Houck, 2007).

fender will be selected, through the above deterministic approaches. So, the crime is one 'manufactured significance' and through forensic science, and is due to biological, psychological and social factors according to the causal of consensual crime theory.

Coroner's Interview Extract:

'We can not cooperate with the police, they do not call us foe autopsies in the place" ... *That we detect gunpowder, but we never see the body of the crime. These are made by police in Greece'.*

Thus, in Greece at present, the official social control is mainly exercised by the police. Moreover, the state and political power determine the role of formal social control agencies. Moreover, as seen from the survey data, the autopsy carried out mainly by the police, when the coroner should be present. Therefore, the formal institutions of social control, according to the degree of power they possess, construct also the way that each crime should be studied and researched as well as the degree of cooperation between them regarding to the exercise of official social control.

Coroner's Interview Extract:

'Like I said we are the 'right hand' of the police and prosecutor's eyes ... *the coroner's like giving information to the prosecutor in order to start the prosecution, and whatever he might need* ... *the police comes and gets us, then leads us to the crime scene, we do the autopsy and then leave.. Yes, the coroner is the one who will help in the role of investigative* ... *we would say that the court usually follows these findings of the coroner...In helping the existing investigative authority to work in solving crimes against life'.*

Nevertheless, according to the forensic theories of conflict, a new field of conflict between the official agencies of social control is created. The aim is, firstly, the dominance of one operator to another and secondly the enforcement of the power in order to protect the dominant values. Of course, all this is linked to political power, which participates in this mode, as well as the criminal law, which is expressed, by the definition of 'crime' and 'criminal'. Besides, 'the class rule, claimed Therborn, is exercised through state power ... through the interventions or policies of the state'. (Scraton, Chadwick 2004: 297). Medical coroners are a good example of the policies of the state. This is reflected by the non-cooperation of official agencies of social control between them.

Coroner's Interview Extract:

'Unfortunately, psychiatrists do not cooperate with us ... We cannot work with the police, we are not called for the investigations of crime scene, they only bring us the corpse the next day or the same, when we should normally be called ... Sure I guess, if a crime is determined after the police is called, without touching anything, the coroner and forensic should be called together. But this does not take place. Sure there are experts to attend and, unfortunately, this does not happen. *The bad aspect is that the police destroy evidence'.*

Therefore, through this, it appears that the selectivity of the official agencies of social control, about who will be introduced in the criminal justice system and will be characterised with the social identity of 'criminal'. Especially when, the bodies of official social control their one 'destroy evidence'.

Also, through research data, future challenges emerge in the field of bioethics[14], in connection with criminology, since human rights are affected and infected through the forensic applications of genetics. A particular example, regarding to the future performance of the 'new formal social control', according to the second hypothesis is the genotypic databases.

According to Jackson & Jackson (2008), 'a major advantage of modern DNA profiling is that the data generated can be readily presented and collected in databases that can be searched with new DNA evidence from a crime scene. In April 1995 the Forensic Sience Service (FSS) in England and Wales set up the National DNA Database (NDNAD), the first database of its kind in the world. Many countries now have or are starting to develop such database'. (Jackson & Jackson 2008: 163).

Coroner's Interview Extract:

'In Germany it was recently declared that the provision of criminal procedure, that provides the possibility to maintain the sample of the same person for future use when there is evidence of further serious crimes, in line with the Constitution. A similar arrangement regarding to the possibility of collecting and using samples exists also in Canada ... *In Australia the creation of personal files with information from the*

---

[14] The term 'bioethics' or (biomedical ethics) means the science that deals with philosophical morals and customs, and ethical standards on issues arising in the provision of health services and especially of medical practice. (Koutselinis, 1999).

process is forbidden ... The federal U.S. legislation, also provides the operation of the FBI database for DNA of persons who are convicted for certain crimes (sexual, against minors, etc.). This bank is linked to similar banks that operate both locally and at the level of the States ... It should be noted, however, that in most jurisdictions no special provisions for the protection of genetic information,are required'.

For the genotyping data bank or biobank of Greece, which is under construction, 'In 2008, the Council of the European Union converted the Treaty of Prum into EU legislation, according to which, every EU-country is required to establish a forensic DNA database which should be available for automated searches by other EU member states'. (Voultsos, et.al., 2010).

According to Guillen, Lareu, Pestoni, Salas, Carracedo, 'There are currently three available approaches concerning forensic DNA databases, each with its advantages and drawbacks. The first one, which is the most permissive, which is based on the genotyping and the inclusion of the general population on the database. The second one, which is more conservative, which permits DNA fingerprinting and the inclusion of profiles on the database only for a specific list of crimes and only for individuals linked to a high degree with a crime. Finally, the third one, which is against the preparation of DNA databases for criminal investigation'. (Voultsos, et.al., 2010).

Furthermore, as regards to the legislative framework, 'in 2009, the law was amended to allow people arrested or charged with an offense, even if subsequently acquitted, to be included in the Greek National DNA Database, which will eventually result in an expanded database, including many innocent people and children'. (Voultsos, et.al., 2010).

Also, through the creation of genotypic data bank, at the national level, concerns arise because, as noted characteristically by Vidali, 'this is especially important in a country such as Greece, where immigrants, both legal and illegal, are rapidly increasing. The rising wave of crime in Greece has often been attributed to immigrants. It seems that negative stereotypes have been constructed and that xenophobic feelings have already been fermented amongst the Greek population'. (Voultsos, et.al., 2010).

Extract content analysis documents:

'The National Bioethics Committee has only advisory powers, directing, either on its own initiative or upon request, to any organ of

*state. **Its mission is to highlight the close association of the applications of biological sciences with modern social values.** Necessary elements of this mission are both reliable public information of the citizens,
as well as adequate **support of relevant state policies** '.*

The main problem lies in the fact that mission is not to highlight
the close association of the applications of biological sciences with
modern social values, but with modern social values, set by powerful interest groups.

Moreover, these committees Worldwide express the criminal law,
since they take part in the adoption of legislation and policy measures.
Therefore, these committees are part of the official agencies of social
control.

Coroner's Interview Extract:

*'Cooperates also with relevant bodies in our country and make
proposals for legislation or the reception of other measures of policy for
the state'.*

At the same time, he who will be employed by society as 'criminals', in the future as far as modern social systems are considered , will
be treated as such by the formal and informal social reaction, is the one
who would be classified as criminal according to the new definitions
based on genetic identity, genetic features and of course on 'evidence'.

The corollary to this is to create a hyper-controlled society, where
the criminal policy of prevention, control, surveillance and suppression
of crime, will be based on genetics through the genotypic information
banks, as we shall see below.

The consensus of the members of the society for these models of
supervision and control of modern societies will occur due to a further
factor, the factor of the 'fear'. As stated characteristically, Davis, 'For
those unfamiliar with legacy of the Chicago School of Sociology and
their canonical study of the 'North American city' , Mike Davis say that
Burgess dart board represents the five concentric Zones into witch the
struggle for the survival of the Fittest (as imagined by Social Darwinist)
supposedly sorts urban social classes and housing types. It portrays a
'human ecology' organized by biological forces of invasion, competition, succession and symbiosis. My remapping of the urban structure
takes Burgess back to the future. It preserves such 'ecological' determi-
nants as income, land value, class and race, but adds a decisive new factor: 'fear'. (Davis 2004: 528).

The concept of 'fear' has central importance to the concept of 'new social control'. Members of modern social systems will accept the new methods and new control models such as the biometric checks, since they will have incorporated the concept of fear.

With regard to urban structure, and concentric circles of Burgess, the difference lies in the fact that the 'social control' concerns not only a specific country, but the European or global community. For example, genotypic databases and the World 'hyper-bank' of information, including genetic information of members of society, will be able to control and identify the elements, to face with the crime in the frame of globalization of crime, perhaps in all countries.

Parallel, between the current social control and the 'new social control', the difference lies in the fact it will not only concern targeted groups of the society (eg immigrants), but all members of the society.

So there is no zoning to protect a country's internal security, but a European or global 'new social control', through genetics and forensics, for the 'alleged' protection of all members of society and the international security, for example to face terrorism.

Furthermore, 'As city life, in consequence, grows more feral, the different social milieux adopt security strategies and technologies according to their means. Like Burgess original dart board, the resulting pattern condenses into concentric'. (Davis 2004: 529). One of these strategies and technologies in security, for the application of 'new social control', will be the Genotyping Data Banks or biobanks[15] and future

---

[15] 'The term biobank refers to collections of biological samples linked with personal data of donors of these samples. The biological samples can be tissues, cells, blood or DNA isolated from them. Personal information includes, beyond the identity of the donor, the genetic information of the samples and medical data. In many cases they also include genealogical data or information related to lifestyle (dietary habits, smoking, alcohol consumption, exposure to pollutants). The "novelty" of biobanks in the medical research is to collect a large number of samples and genetic information from these samples and, especially, the continuous updating of the database with medical and / or social information to the donor. The establishment and use of biobanks raises issues of security and confidentiality of data involved, due to the novelty of the proposed concentration. Also, the fact that the results of research in biobanks concerning groups of persons raises issues of discrimination and / or stigmatization of these groups based on genetic criteria, geographical / ethnic origin or social behaviour (eg eating habits). Moreover, ownership (public or private) of samples and data associated with them as well as the profit entities involved in recovery, and sometimes the establishment, biobanks to research and develop new and effective medicines were a concern. Finally, the recognition of the need of control and surveillance operation led to several countries in the legislative framework for the smooth functioning and ensuring social acceptance of these research programs. One issue dominated the debate on biobanks, and continues to be a point of controversy is that of the consensus of the participants; it relates to the fact that the analysis will be

'the hyper-bank of genotypic information' that will include data on a global level. Thus, 'the new globalized social control' is structured. In this context, the concentric zones are not regions of a country, but countries more secure and others less safe.

For example, 'As the Los Angeles Business journal recently pointed out in a special report, the riot-tested success of corporate Downtowns defenses has only stimulated demand for new and higher levels of physical security. As Mike Davis said, the LAPD have become central players in the downtown design process. So, inevitably the workplace or shopping mall video camera will become linked with home security systems, personal 'panic buttons', car alarms, cellular phones, and the like, in a seamless continuity of surveillance over daily routine. Then, as Mike Davis remarks for example, some architects now predict the day when buildings own AI security computer will be able to automatically screen and indentify its human population, and, even perhaps, respond to their emotional states (fear, panic etc.)'. (Davis 2004: 530).

Moreover, the genetic science in the future will be the main method of prevention and suppression of crime. In this context, the 'new social control' associated with the use of 'new technologies' to implement a comprehensive and screening of members of modern societies. For example, 'Although no LA housing project is yet as technologically sophisticated as Chicago's Cabrini-Green, where retinal scans (cf, the opening sequence of Blade Runner) are used to check ids, police exercise increasing control over freedom of movement'. (Davis 2004: 532).

Also, the spatial and geographical structure of modern societies will consist a factor that will help to build the 'new social control'. Another emerging technology 'is the police utilization of LANDSAT satellites linked to Geographical Information System (GIS). Almost certainly by the end of the largest US metropolitan areas, including Los Angeles will be using geosynchronous LANDSAT systems to manage traffic congestion and oversee physical planning. The same LANDSAT - GIS capability can be cost - shared and time-shared with police departments to surveil the movements of tens of thousands of electronically tagged and their automobiles'. (Davis 2004: 535).

---

performed on biological samples taken from a biobank, samples that are not necessarily known at the sampling. Consequently, the emphasis on the issue of consent, the debate distracts from the core issue of the establishment and / or exploitation of biobanks that are collective in nature and concern for public health, (According to the proponents of this view, the innovation of biobanks is precisely to serve the public interest either in terms of public health or public policy (see DNA banks for criminological purposes)' (Vidalis, Manolakou 2010).

This 'new electronic social control' will be one of the levels of 'new social control', since after electronic surveillance; there will be genetic tests for identification, for example from a database. Through these modern geographical surveillance systems such as GIS, the geographic range that social control can be exercised changes. Thus, the concept of 'new globalized control' is constructed.

In addition, through globalization, changes 'the relationship between the places where we live and our cultural practices, experiences and identities'. (Tomilnson 1999: 106).

At this point we should mention the concept of the geography of social classes. For example, according to Davis (2003), 'the gang develops as one manifestation of the economic, moral and cultural frontier which marks the interstice - a gang map of Los Angeles today is coextensive with the geography of social class'. (Davis 2004: 531).

An example of a contemporary 'new social control' using new technologies 'is FLINTS which can be used to identify criminal networks, make connections between offenders and places, and establish patterns of crime (including, through geographical profiling, crime 'hotspots'). Although, FLINTS[16] concentrates mainly on current offenders, it can also provide information that may be useful in predicting future crimes. This intelligence system (nicknamed the 'digital detective') haw already been adopted by other forces, such as Staffordshire police'. (Jackson & Jackson 2008: 7).

In this sense, there are differences between the concept of social class, since with the use of new surveillance technologies and methods of identification with the help of genetics to the new formal social control, there will be 'new geographic social classes' in a global social environment that will concern all the population. In this context, the main concern, is whether these geographic social classes will be separated also with their genetic characteristics.

For example, as Mike Davis observe, 'although such monitoring is immediately intended to safeguard expensive sports cars and other toys of the rich, it will be entirely possible to use the same technology to pull the equivalent of an electronic handcuff on the activities of the entire urban social strata. Drug offenders and gang members can be 'bar-coded' and paroled to the omniscient scrutiny of a satellite that will track their

---

[16] FLINTS is a forensic – Led intelligence System: a computer software package jointly developed by West Midlands Police and the Forensic Science Service (FSS). (Jackson & Jackson 2008: 7).

24 - hour itineraries and automatically sound an alarm if their stray out-side borders of their surveillance district. With such powerful Orwellian technologies for social control, community confinement and the con-finement of communities may ultimately mean the same thing'. (Davis 2004: 535).

Therefore, the evolution of consensual crime theories through ge-netic forensics, where biological factors explaining the crime are repro-duced using methods of genetics, in modern social systems, will lead to a new area of conflict, where the dominant groups will define, according to the dominant values the crime against the weak and implement mod-els of supervision and control of crime based on genetic characteristics of members of society, is the 'new genetic control'.

The state and political power in this new area of conflict will both protect the institutions of formal social control, with the use of genetics, while establishing institutions, in which groups that have power and au-thority will again be involved, groups that will seek to bring the consen-sus of the members of society. Furthermore, «the smooth and successful operation of power by the formal social control is dependent on social arrangements, forms of political management and cultural traditions which together contribute towards hegemony. (Scraton, Chadwick 2004: 295). Moreover, as Sim remarks, 'power is dispersed through the body of society and exercised through the processes of discipline, surveil-lance, individualization and normalization'. (Scraton, Chadwick 2004: 294), A typical example is the International Bioethics Committees which establish rules, sometimes law, relating to forensic applications of ge-netics.

Thus, the concept of 'world domination' is structured (Gilipin, 2001). In this context, the objective is the official institutions of social control to develop a 'global hegemony' through the control administered to members of their communities. Furthermore, genetics will be the pri-mary method of developing this global hegemony, since through the ap-plications massive members of modern social systems will be able to be controlled.

Besides, 'criminalization, the application of the criminal label to an identifiable social category, is dependent on how certain acts are la-beled and on who has the power to label, and is directly limited to the political economy of marginalization'. (Scraton, Chadwick 2004: 299). According to the above, and as evidenced by this research, forensics has the power to classify an act as criminal and give it this label objectifying the criteria for an act to be classified as 'criminal'.

These issues arise because 'the genetic information contained in DNA (deoxyribonucleic acid), of the individual is unique and the information provided does not only concern the present of the person but also the person's past and future. Since the establishment of the genetic footprint requires access to DNA for the individual, the information that can potentially be extracted is far more stringent than those required to identify the genetic fingerprint'. (Georgiou 2008: 205). Furthermore, DNA in forensic investigation, as mentioned characteristically, 'is the most important progress in recent years to investigation and identification of the perpetrator'. (Michalodimitrakis 2001: 71). So, it consists, along with the rapid technological development will consist, the main method for the study, prevention and suppression of 'criminality'.

Coroner's Interview Extract:

'Since the biological material of each person is written it is like having him in front of you, it is not always used for good purpose.. We can find everything with DNA".. "To keep an individual, who has been accused of something and he is now free, under arrest so as to have the possibility to search his material if anything happens agin any time?...I don't think that it is right... it is a violation of human rights because it is actually like someone supervise you permanently...You are under permanent monitoring. Yes, maybe in 100 years we could have genetic data bank in Greece'.

An outstanding example of such methods through which human rights are violated, is eugenics[17]. The aim of this method is the 'advancement of the human race so as the creation of another kind of human scale organically high - in modern terms - standards in every physical, mental, cognitive'. (Koutselinis1999: 211-212).

While in the past, eugenics was used for 'the selection of species and the survival or rather say it was used for the need to survive against the stronger and weaker difficulty, in modern approaches, eugenics is linked to biology and genetic engineering, and aims for example to achieve the process of transfer of hereditary characteristics through genetics, the analysis of the role played by hereditary and environmental

---

[17] The term 'eugenics' Francis Galton (1904), means the science of improving the breed with the study of socially controlled parameters that can enhance or reduce the racial profile of future generations, both physically and mentally or psychologically. (Koutselinis 1999: 211). EUGENICS is the science which deals with all influences that improve the inborn qualities of a race; also with those that develop them to the utmost advantage. (Galton 1904).

influences on personality development, according to psychology or information related to hereditary disorders, according to medical genetics'. (Koutselinis 1999: 212).

Respectively, these methods are related to forensic science, since hereditary or environmental influences or hereditary defects, for forensic consensual theories are causes that lead someone to commit crimes.

At the same time, these methods will involve the construction of modern crime, branding and giving the label of 'criminal' members of modern societies, according to their genetic characteristics. Moreover, the goal of modern institutions of social control is the genetic response to causative factors governing the evolution of man, to the 'perfect' man, who is not deviant.

Under this framework, the concept of 'new genetic social control' is also supported. The study - control of the genetic characteristics of the individual, starting from the prenatal testing[18], will continue during the life of the individual and will be completed with the control over the dead body, as stated above.

For example, in prenatal diagnosis, 'the aim is to diagnose and identify problematic embryos. Ovulation is induced pharmaceutically, then the eggs from the ovary are separated, trying to achieve in vitro fertilization technique and when the embryos are divided into eight cells, one of them is taken to check the genetic codex. Then the 'problematic' embryos are discarded and the healthy ones are implanted in the uteri. (Koutselinis 1999: 213).

Therefore, at all stages of life and death, genetics will be the method to control the individual. The ones that will have a 'problem' will be rejected prenatally, in life will be 'marginalized or imprisoned' while when it comes to death the ones that had these characteristics will be studied and labelized.

Moreover, as noted in Ethical problems concerning the application of modern eugenics, but also studying the Contracts for the Protection of Human Rights[19], multi-level thinking is created concerning the applications, such as for example when it comes to, 'eugenics' immediately after birth, when carrying out euthanasia genetically stigmatized or inva-

---

[18] The term 'prenatal testing' means the eugenics during pregnancy, carried out mainly by amniocentesis to diagnose any defects on the conformation and abortifacients. (Koutselinis 1999: 212- 213).

[19] See Convention for the protection of human rights and human dignity in relation to the application of biology and medicine: Convention on Human Rights and Biomedicine.

sive insemination, where according to Muller, the collection of used sperm from men with superior characteristics and lineage as far as possible free of defects is proposed that and to keep the sprem frozen for as long as possible , perhaps even more than the lifetime of the donor.

The sperm will then be available for women who want to have children whose superior genetic characteristics are tested (sperm bank). Finally, many discussions are created also when it comes to 'cloning' which means the genetic selection. (Koutselinis 1999: 213).

Moreover, official statistics do not record 'crimes' that affect the interests of the powerful groups of the society. As stated characteristically, today there are, for example, no official statistics on human rights abuses and political violence (Aas 2010: 427 – 446).

Therefore, the 'new social control', is structured with the applications of genetics to achieve human intervention in nature, the stigmatization of 'problematic – lower' species as well as to create people with a high level standard in any physical, mental or emotional operation. This, the type of person, according to this perspective, it would not 'commit crimes', but this man is created to act smoothly in society, will be the new ready 'product' of modern societies.

In addition, through the above, we can see the structure of the 'new global social control' that is exercised by the competent bodies, institutions of formal social control are strengthened and grow and their role is enforced while the 'filtering' open to the each 'alleged perpetrator' is also more intense. The evidence - evidence gathered through the analysis will provide the springboard for the next stage until the end of the process in court.

Also, as mentioned in the excerpt of the interview of the coroner, the biological material can be used also for purposes prohibited. For example, the use of DNA in research that involves the cloning is one of those prohibitive cases.

Besides future goal is to create a 'hyper-bank' genotypic information, which includes genetic data of people worldwide. As pointed out characteristically, 'in hyper-banks' will be saved not only the DNA of convicted but also of suspected of terrorist and criminal acts. The prosecuting authorities of the states-members should have as far as their research is concerned, free access. It is not clear whereas, whether law enforcement authorities of third countries like the U.S will also have the same access Furthermore, the storage and exchange of information related to DNA not only for heavy crimes but also for a series of light offences. Under the Treaty, the States – members must register the information to database and for suspects generally when they have to travel so as to watch sporting events or participate in pan-European demonstrations. (Georgiou 2008: 224).

A typical modern example of the use of technical analysis of DNA, are the studies in the U.S. Where 'the method of genetic fingerprinting has found many fans in the hot cycle of organizations against the death penalty, requesting review and demonstrating   several times the innocence of people sentenced to death penalty. Such actions prompted the governor of Illinois George Ryan on 30 January 2000, to suspend all executions in that state, since in most cases the innocence of persons sentenced to death was proved'. (Georgiou 2008: 195).

Coroner's Interview Extract:

'I think that each laboratory as well as our own has become one study by our biologist who has taken a sample of Greeks, I do not know now, 1000-2000 people, and knows the limits on which moves the Greek DNA ...« I think this is not moral, it is like you abuse many human rights when you take genetic material of an individual, keeping it in a bank and having the possibility to use it. Cause it may be used also for non-scientific reasons that do not have to do with this kind of research. No, I do not think this is right'.

As seen from the above, forensic science interacts with criminology, developing methods and applications of crime prevention. Applying the principles of consensual crime theories, in the future, genetics will be the main method of new formal social control.

Furthermore, the violation of human rights as already mentioned characteristically by the coroner, a breach of personal data would create 'new biological rights'20 or 'new genetic rights'. Government policies and actions of official institutions of social control, led to the creation of 'Fundamental Human Rights'. In future, the prevention and combating of crime based on surveillancing patterns of the members of modern societies through genetics. So, the lack of measures of protection for human rights through the existing framework, will lead to the necessity of 'new biological rights'. A typical example is the special care to protect the human genome that is found in Article 13 of the Convention of the Council of Europe.

Moreover, as mentioned characteristically, 'The revolution in the area of criminal law sought to protect the individual rights of citizens

---

[20] Iliadou 2007: 402.

who were then playthings to arbitrary judicial and state institutions' (Michalodimitrakis 2001: 3).

Furthermore, the connection between criminology and the Coroners are inseparable, since it is considered that these two sciences share common methodological tools.

Coroner's Interview Extract:

'Sure is great to link forensic science with criminology Yes ... well, the two sciences share common methodological tools and methods and techniques that show off forensic interest'.

Thus, the modern social control will be linked to social evolutions, in the terms of which, the applications of genetic science are used as methods to face with criminality , where genotypic databases will be the 'technocratic forms of control with proactive content'.(Lampropoulou 2001: 69).

Epilogue

In modern societies who are dealing with the globalization of crime, strong teams, according to the dominant values, are required to implement prevention and suppression of "crime." Bodies of official social control and the new operators of the formal social control, such as genetic Coroners are asked to apply new methods of surveillance towards the members of social systems and subsystems. The gene is and will be the central method of implementing these policies. Similarly, the criminal law legalizes and legitimizes these applications in order to suppress the 'modern crime'. A typical example is the goal of creating a common genotypic Information Bank, where you can check after you have filed a joint database of the genetic identity of the members of the Society for the Suppression of the 'crime'.

As seen from the above, forensic interacts with criminology, developing methods and applications of crime prevention. Applying the principles of consensual crime theories, in the future, genetics will be the primary method of new formal social control. Furthermore, the violation of human rights through an infringement of personal data would create "new biological rights." All this will take place in the globalization of the 'crime' and to develop methods for monitoring and control of members of contemporary social systems.

Thus, the modern social control will be linked to social development, in the terms of which the application of genetic as methods in prevention and suppression of crime, where genotypic databases will be the technocratic forms of control with proactive content.

References

Anthony, T. Cunneen, C., (eds), (2008) *The Critical Criminology Companion.* Sydney: Hawkins Press.

Aas, K.F. (2010) Global Crime, in McLaughlin, E., Newburn, T., (Eds), *The sage handbook of criminological theory.* London: Sage Publications Ltd.

Becker, H. (1963) *Outsiders,* New York: The free press of Glencoe.

Becker, H. (2004) Outsiders, in McLaughlin, E., Muncie, J., Hughes, G., (Eds), *Criminological Perspectives,* 2nd ed., London: Sage.

Bell, S. (2008) *Encyclopedia of forensic science.* America: Facts on file.

Bell, S. (2004) *The facts on file dictionary of forensic science.* America: facts on file.

Cohen, L. Manion, L. (1980) *Research Methods in Education.* London: Routledge.

Craib, I. (2002) *Modern Social Theory.* From Parsons to Habermas. 8th ed. Translated from English by P. E. Lekkas. Athens: Ellinika Grammata (in Greek).

Dahrendorf, R. (1959) *Class and Class Conflict in industrial Society.* London: Routledge

Daskalakis, I. (1985) *Criminology of social reaction.* Athens - Komotini: Sakkoulas. (in Greek).

Davis, M. (2004) Beyond Blade Runner: Urban control. The ecology of fear, in McLaughlin, E., Muncie, J., Hughes, G., *Criminological Perspectives,* 2nd ed. London: Sage.

Fisher B., A., J., Tilstone, W., J., Woytowicz, C. (2009) *Introduction to criminalistics. The foundation of forensic science*. USA: Academic press Elsevier.

Galton, F. (1904). Eugenics. Its definition, scope and aims. *The American Journal of Sociology*,10,pp.1-6.

Georgiou, M. (2008) *Forensic Genetics*. Athens: Parisianou. (in Greek).

Gilpin, R. (2001) *Global Political Economy: Understanding the International Economic order*. Princeton: Princeton University Press.

Hatty, E. Schwartz, D. (2003) *Controversies in critical criminology*. England: Anderson.

Houck, M., M. (2007) *Forensic science: modern methods of solving crime*. Praeger: America.

Houck, M., M., Siegel, J., M. (2010) *Fundamentals of forensic science*. USA: Academic press Elsevier.

Hulsman, L. (2004) Critical Criminology and the concept of crime, in McLaughlin, E., Muncie, J., Hughes, G., (Eds), *Criminological Perspectives*, 2nd ed., London: Sage.

Hulsman, L. (1986) Critical Criminology and the Concept of Crime. *Contemporary Crises*, 10 (1) pp. 63-80.

Iliadou, A. (2007) Bioethics and law. The developments in biomedical by the law, in Kotsalis, L., Triantafillou, G., (eds), *Human Rights and Criminal Law*. Athens - Komotini: Sakkoulas. (in Greek).

Jackson, A., R., W., Jackson, J., M., (2008) *Forensic Science*. 2nd ed. England: Pearson Education Limited.

Koutselinis, A. (1999) *Principles of Medical Ethics and Bioethics*. Athens: Parisianou. (in Greek).

Lampropoulou, E. (2001) *Internal Security and the society of control.*

Athens: Kritiki. (in Greek).

Lee, H., C., Harris, H., A. (2006) *Physical evidence in forensic science.* America: Lawyers & Judges publishing.

Mead, H.G. (1934) *Mind, Self and Society.* Chicago: University of Chicago Press.

Merton, R. K. (1957) *Social theory and social structure.* Glencoe: Free press.

Michalodimitrakis, M. (2001) *Forensic.* Athens: Parisianou. (in Greek).

Rafter, N. (2008) Criminology's Darkest Hour: Biocriminology in Nazi Germany. *Australian and New Zealand journal of criminology*, 41 (2), pp.287-306.

Sargiacomo, M. (2009) Michel Foucault, Discipline and Punish: The Birth of the Prison. Allen Lane, London, 1977, Trans. by Alan Sheridan. *Journal of Management and Governance*, 13(3), pp. 269-280.

Scraton, P., Chadwick, K. (2004) The theoretical and political priorities of critical criminology, in McLaughlin, E., Muncie, J., Hughes, G., (Eds), *Criminological Perspectives*, 2nd ed., London: Sage.

See, E. (2004) *Criminological Theories: Introduction, Evaluation, and Application.* Los Angeles: Roxbury Publishing Company.

Sellin, T. (1938) *Culture Conflict and Crime.* New York: Social Science Research Council.

Tomilson, J. (1999) *Globalisation and culture.* Chicago: University of Chicago press.

Ruggiero, V., South, N., Taylor, I. (1998) *The new European criminology: crime and social order in Europe.* London and New York:Routledge.

Vidalis, T., Manolakou, K. For the biobanks of human source in biome-

diacal research. Available at:
www.bioethics.gr/media/pdf/reports/biobanks_report_gr.pdf. [Accessed 20 February 2011].

Vold, G. Bernard, T. Snipes, J. (2002). *Theoretical criminology.* 5th ed. Oxford: Oxford University Press.

Vold, G. Bernard, T. Snipes, J. (1998) *Theoretical criminology.* 4th ed., Oxford: Oxford University Press.

Voultsos, P. Njau, S. Psaroulis, D. Tairis, N. Kovatsi, L. (2010) Focus: Launching the Greek forensic DNA database. The legal framework and arising ethical issues. Forensic Science International: Genetics. Available at:
www.sciencedirect.com/science?_ob=MImg&_imagekey=B8CX5120CJ D31&_cdi=40079&_user=632480&_pii=S1872497310001316&_origin =search&_coverDate=09%2F18%2F2010&_sk=999999999&view=c& wchp=dGLbVlbzSkWb&md5=40a23d0fd809a7ccaeee5447ac2f685f&ie =/sdarticle.pdf [Accessed 22 February 2011].

Walkers, P., Wood, E. (2010) *Forensic science experiments.* N.Y: Infobase.

INDEX

Stratos Georgoulas

Critical Criminology of Leisure

Theory, Methodology and a Case Study

Soziologie: Forschung und Wissenschaft

L<small>IT</small>

Stratos Georgoulas
Critical Criminology of Leisure
Theory, Methodology and a Case Study
Critical Criminology of Leisure aims to play the role of an introductory essay, of a concise guide for the theoretical study and research on a social field which emerges as the point of intersection of two establis-hed scientific subjects: leisure and crime.
The concept of 'leisure' is used as a methodological tool, as privileged social time for the study of the social problems of modern societies and more specifically for the study of the issue of criminalization or the forms of action (or inactivity) of formal social control agents and the legitimization of this action by the public.
Bd. 29, 2009, 104 S., 19,90 €, br., ISBN 978-3-643-10350-5

L<small>IT</small> Verlag Berlin – Münster – Wien – Zürich – London
Auslieferung Deutschland / Österreich / Schweiz: siehe Impressumsseite

Gunter Runkel

EVOLUTION and SEXUALITY

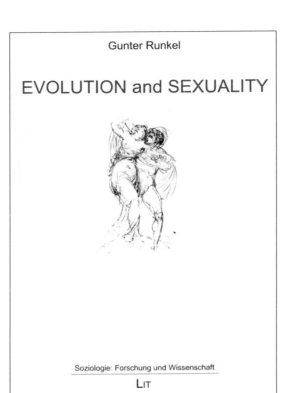

Soziologie: Forschung und Wissenschaft

LIT

Gunter Runkel
Evolution and Sexuality
The work encompasses two subject areas which have attained great meaning for various sciences and humans as well: evolution and sexuality. First, I will lay down the foundation of evolution, a process on which the emergence of the world and the subsequent developing living human beings is based upon. The subject will be societal and cultural change in society from its beginning until the present, and I will take a closer look at the growing meaning of an orientation toward the future. I will then apply the general views of Function Systems to intimate relationships. In the end I will take a look at forthcoming development, such as the increasing separation of sexuality and producing offspring and the effects on family and reproduction.

Bd. 30, 2010, 208 S., 19,90 €, br., ISBN 978-3-643-10383-3

LIT Verlag Berlin – Münster – Wien – Zürich – London
Auslieferung Deutschland / Österreich / Schweiz: siehe Impressumsseite

Hamburger Studien zur Kriminologie und Kriminalpolitik

hrsg. von Prof. Dr. Susanne Krasmann. Prof. Dr. Fritz Sack, Prof. Dr. Sebastian Scheerer, Prof. Dr. Klaus Sessar, Prof. Dr. Bernhard Villmow und Prof. Dr. Peter Wetzels

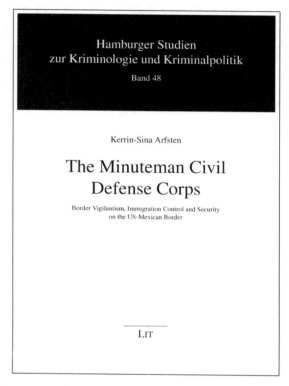

Hamburger Studien
zur Kriminologie und Kriminalpolitik

Band 48

Kerrin-Sina Arfsten

The Minuteman Civil Defense Corps

Border Vigilantism, Immigration Control and Security
on the US-Mexican Border

LIT

Kerrin-Sina Arfsten
The Minuteman Civil Defense Corps
Border Vigilantism, Immigration Control and Security on the US-Mexican Border
Using the *Minuteman Civil Defense Corps* as a case study, this work explores the emergence and recent proliferation of civilian border patrol groups at the US-Mexico border. It is shown that the emergence of these groups can be linked, on the one hand, to an increasing criminalization and securitization of immigration. On the other hand, it is shown that it can also be connected to globalization and its associated forces of political and economic liberalization, which have transformed the security landscape in such a way that this form of citizen activism is not only tolerated, but arguably even encouraged.
Bd. 48, 2010, 128 S., 19,90 €, br., ISBN 978-3-643-10703-9

LIT Verlag Berlin – Münster – Wien – Zürich – London
Auslieferung Deutschland / Österreich / Schweiz: siehe Impressumsseite

Hamburger Studien
zur Kriminologie und Kriminalpolitik

Band 50

Laura Naegler

Gentrification and Resistance

Cultural criminology, control, and the
commodification of urban protest in Hamburg

LIT

Laura Naegler
Gentrification and Resistance
Cultural criminology, control, and the commodification of urban protest in Hamburg
Based on ethnographic research in Hamburg *Sternschanze* and utilizing the cultural criminological perspective as an underlying theme, this work explores the contested spaces of gentrified inner city neighborhoods. It examines the complex and sometimes paradox interplays of urban revaluation, criminalized anti-gentrification resistance and urban control. The main focus lies on the spatialized commodification of urban counter-culture and its incorporation into the process of gentrification. It is shown that by these processes, "authentic" anti-gentrification resistance becomes increasingly sanitized: blurred and hardly distinguishable from commodified rebellion it eventually loses its subversive power and political vigour, and – unwillingly – turns into an integral of the process of urban revaluation it is originally meant to defend.
Bd. 50, 2011, 184 S., 29,90 €, br., ISBN 3-643-90114-9

LIT Verlag Berlin – Münster – Wien – Zürich – London
Auslieferung Deutschland / Österreich / Schweiz: siehe Impressumsseite

Swiss: Forschung und Wissenschaft

Thomas Austenfeld; Dimiter Daphinoff; Jens Herlth (Eds.)
Terrorism and Narrative Practice
Terrorism as a factor of public life has generated far-reaching and as yet underexplored questions about narrative and representation. Different textual forms can investigate both the symbolic and the performative character of terroristic acts. Diverse literary traditions, ranging from countries of Eastern and Western Europe to North America and the Middle East, bring their respective historical imaginations to bear on such representations. The essays collected in this volume join together in a transdisciplinary effort that seeks to further our understanding of the role of narrative practice in all its varieties in approaching the phenomenon of terrorism, whether historical or contemporaneous.
vol. 7, 2011, 248 pp., 18,90 €, br., ISBN-CH 978-3-643-80082-4

LIT Verlag Berlin – Münster – Wien – Zürich – London
Auslieferung Deutschland / Österreich / Schweiz: siehe Impressumsseite

0 1341 1501015 6